INTROSPECTIVE

EXPANSION THROUGH INTROSPECTION   **VOLUME | 01**

EXPANSION

**DELIBERATELY CREATED
WITH GRATITUDE AND
PURPOSE BY...**

BRANDON THOMAS

EXPANSION

JOURNAL SERIES

Expand mindfully into the greatest and grandest version of yourself that your physical vessel can hold. Daily Mindfulness, Introspective writing, Creative expression and Wisdom reflection. Available now. Welcome to you.

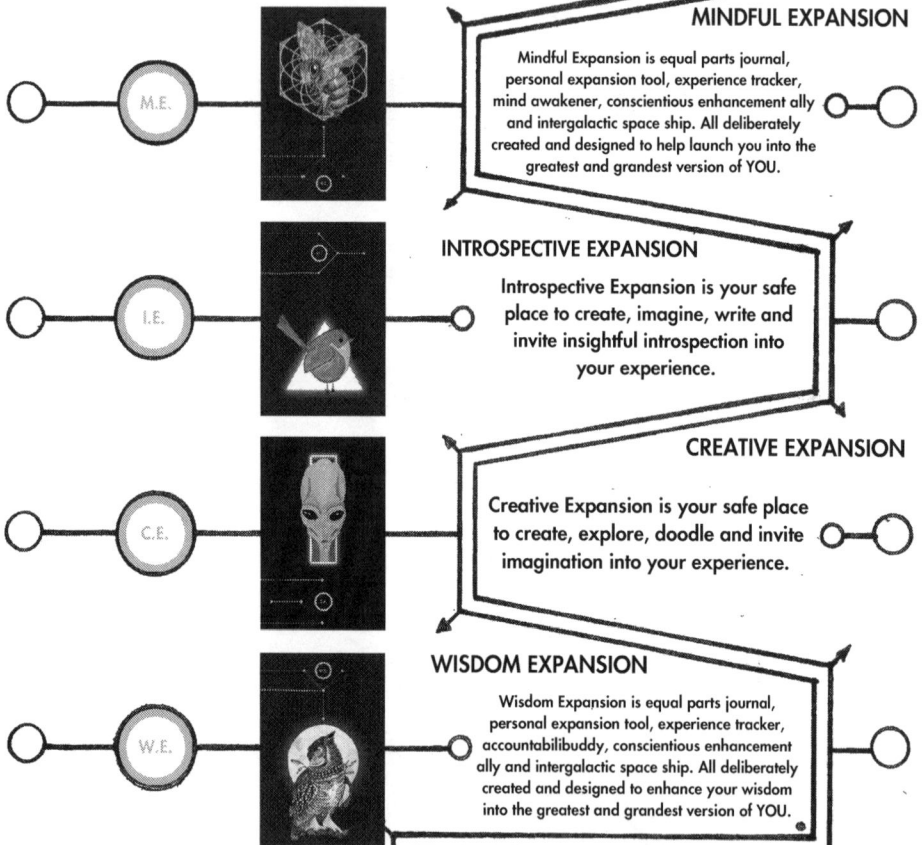

MINDFUL EXPANSION

M.E.

Mindful Expansion is equal parts journal, personal expansion tool, experience tracker, mind awakener, conscientious enhancement ally and intergalactic space ship. All deliberately created and designed to help launch you into the greatest and grandest version of YOU.

INTROSPECTIVE EXPANSION

I.E.

Introspective Expansion is your safe place to create, imagine, write and invite insightful introspection into your experience.

CREATIVE EXPANSION

C.E.

Creative Expansion is your safe place to create, explore, doodle and invite imagination into your experience.

WISDOM EXPANSION

W.E.

Wisdom Expansion is equal parts journal, personal expansion tool, experience tracker, accountabilibuddy, conscientious enhancement ally and intergalactic space ship. All deliberately created and designed to enhance your wisdom into the greatest and grandest version of YOU.

Connect with the Author and Creator

BRANDON THOMAS
instagram.com/brandonthomas369

Might as well check out his podcast
Expanding Reality

RIDICULOUSLY ORIGINAL AUTHORS

RIDIGINAL
PUBLISHING

instagram.com/ridiginalpublishing

The Expansion series is all about Creation, Creativity, Imagination, Introspection, Growth, Authenticity, Expansion (of course) and the confidence to feel empowered in your greatest quality, YOU.

I.E.

INTROSPECTIVE EXPANSION

The idea behind Introspective Expansion is one's desire to write, journal, document, examine, creatively formulate and expand one's view of reality through consciously noting your observation of this wild ride along the journey. List keeping. Goal setting and smashing, etc. . .

There are sample pages of the full Introspective Expansion vol 02 located in the last bit of this book. Designed with your enjoyment of the experience in mind. Expand your reality and discover the joy in the journey with the rest of the expansion series journals available now.

INTROSPECTIVE EXPANSION
volume 02

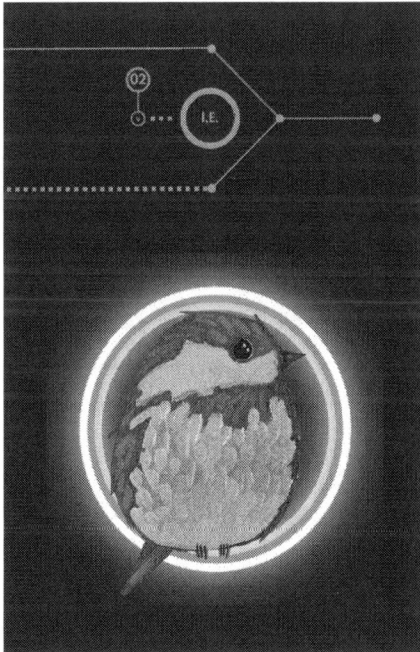

Cover art by Ashley Rose

Go forth boldly and create deliberately.

INTROSPECTIVE

DEDICATION

Dedicated to my perfect partner Mary, who's love and belief in me make every heartbeat better than the last.

Dedicated to the deliberate creator in all of us that is dedicated to our well-being at every level. Empowering life to breathe life into creation's greatest creation-YOU.

Dedicated also to all of the deliberate creators who have moved on and away from us in the physical. May you find your peace.

RIDIGINAL RIDIGINAL PUBLISHING

EMPOWERING & AMPLIFYING THE VOICES & VISIONS OF RIDICULOUSLY ORIGINAL AUTHORS AND CREATORS.

For all things Ridiginal, connect with us on Instagram/ridiginalpublishing

ADDITIONAL AWESOMENESS AVAILABLE FROM RIDIGINAL PUBLISHING

EXPANDING REALITY

EXPANDED INSIGHT & EPISODIC REFLECTION | VOLUME 001

Expanding Reality is The expansion of consciousness cleverly disguised as a podcast. This is the handbook that accompanies that journey.

Follow along with your favorite show. Noting the wisdom and awesomeness from mind expanding guests & asking larger questions inspired by the insights gleaned from each episode.

AVAILABLE NOW AT EXPANDINGREALITYPODCAST.COM & AMAZON

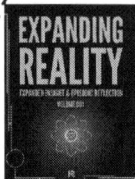

EXPANSION

EXPANDING

WRITE RIGHT, RIGHT?

The way I write would definitely not be taught in school. I never start on Page 1 and end on Page 500. That would totally mess me up.

Instead, I bounce all over the place and create documents on different topics then later assemble them all together in a way that flows. When I'm finished writing a book I would end up with 50 different files covering eight major themes, then I would write all 50 topics on yellow sticky notes and put them together on my dinner table in the correct order in eight columns, one for each major theme.

After this, I will create a new document for each of the eight columns and get to work assembling the 50 chapters accordingly. Once that is complete, I then create the overall master document and fit the eight documents inside of that in the correct order. Basically, I go from 50 down to eight down to one.

All three of my books are written in eight parts, and they have all been written in this unusual fashion. There are no rules, my friends.

| CHARLIE ROBINSON |

EXPANSIVE INTROSPECTION

You know that delicious feeling you get when you're reading a really good book? Writing is like that, only even more delicious. There's nothing quite like filling a blank page with your own words and ideas, breathing life into a hidden world and sharing it with others, leaving your immortal footprints to live on forever. We all enjoy our own unique perspective to All That Is. And yet, we are all one, together in this amazing infinite universe. And we have all the power of the universe within us. So, open your heart, expand your mind, shine your light, let your spirit soar. Now is the time to bring forth the invaluable treasures that only you possess and share them with the world so that all may gaze upon their wisdom and beauty. Peace and love!

| PRESTON DENNETT |

INTROSPECTIVELY

• INSPIRING INSPIRATION •

Words on the page serve as truths we have forgotten. If we're not creating, we've misunderstood what it is to be human.

| MARISA LOVE |

Life experiences, and the path that it has taken you on, are the basis for what motivates and inspires us to put pen to paper and ultimately the hope that what you have written will be meaningful to others.

| LESTER VELEZ |

REMAIN CURIOUS

Like the warriors of old, take up your sword of justice and proclaim within the heart that all you encompass is truth, love and integrity. Allow your light to smite the darkness and bring you into unlimited potential. You are the source of all that was, is and will be.

| PHILP KINSELLA |

REMAIN IN FLOW

I remember back in high school how I loved to put pen to paper. Seeing my thoughts and my words splayed out before me was almost like magic. Never in a thousand years did I think that my thoughts and words would end up in a variety of books and in several different languages. We can all write and there is no reason why you, like me, cannot see your words, thoughts and feelings made available for everyone to share.

You can write your own magic.

| PHILP MANTLE |

• INSPIRING INSPIRATION •

Be true to yourself and follow your passion -- the art of self-expression comes from the heart. Watch, read, and learn from those that came before you, and don't be afraid to ask for help along the way. We're all here to learn from one another and pass our knowledge on to the next generation; what you have to express is important, and you will be surprised to discover who is listening. There are going to be some ups and downs along the way, but keep pushing forward.

The only one who can truly stop you is yourself.

| MIKE RICKSECKER |

EXPRESS SELF

Life is magic.

| DR IREANA SCOTT |

PROCLAIM SELF

We are all influenced by the environment we surround ourselves with and inspiration is often received in random moments when we are relaxed and more open to the universe.

| PAUL ASCOUGH |

Creativity is the souls expression of it's divinity.
We are but mortal; until we create.
Our work transcending time and space, living beyond us, through us and with it, the information of a 1000 lifetimes.

| LEWIS SNOOKES |

In my own experience, writing only emerges when there is a deep passion for something. And at that point, it's hard to focus on much else until the ideas have been expressed to my satisfaction. Long periods of uninterrupted time are critical in this process, as well. There's a certain "flow" that is enabled by eliminating interruptions.

However, if the passion isn't there, writing doesn't happen and it's not even of interest.

| MARK GOBER |

DISOBLIGE REALITY

What I once believed is no more, and what i've witnessed, defies all that I have ever imagined.

| JIM PENNISTON |

DISCOVER MORE

Whether it be writing, or creating music or art, the best advice I can offer is to not overthink, but simply to get in touch with your source of inspiration, and then to get out of your own way. Oftentimes the greatest creative works will come to you without even trying, and if you can access this strange flow state, it can almost seem like the ideas come from another source and you are simply a conduit. Whether it be accessing some mysterious creative frequency, or tapping into our higher selves, it helps to not try too hard. All you need to do is find something that inspires you, latch onto whatever feelings that inspiration evokes, and then start to write down or paint whatever comes out. You can always go back later and finely edit and refine what results come through from the raw, unfiltered creative flow. Inspiration is the true key.

| BEN TEJADA INGRAM |

Most likely if you are a budding author, you have something to say that stems from some deep message inside you. I also had this urge and my whole book project took on a divine life of its own. I only wrote when inspired to do so, so I could hear that deeper quiet inner message. Due to this process my book took five years to write, yet I was motivated since I had a famous coauthor and a publisher waiting to publish from the beginning. This hearing your inner voice is akin to channeling your deeper self, that exists outside time, so you already know how the book will end. From that state of mind, you will be inspired to write/say things you didn't know you knew. Every time that happens, you can rejoice that you are on the right path and getting help from your guides.

| DR DOUG MATZKE |

SCRIBE TRUTH

You have to get comfortable with writing when no one is reading - creating when no one is consuming - putting in the hours when you know no one is clapping - no one is listening - no one is watching - without support - that's it - that's the secret of writing.

| MARK OLLY |

IN AUTHENTICITY

The greatest method of imagination and belief, certainly when writing, is to actually take on the persona of the characters themselves; to literally live and breathe as them. Even if they're alien! I recall an amusing moment, upon writing a sci-fi book called 'THE UNGODLY AGENDA,' whereby I actually envisioned myself as an alien Commander, a reptilian brute with attitude named Cruex. So, I focused on the dinosaurs, encapsulating their movements, and pouring these simulated motions into his complex character. And, guess what? It appeared to work! It can be achieved. Just believe in yourself and your creations, no matter if they're from here, or a zillion Light-years away.

| RONALD KINSELLA |

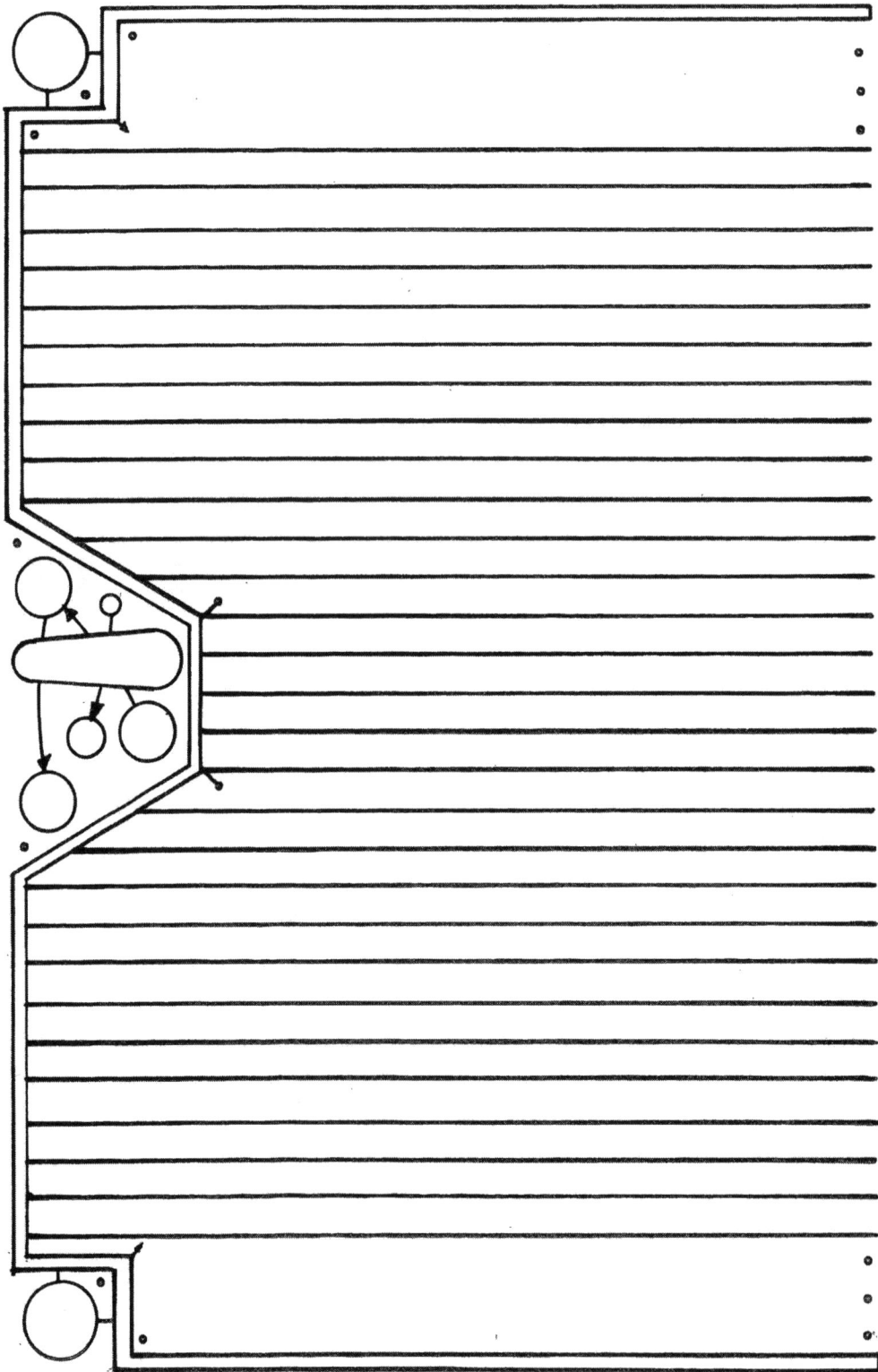

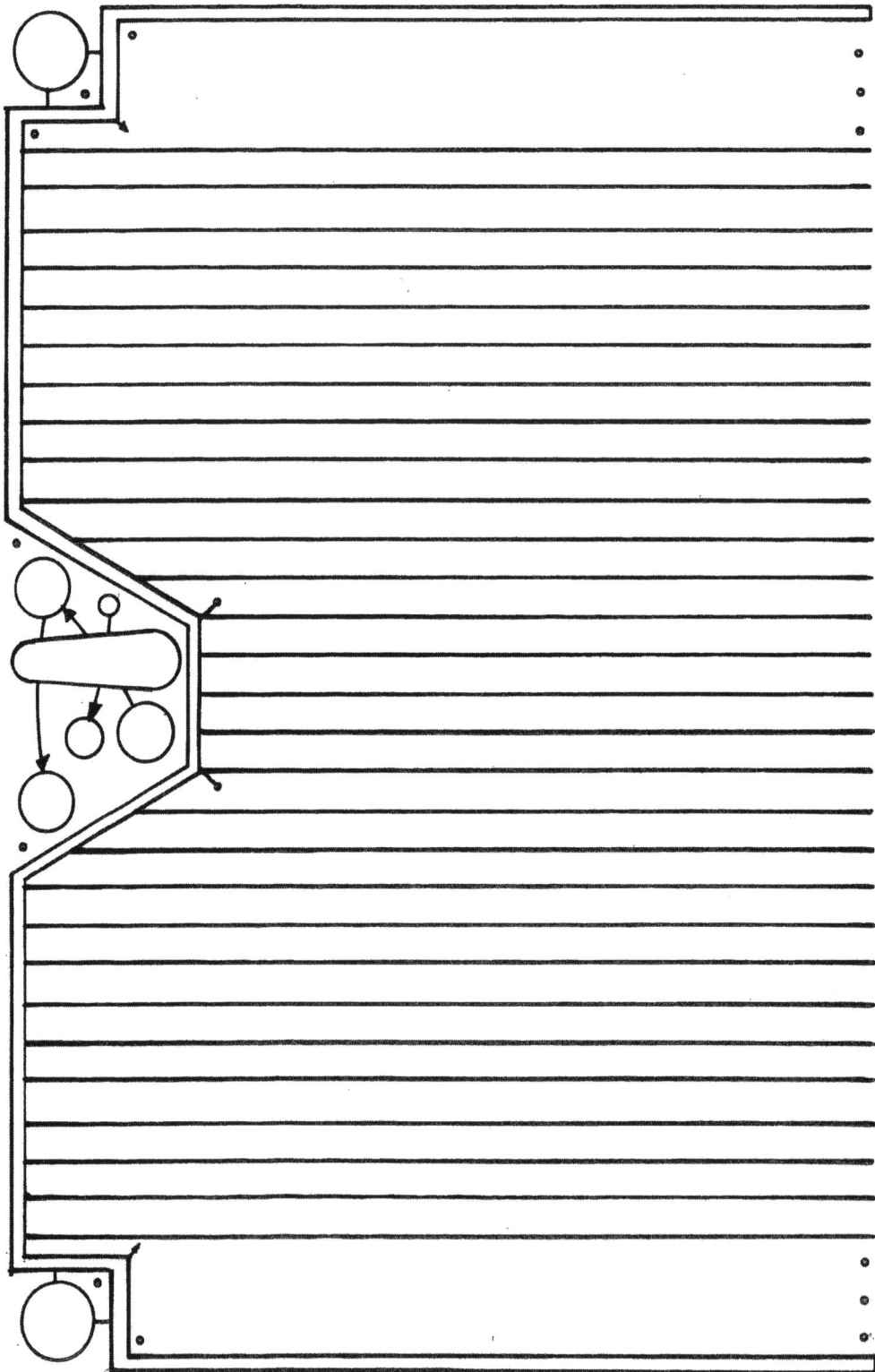

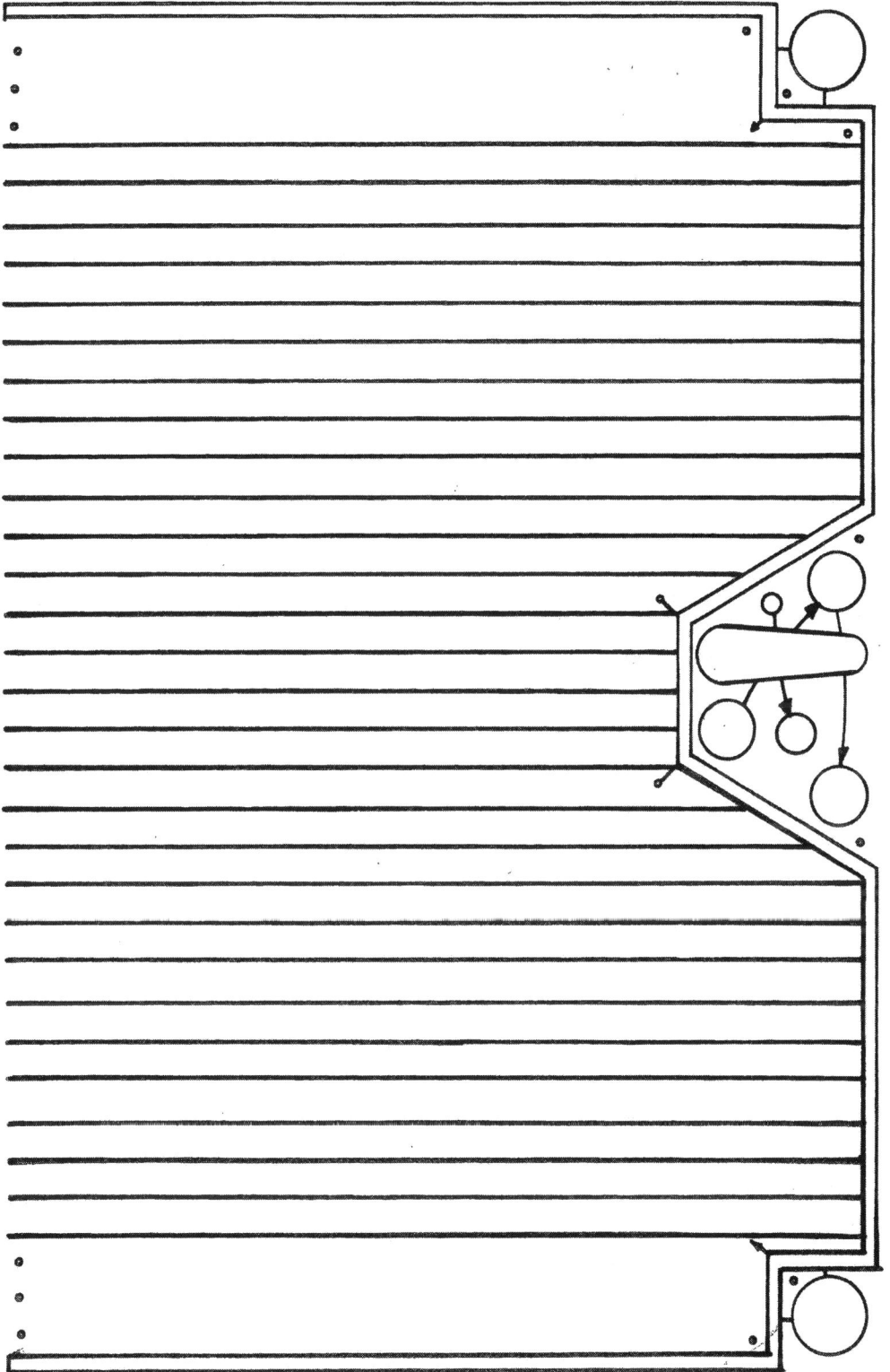

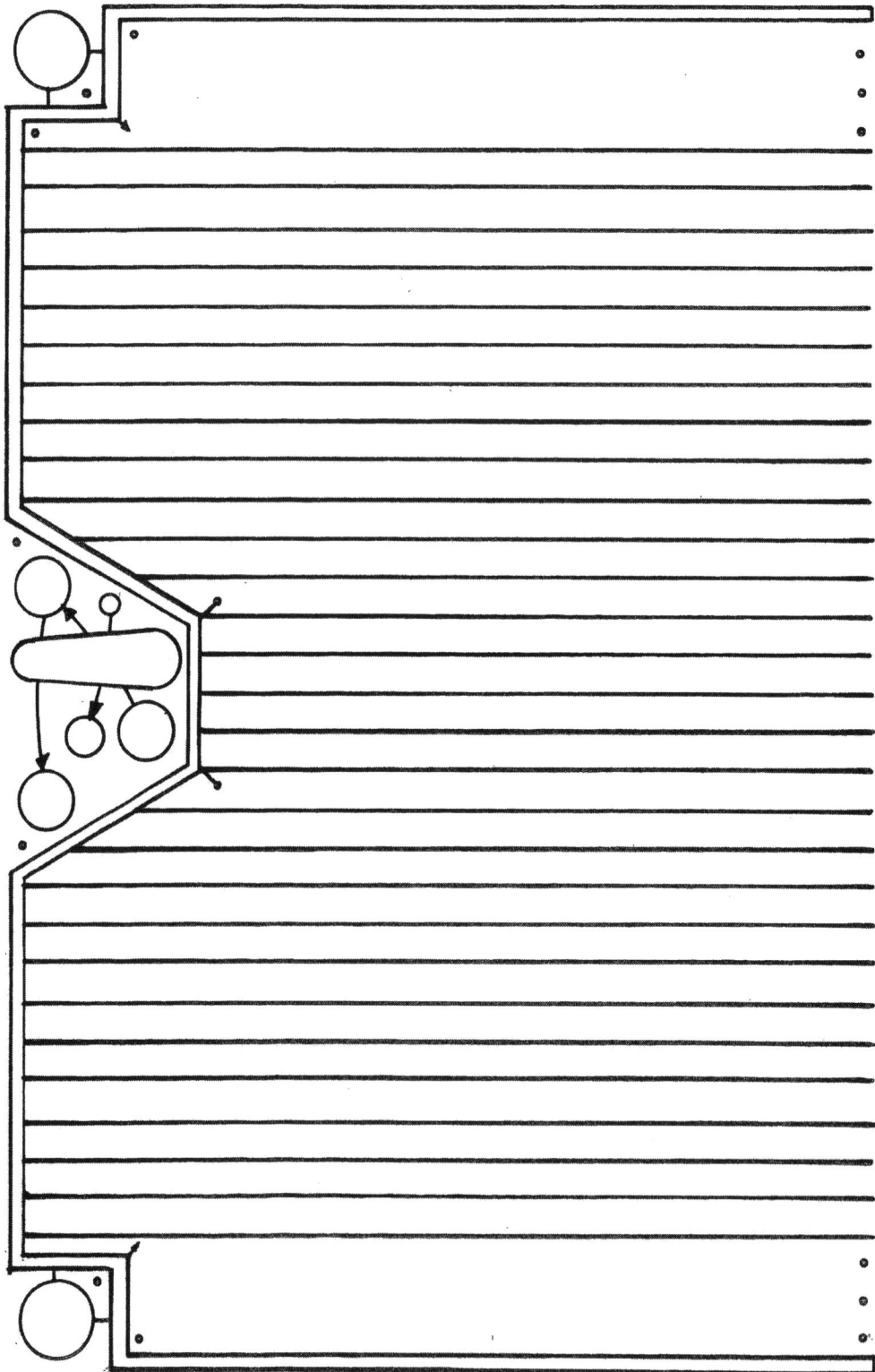

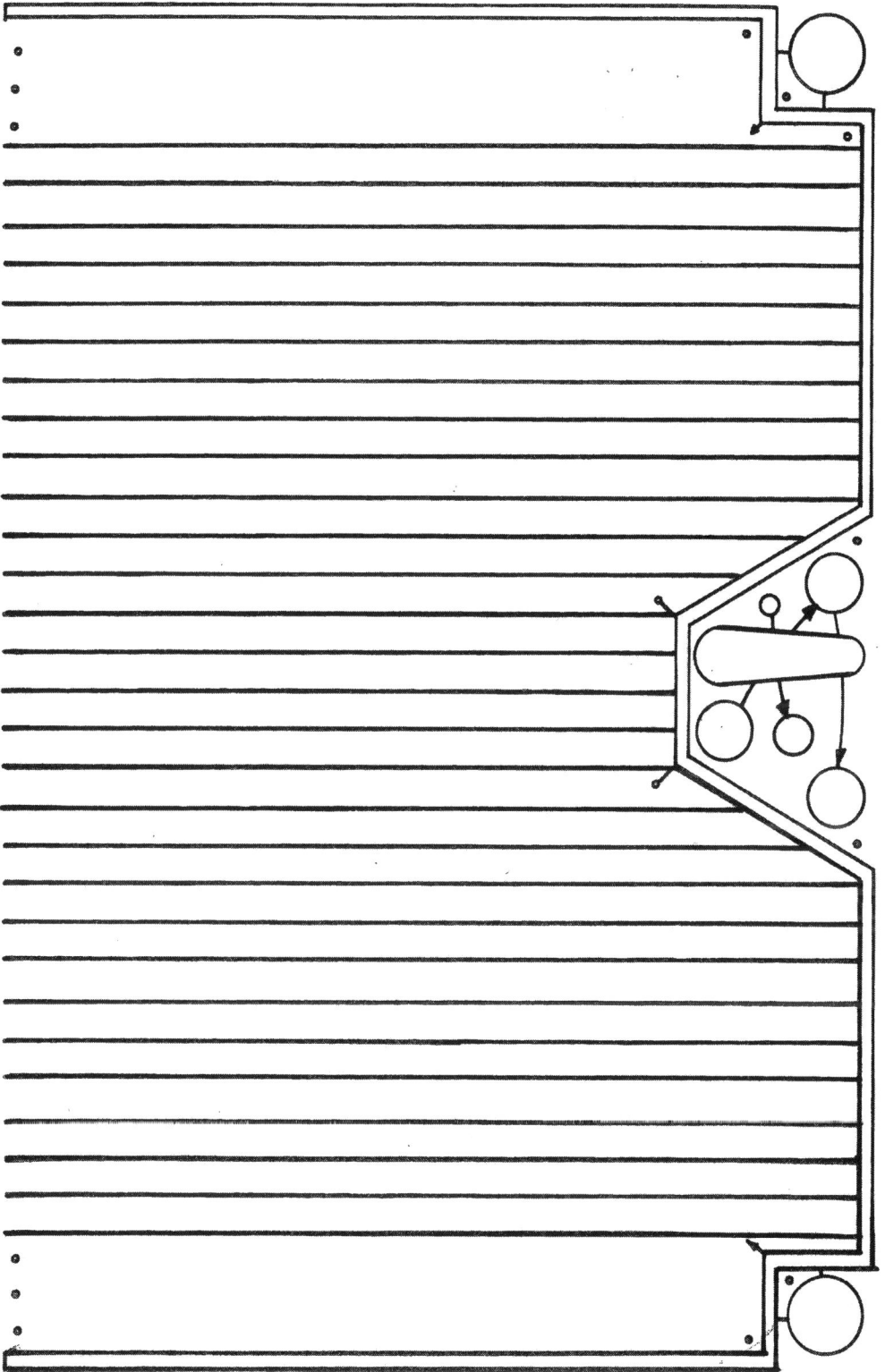

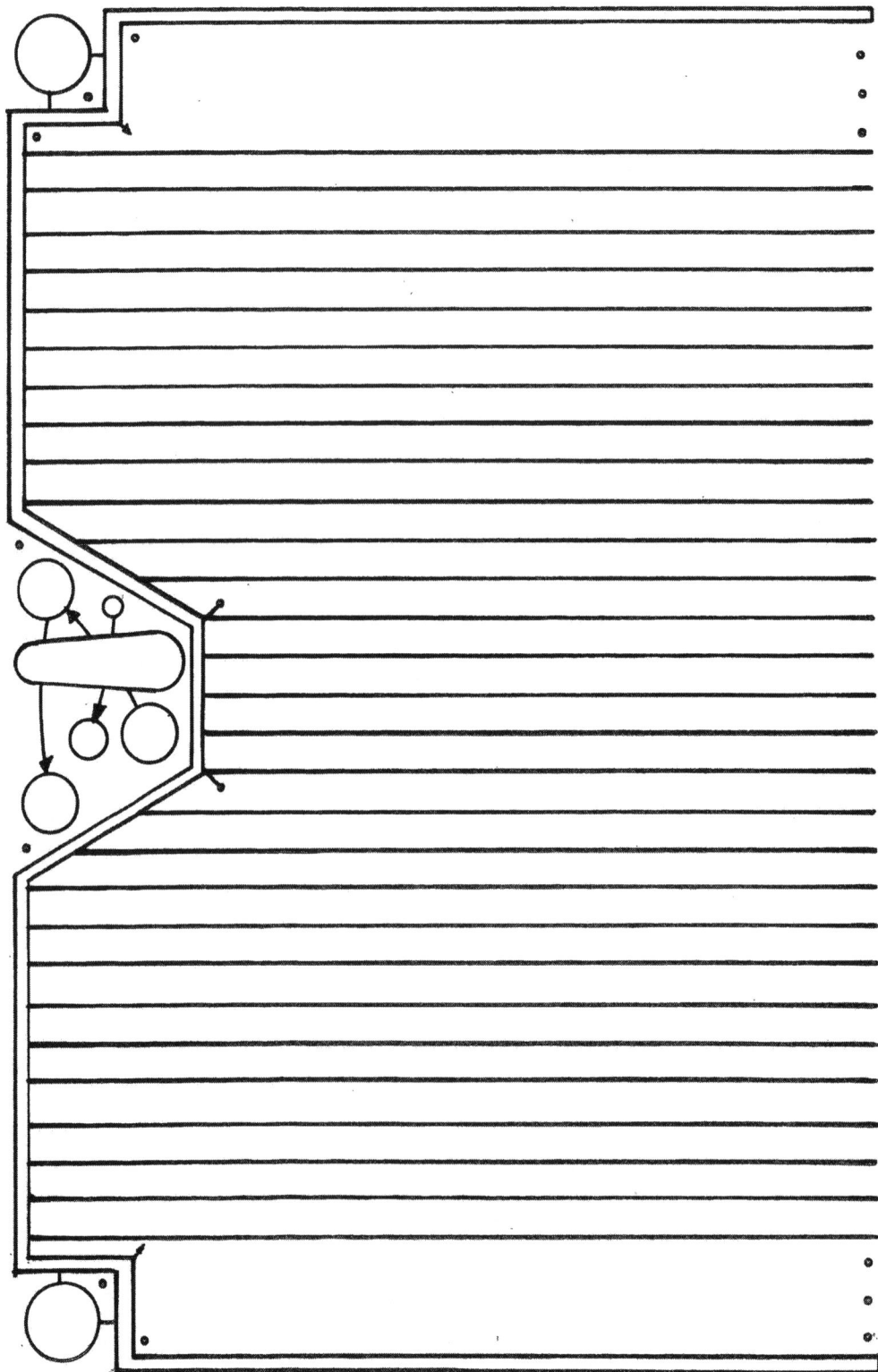

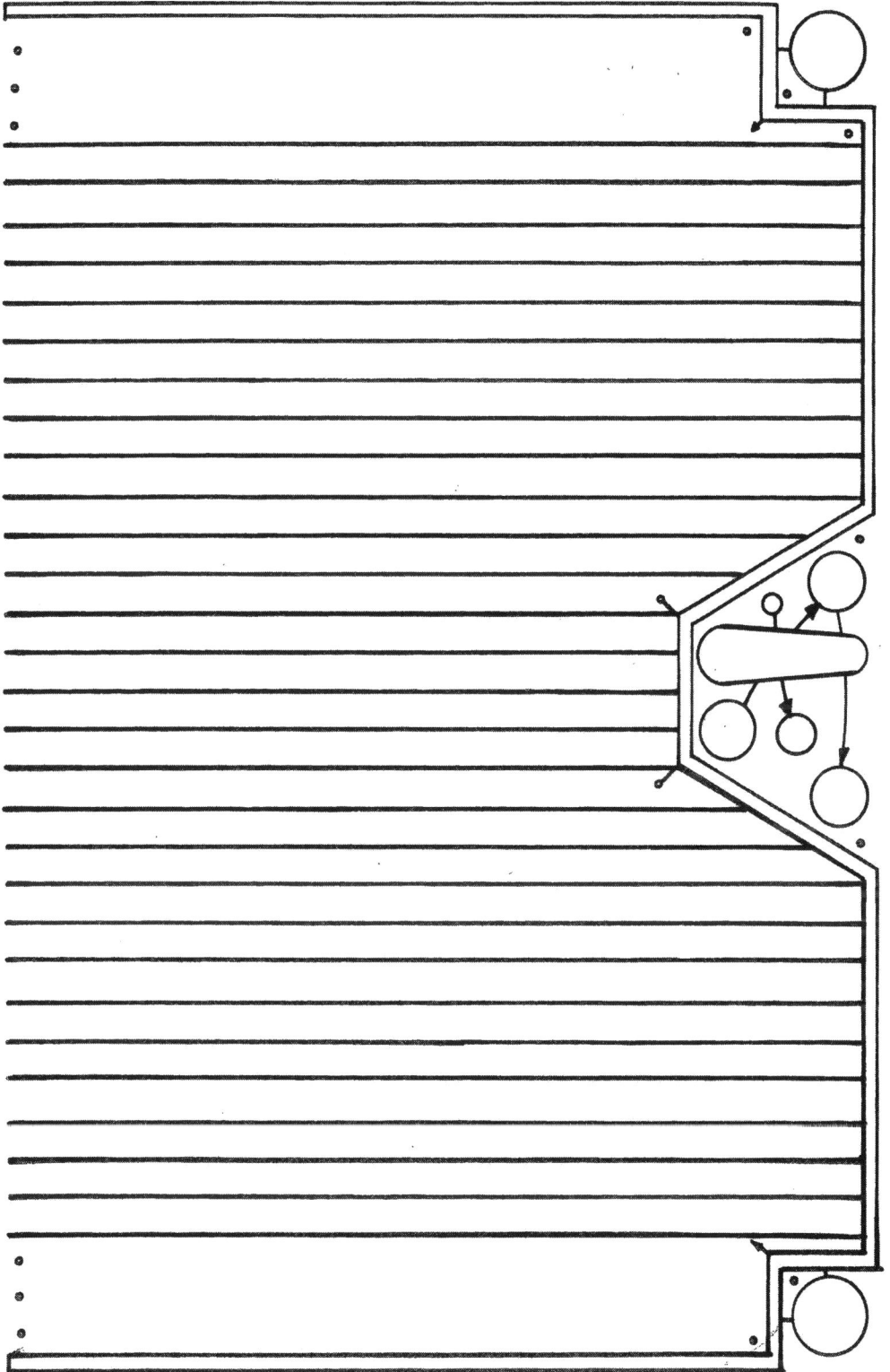

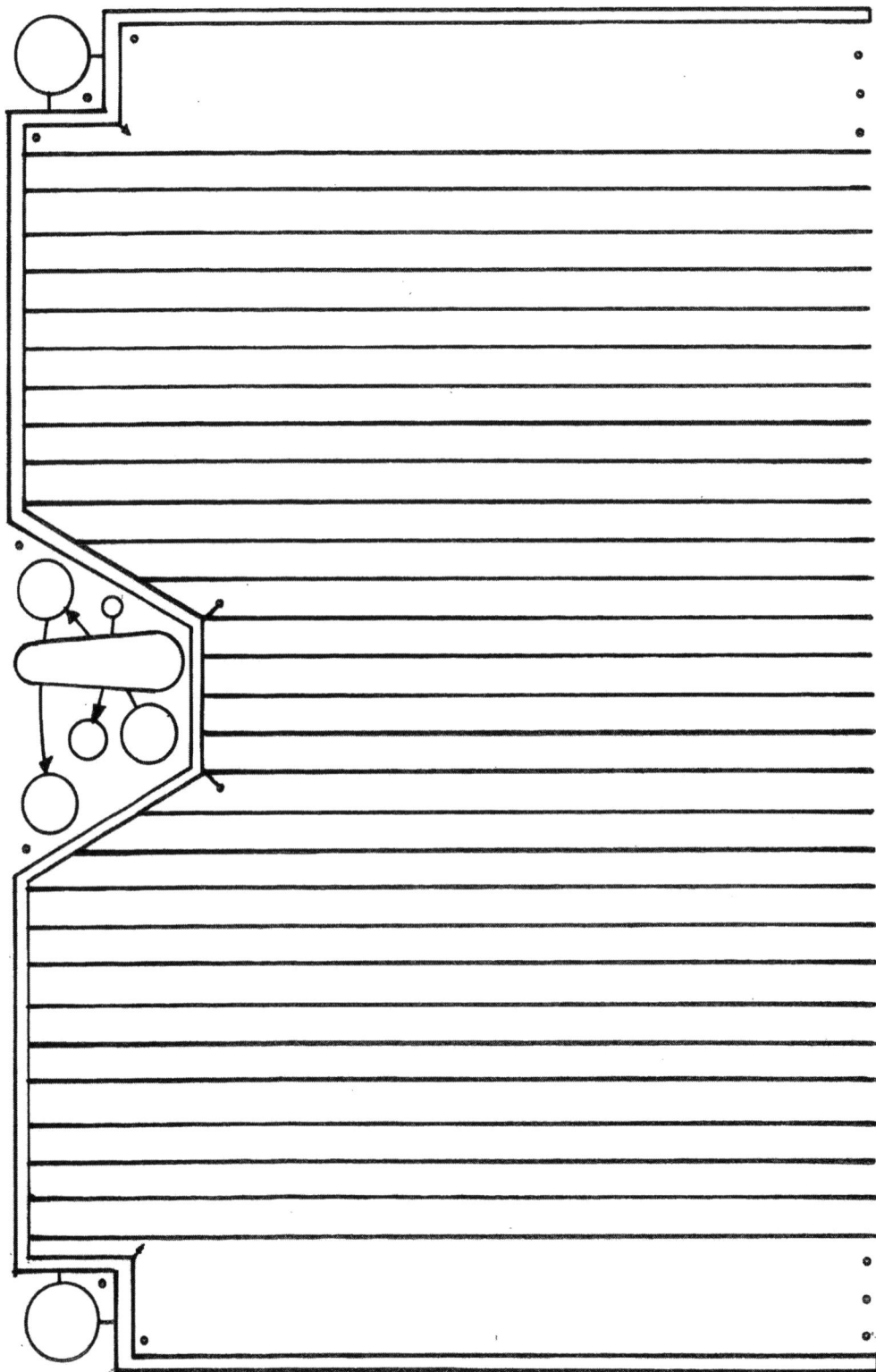

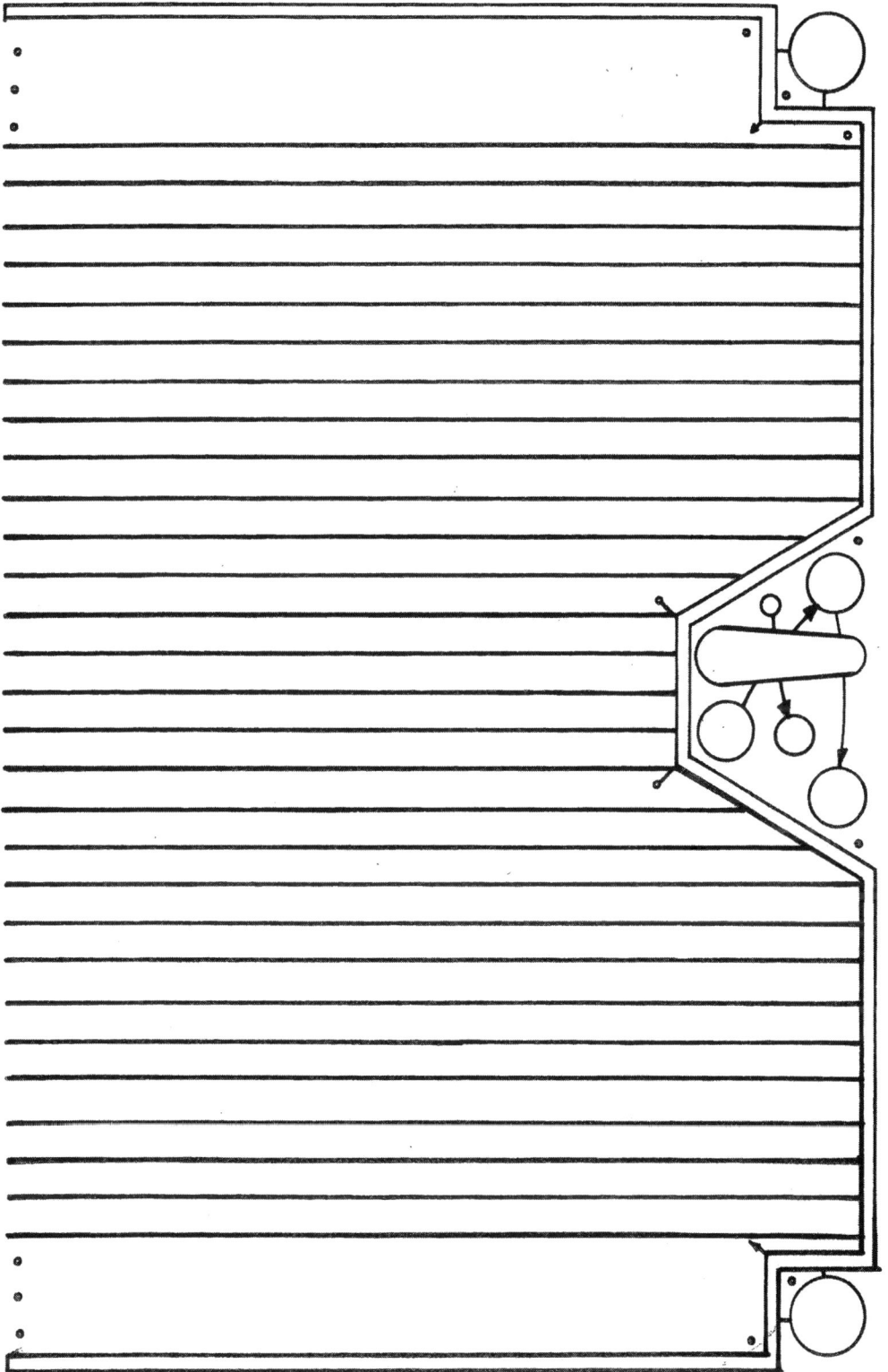

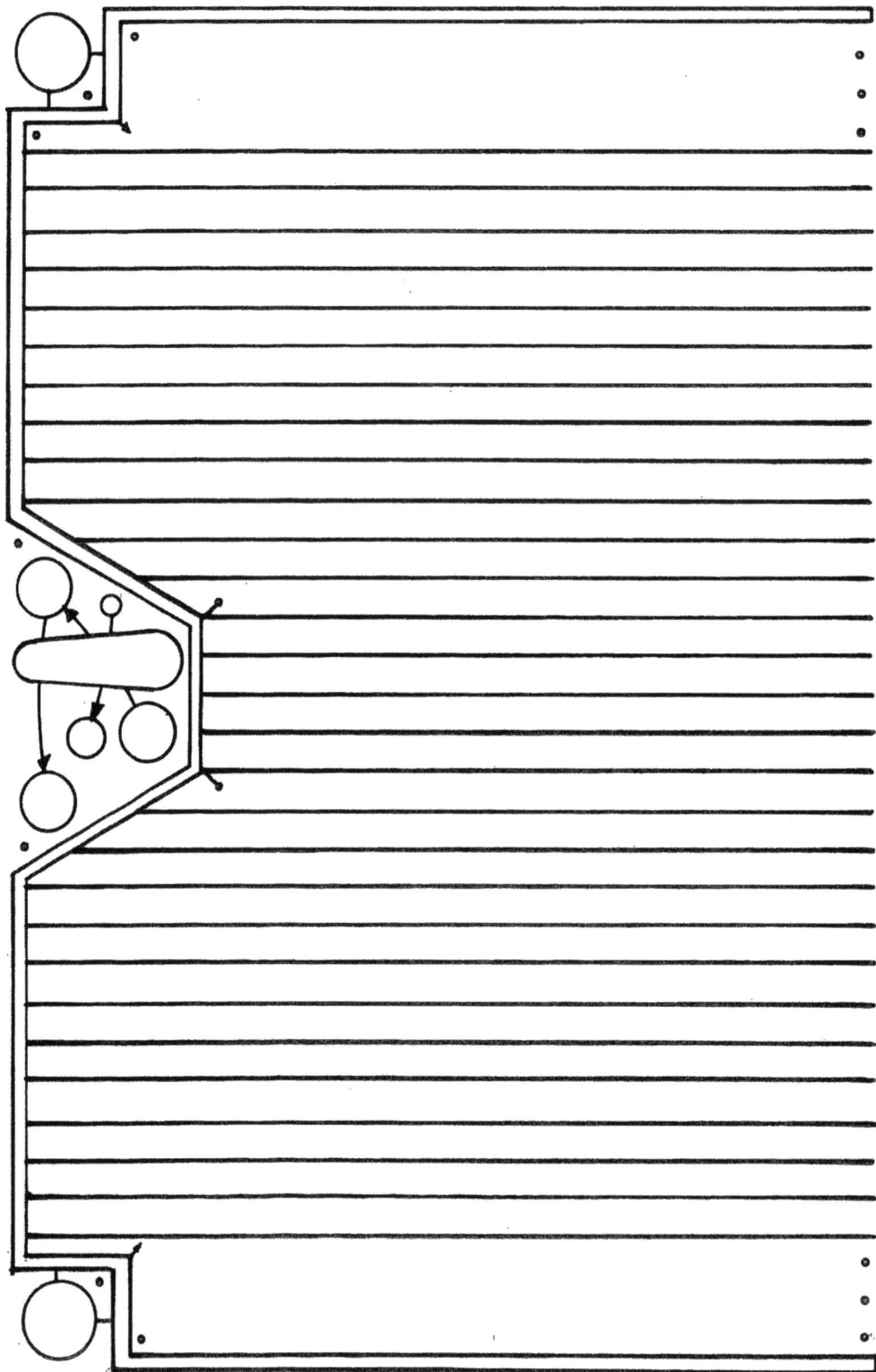

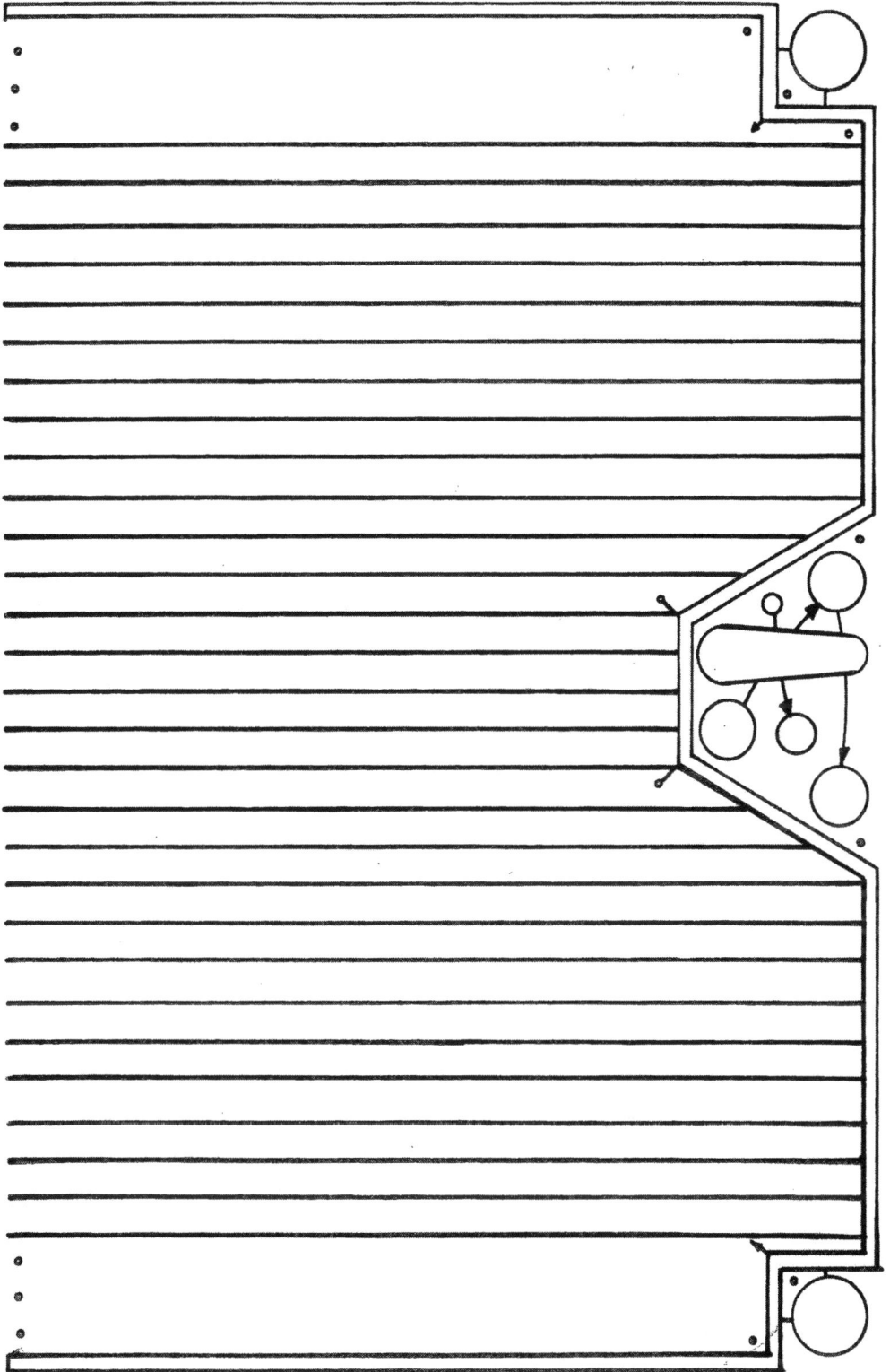

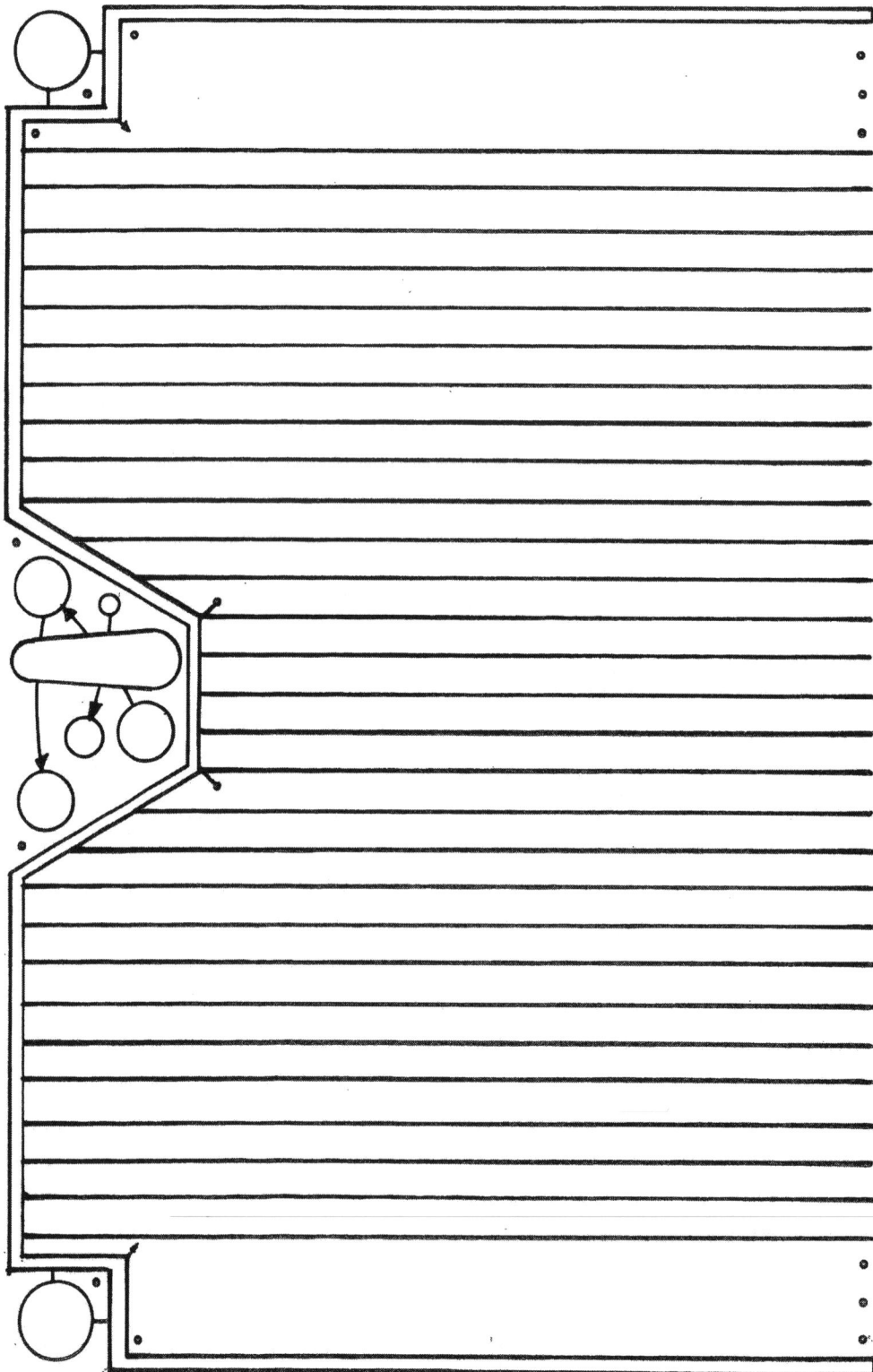

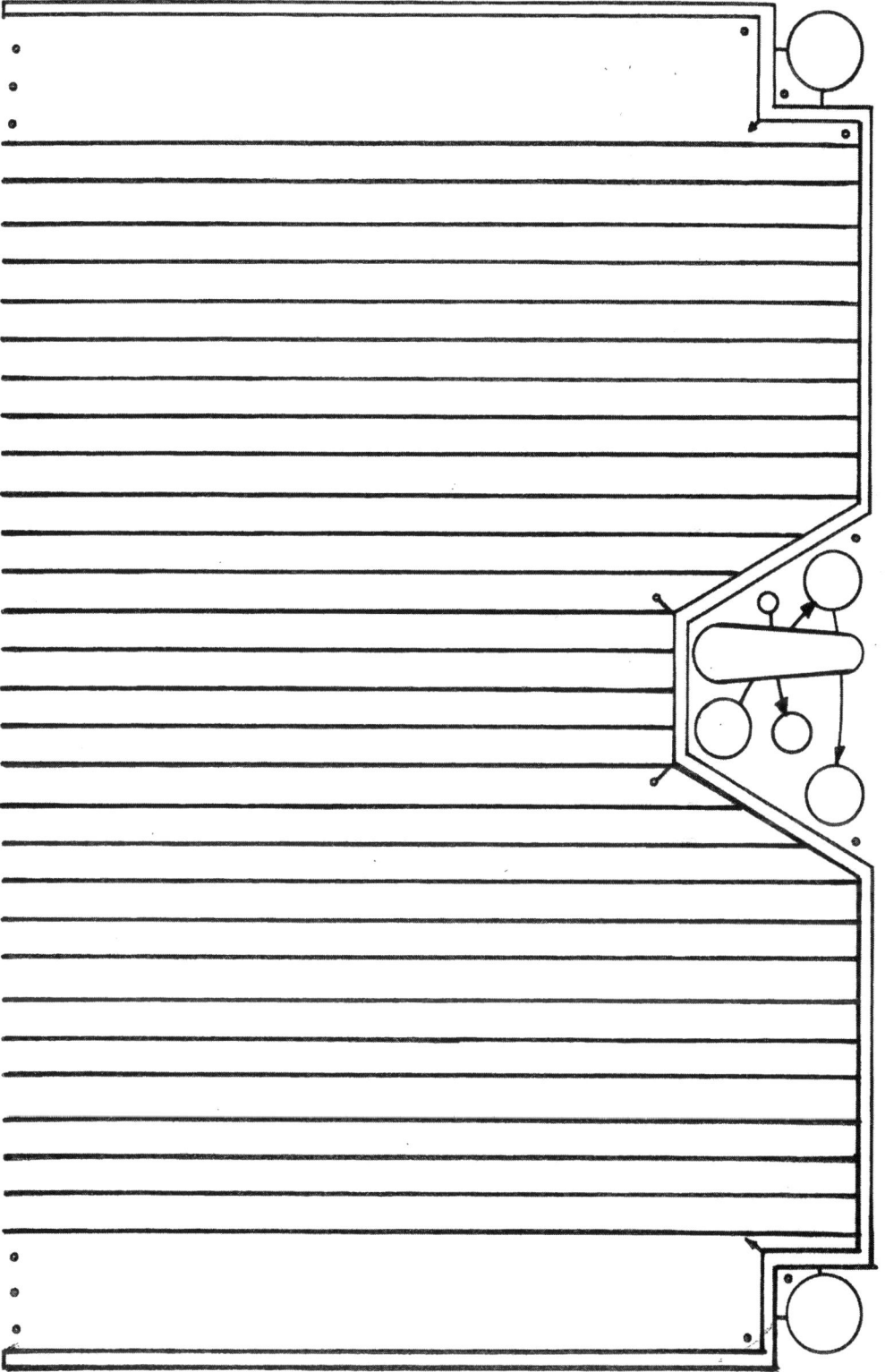

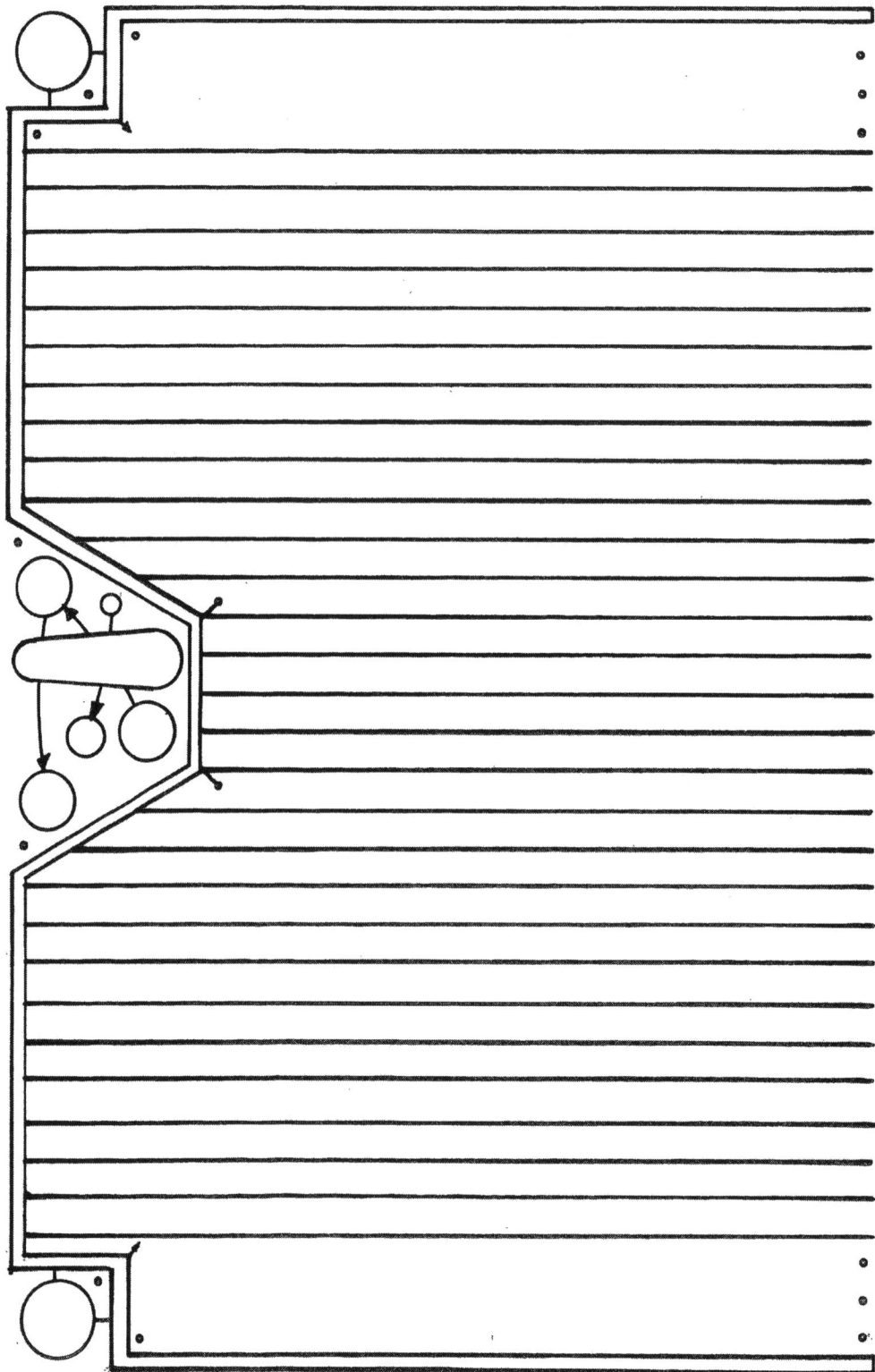

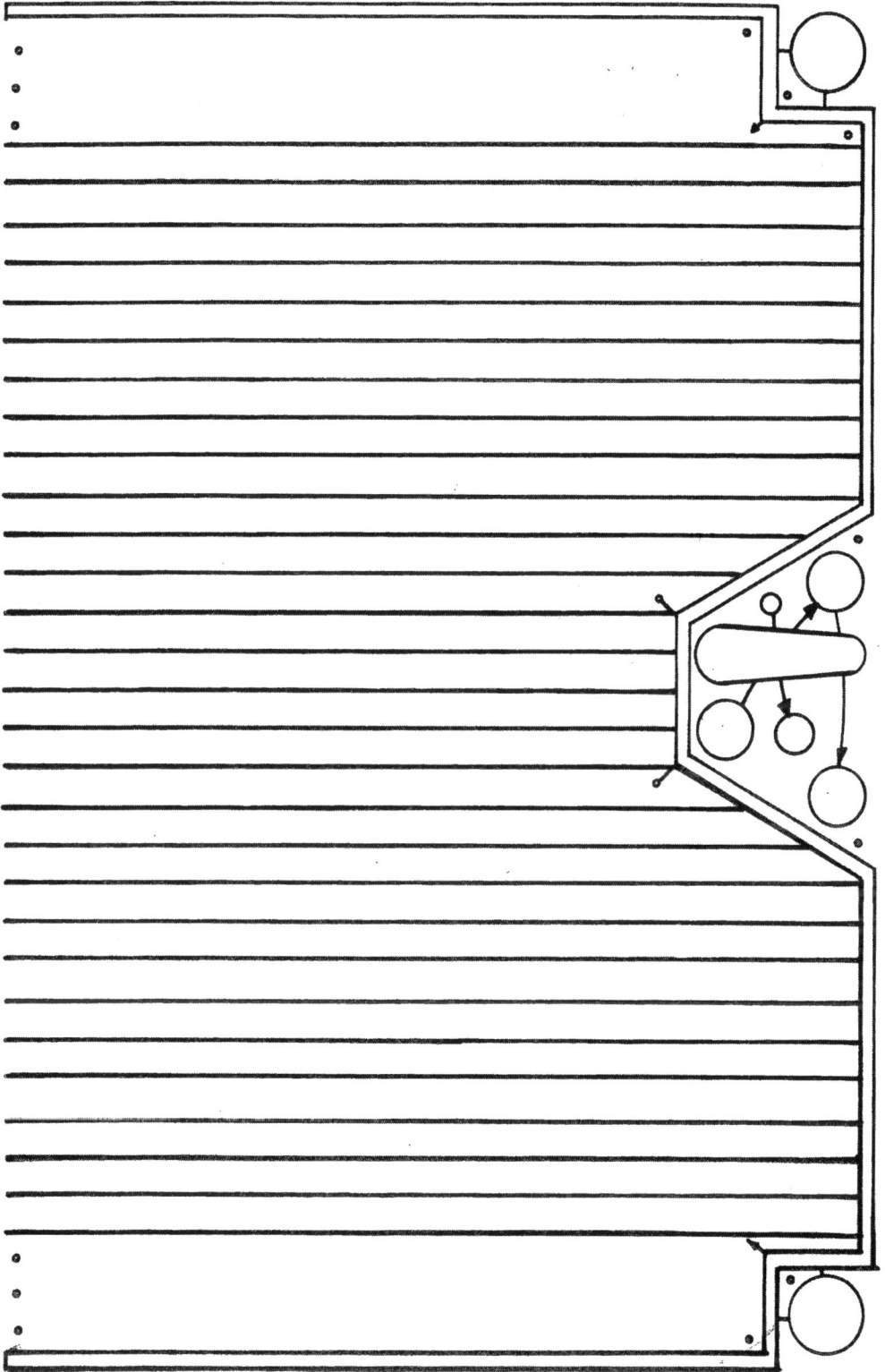

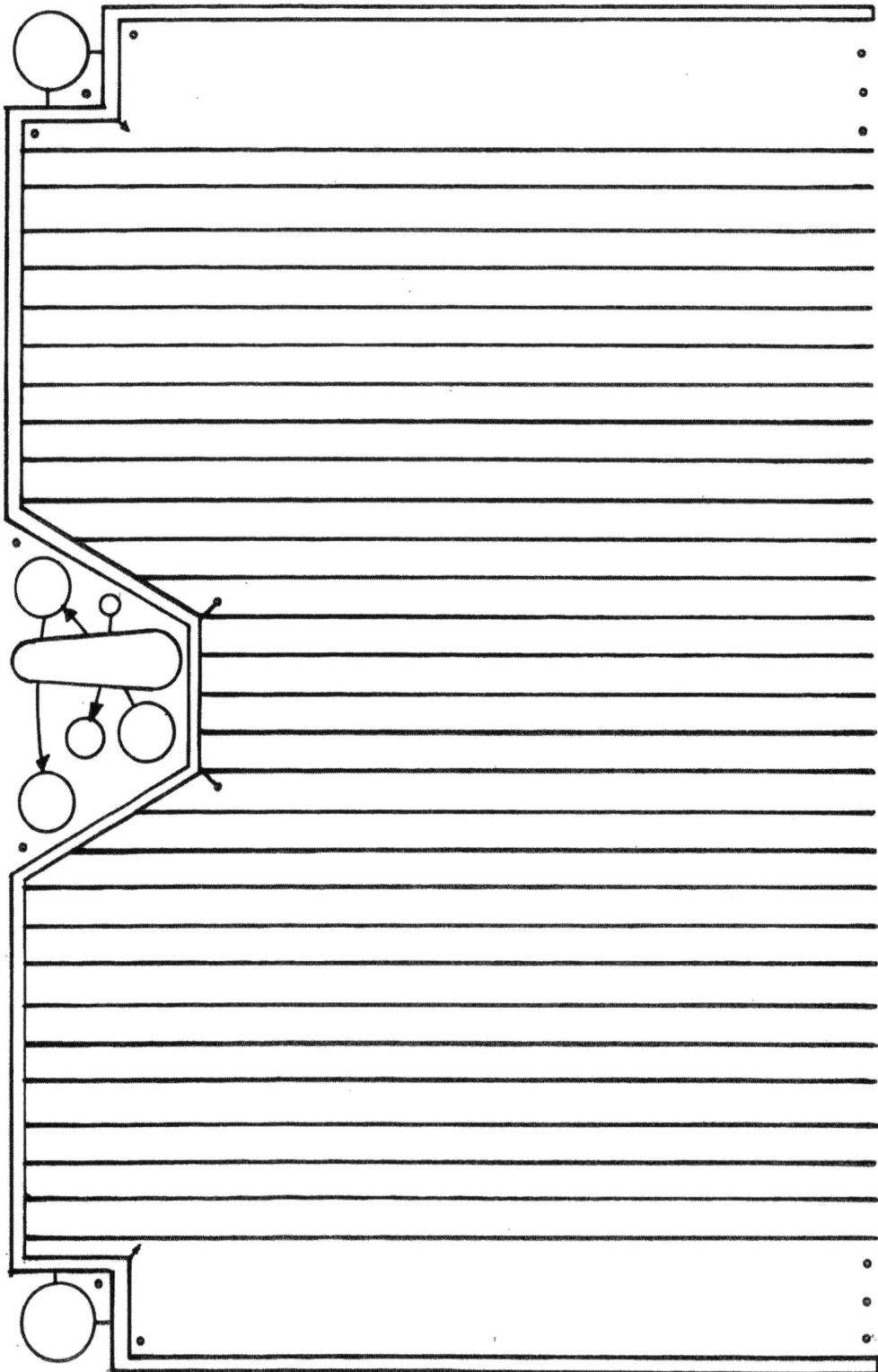

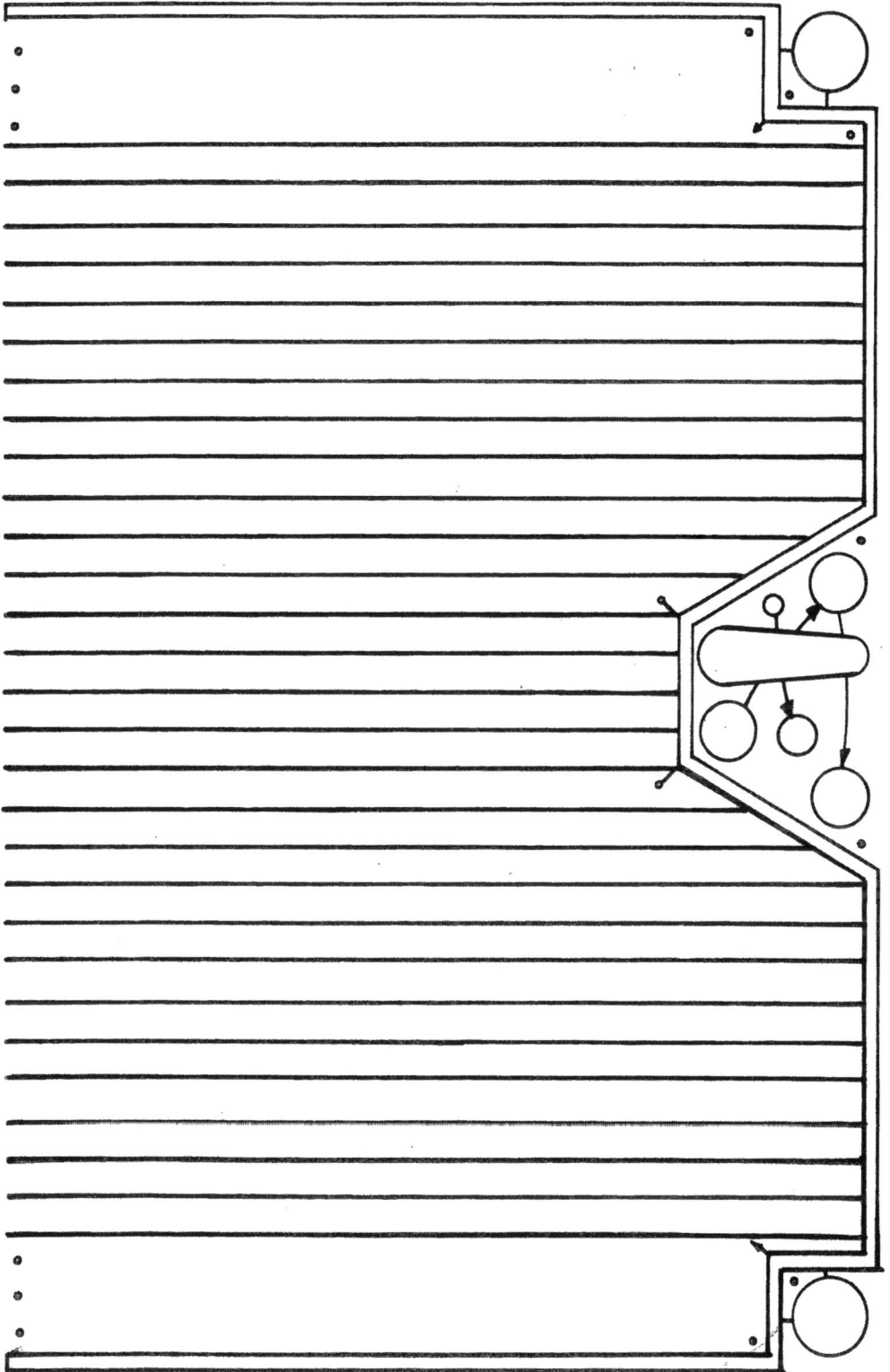

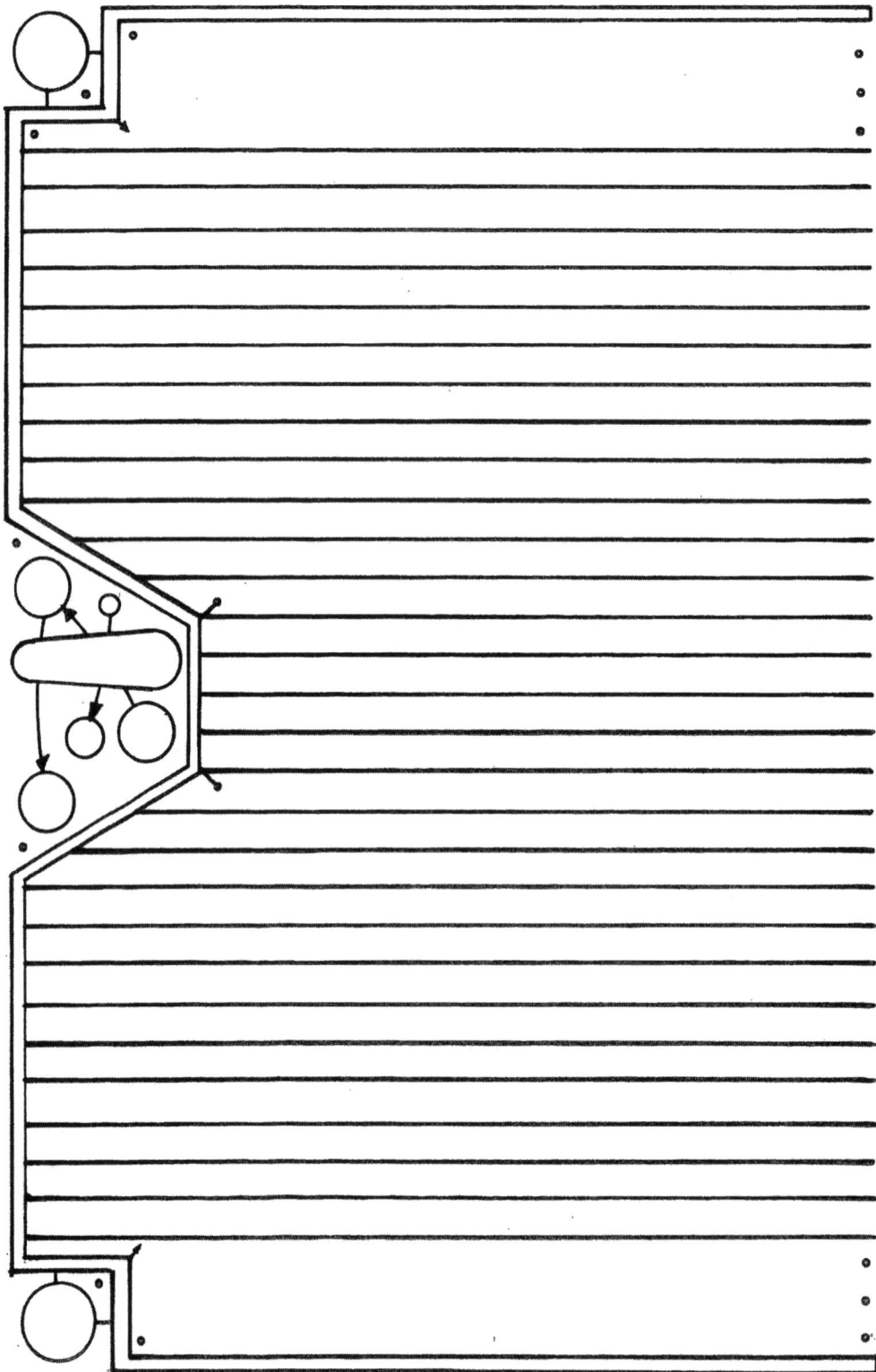

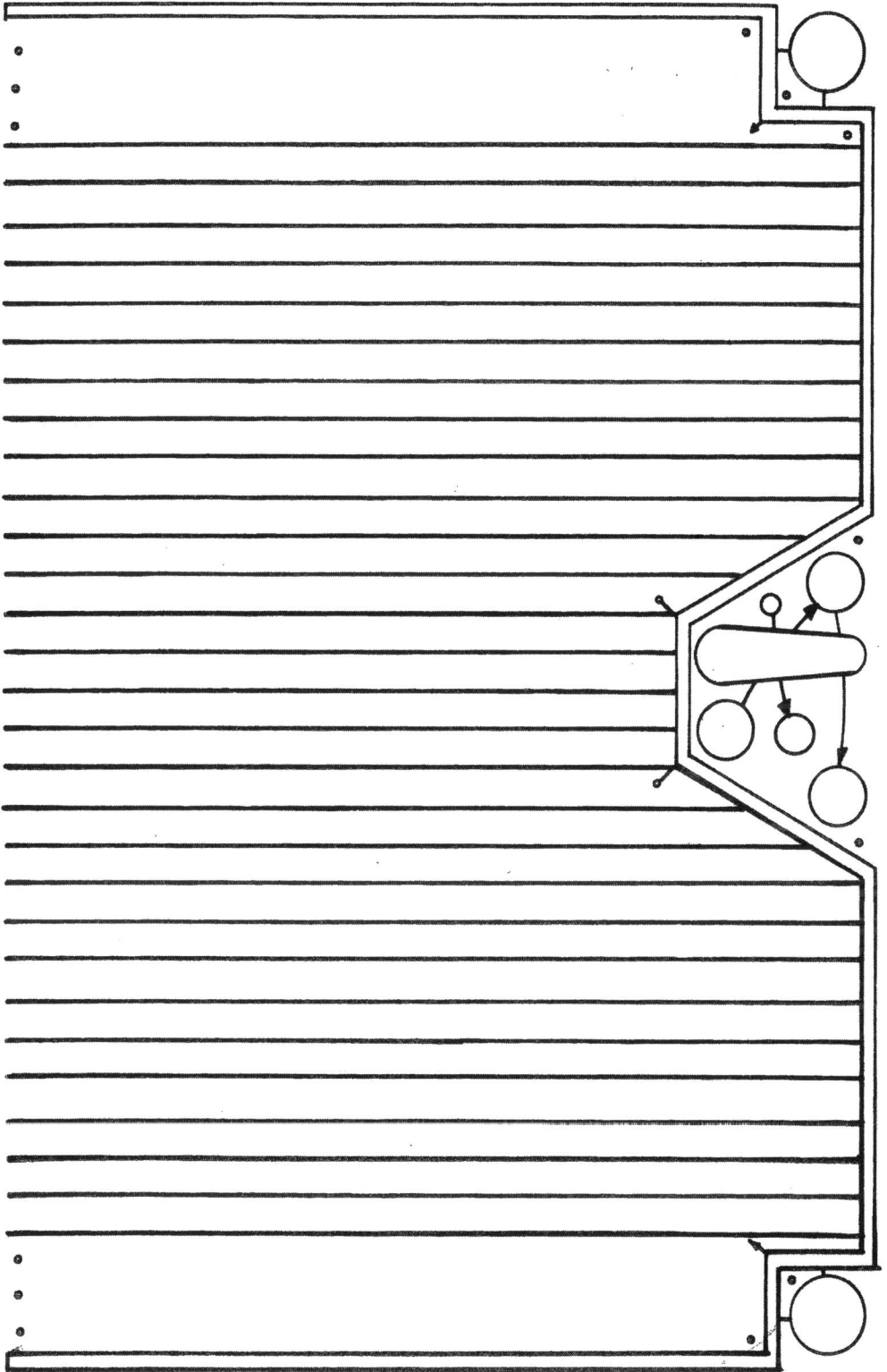

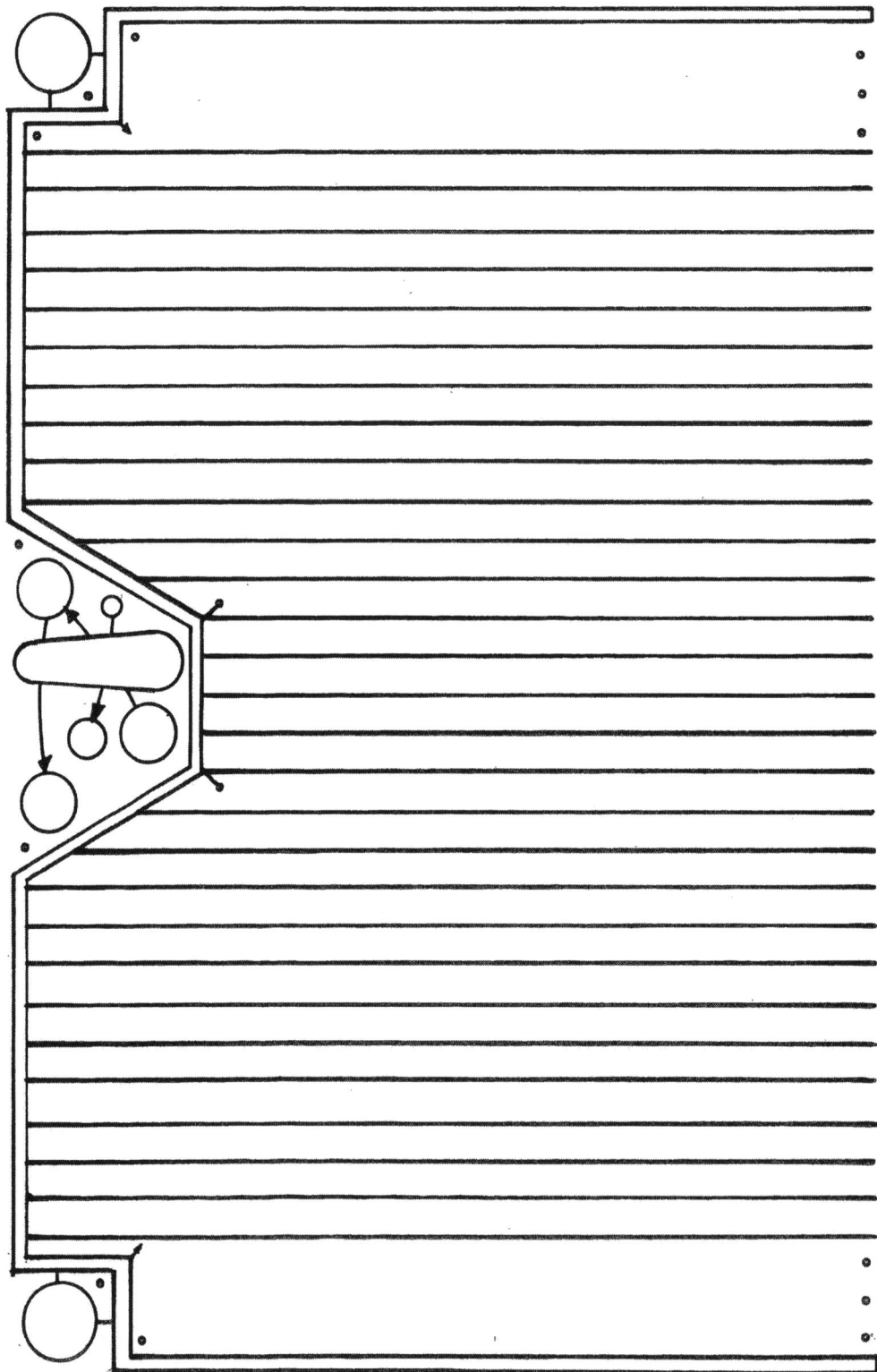

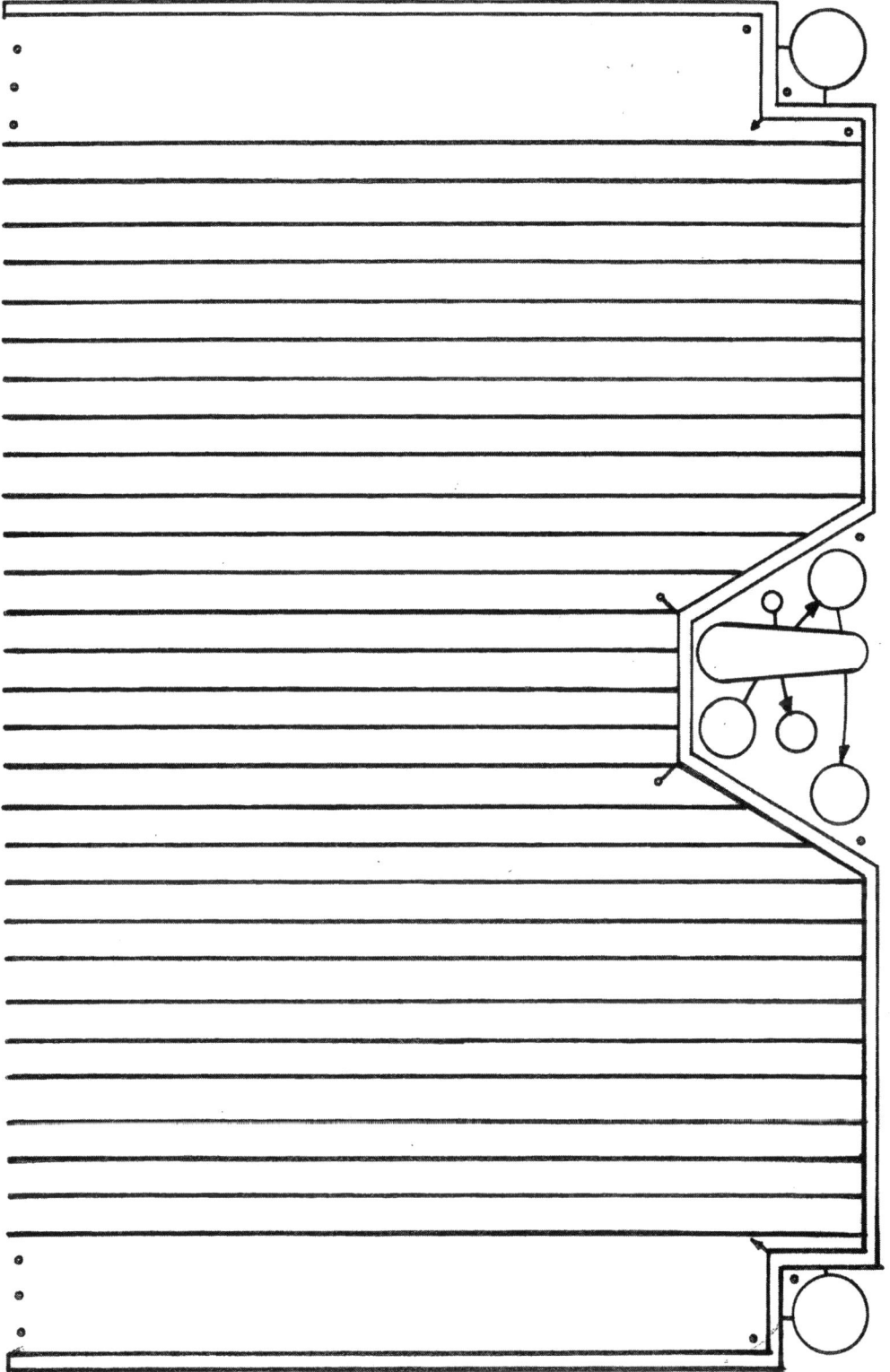

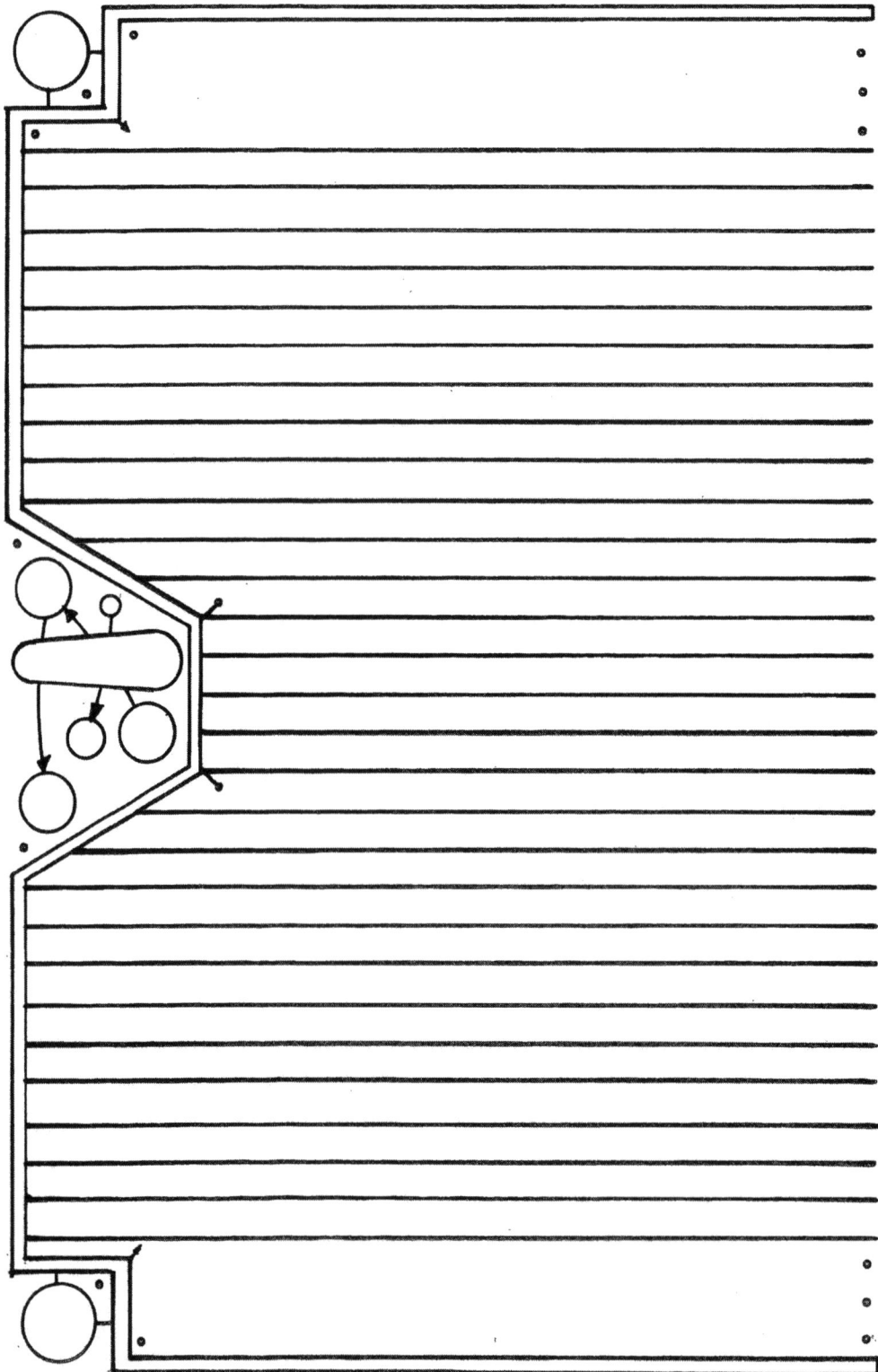

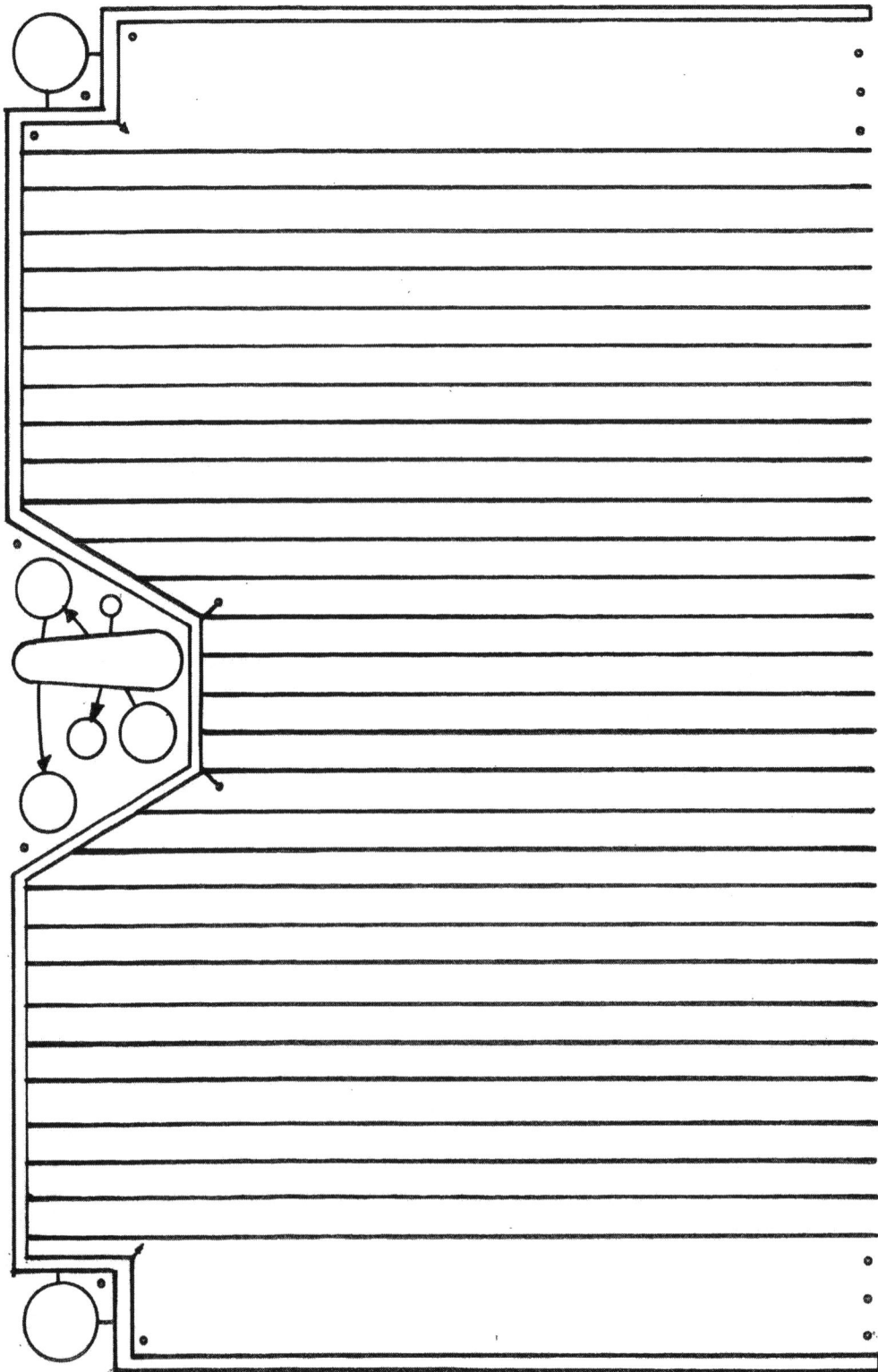

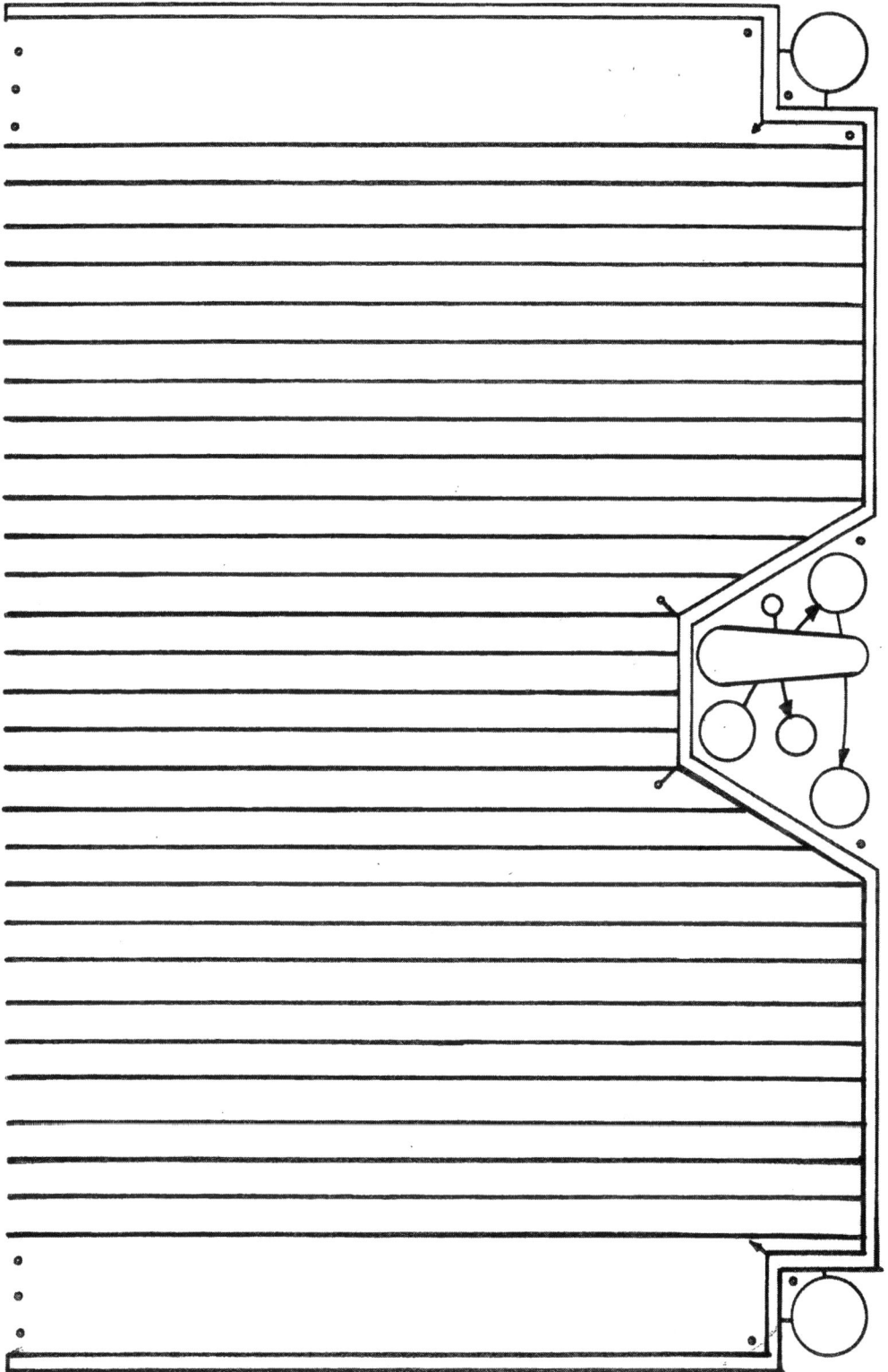

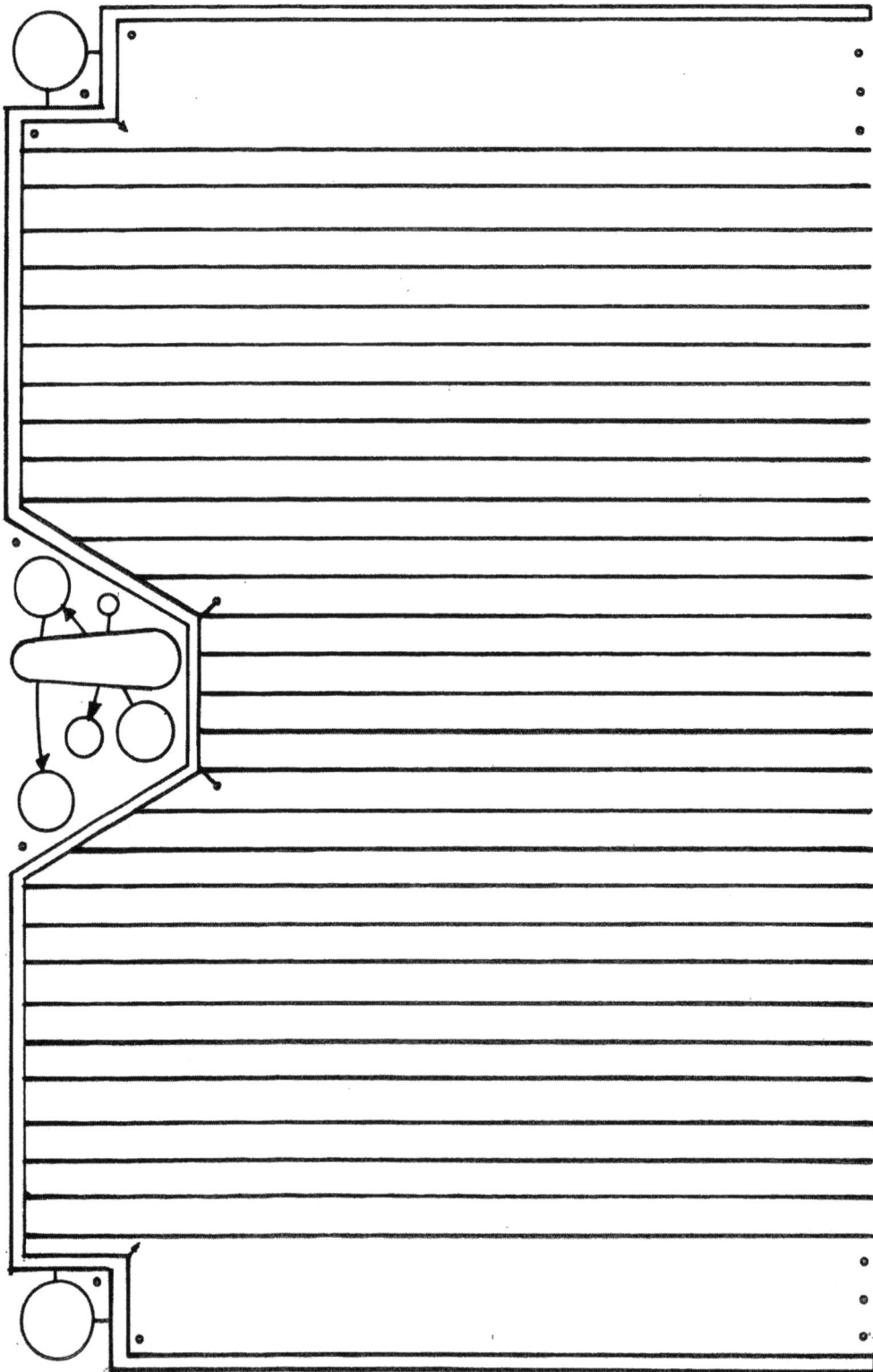

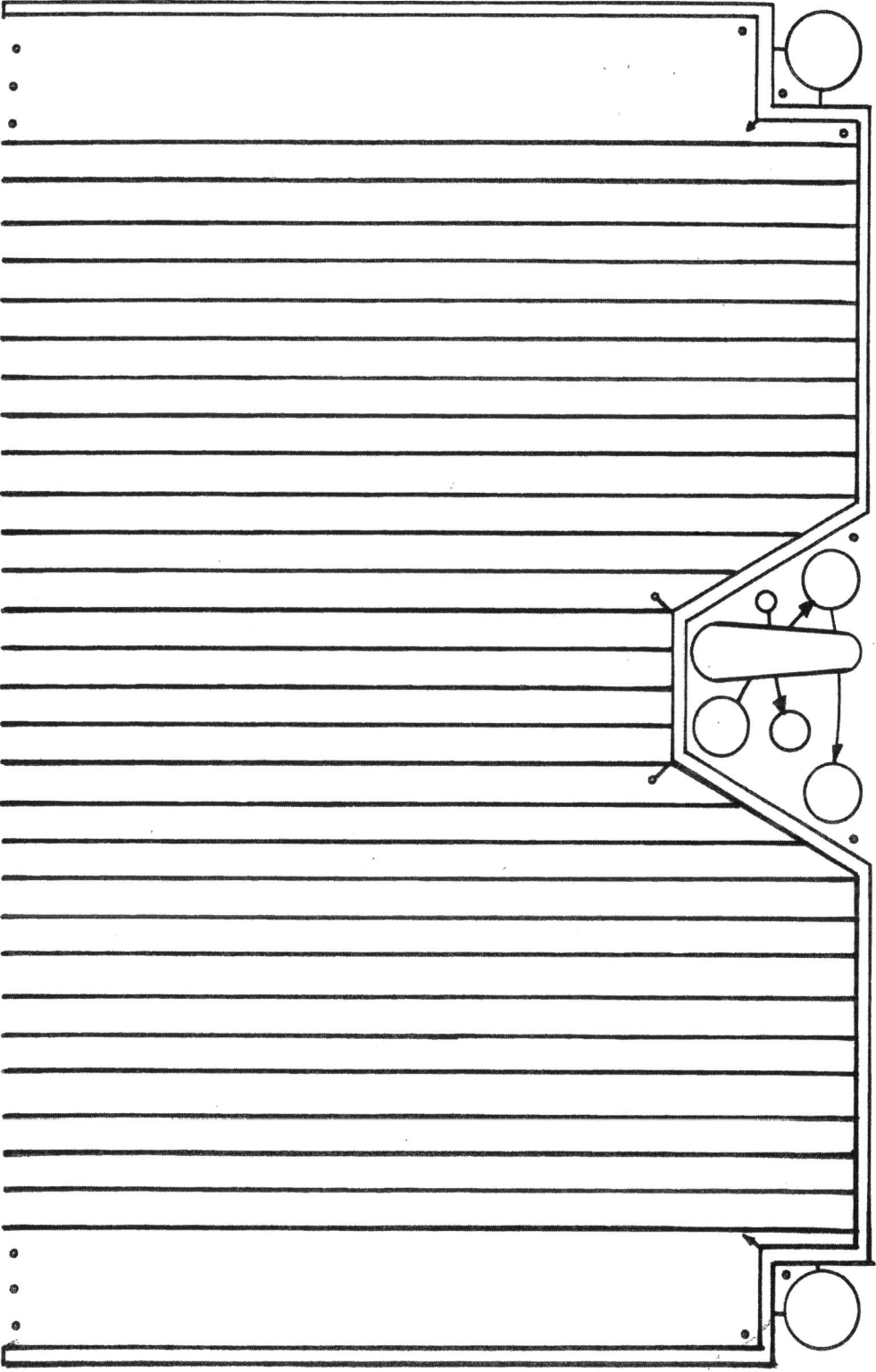

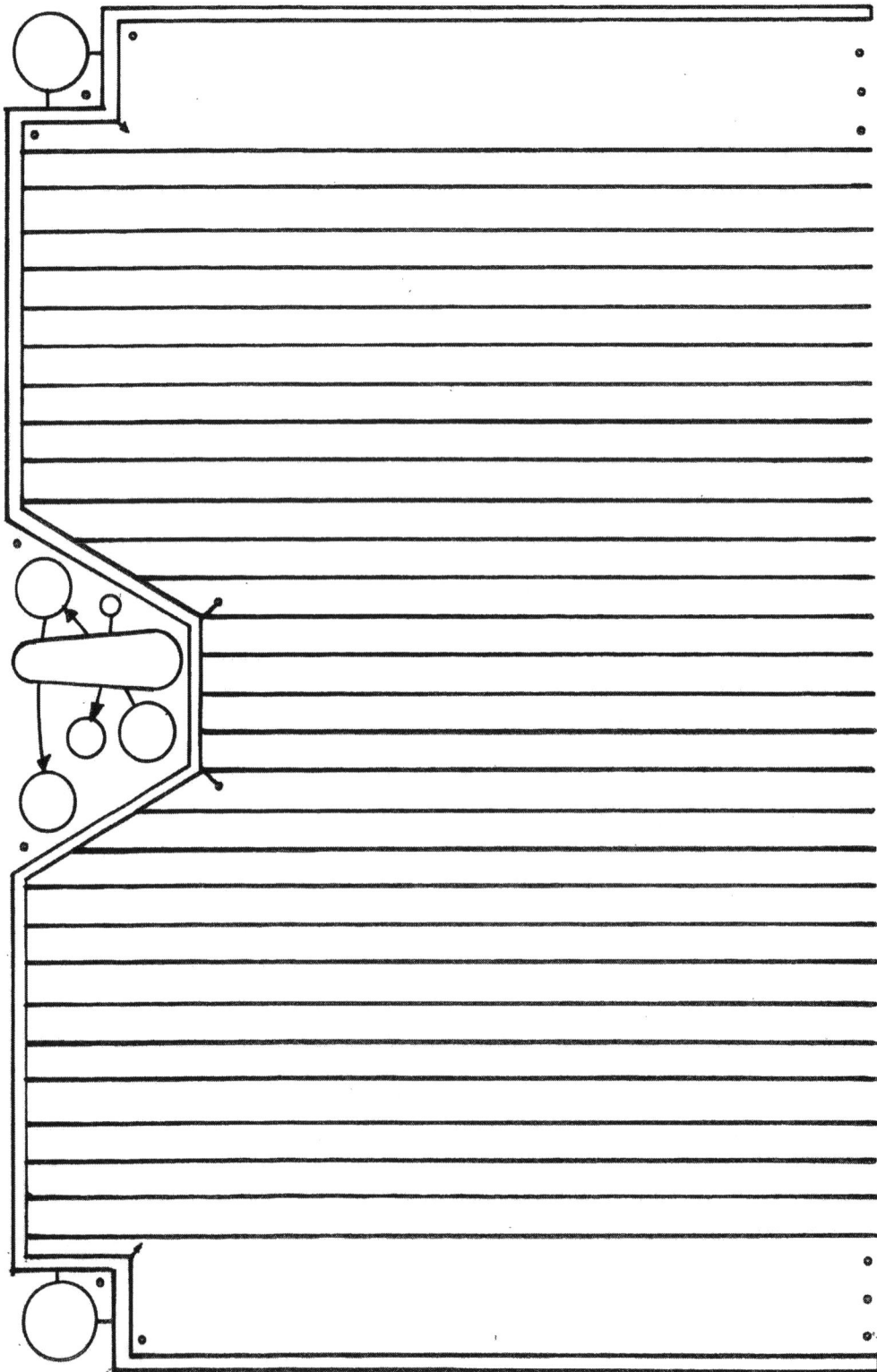

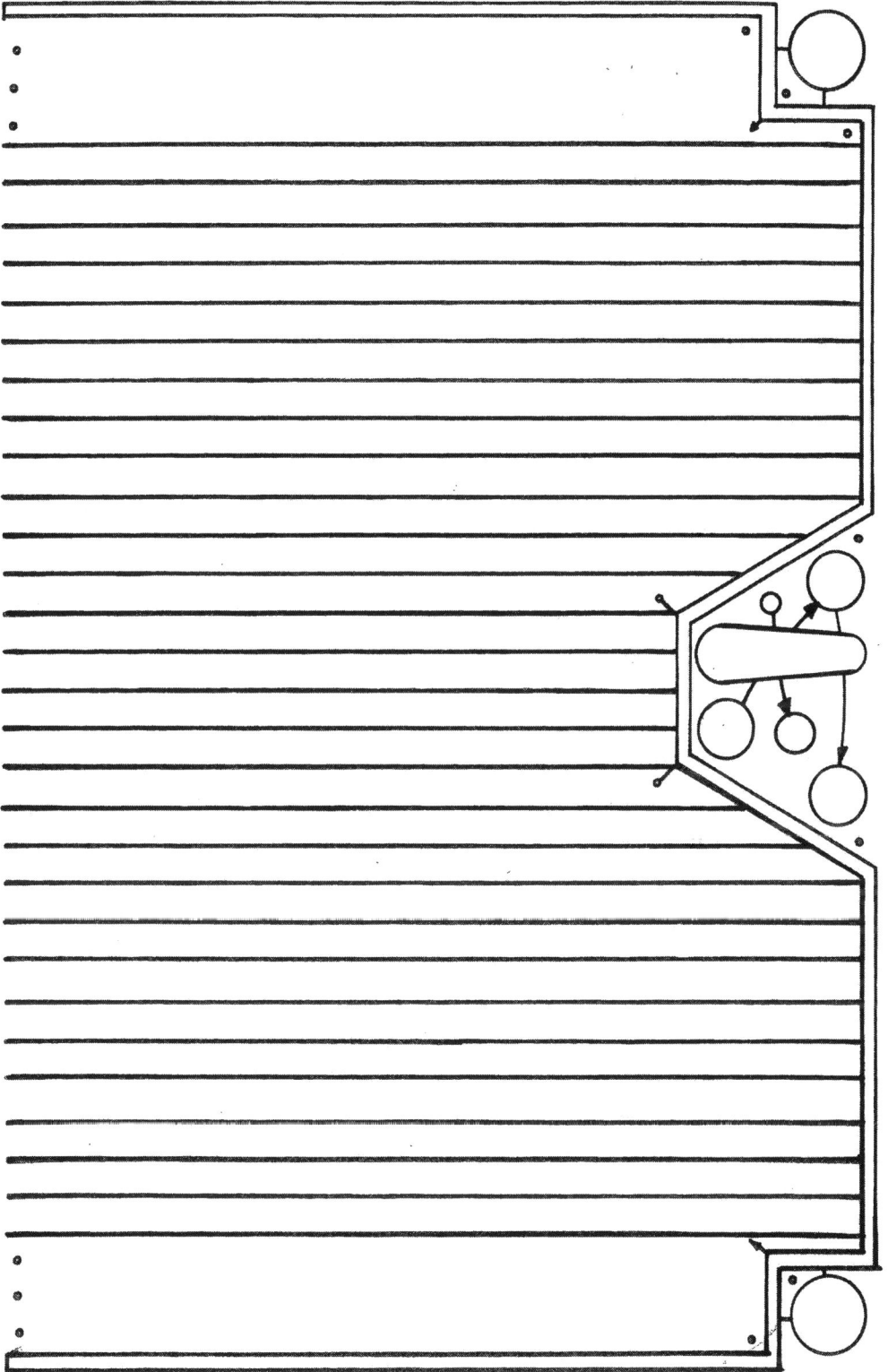

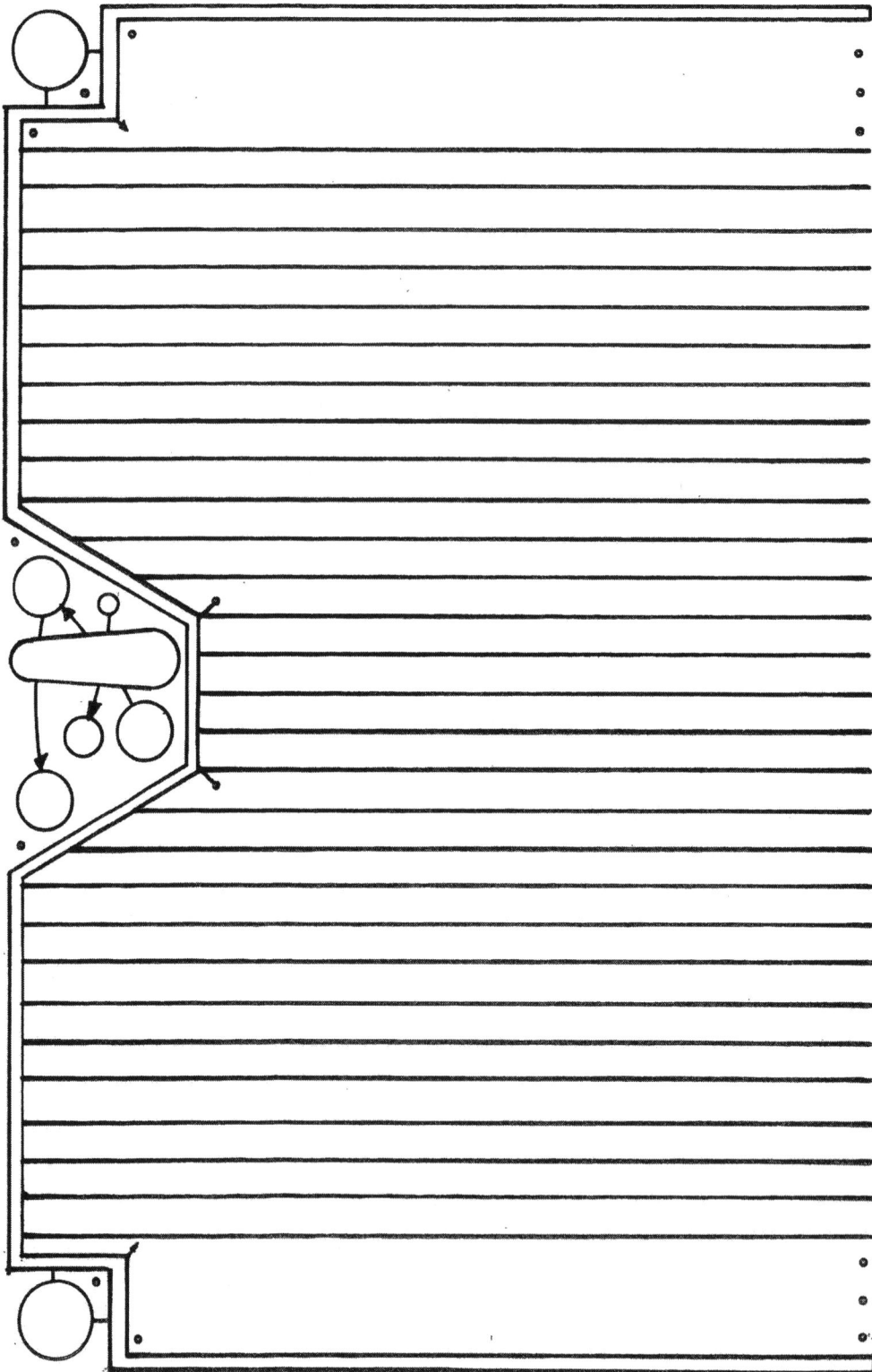

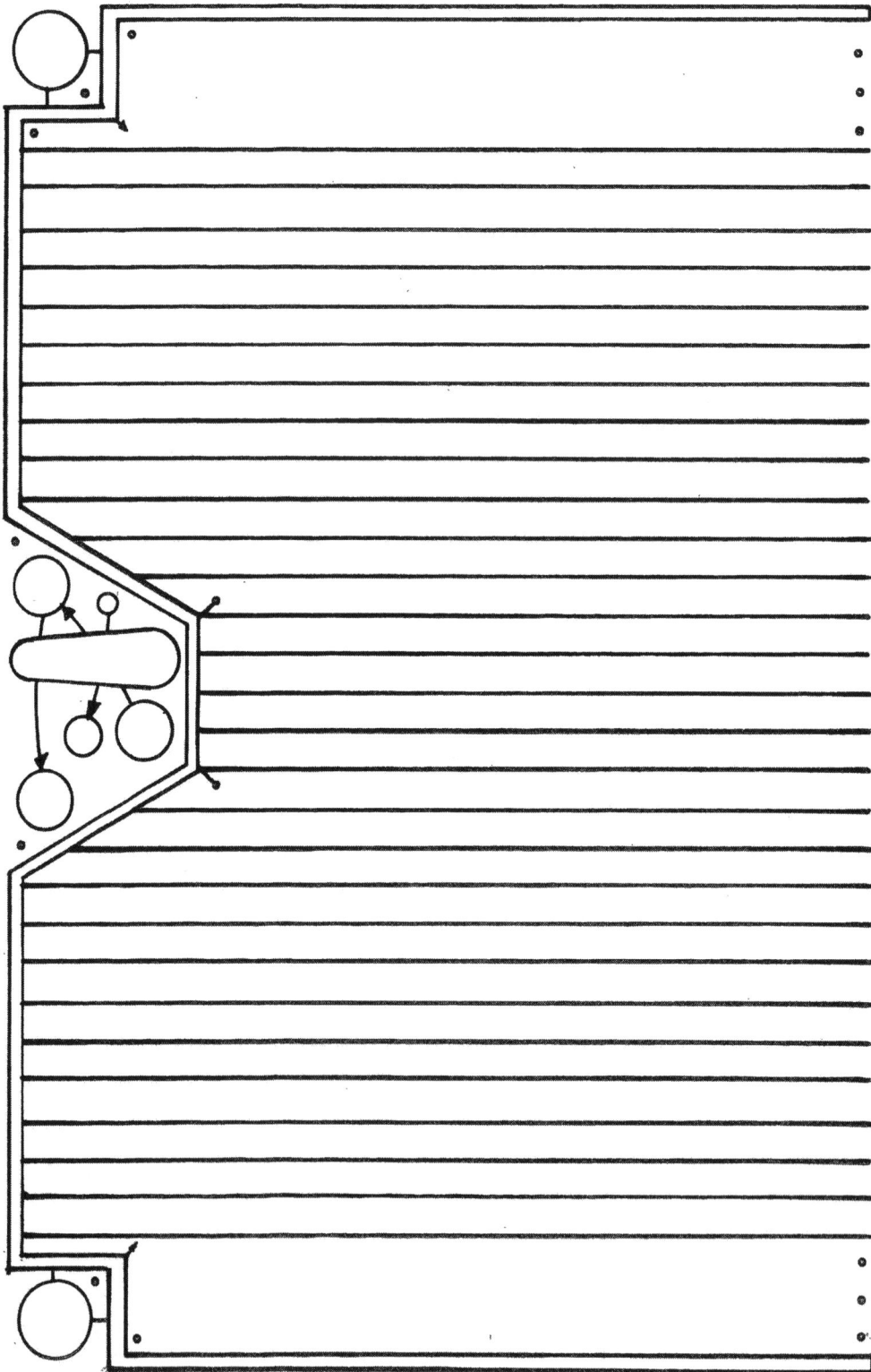

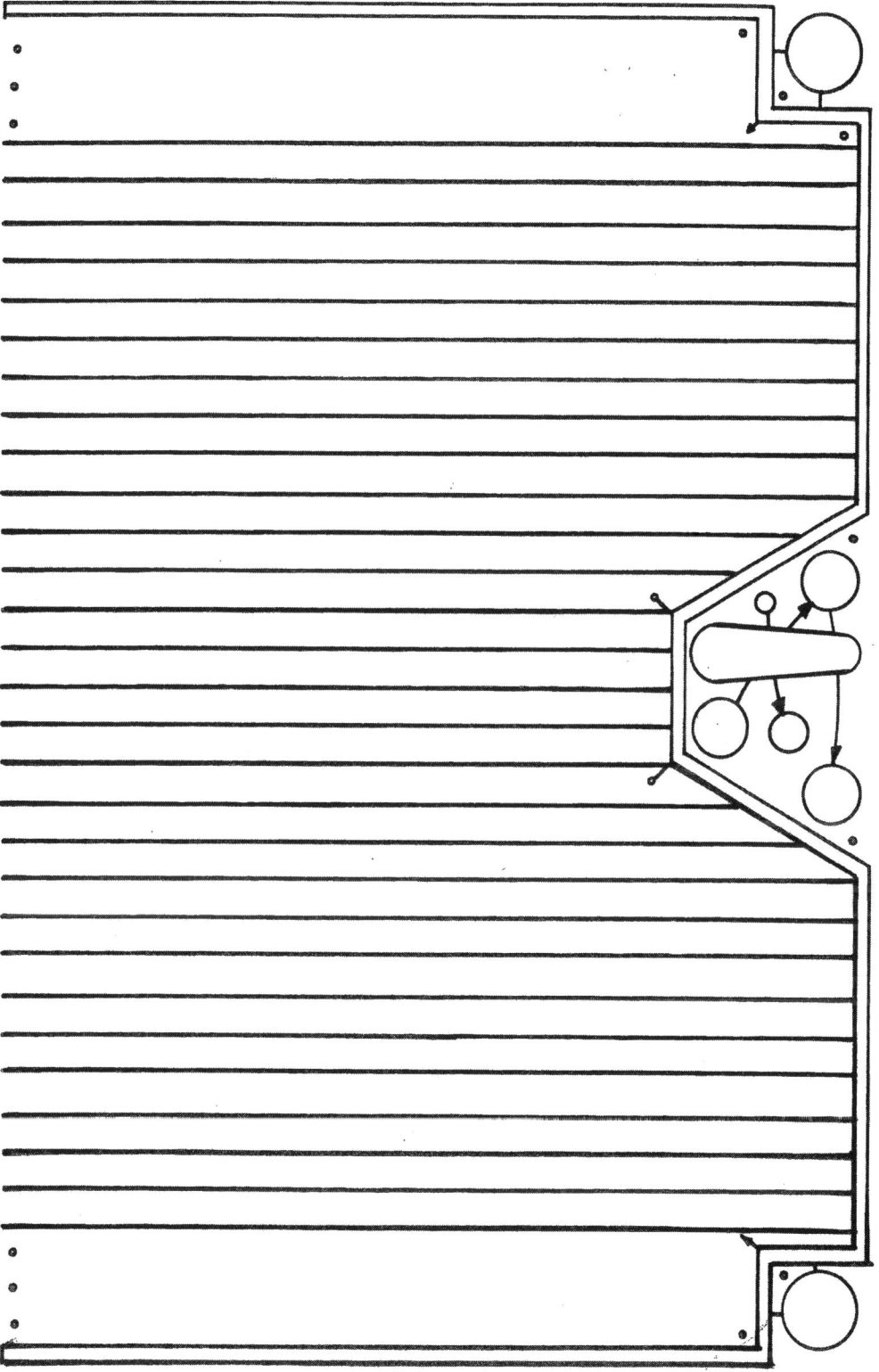

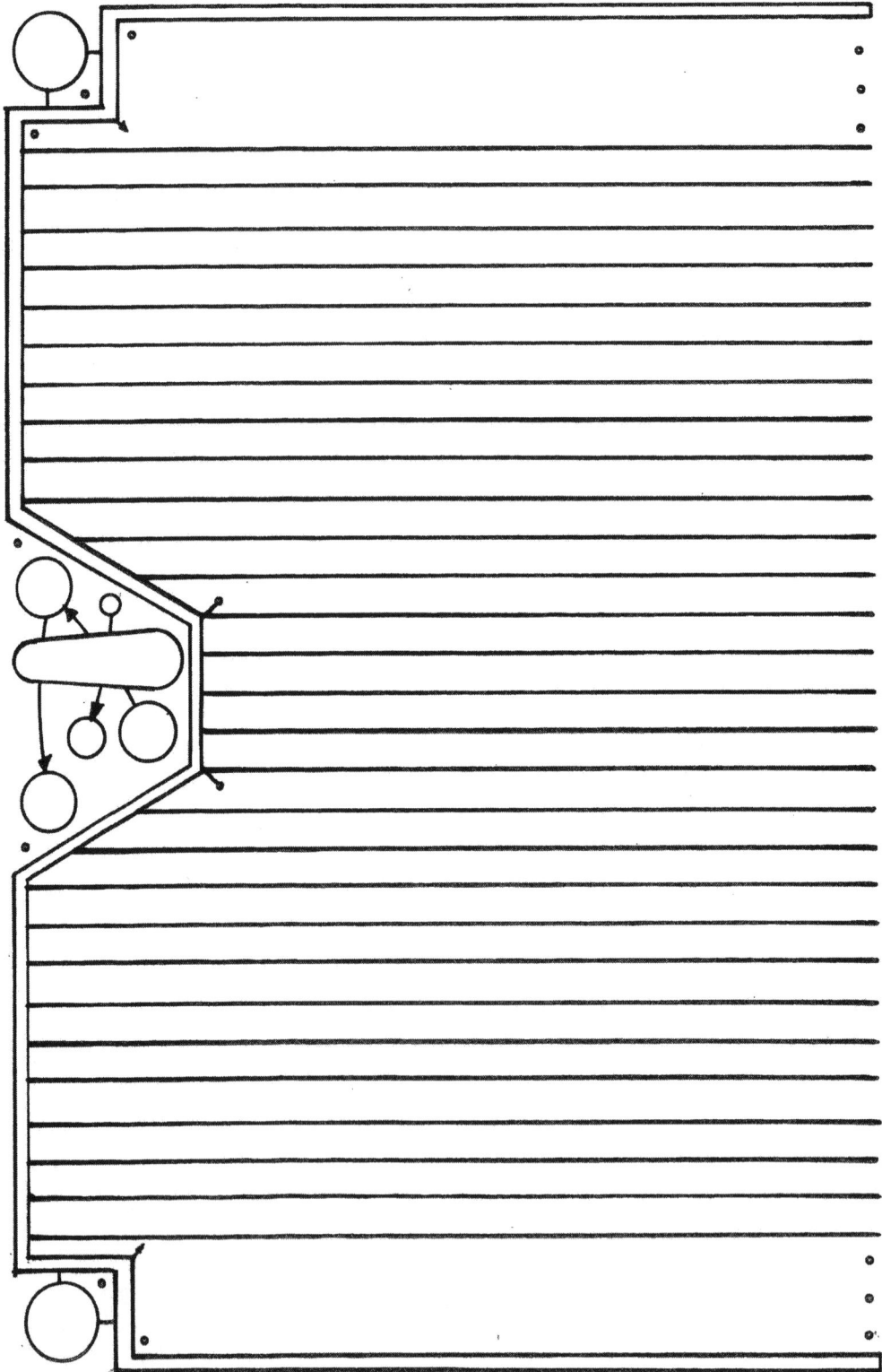

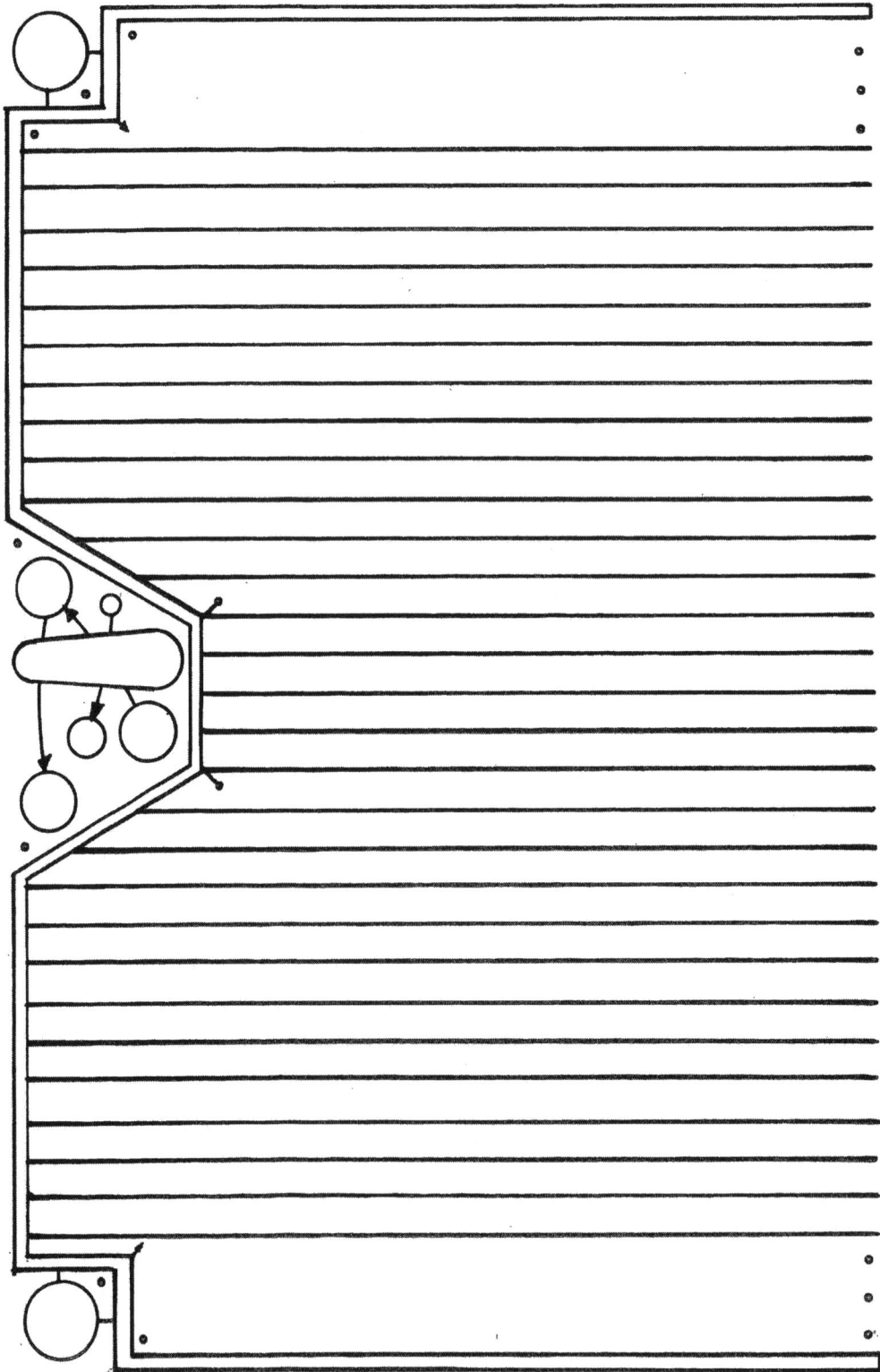

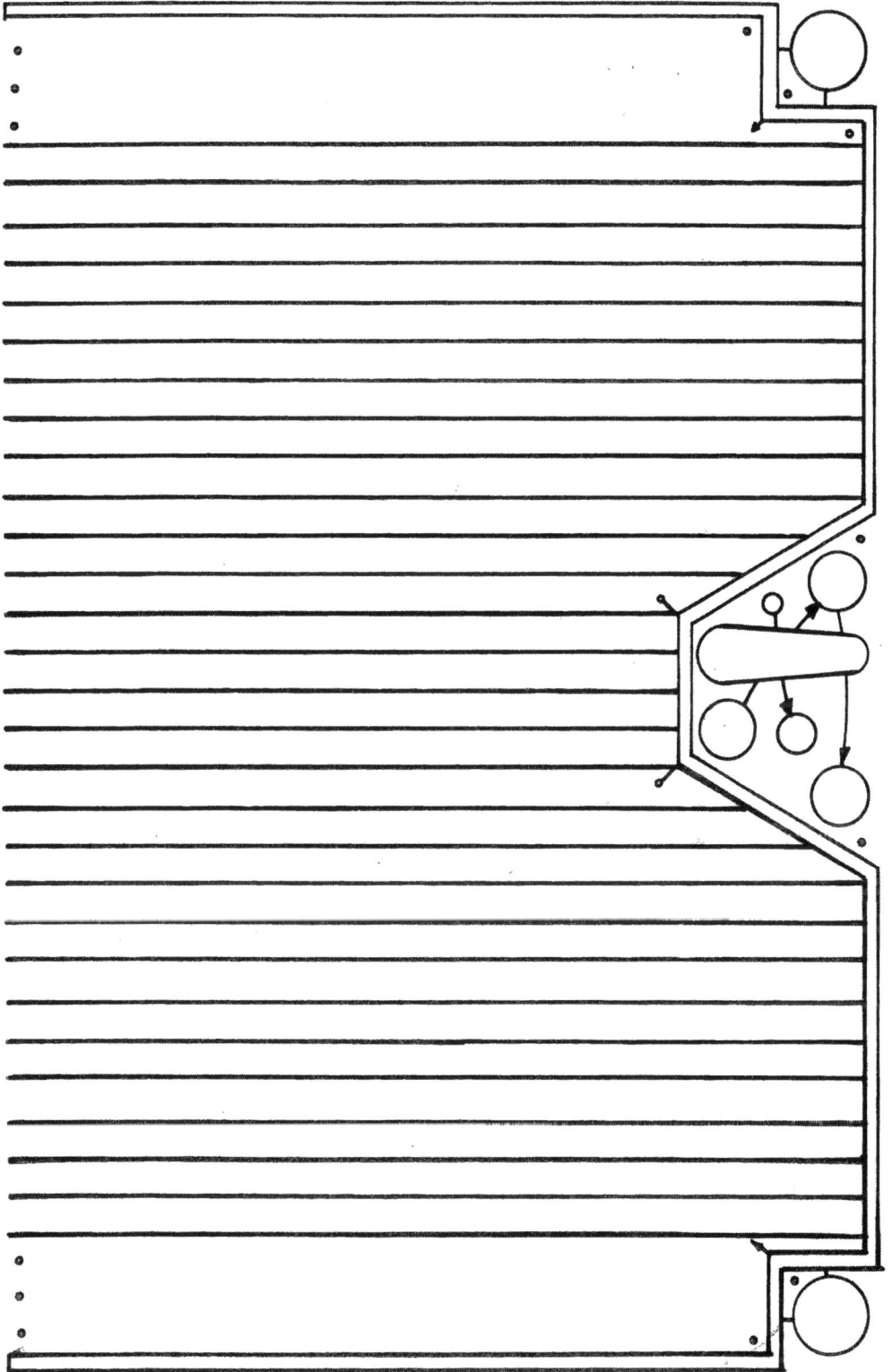

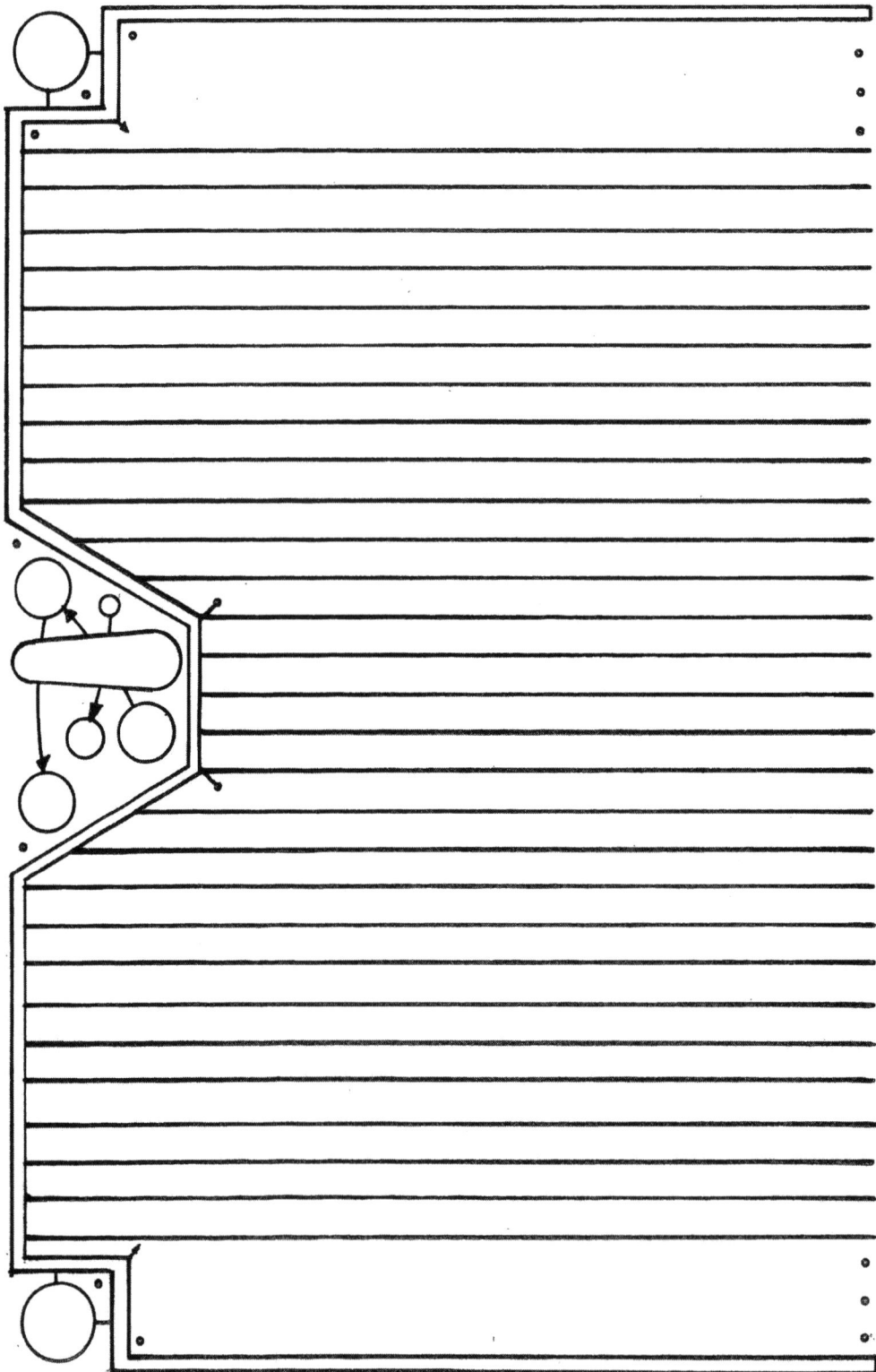

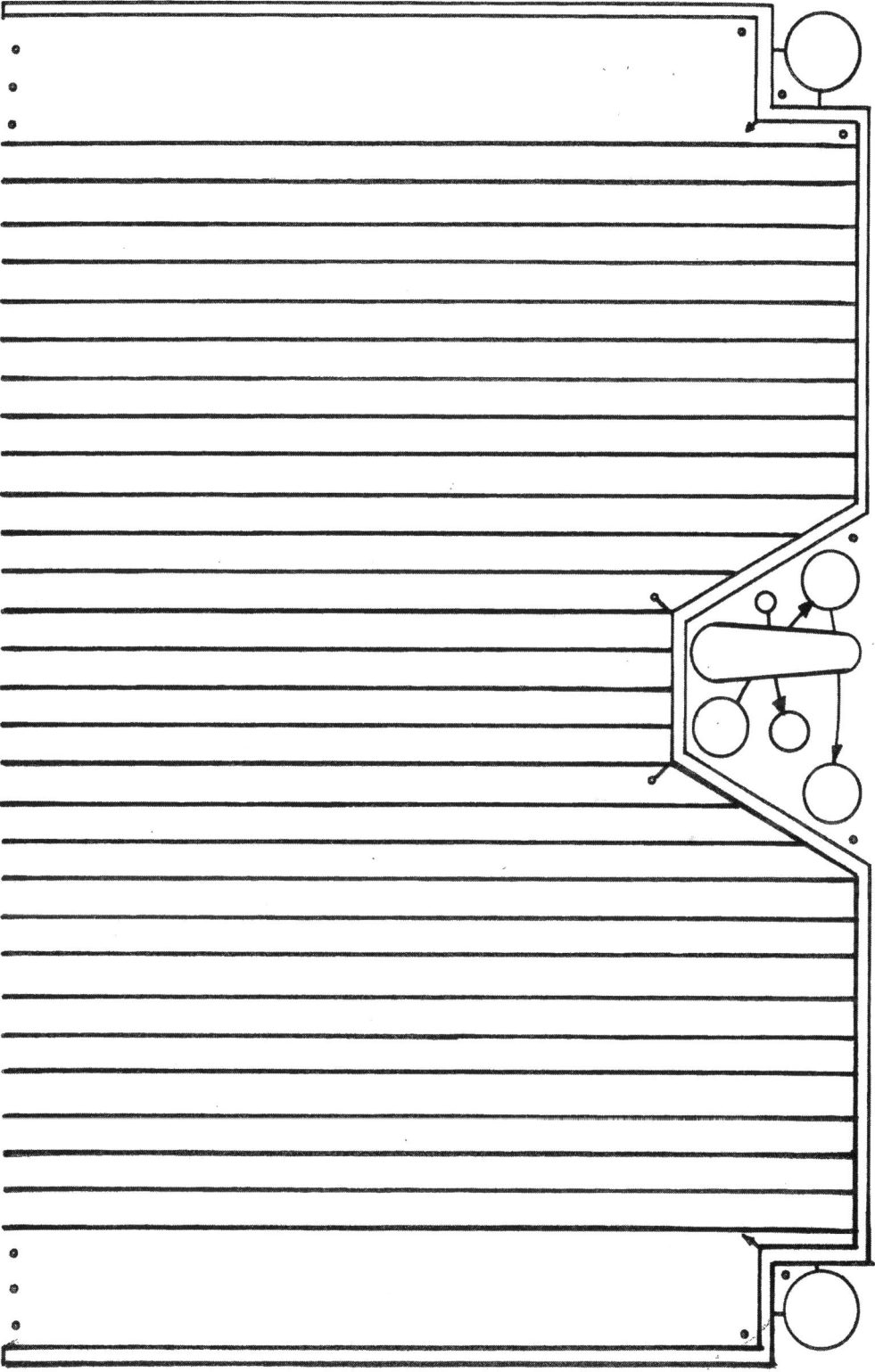

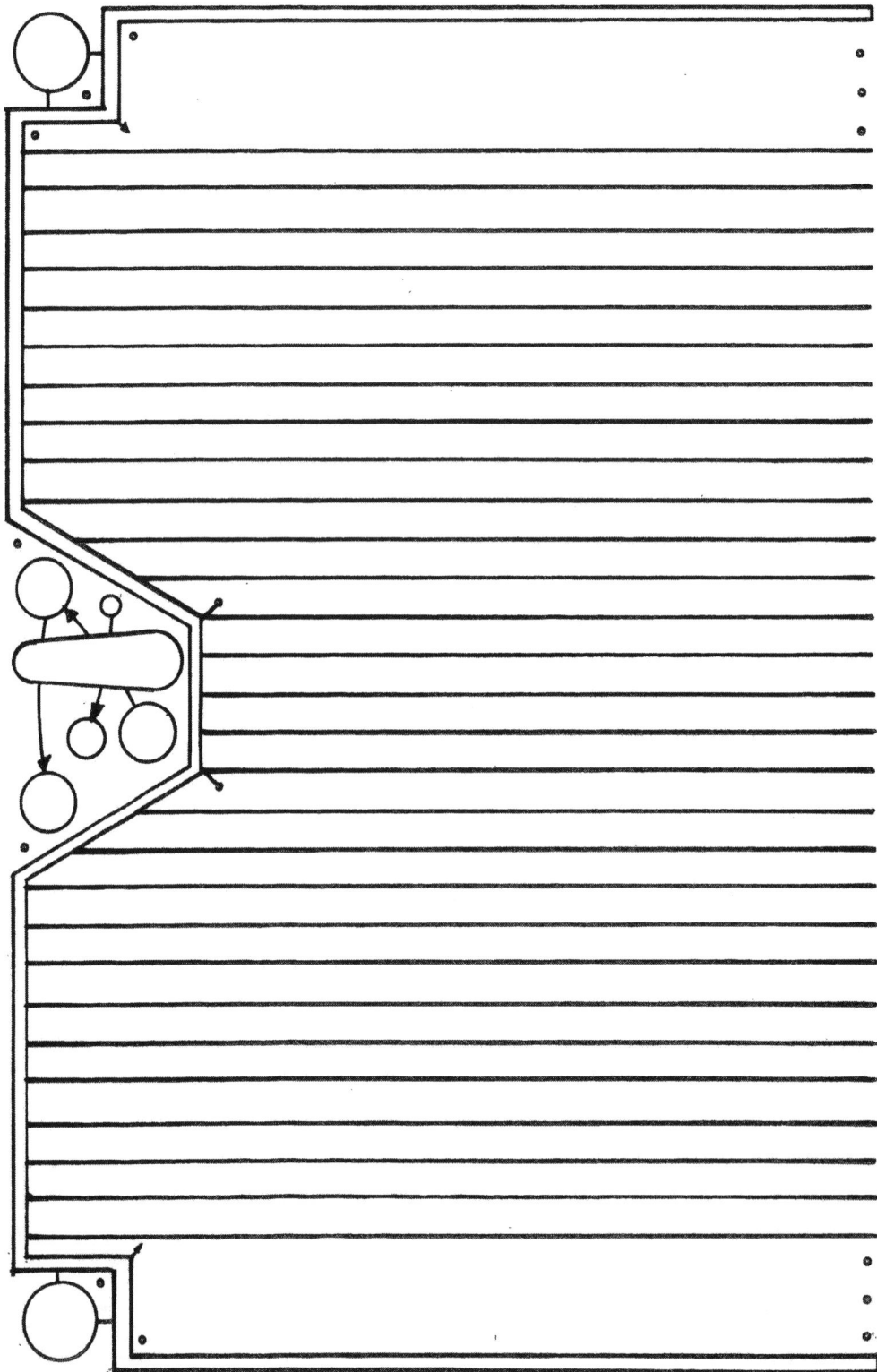

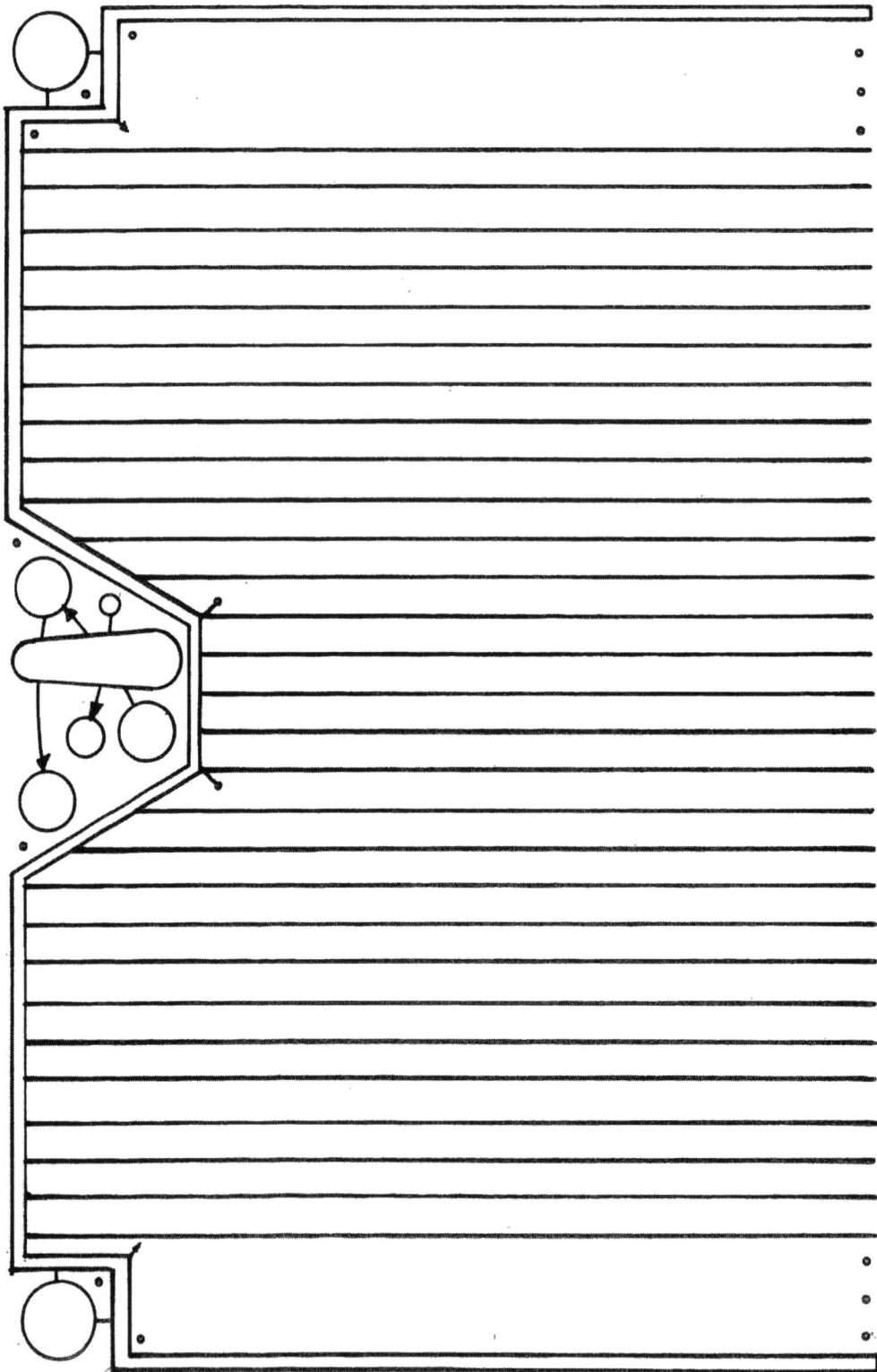

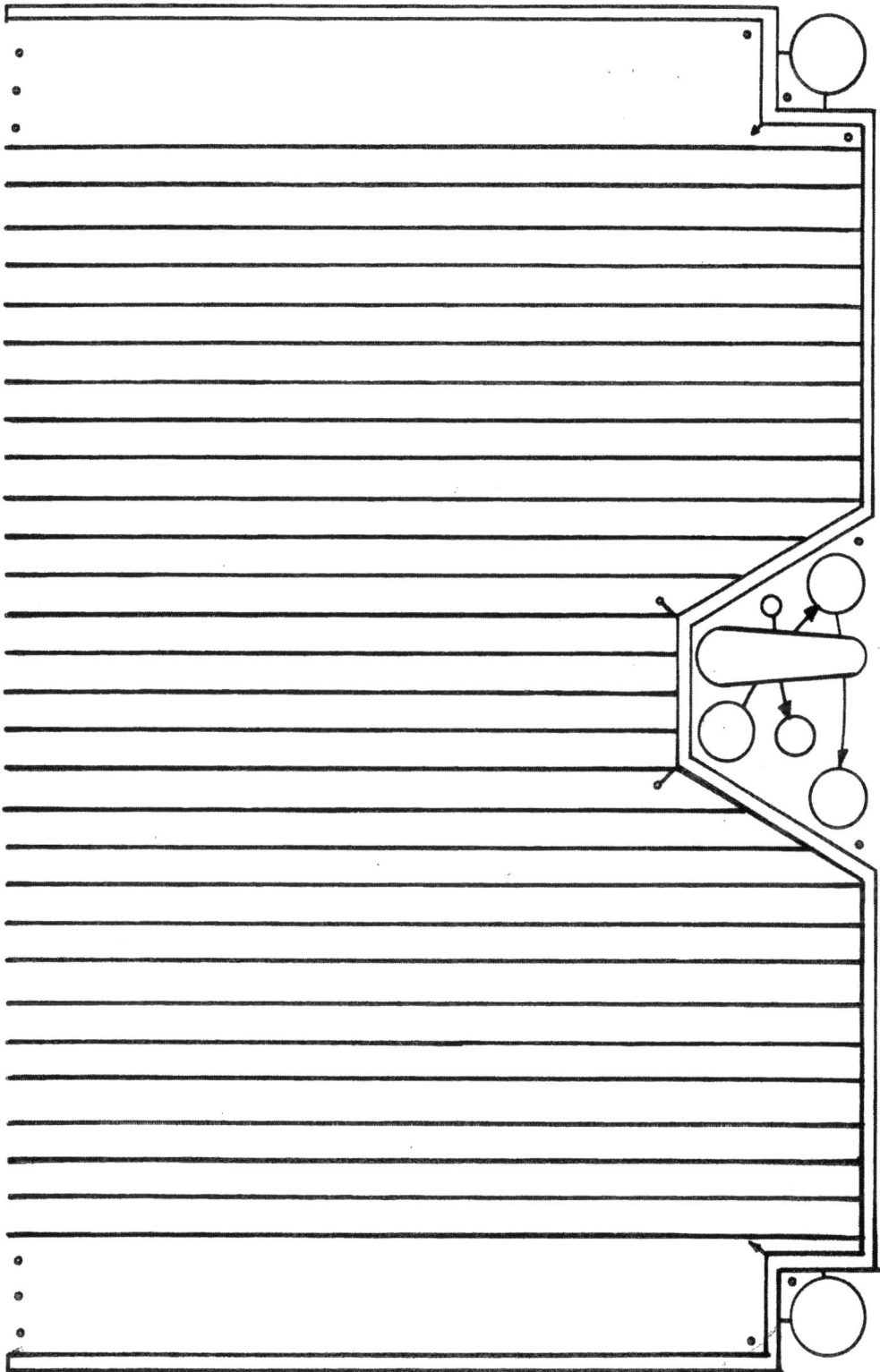

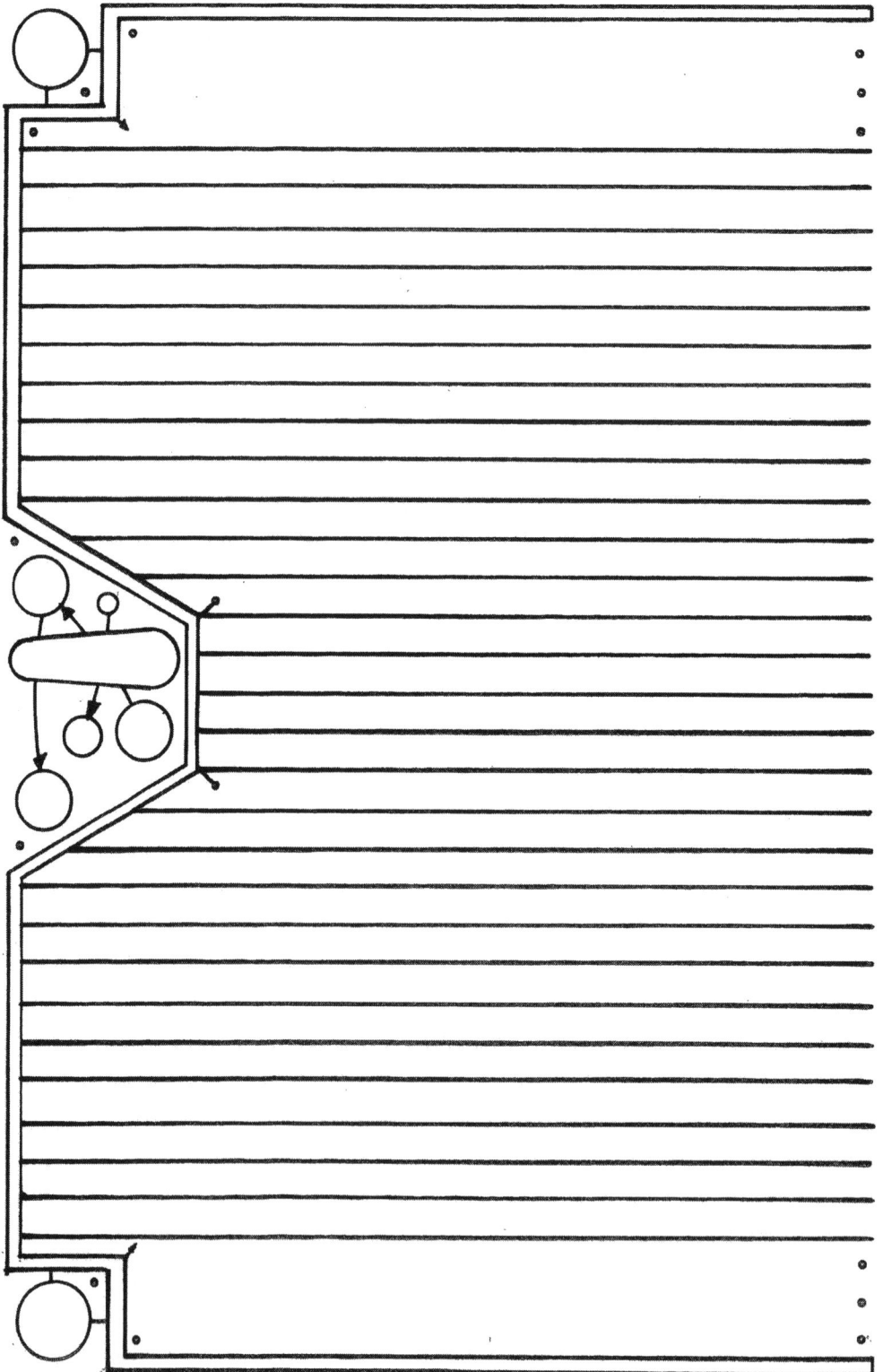

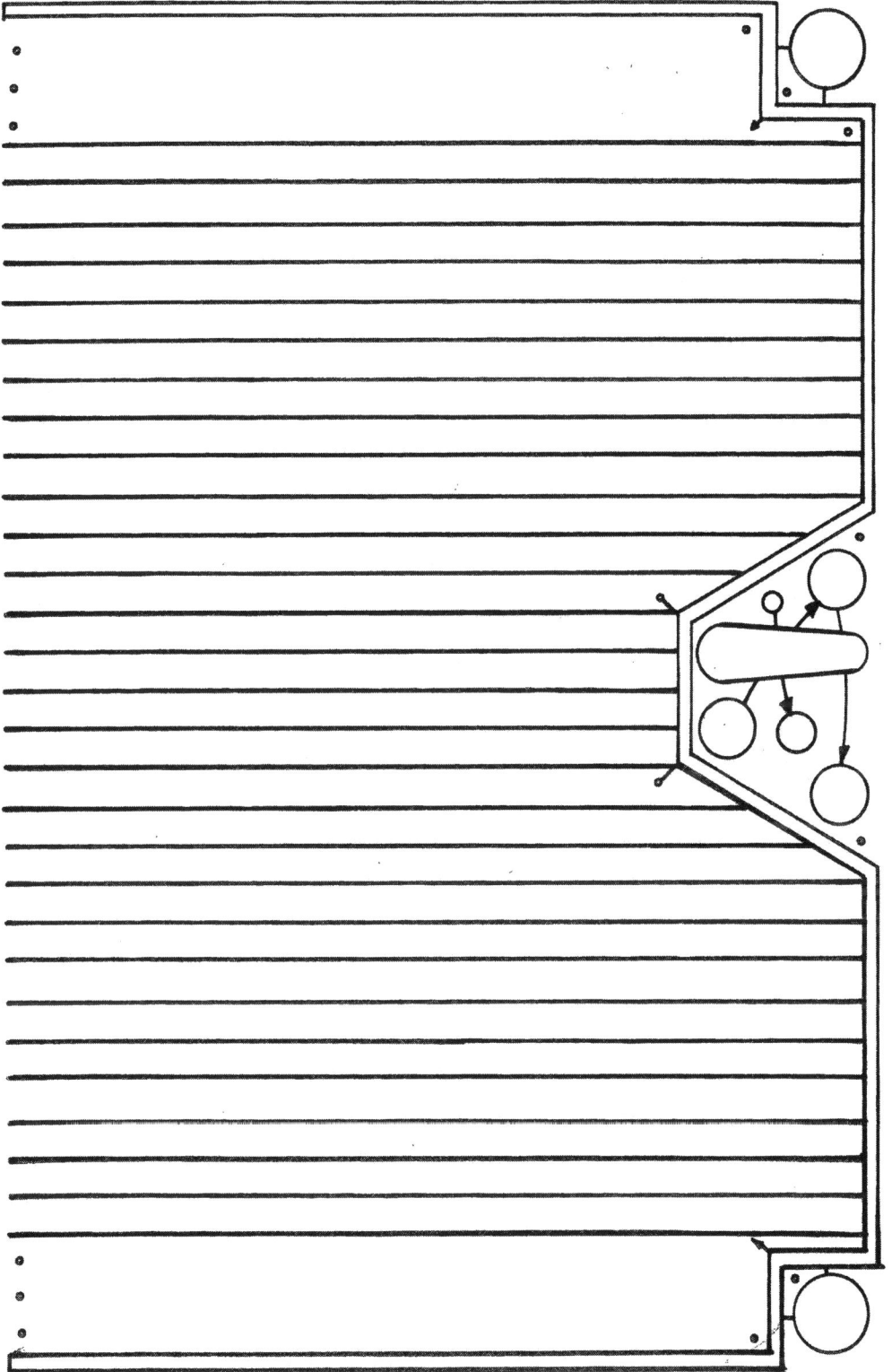

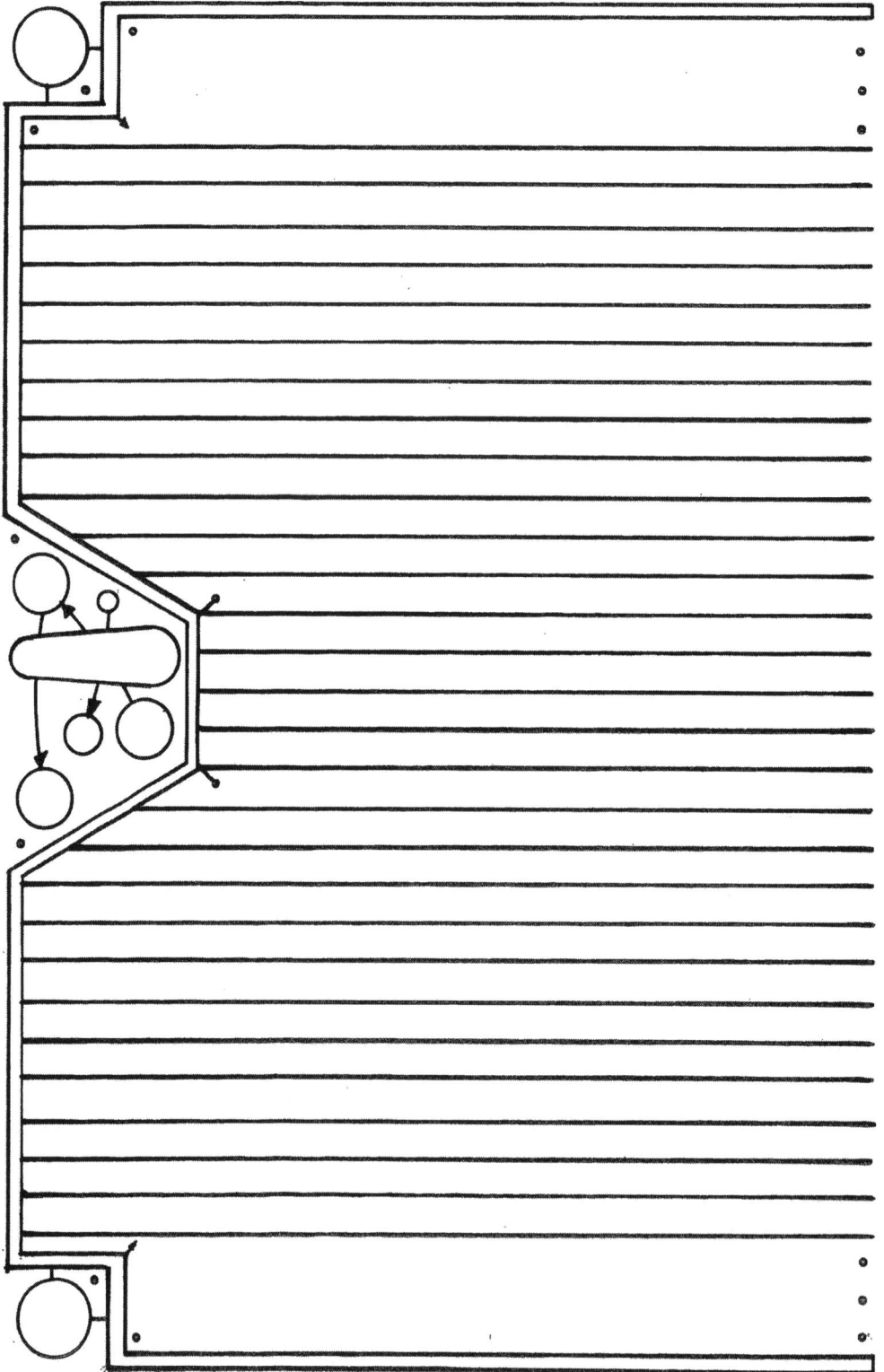

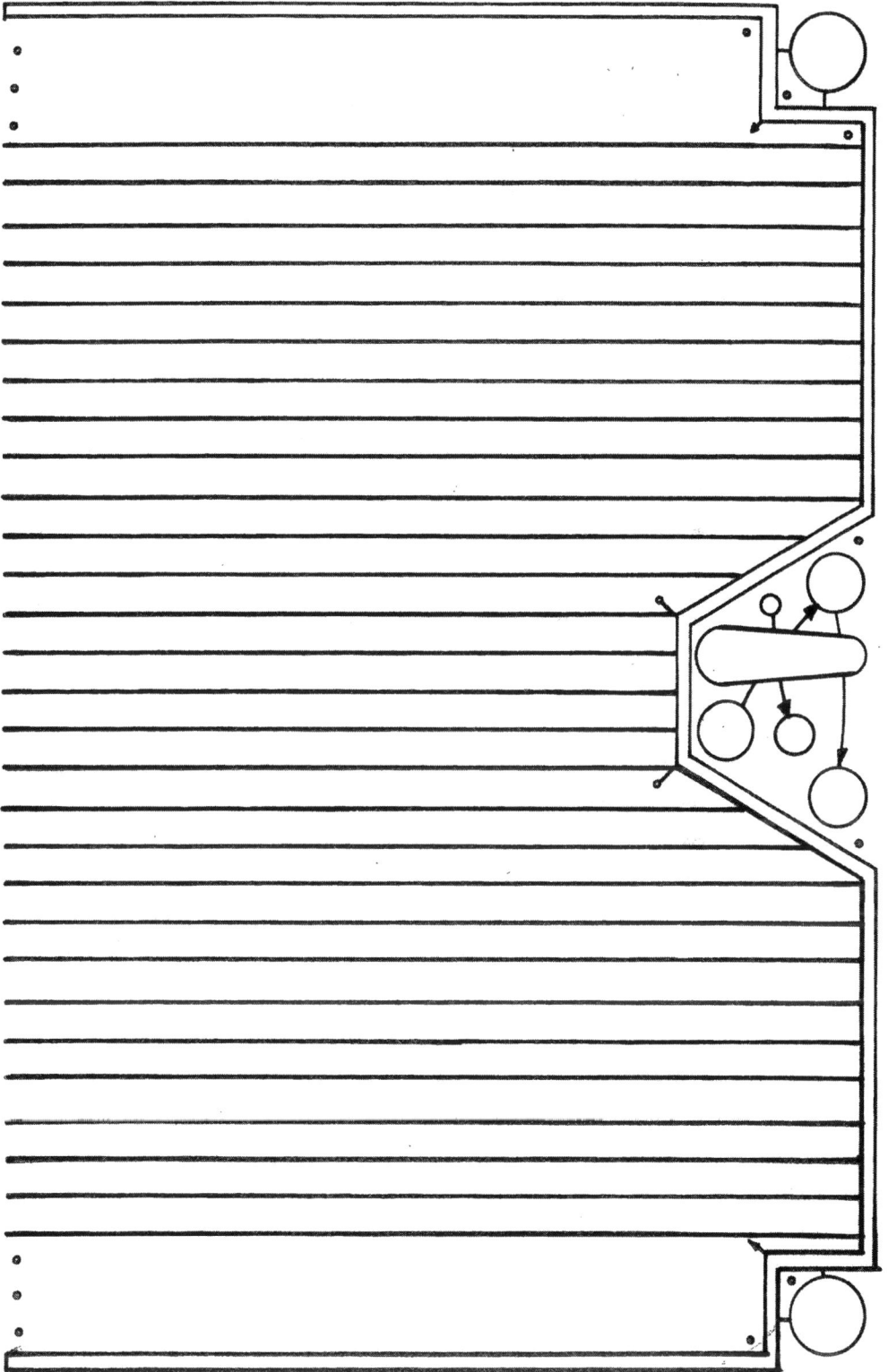

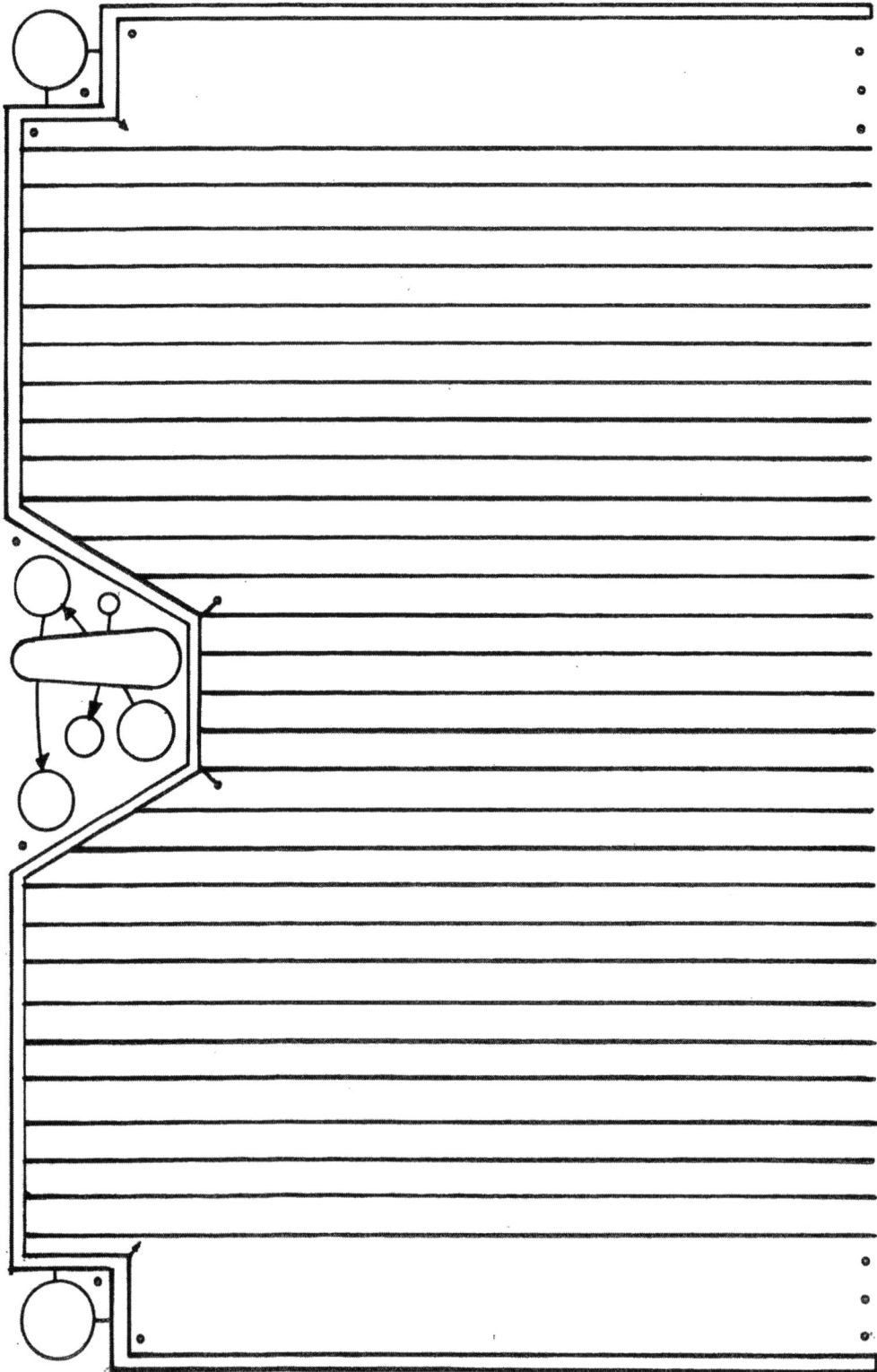

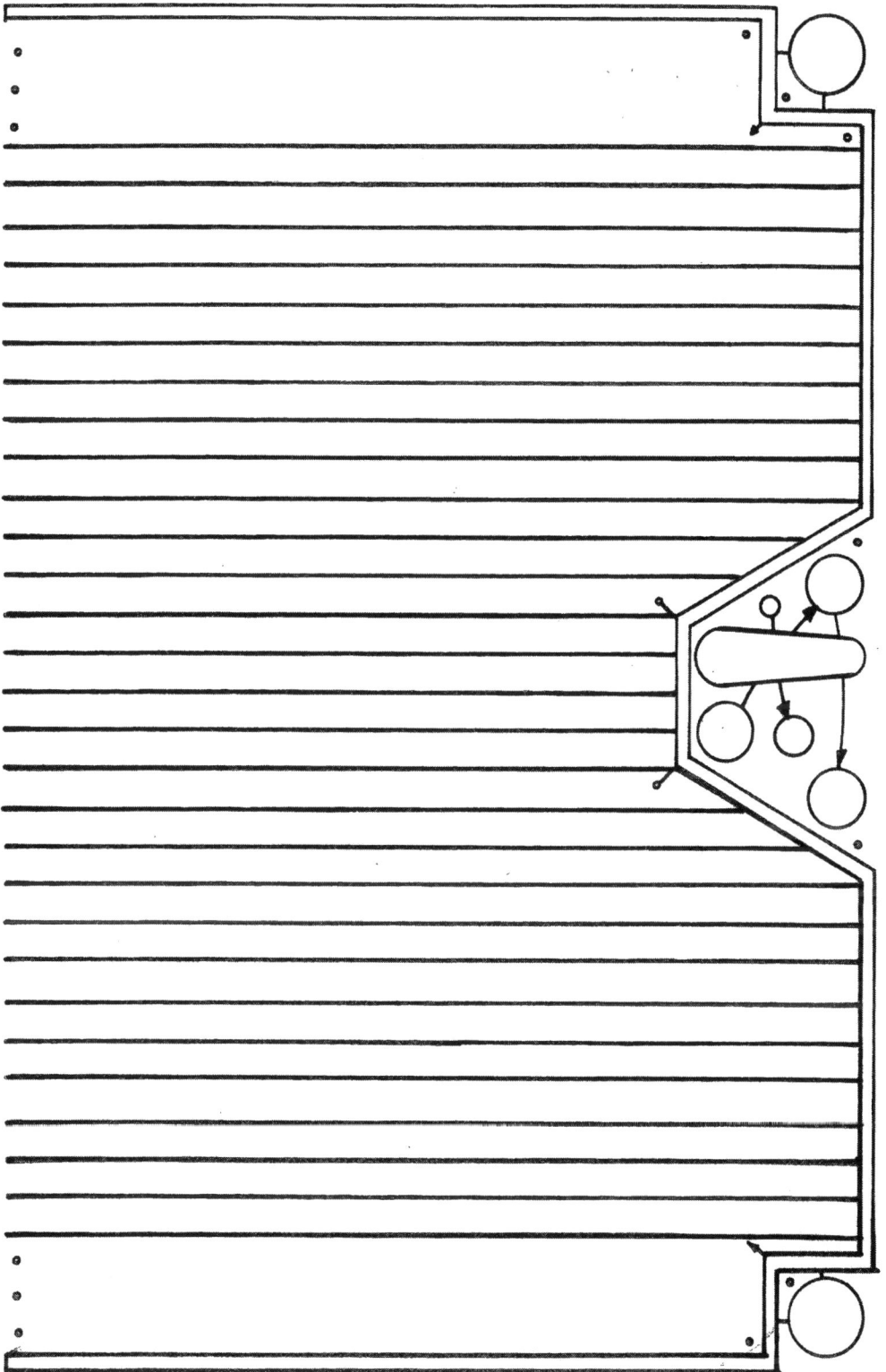

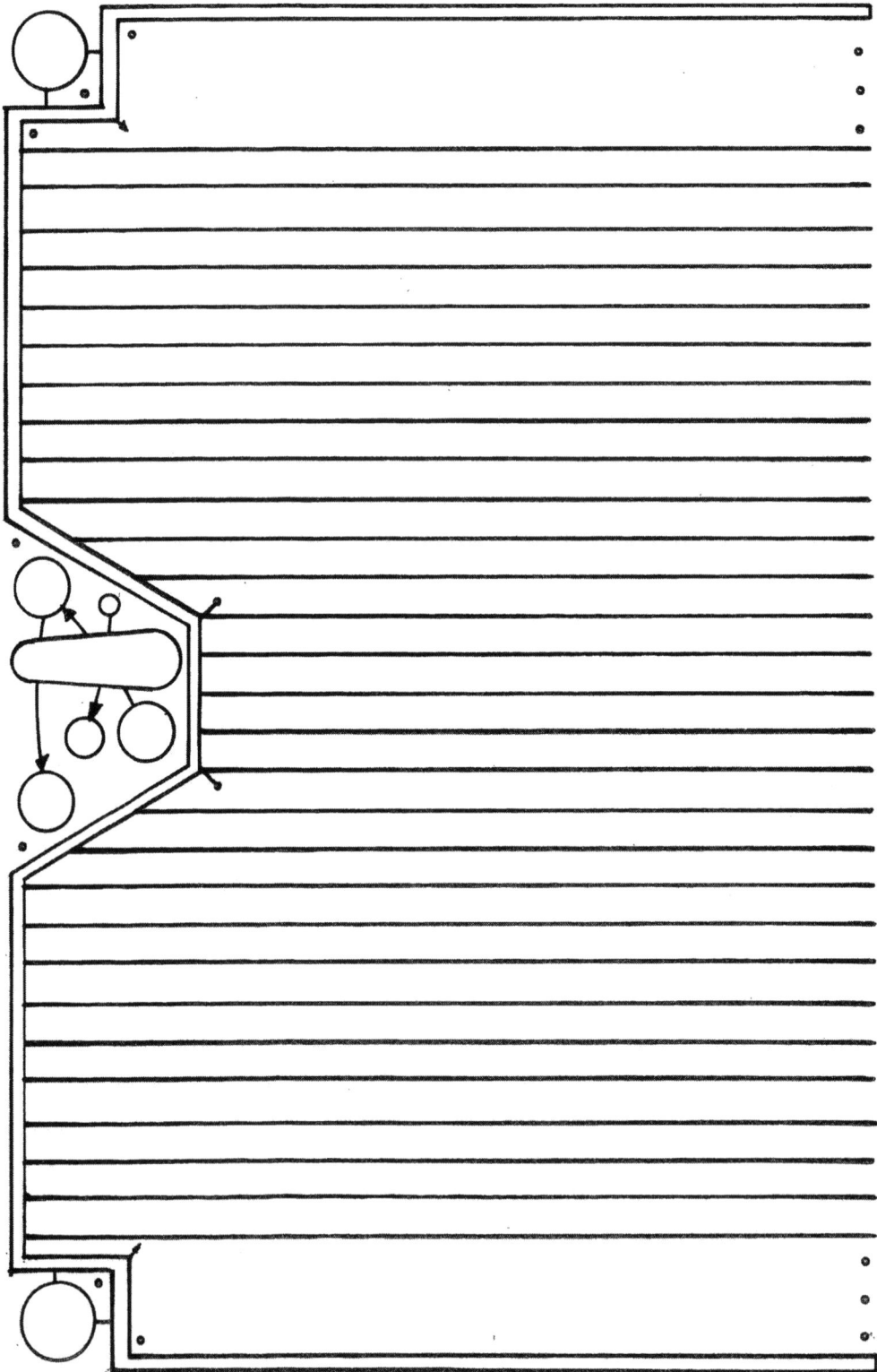

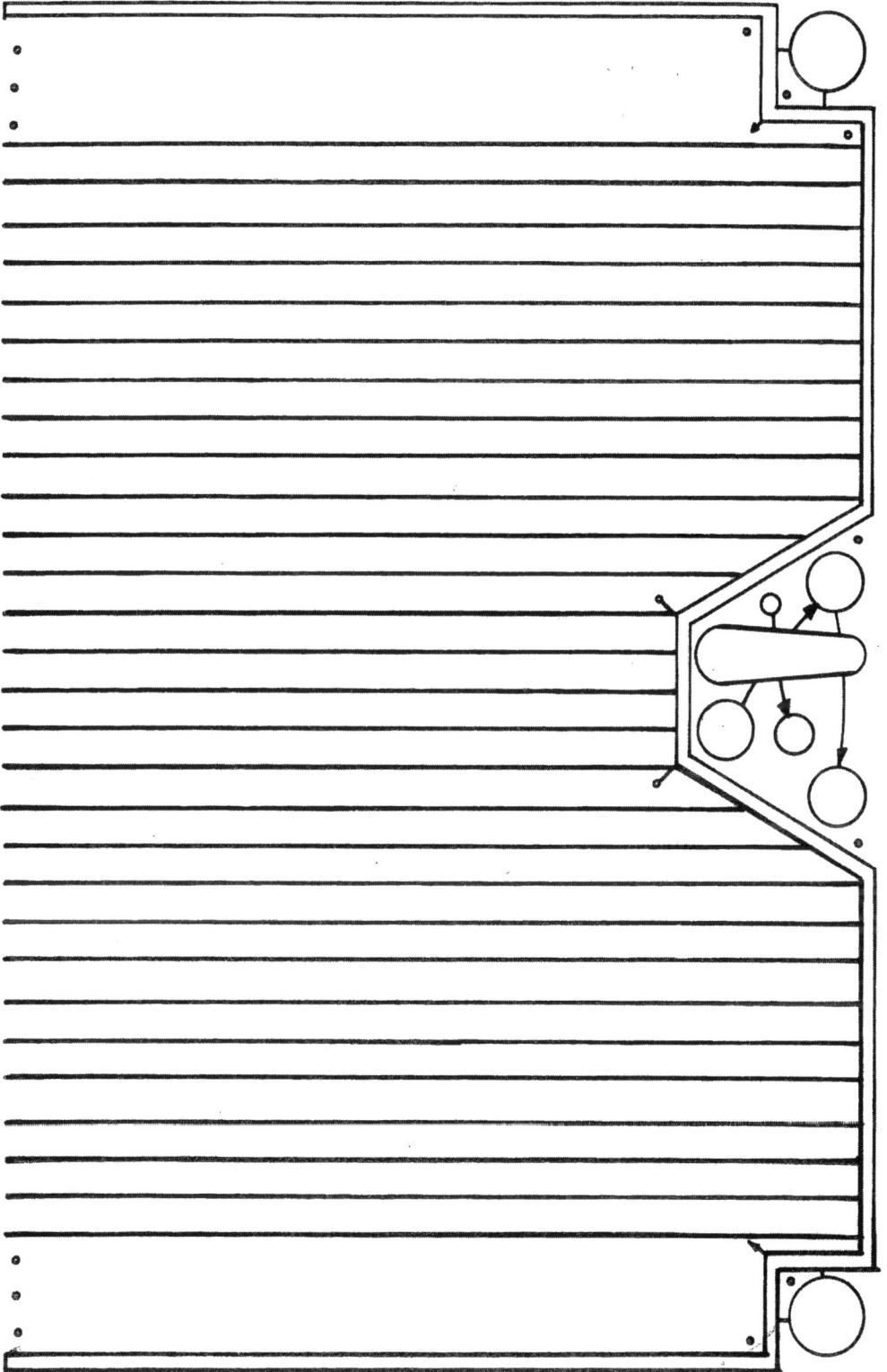

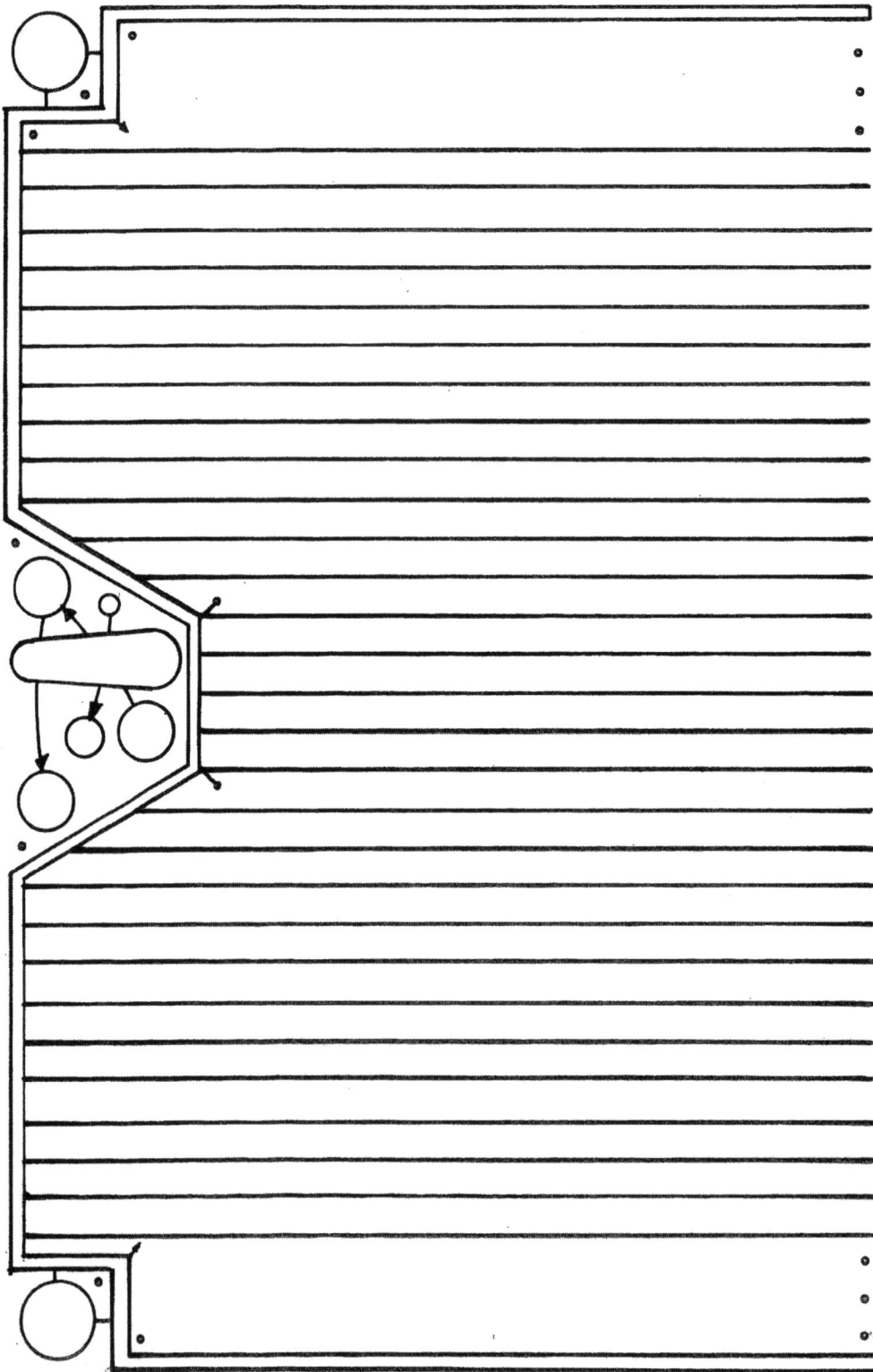

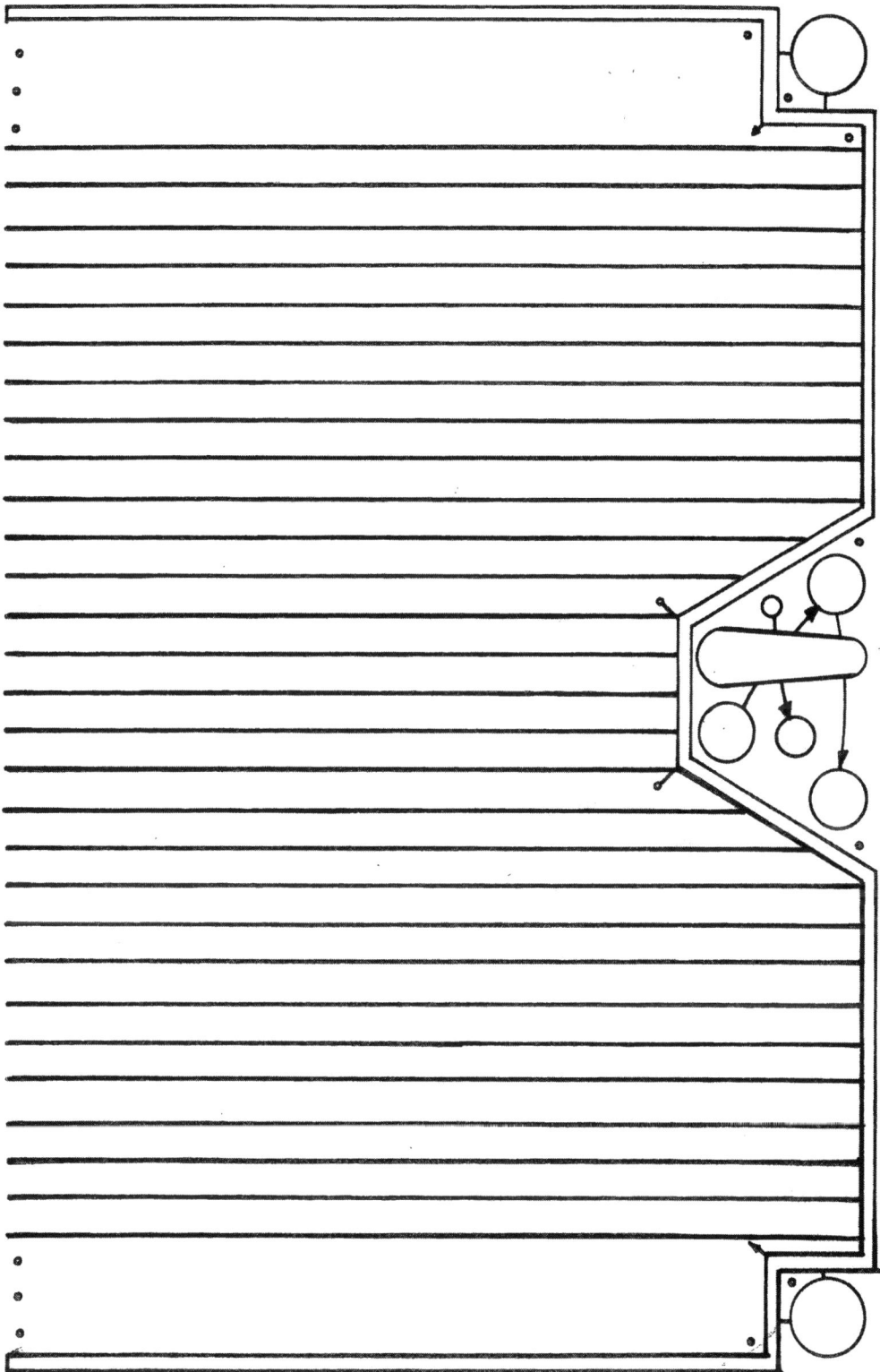

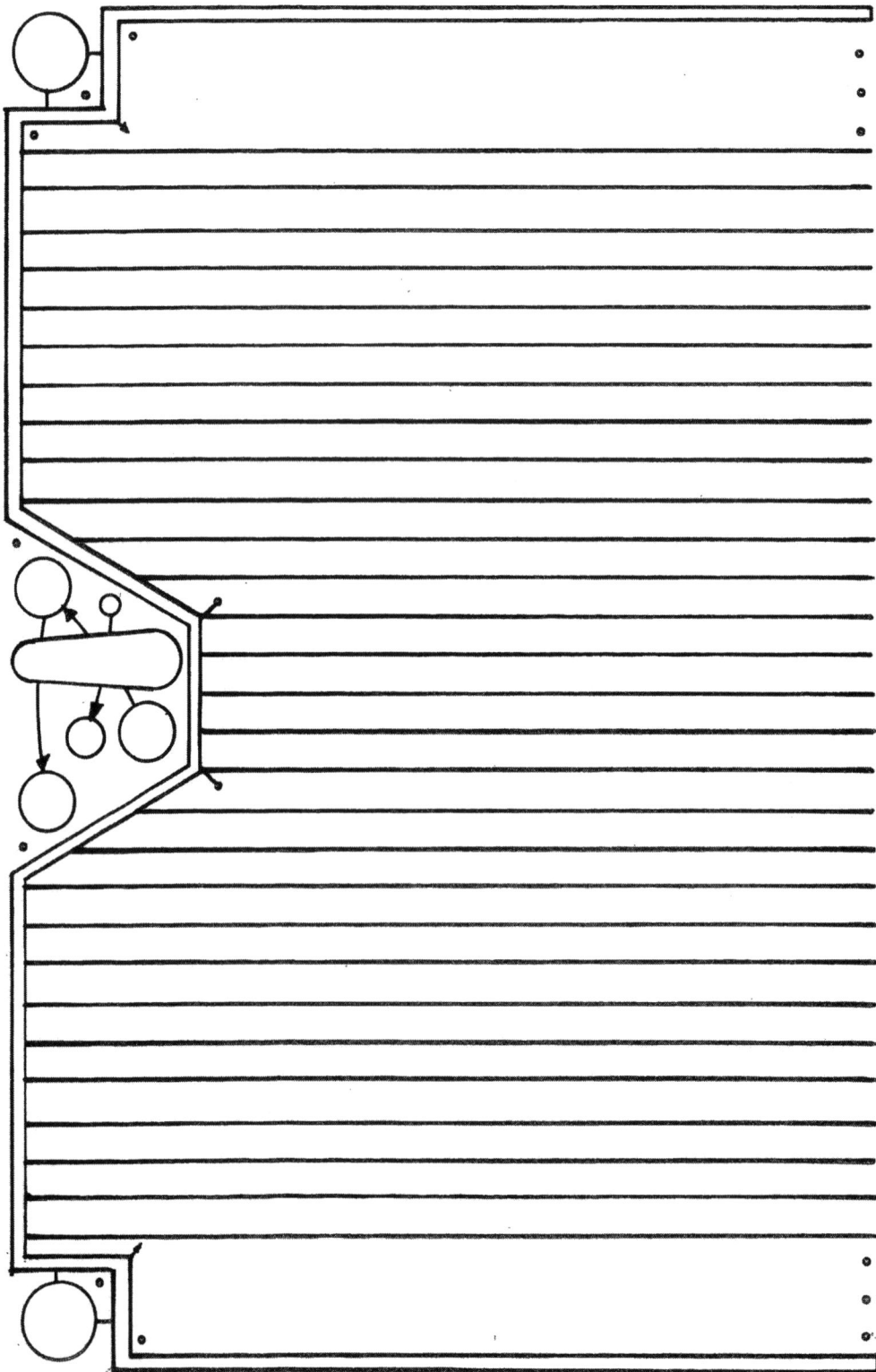

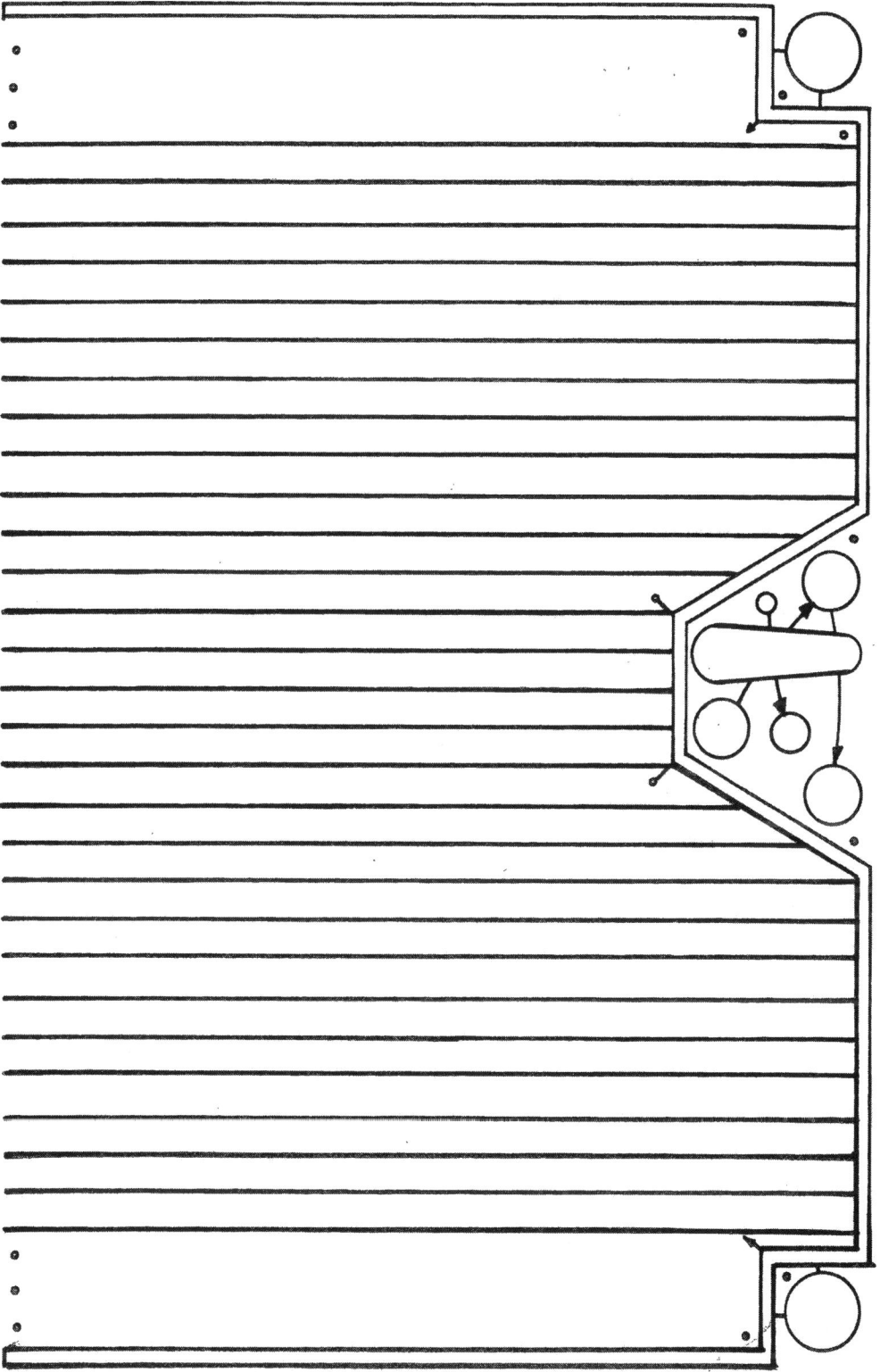

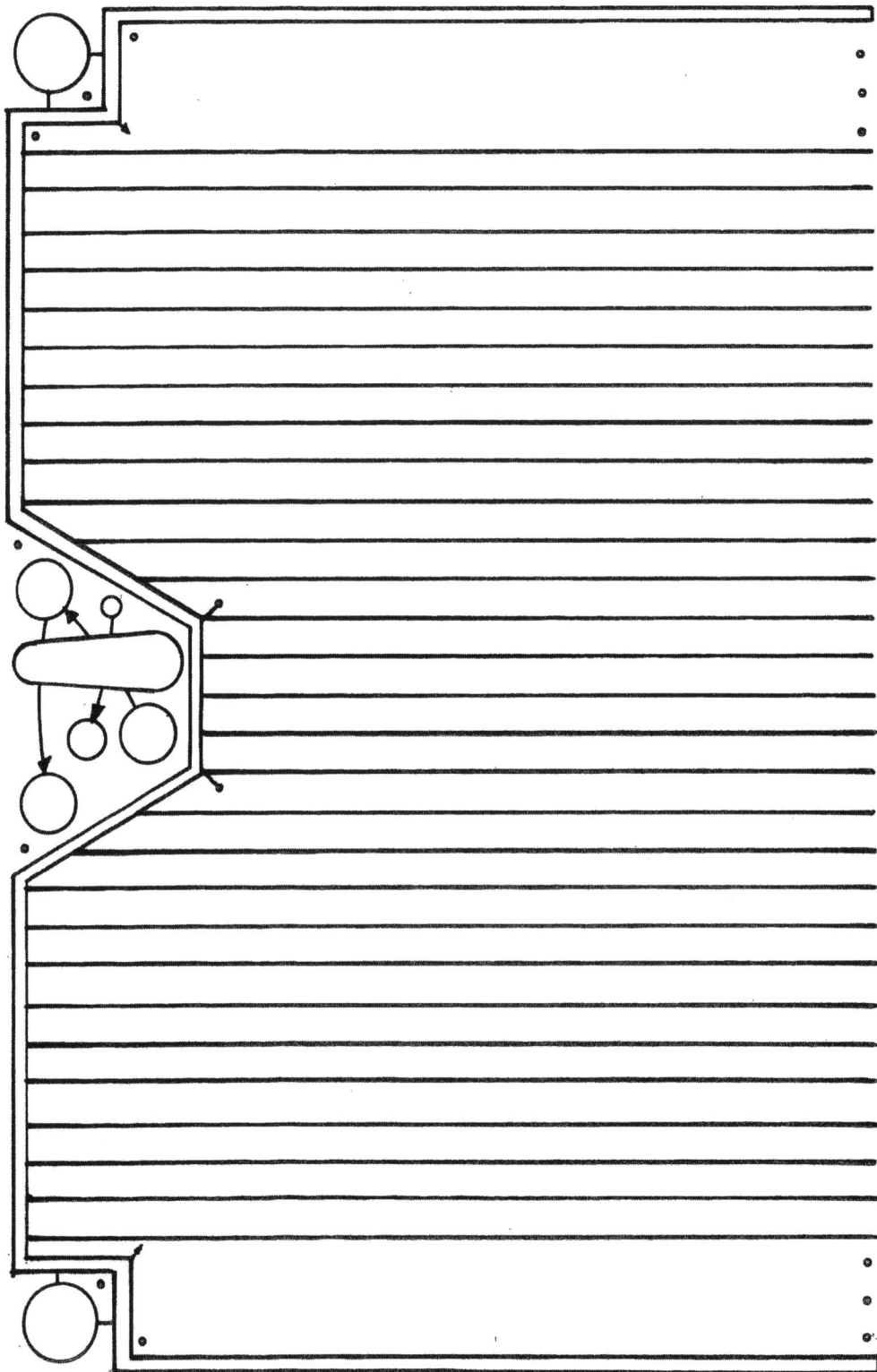

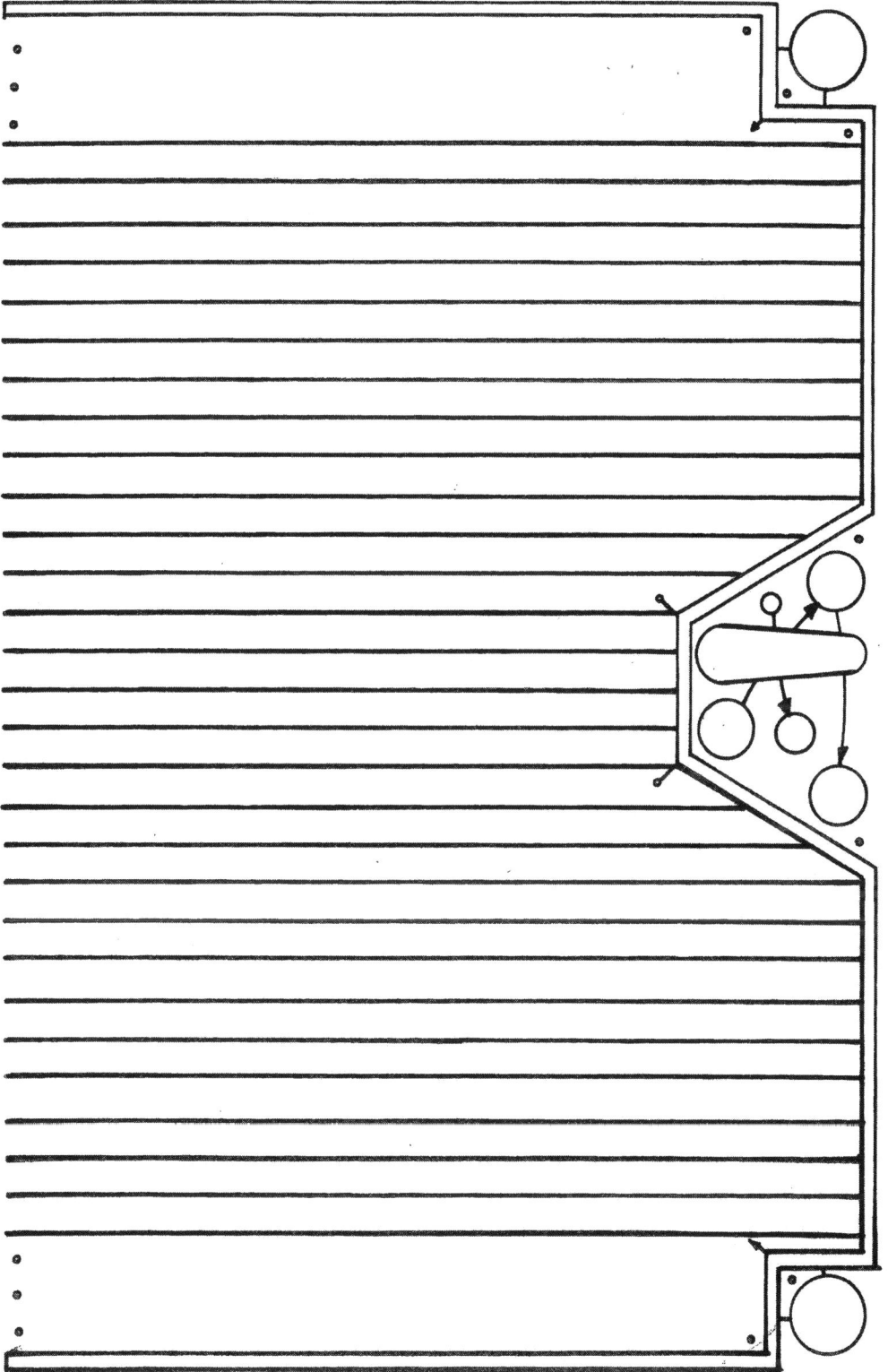

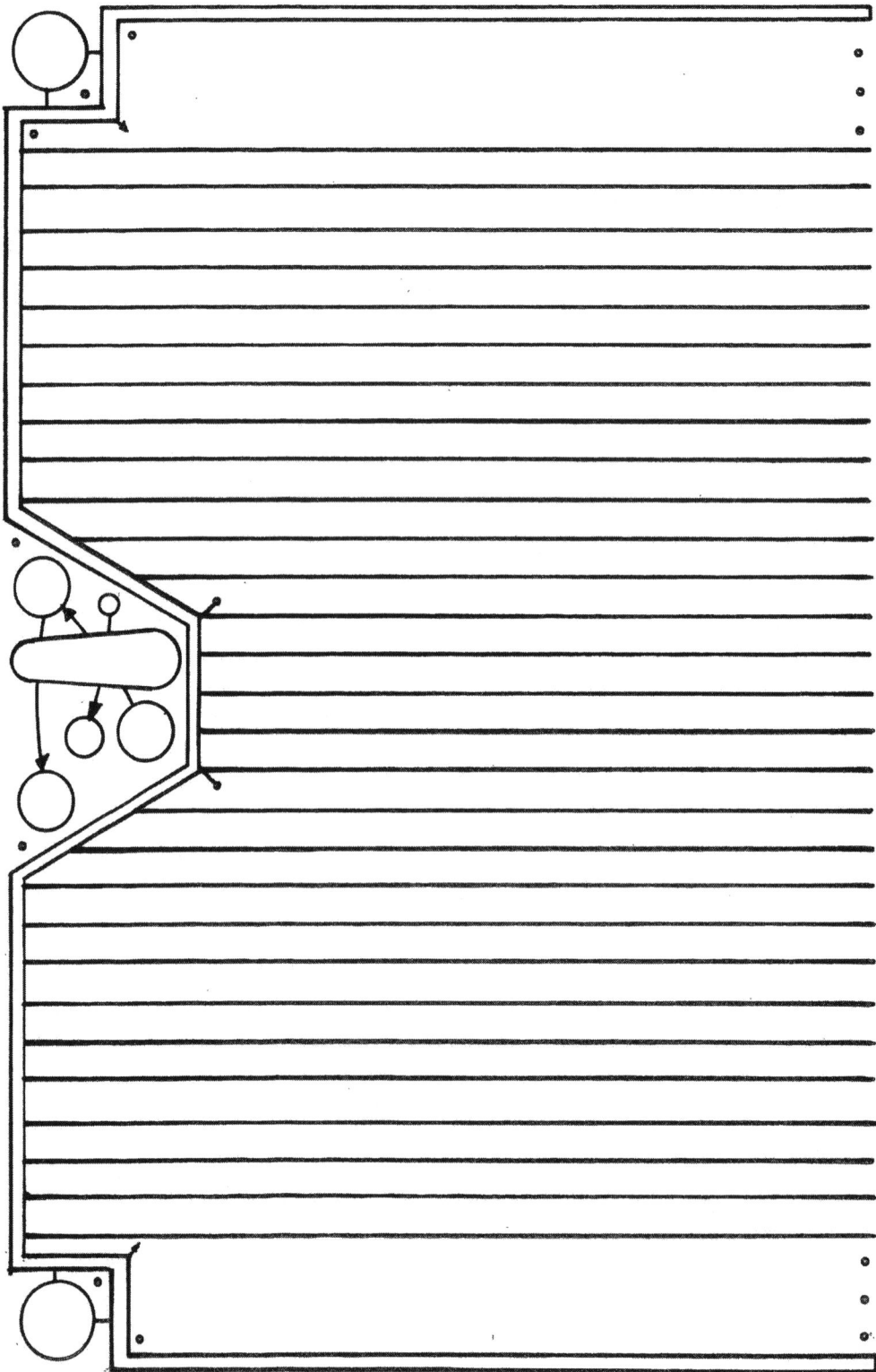

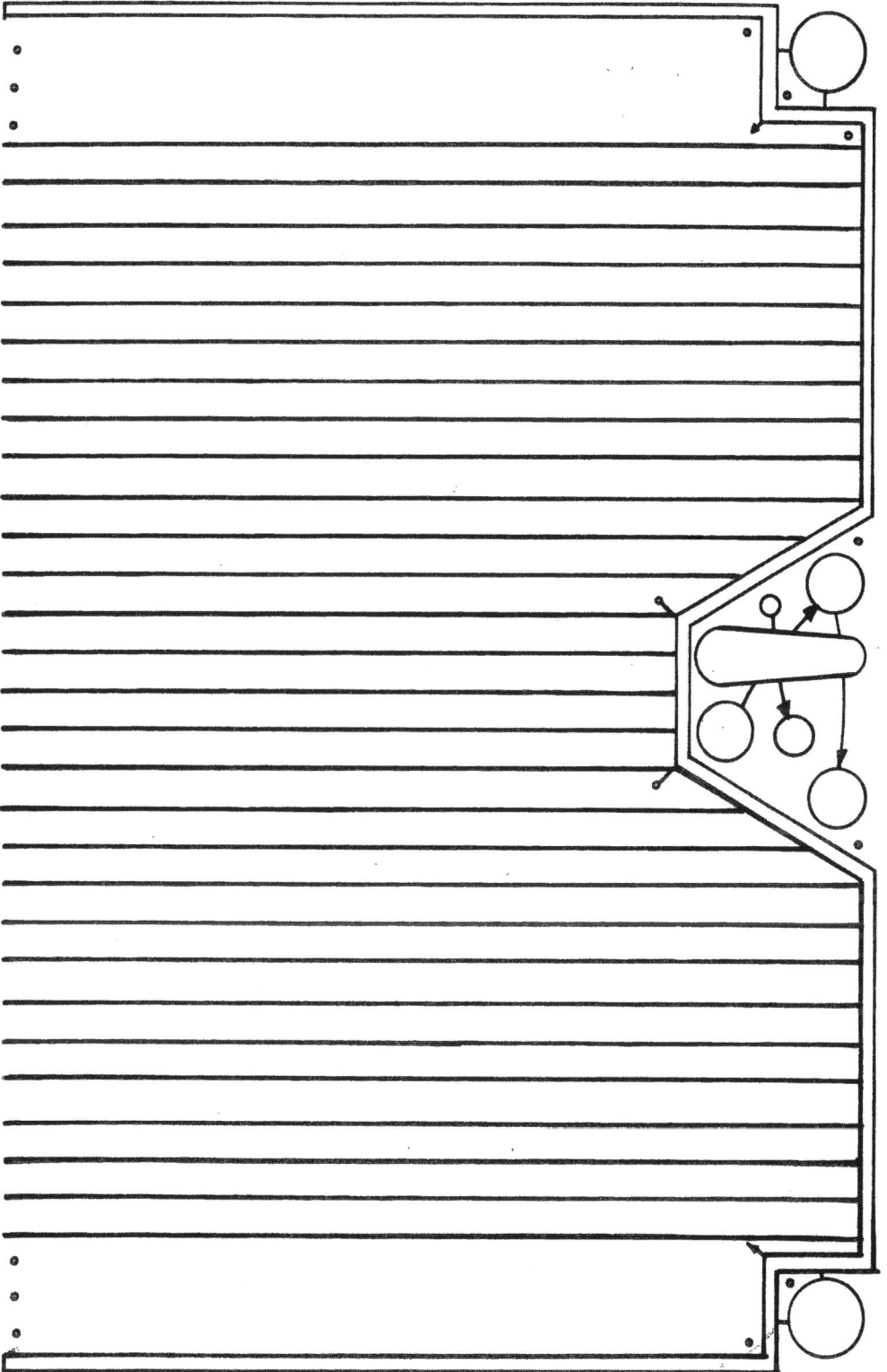

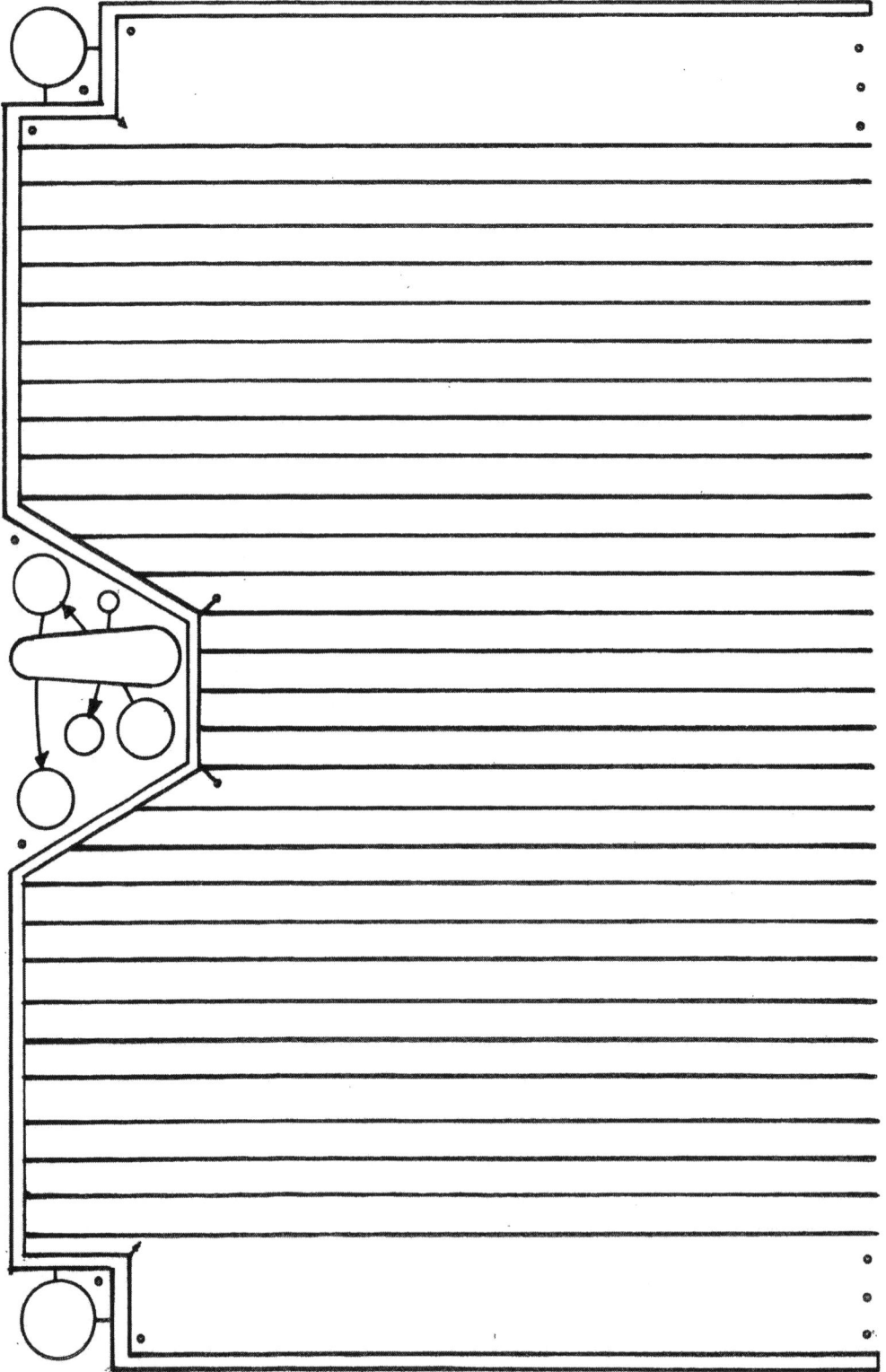

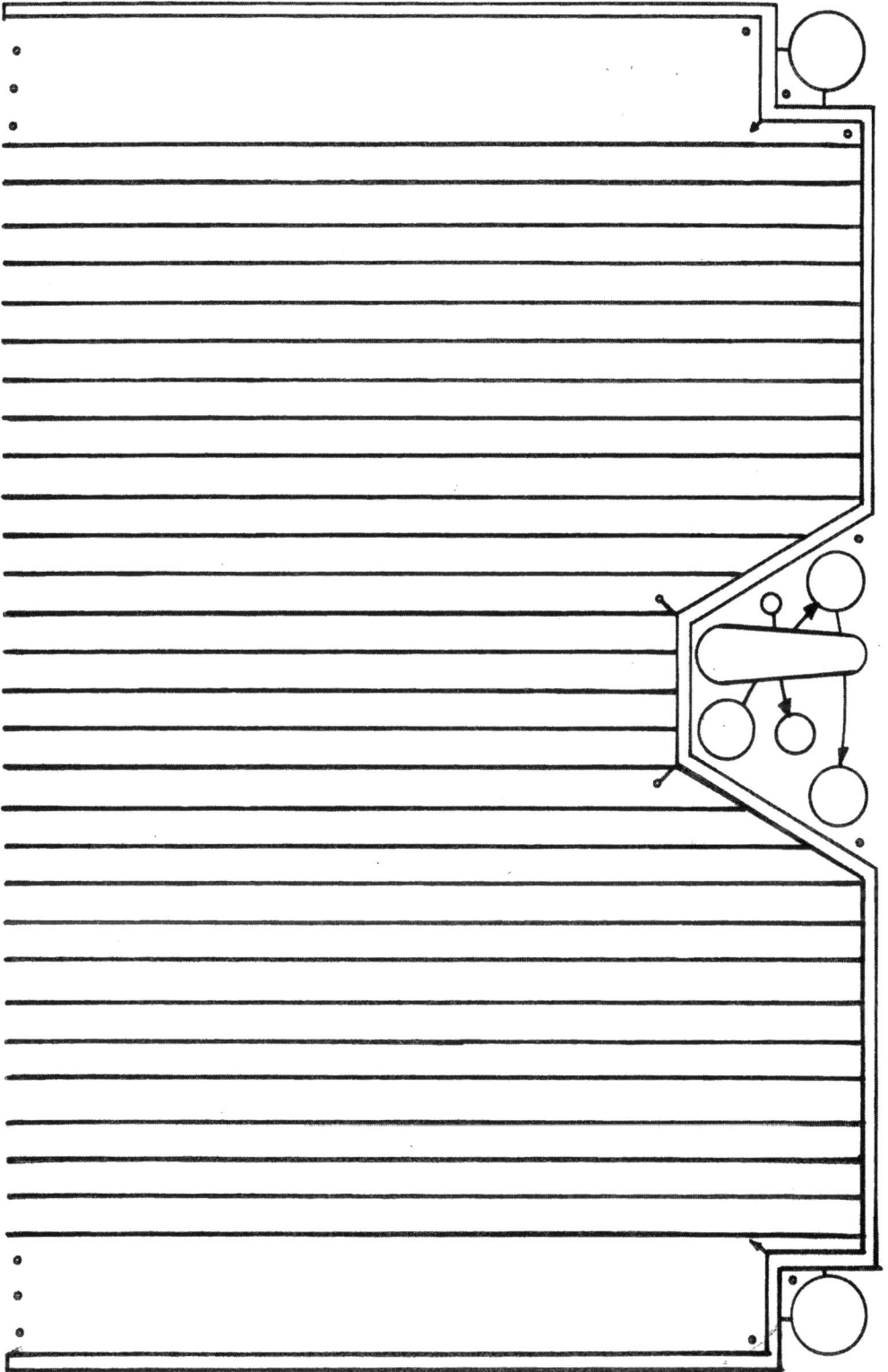

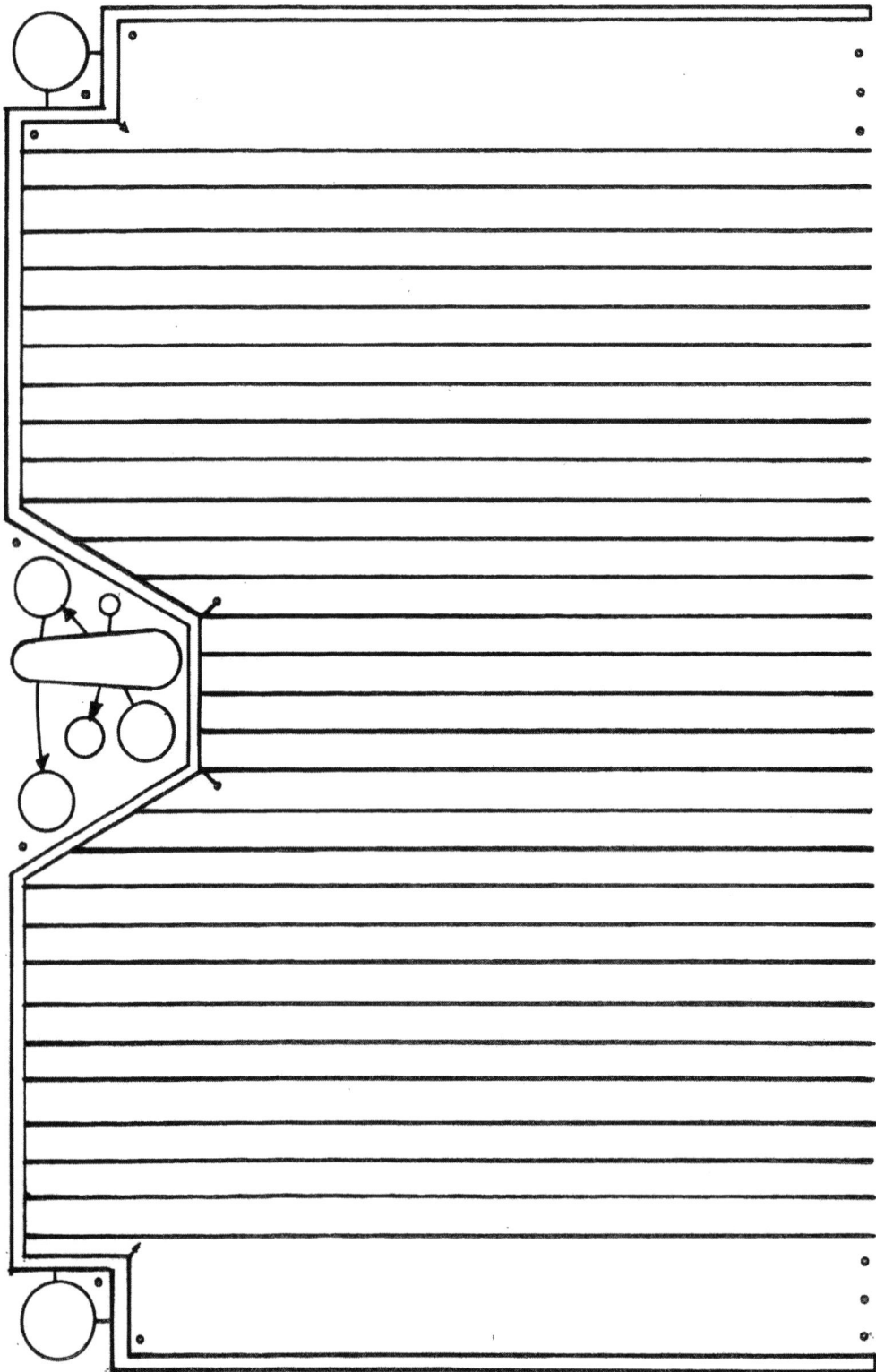

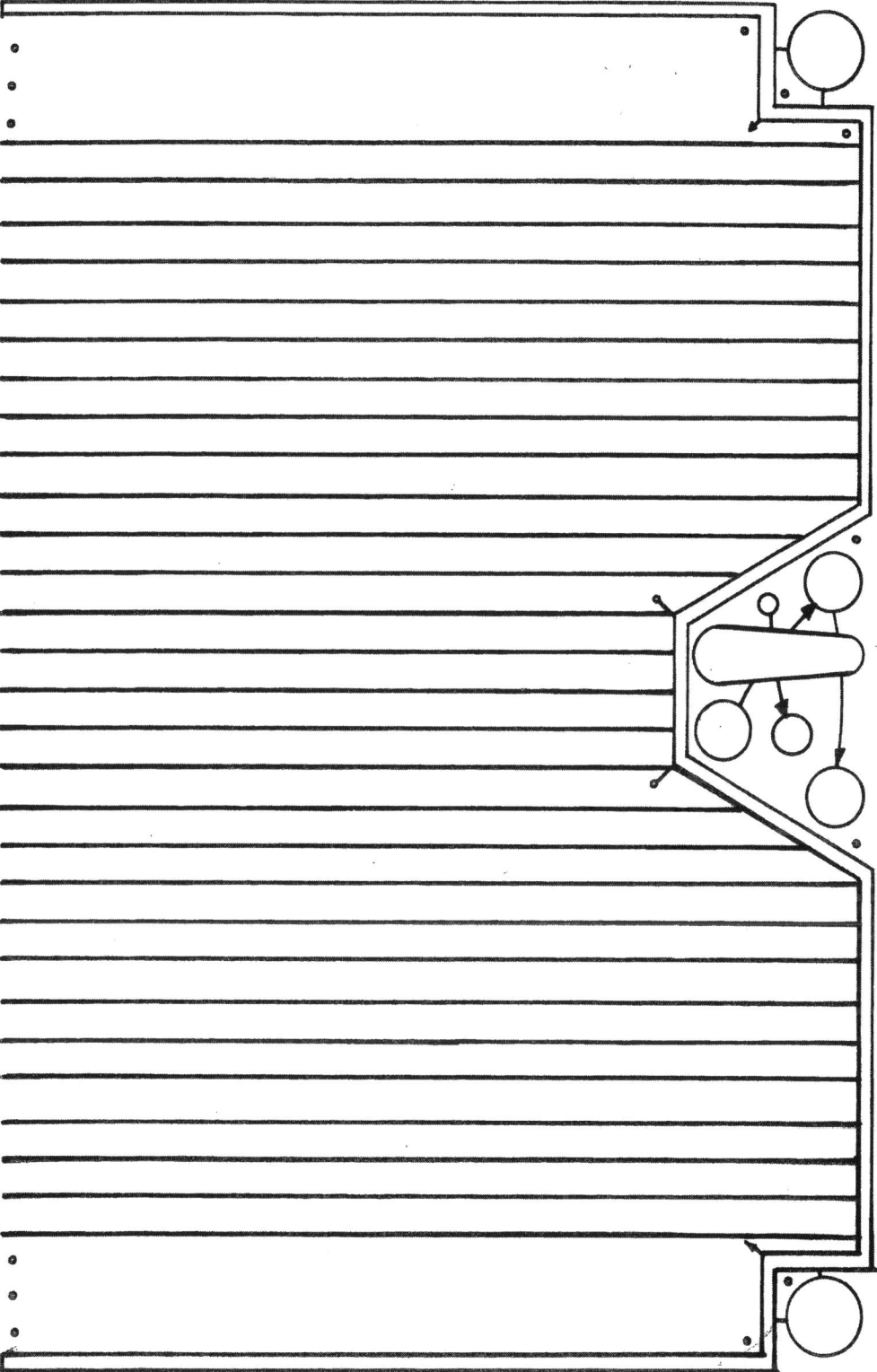

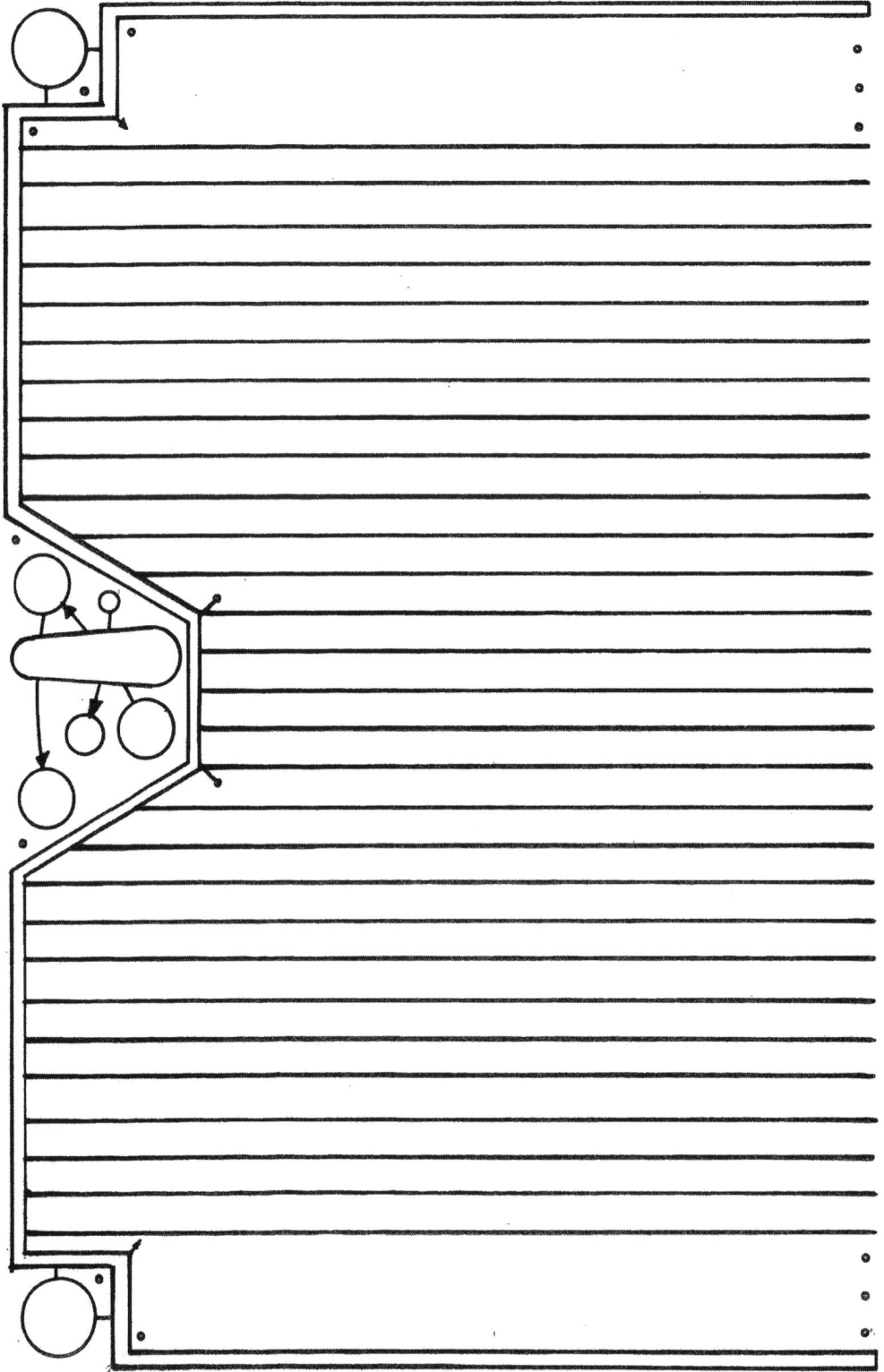

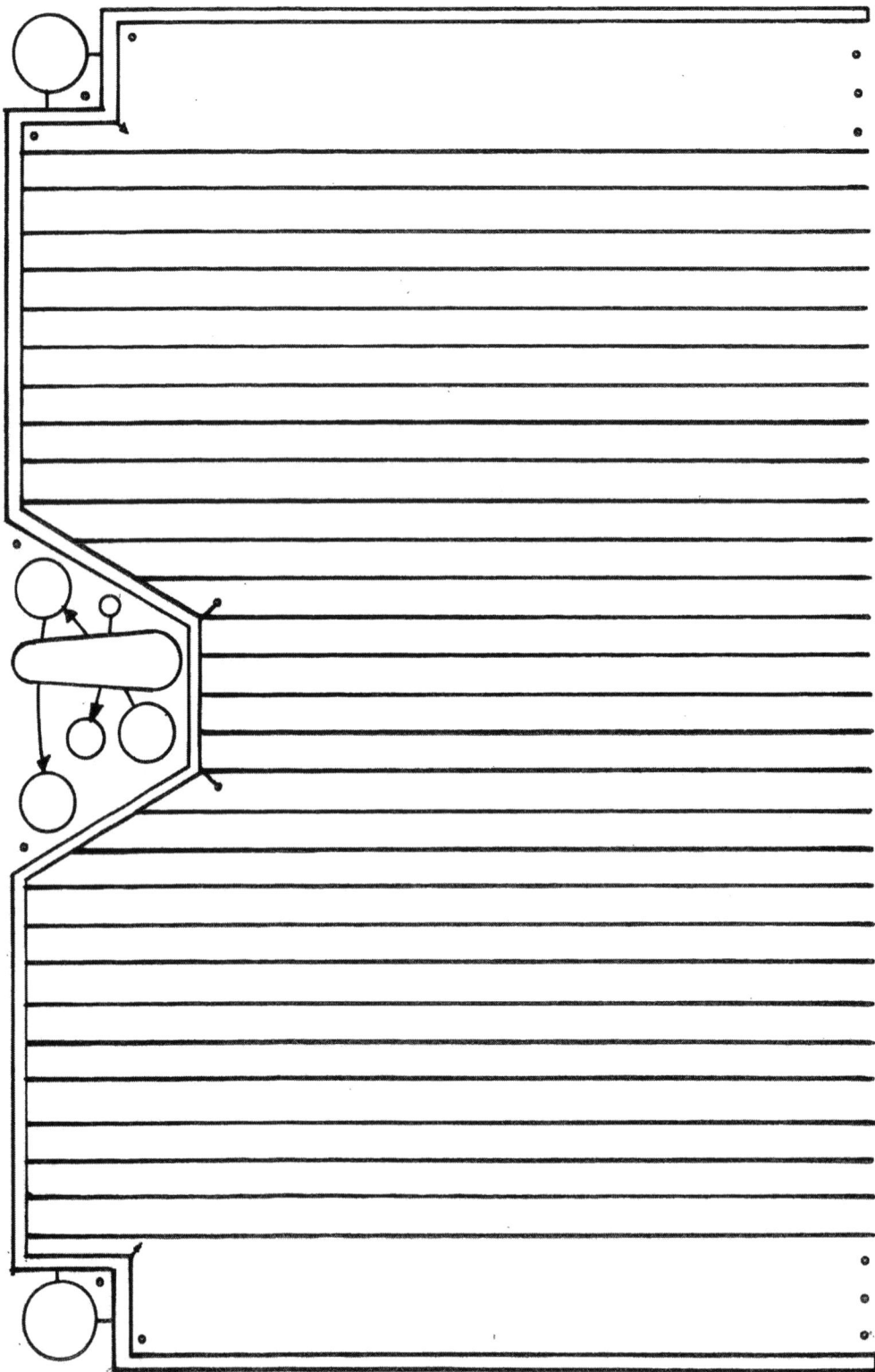

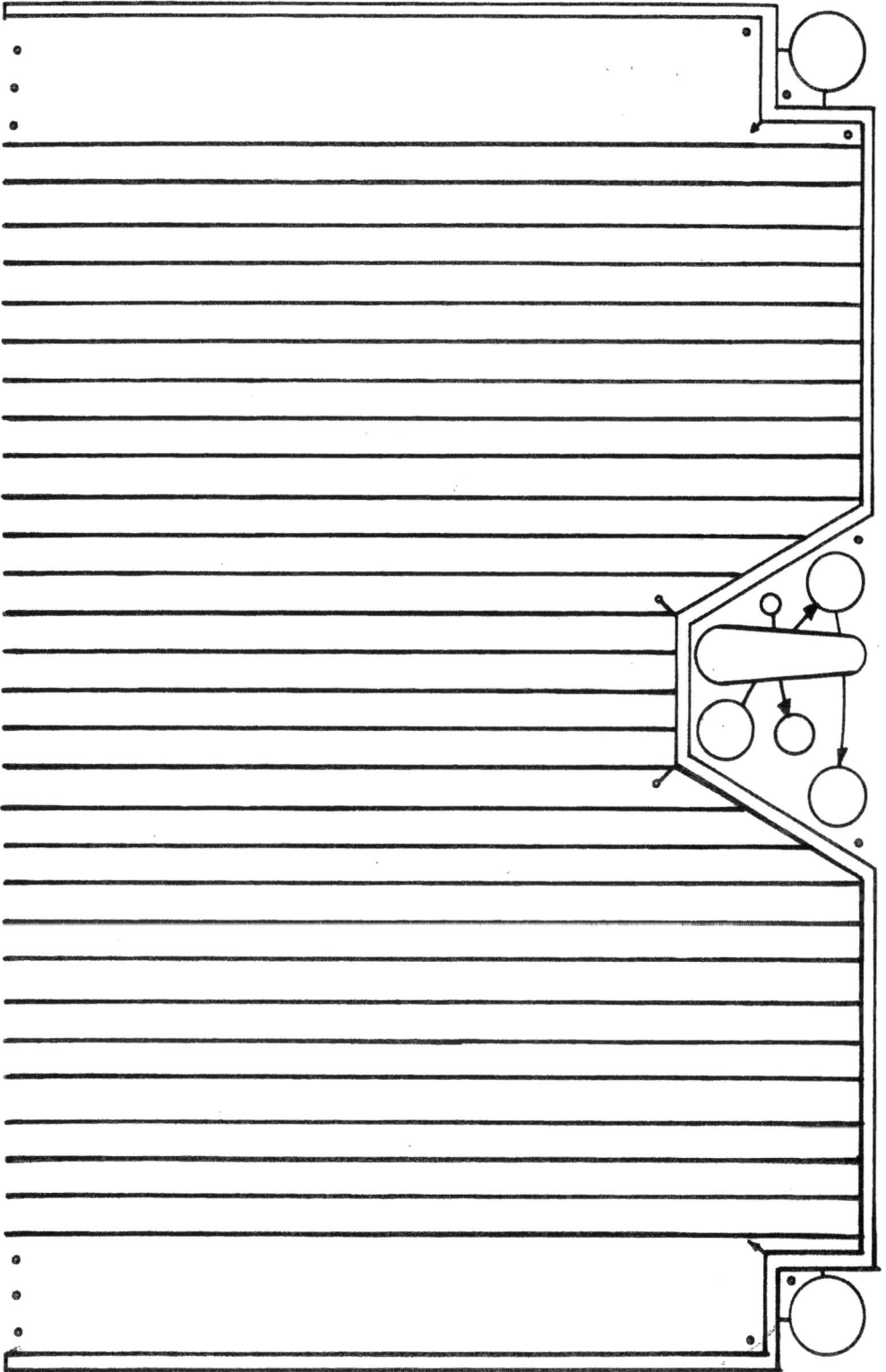

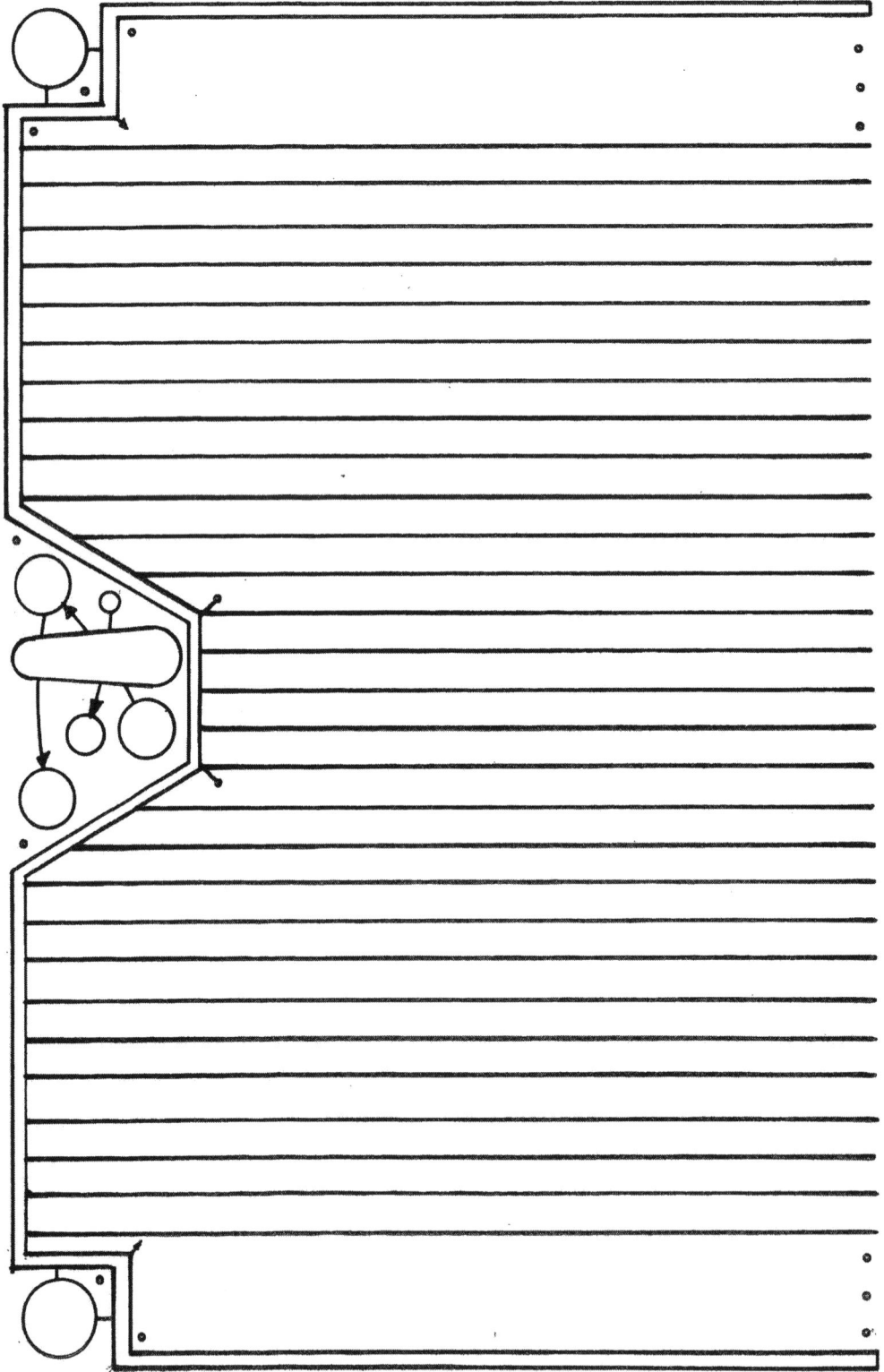

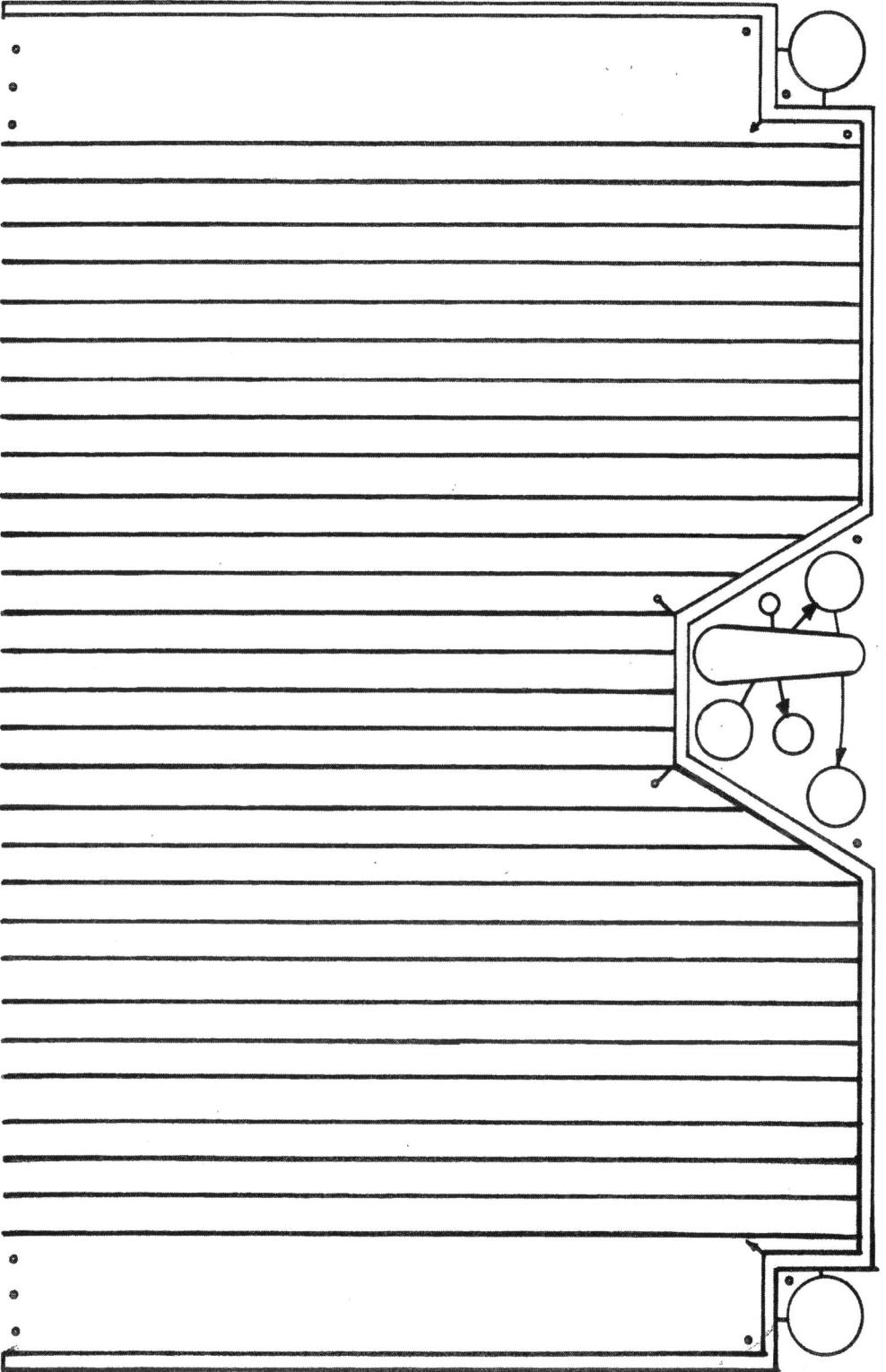

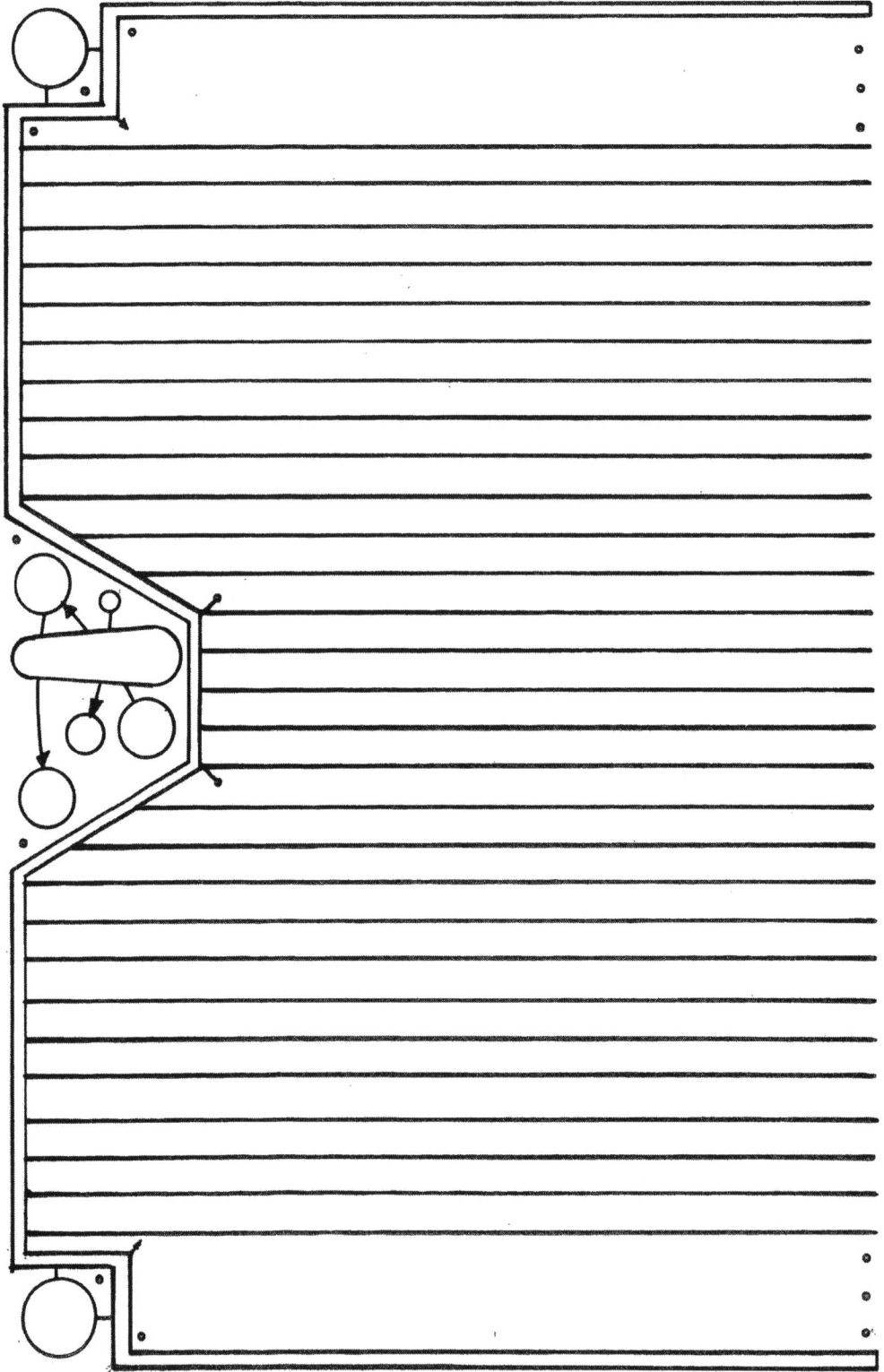

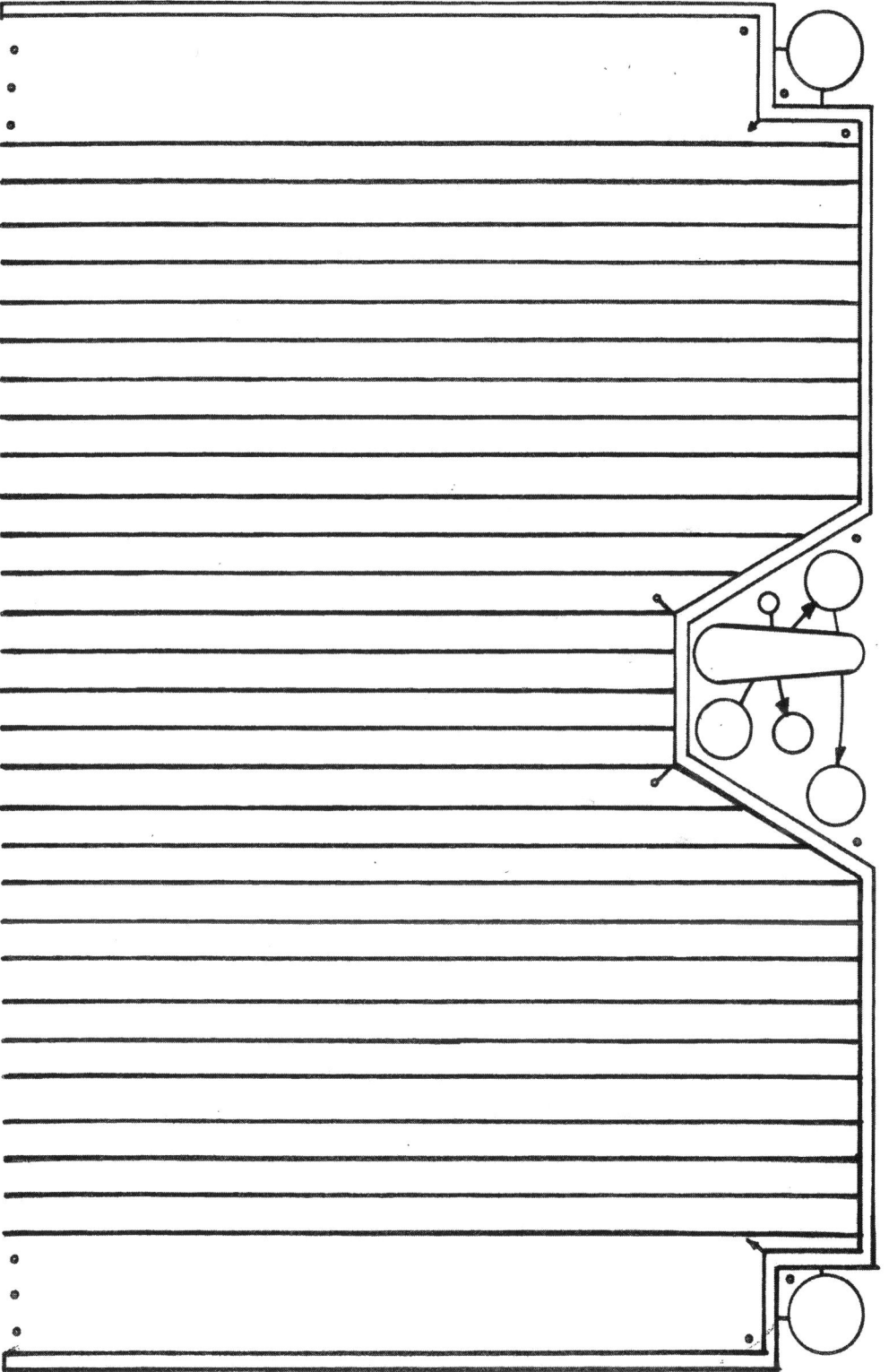

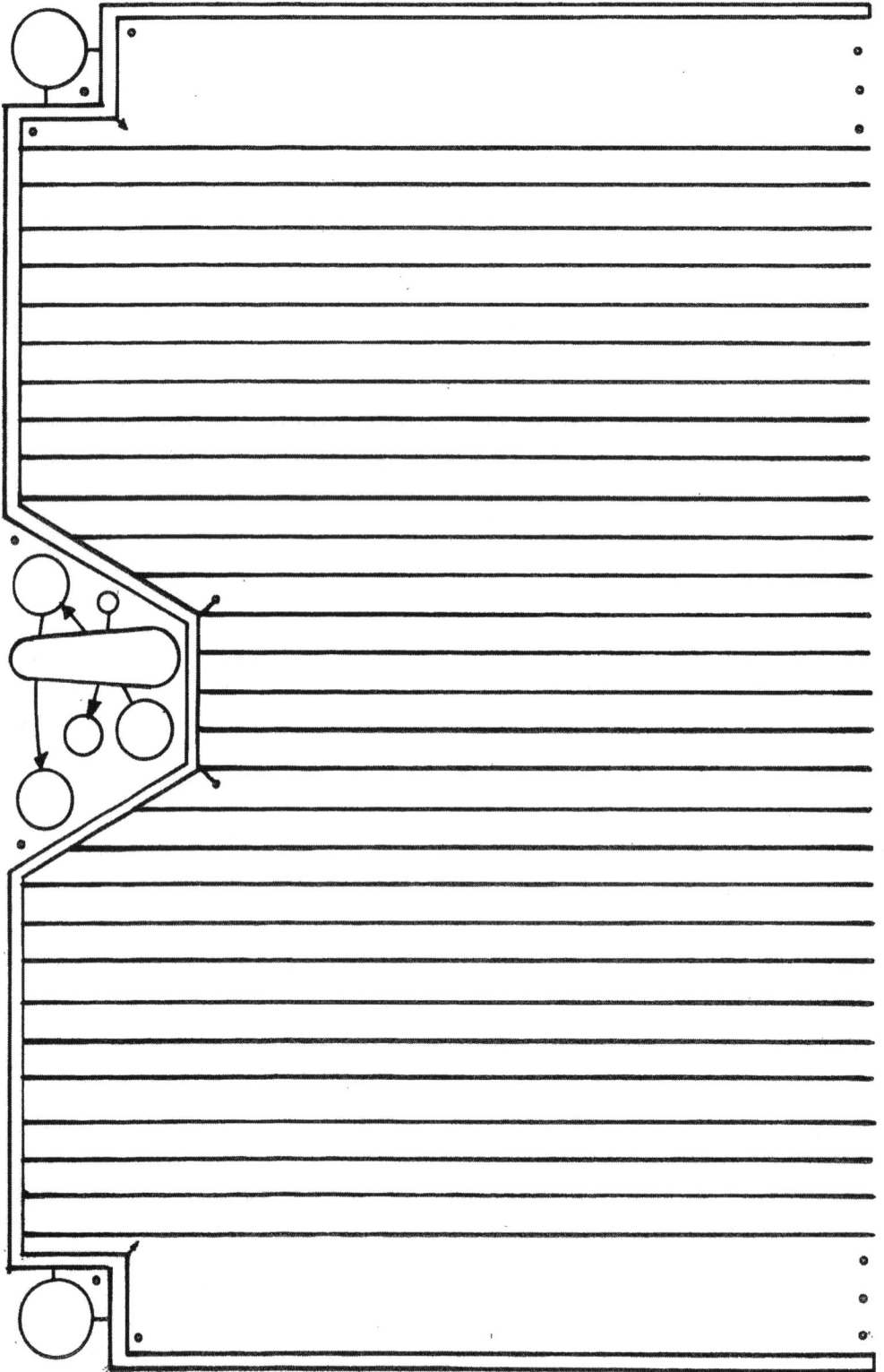

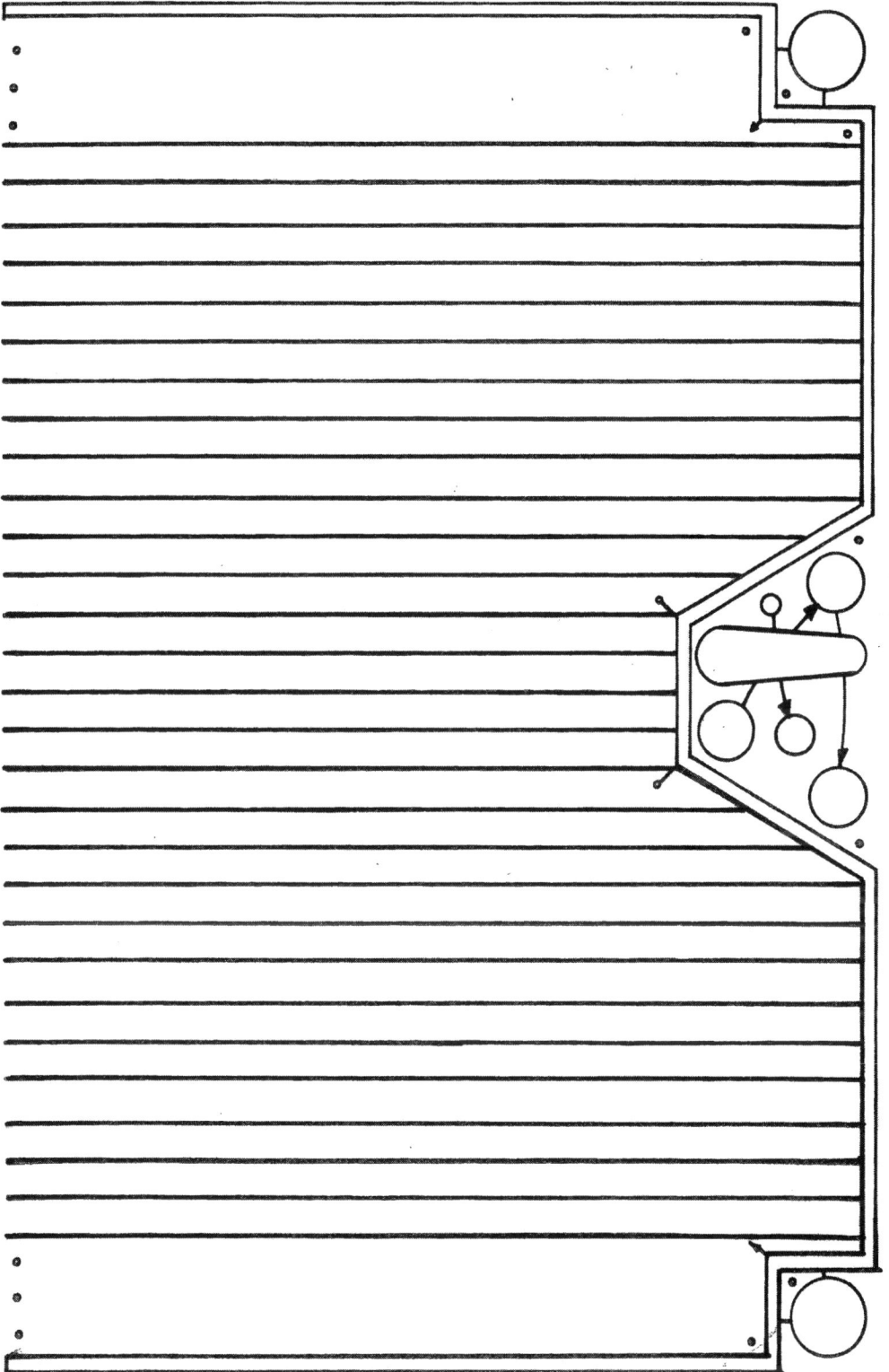

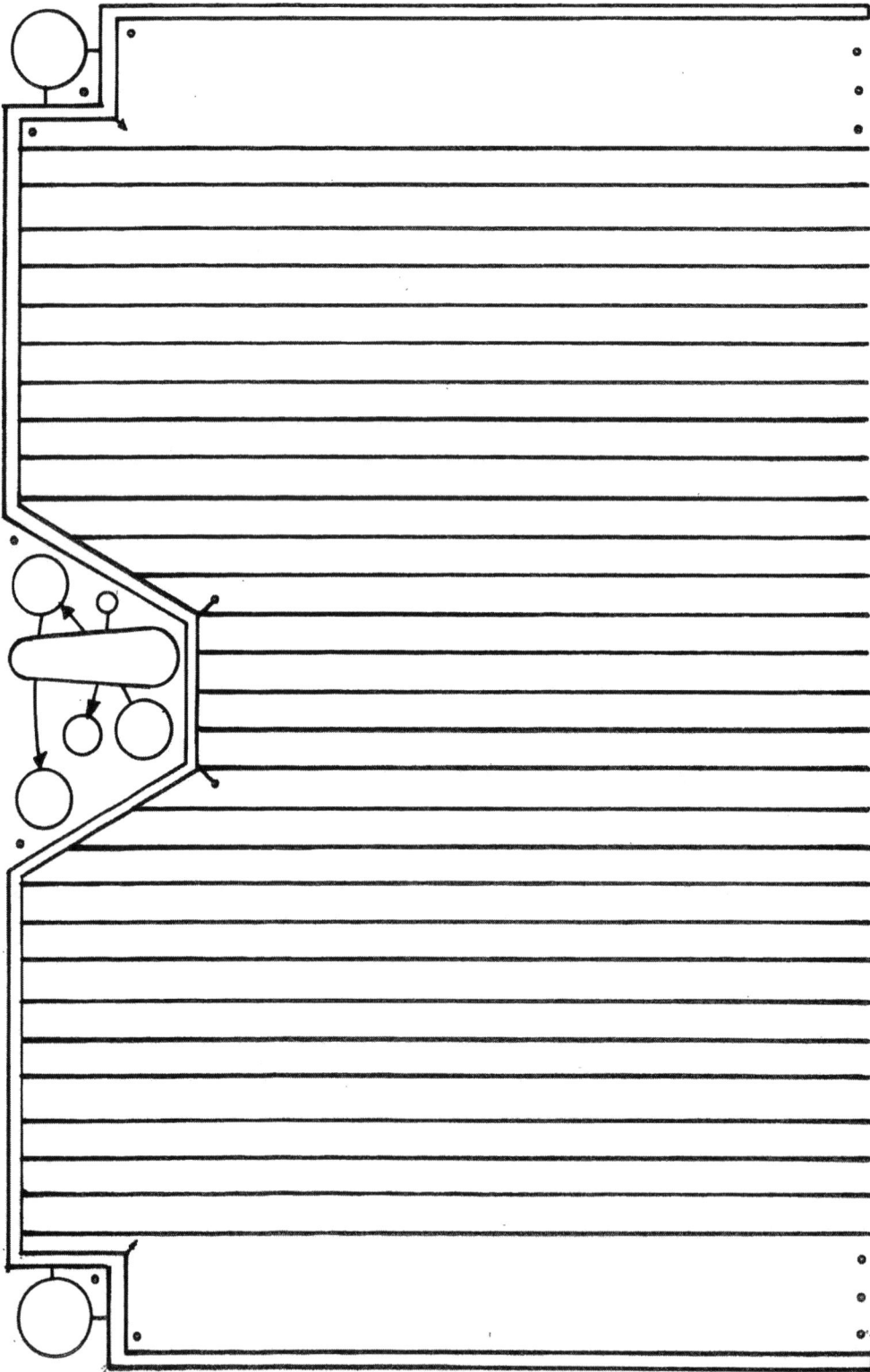

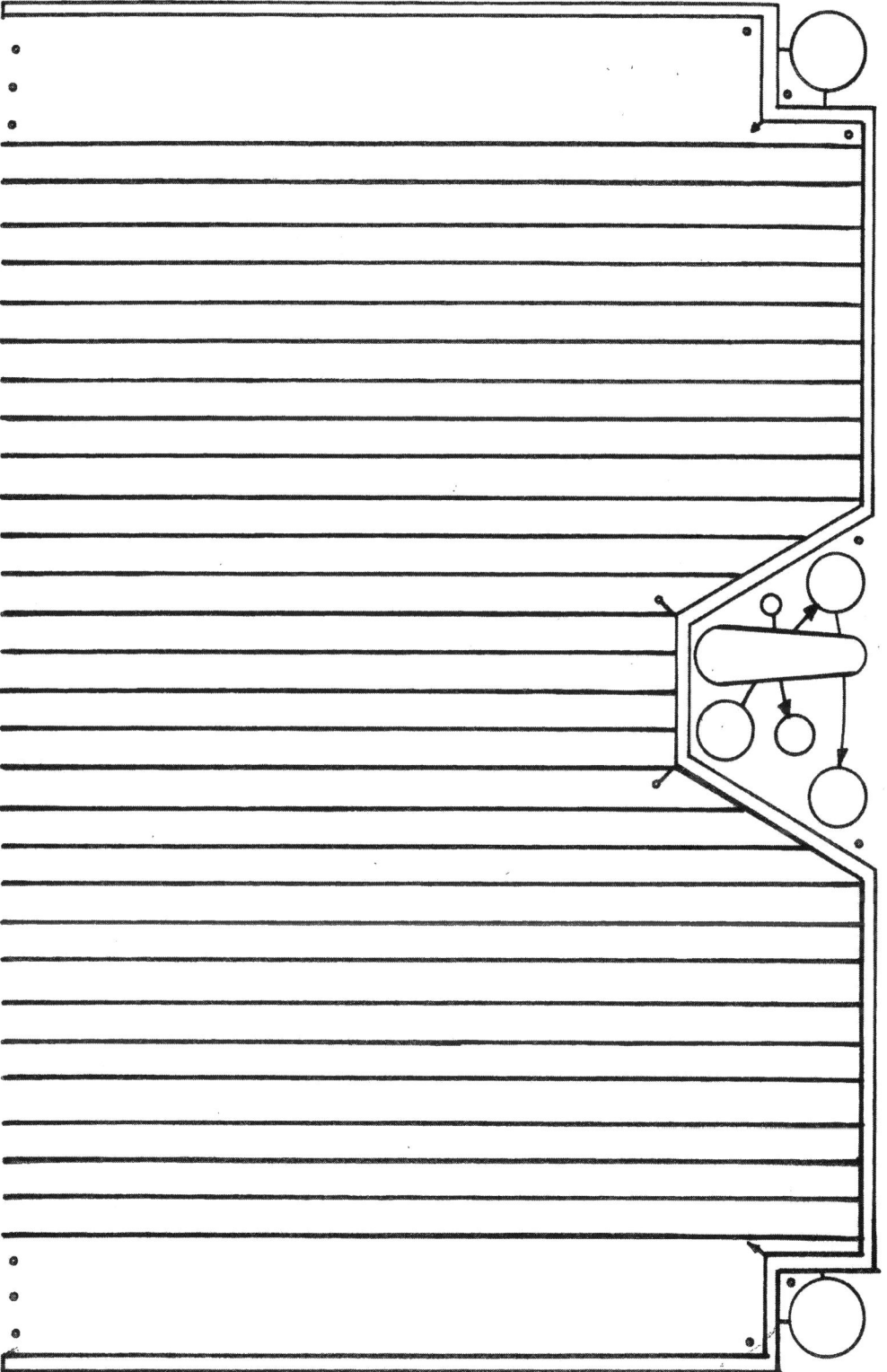

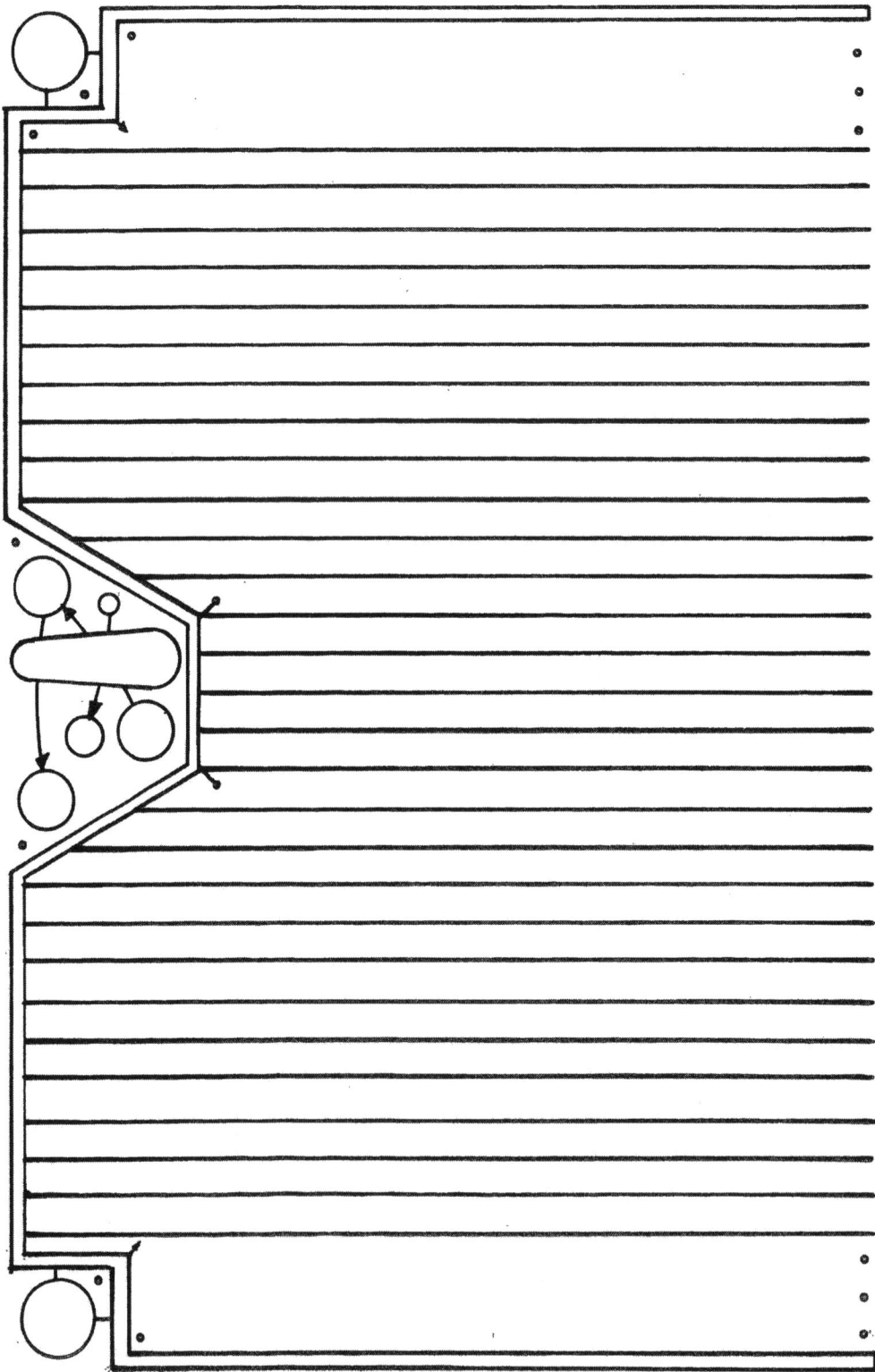

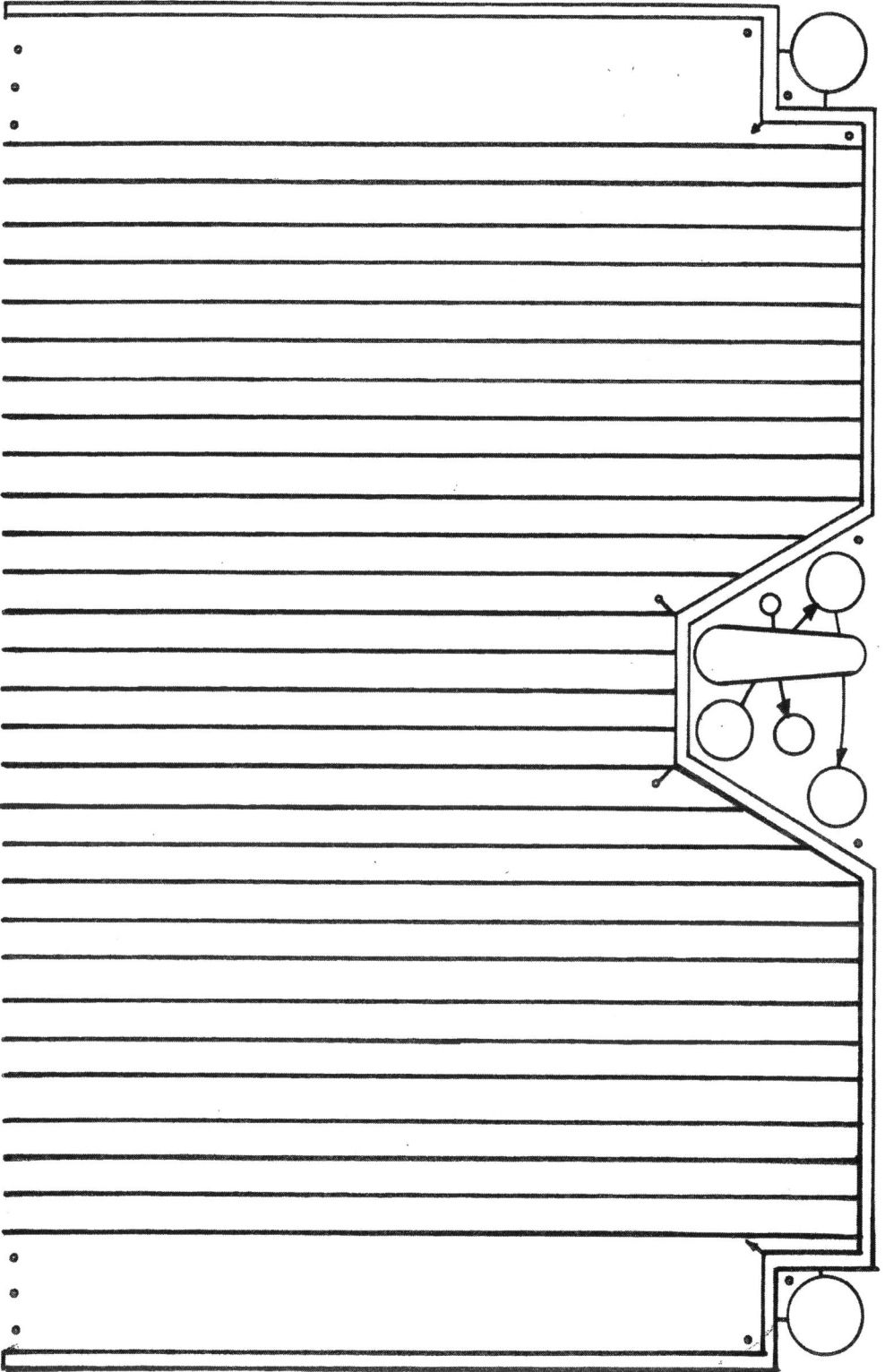

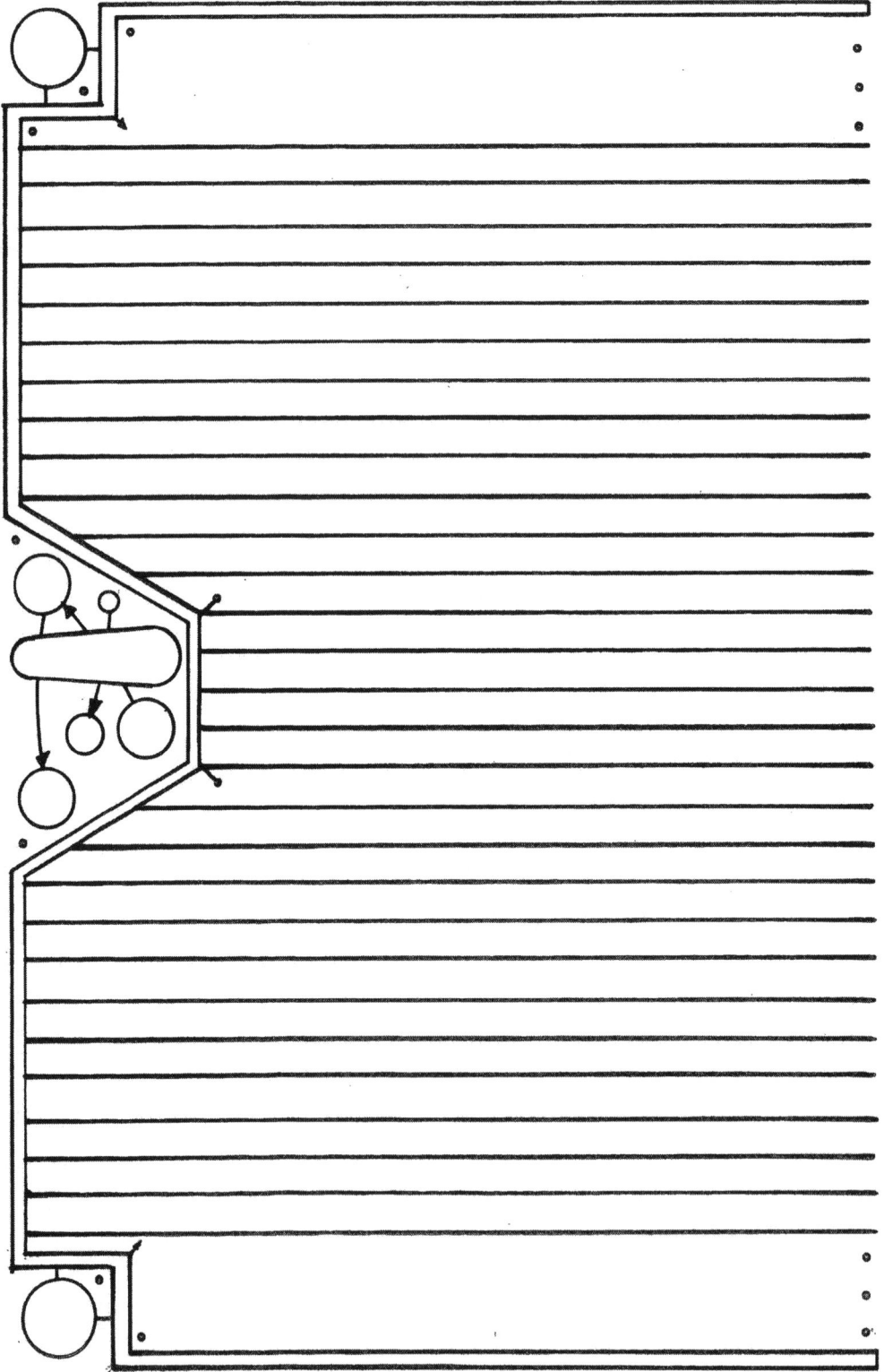

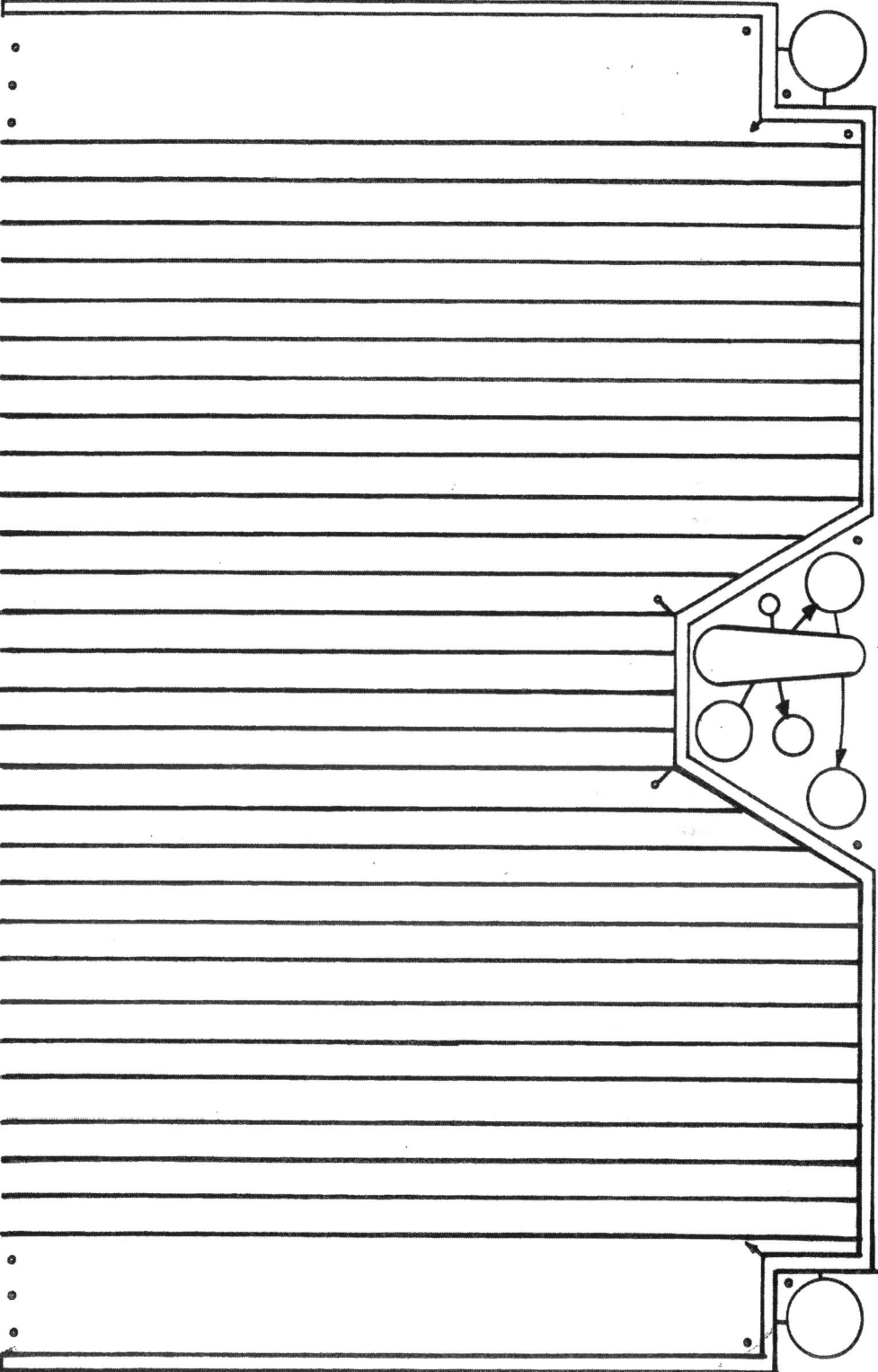

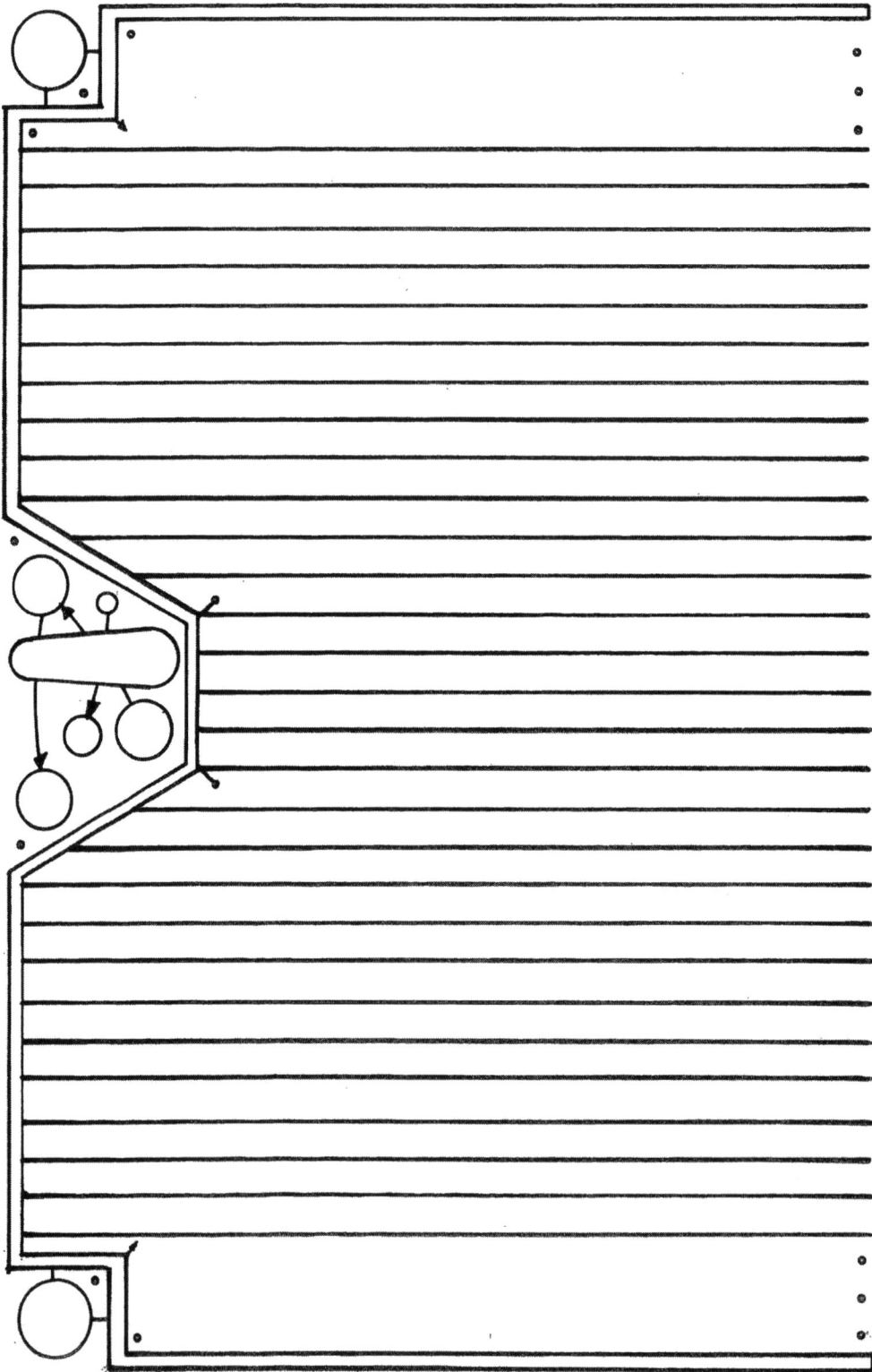

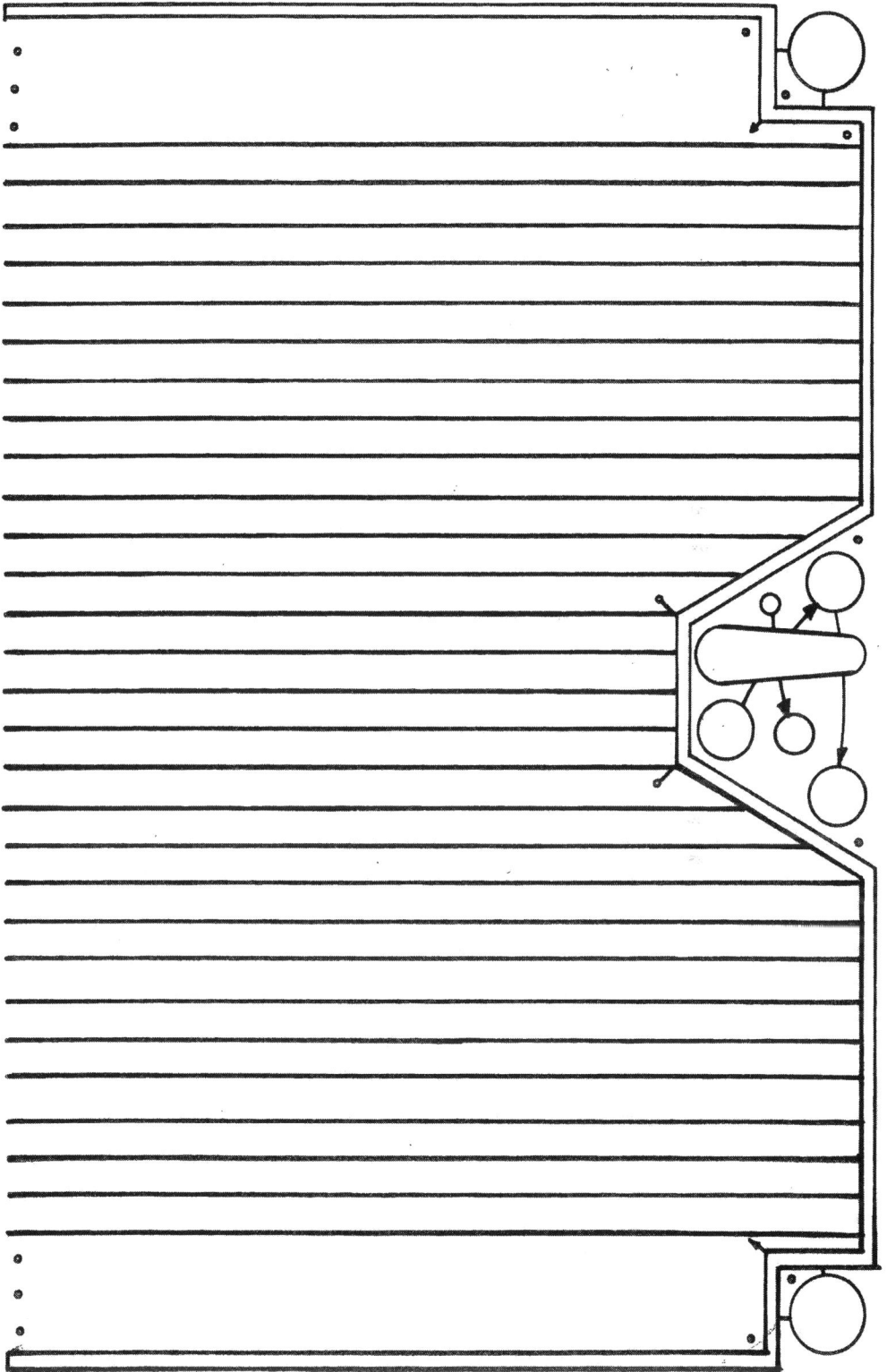

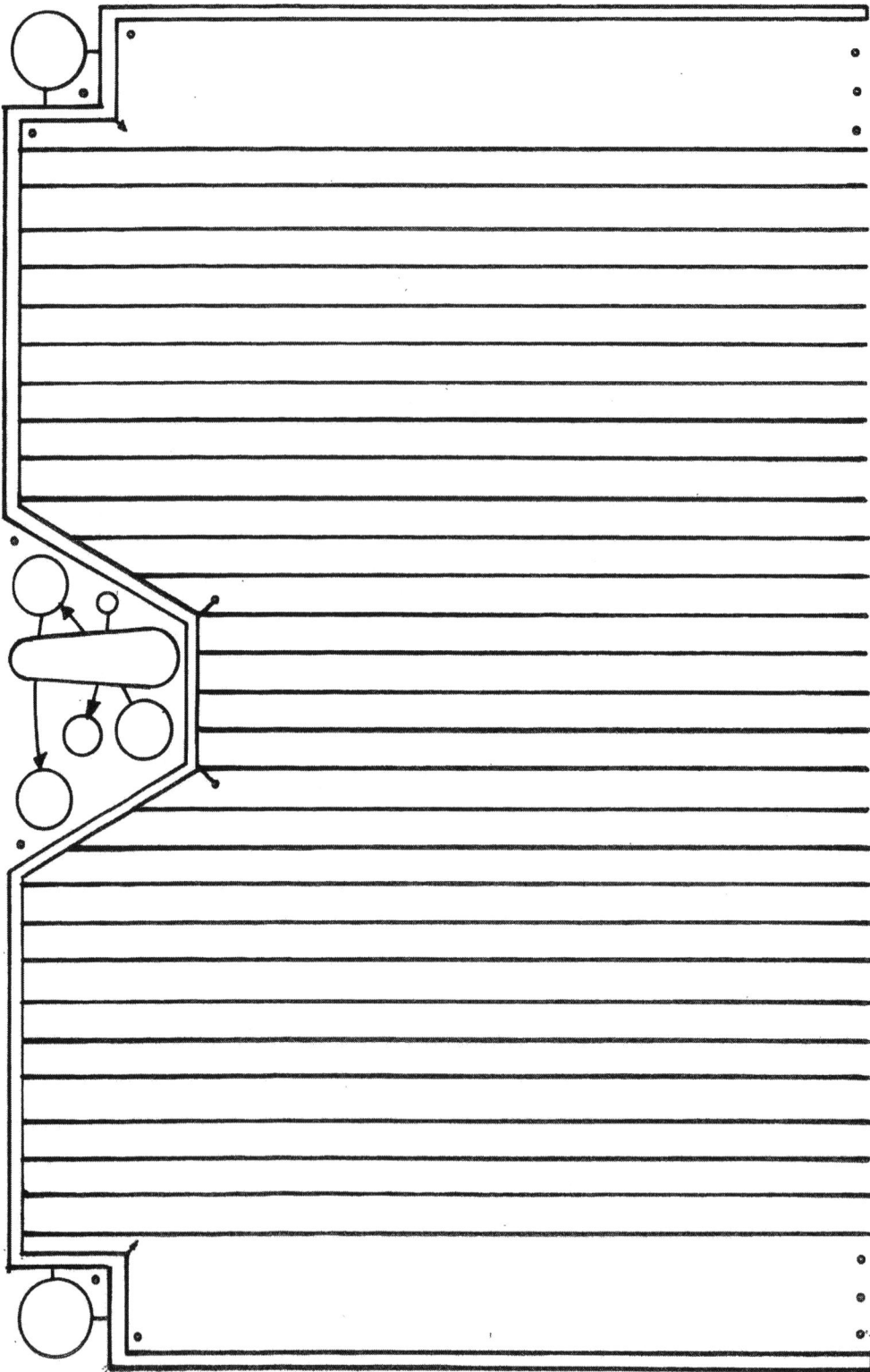

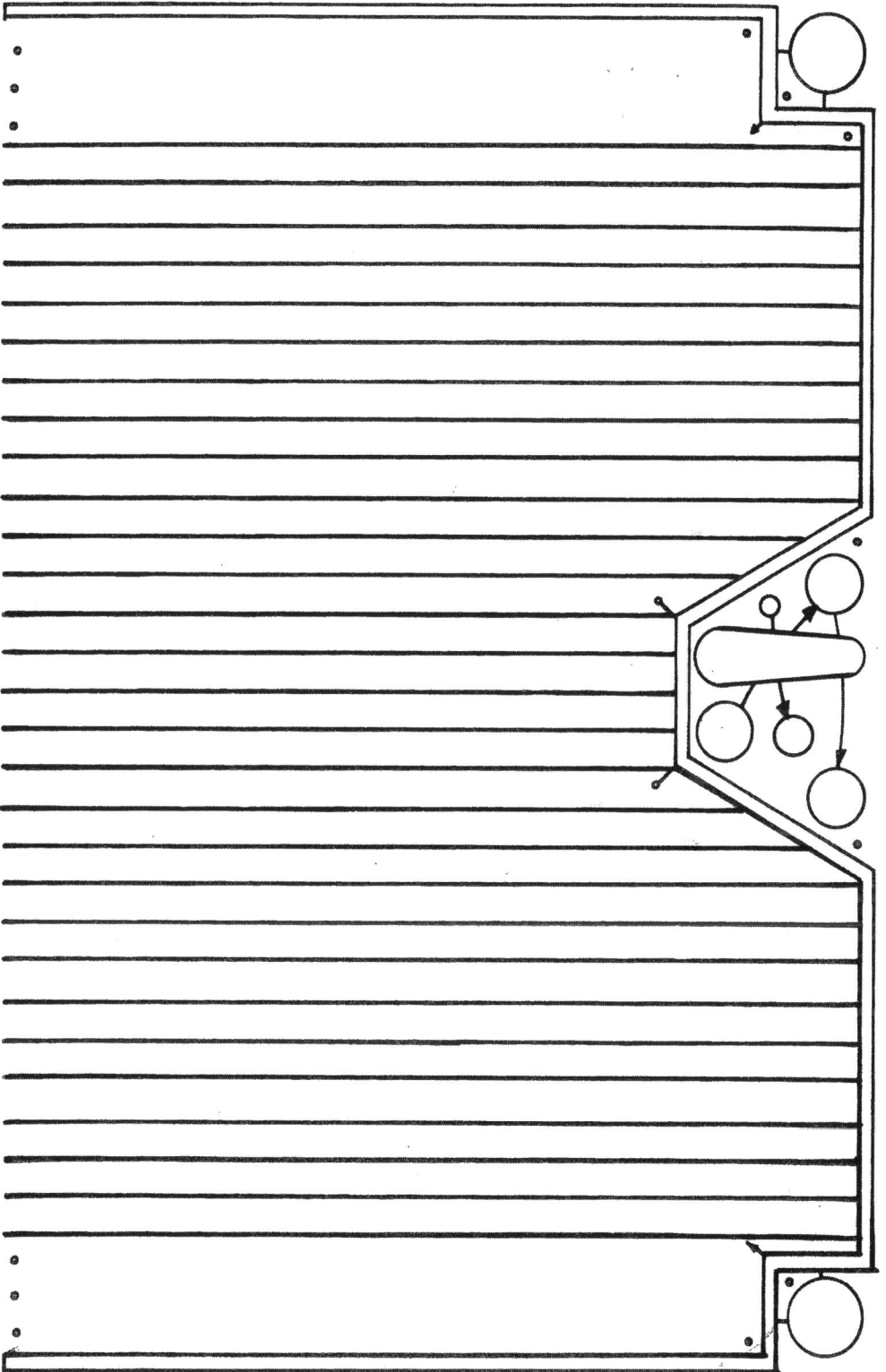

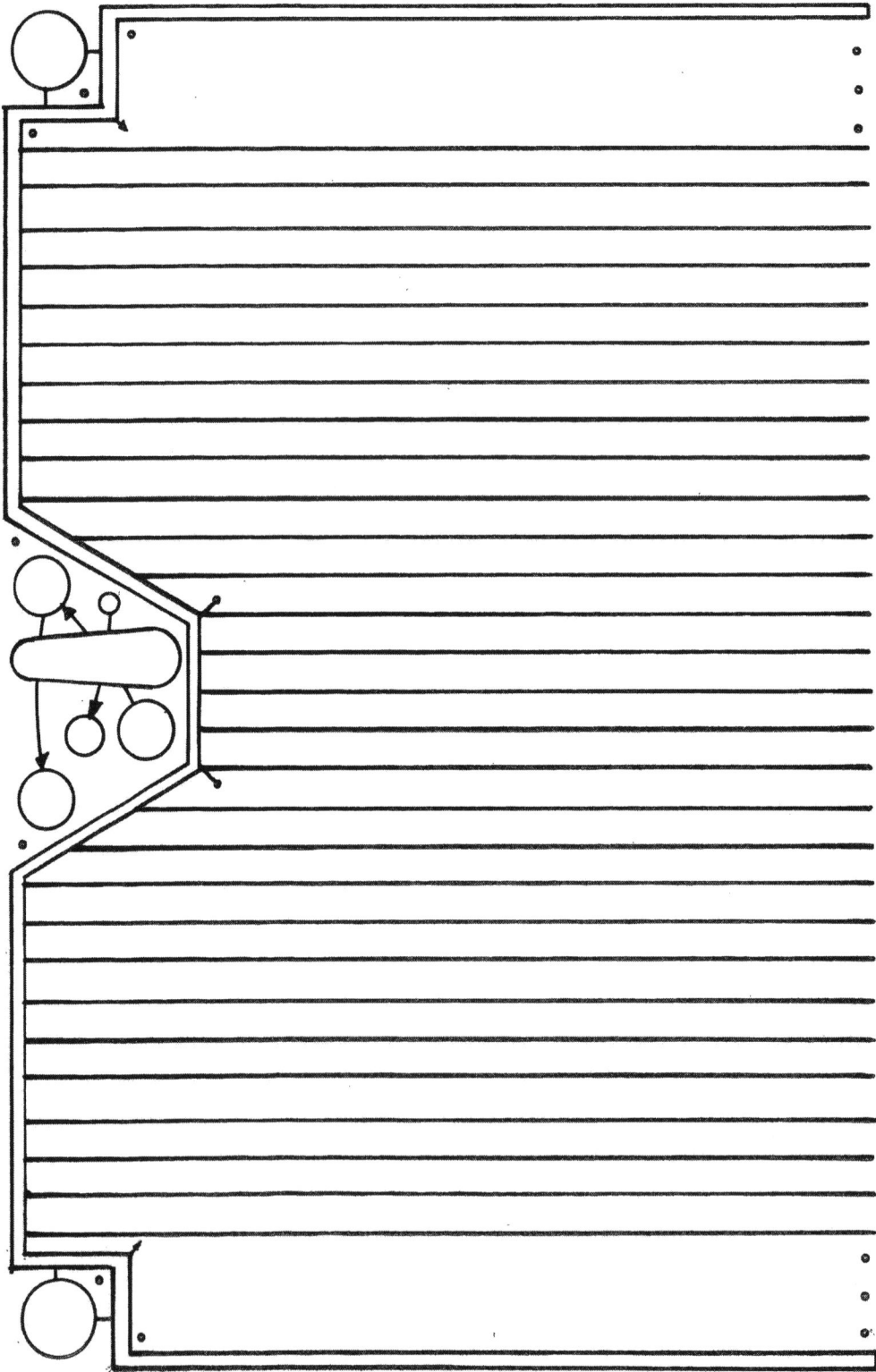

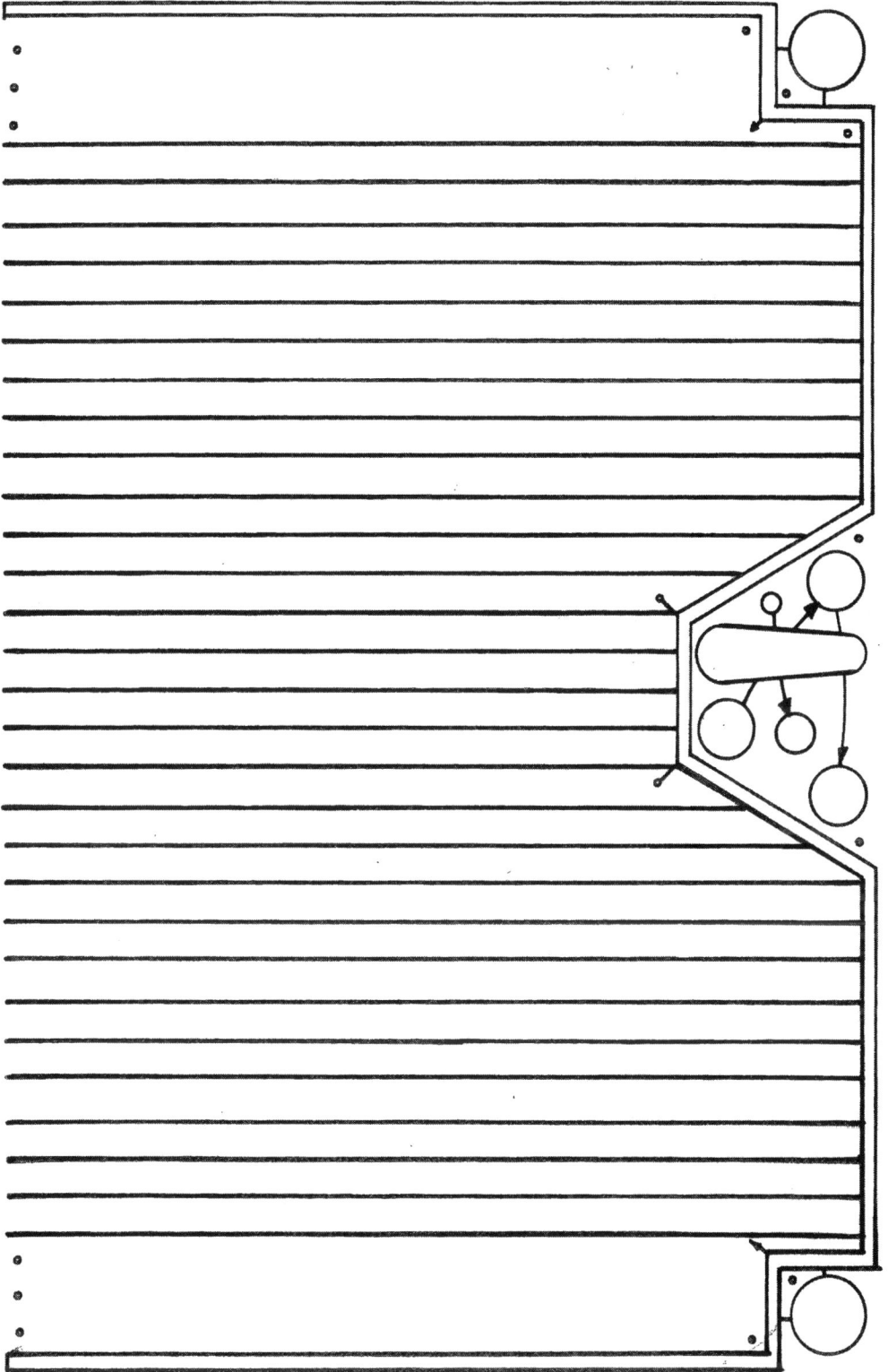

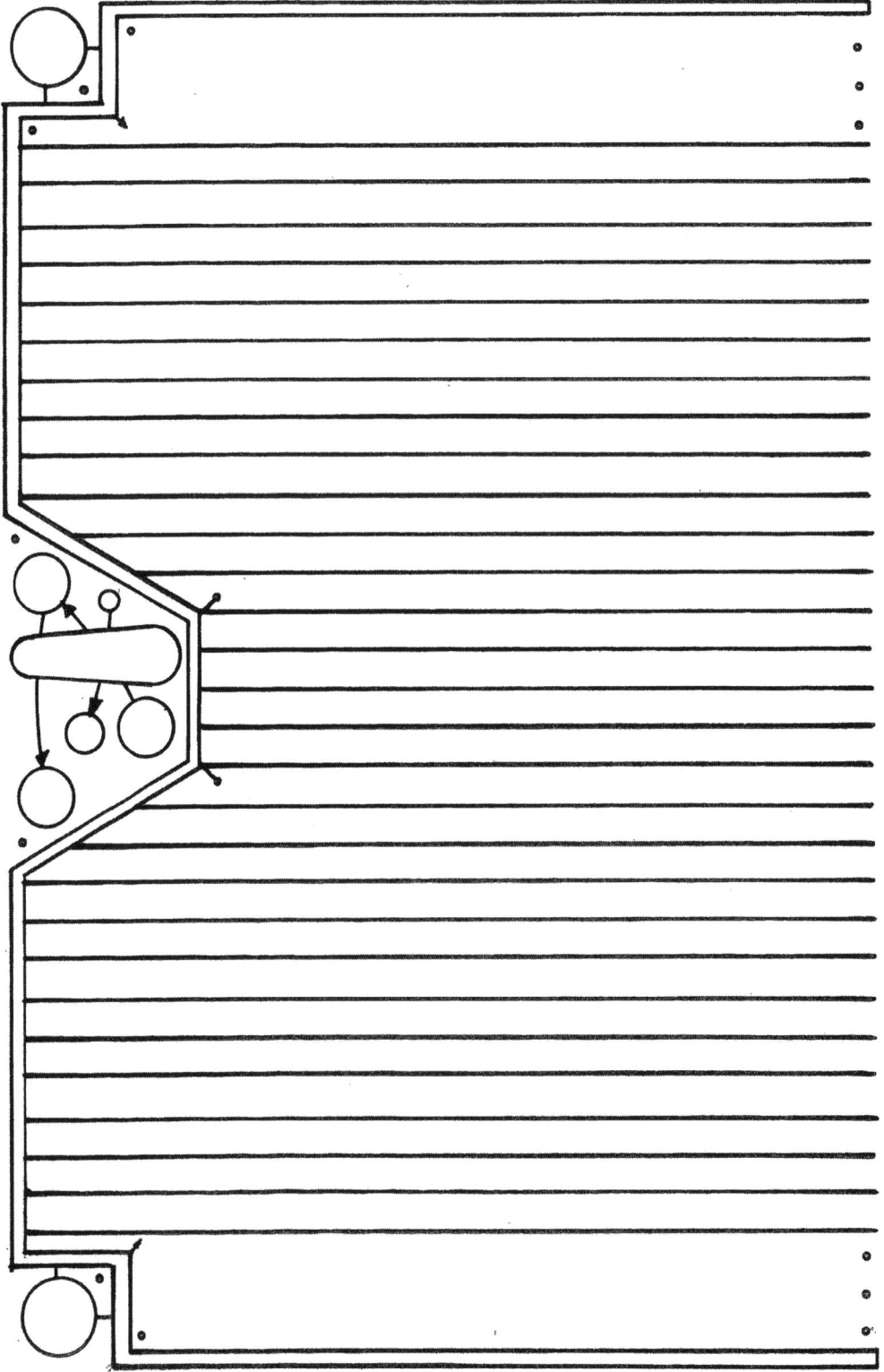

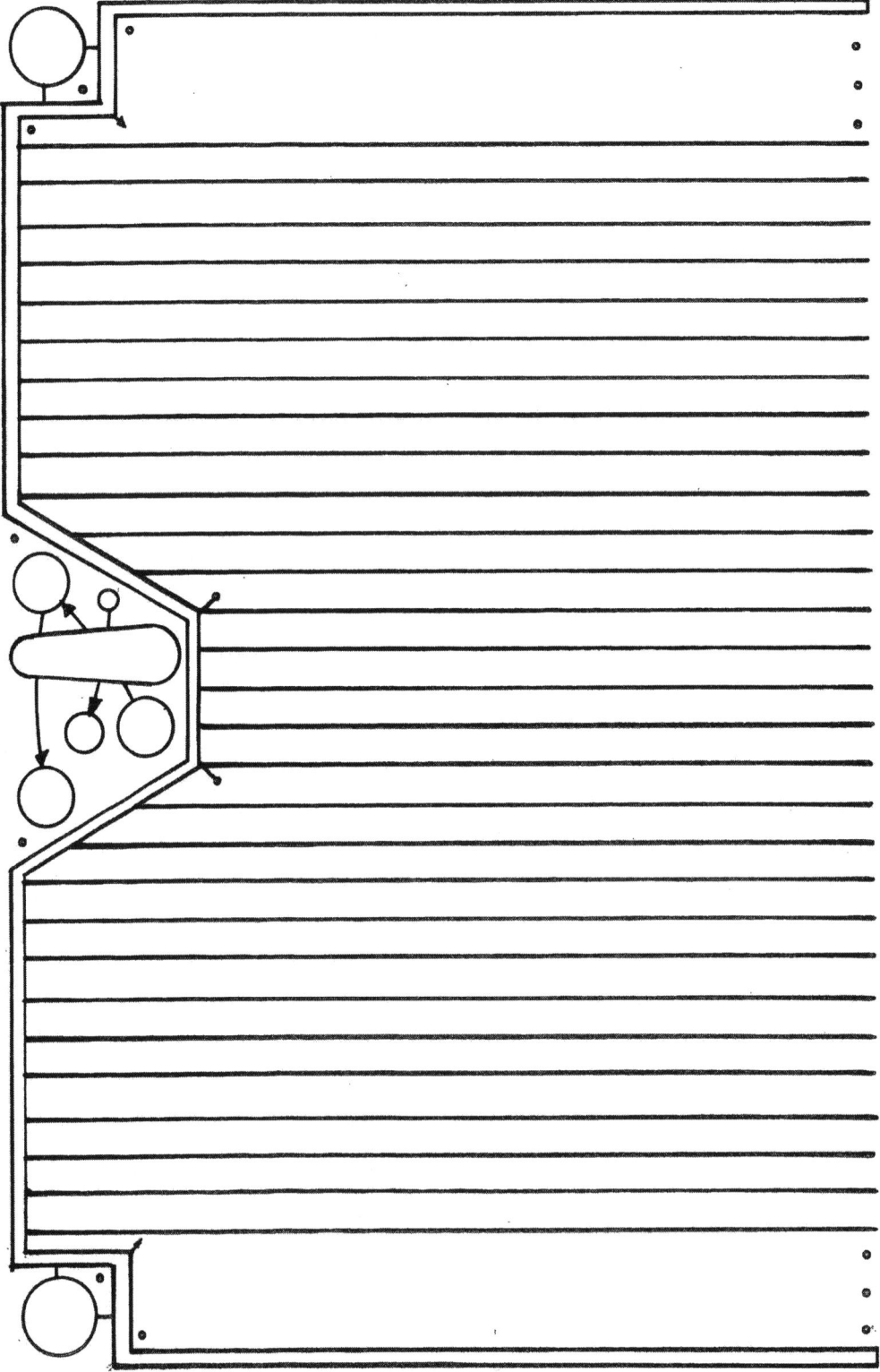

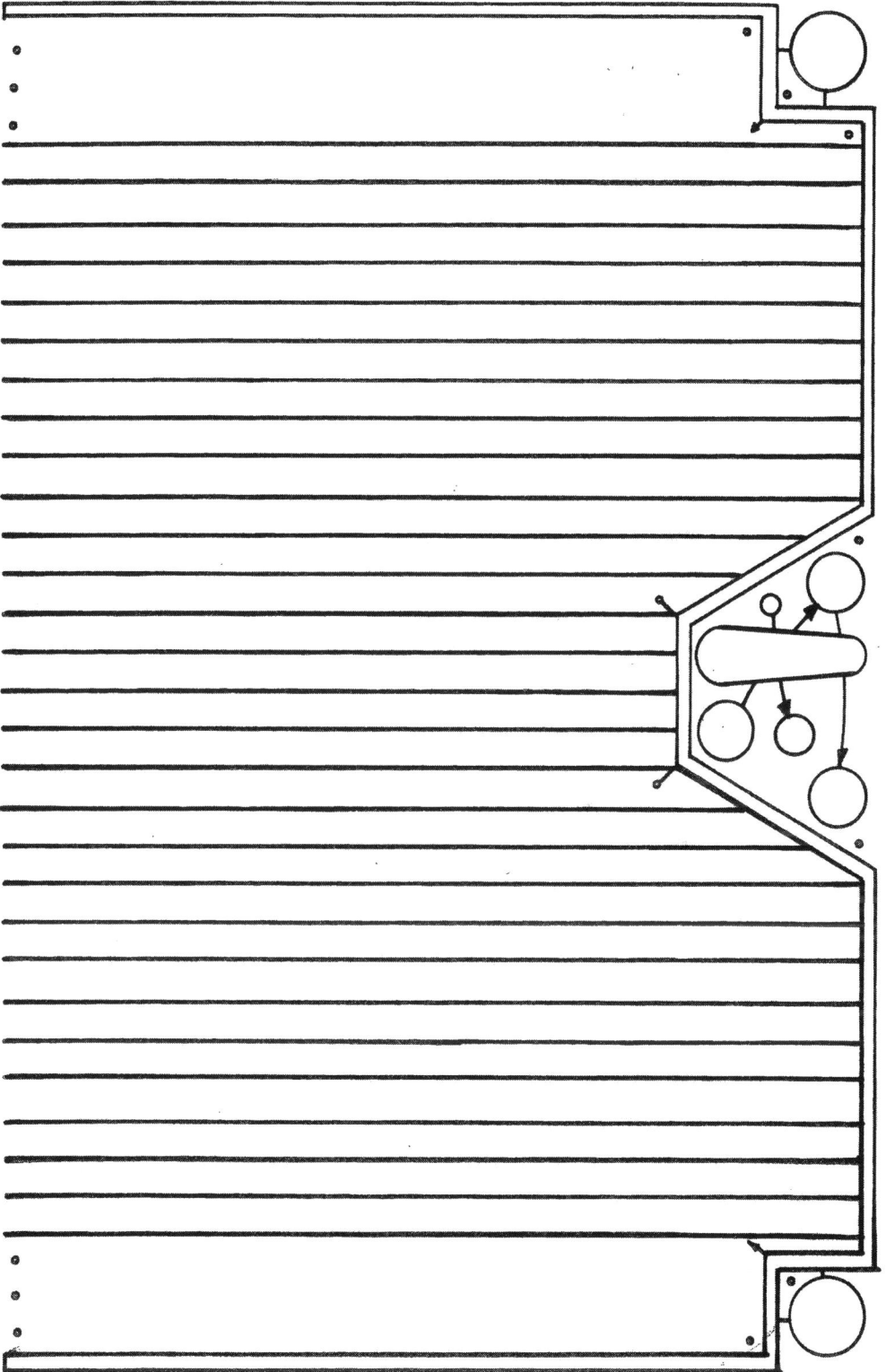

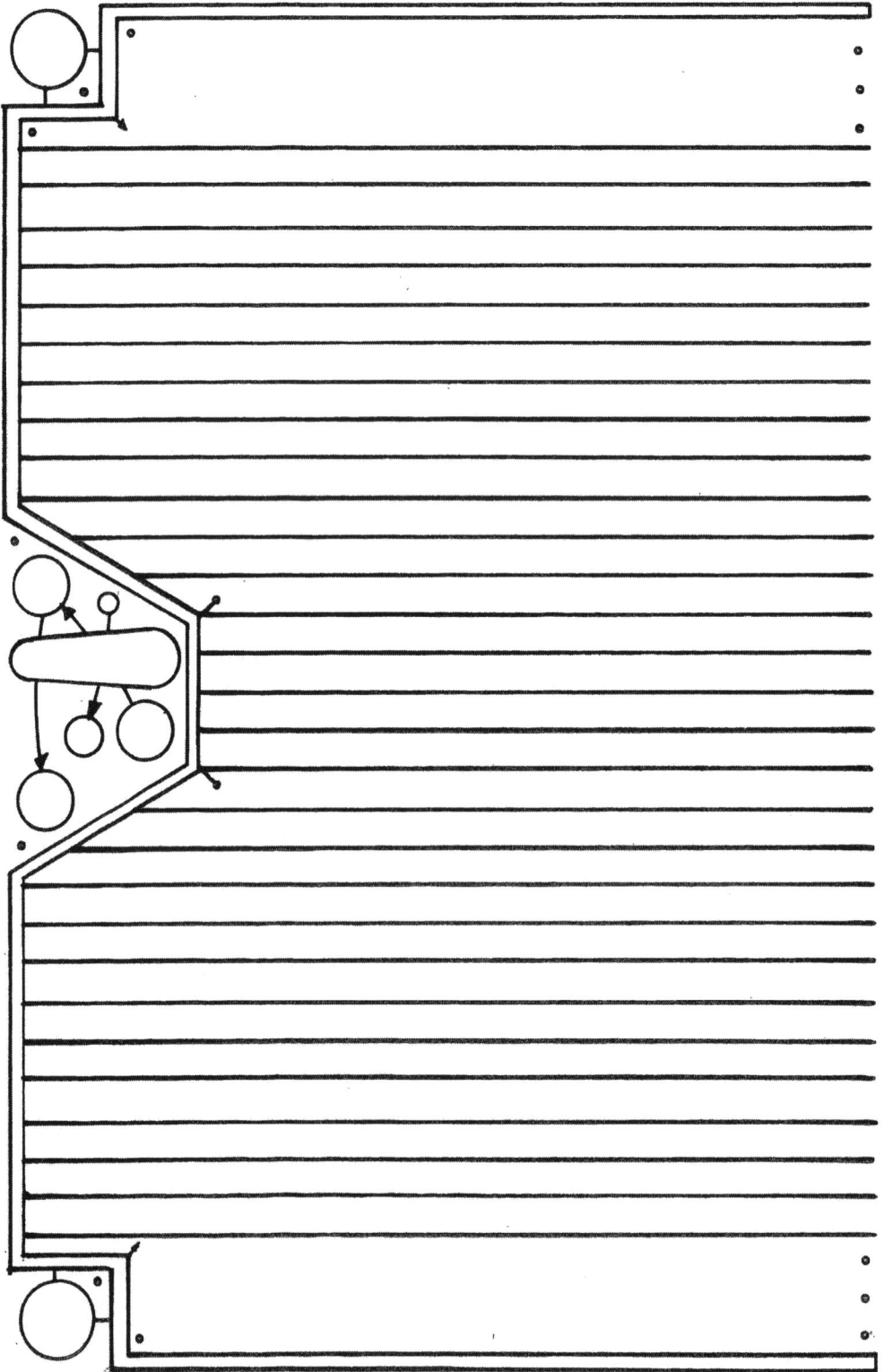

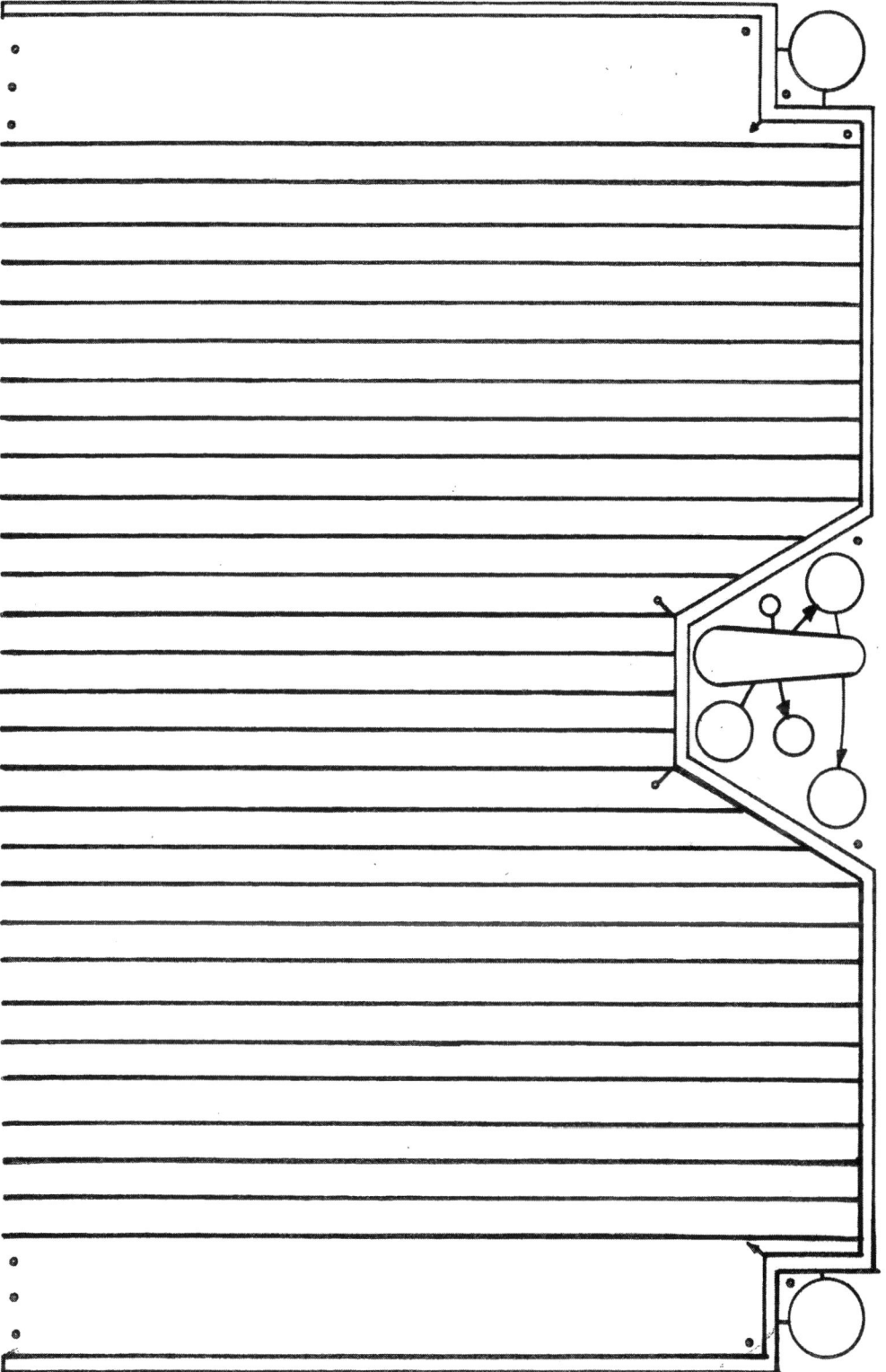

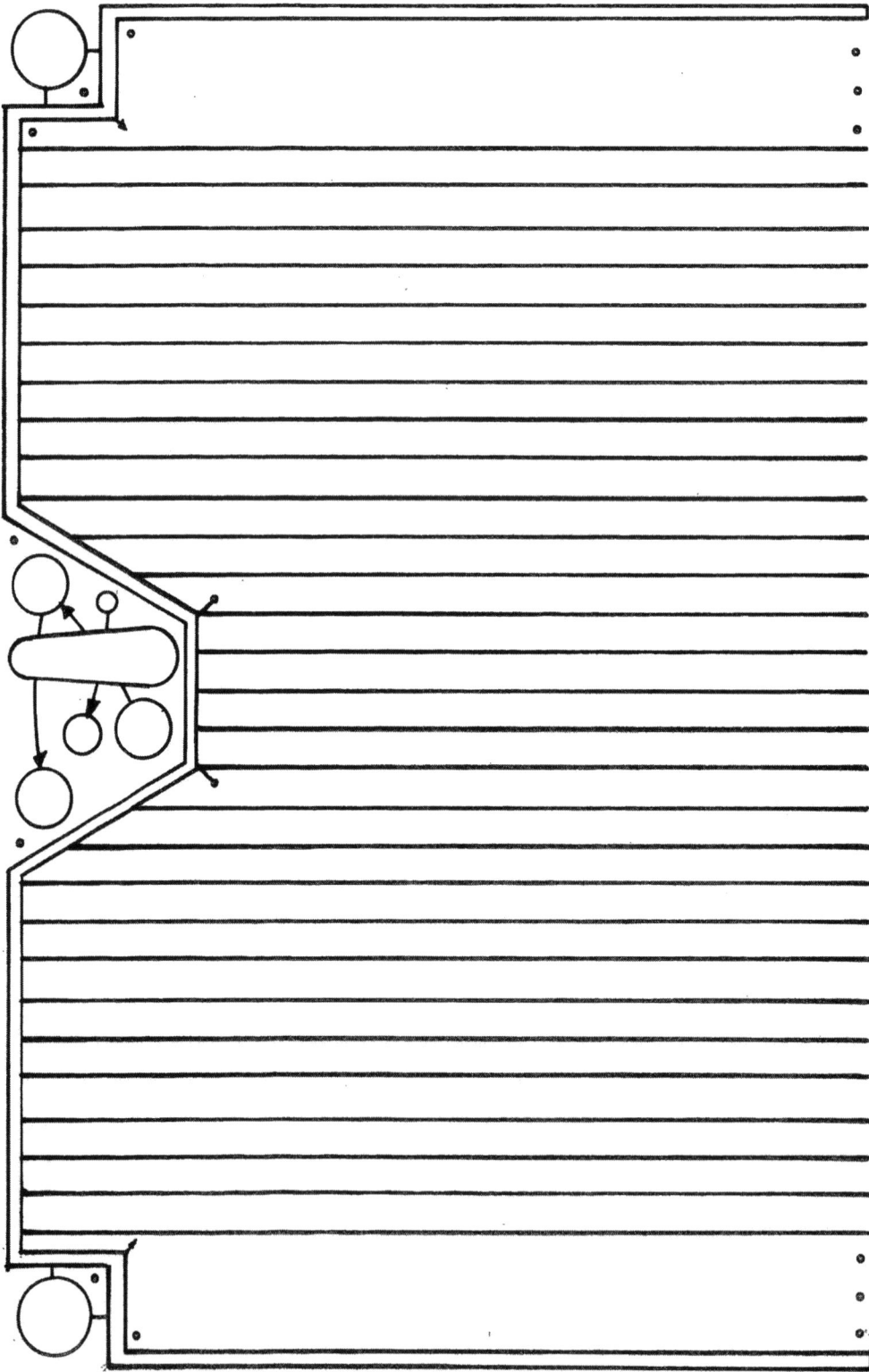

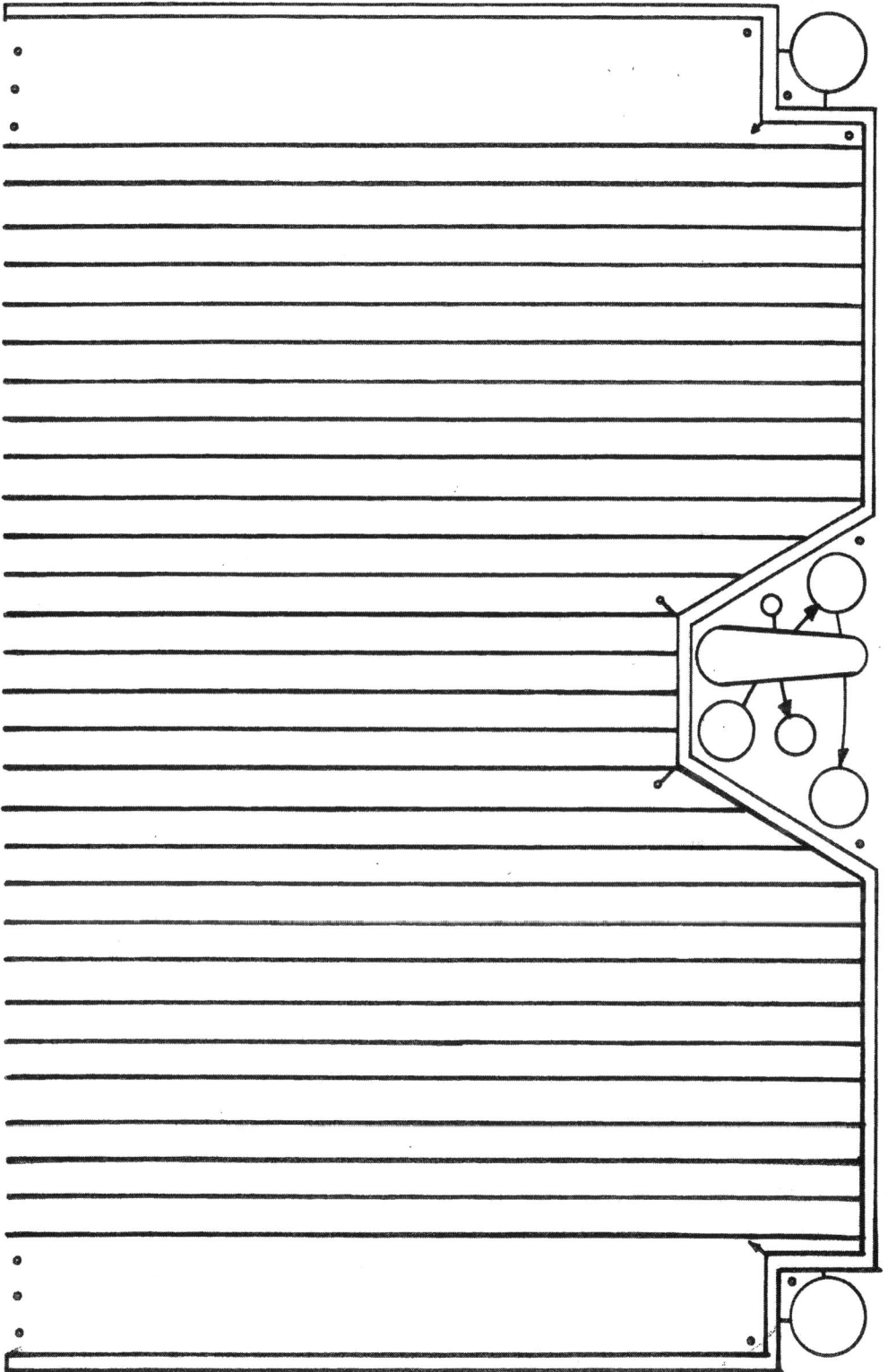

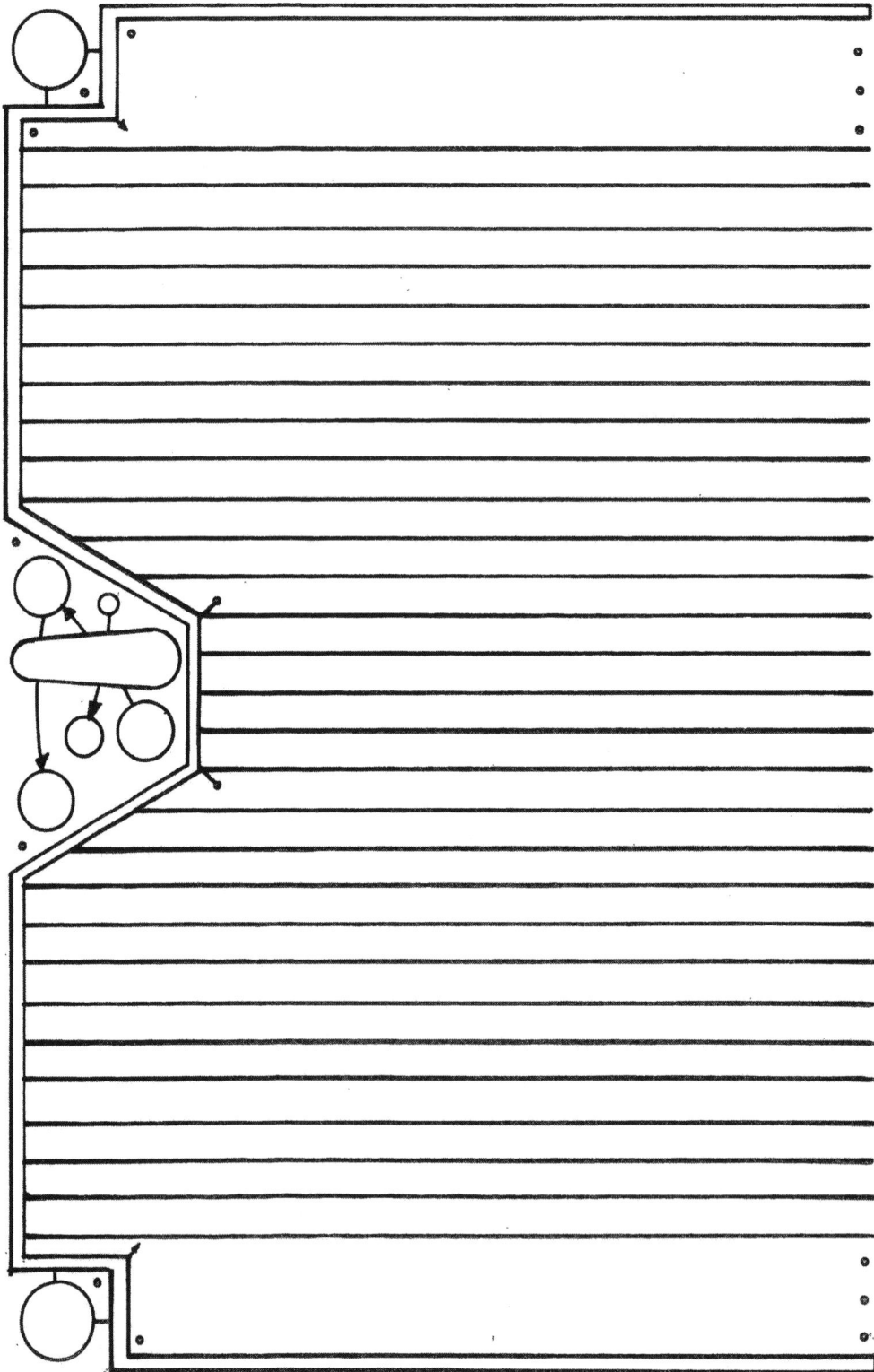

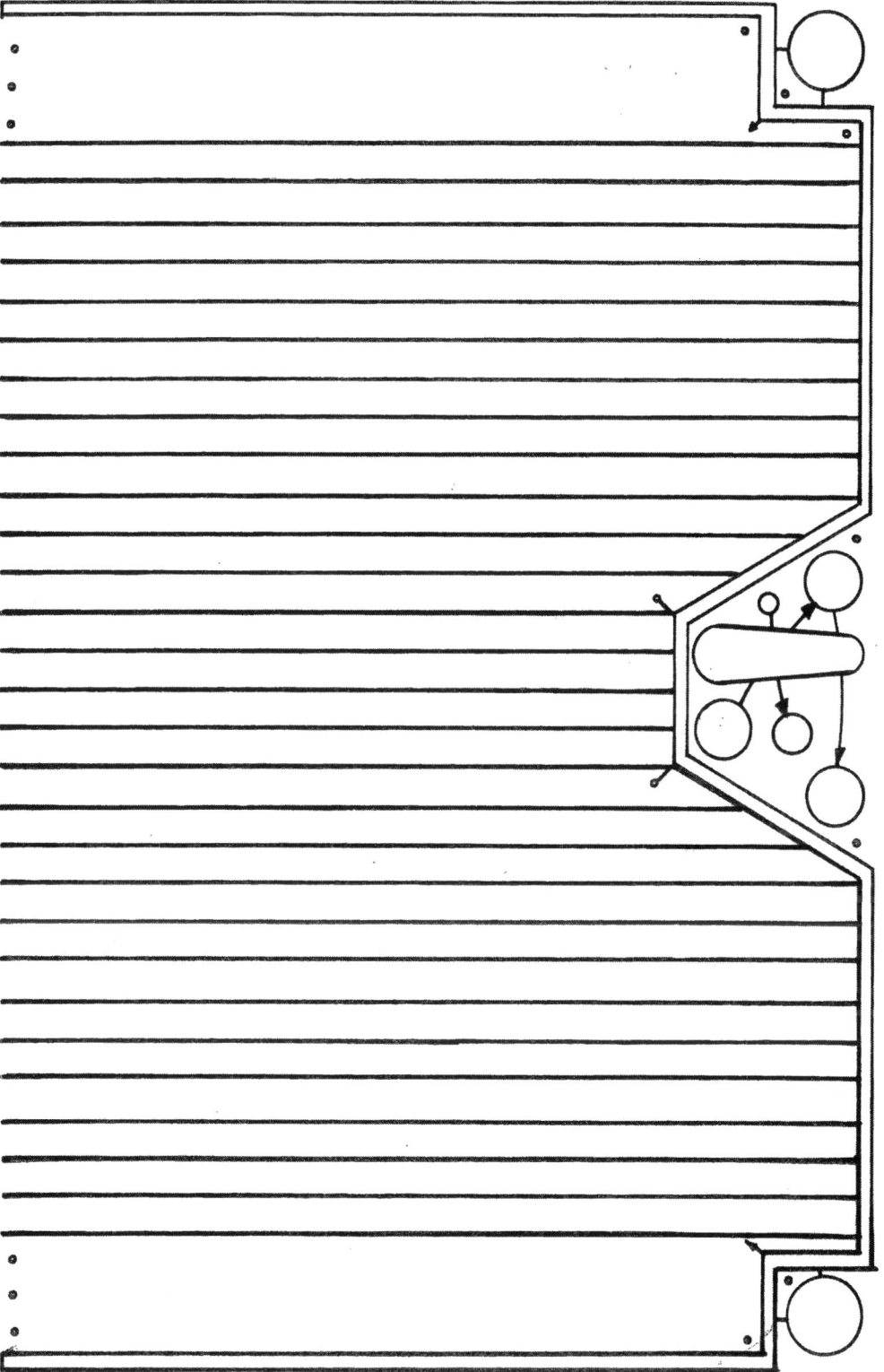

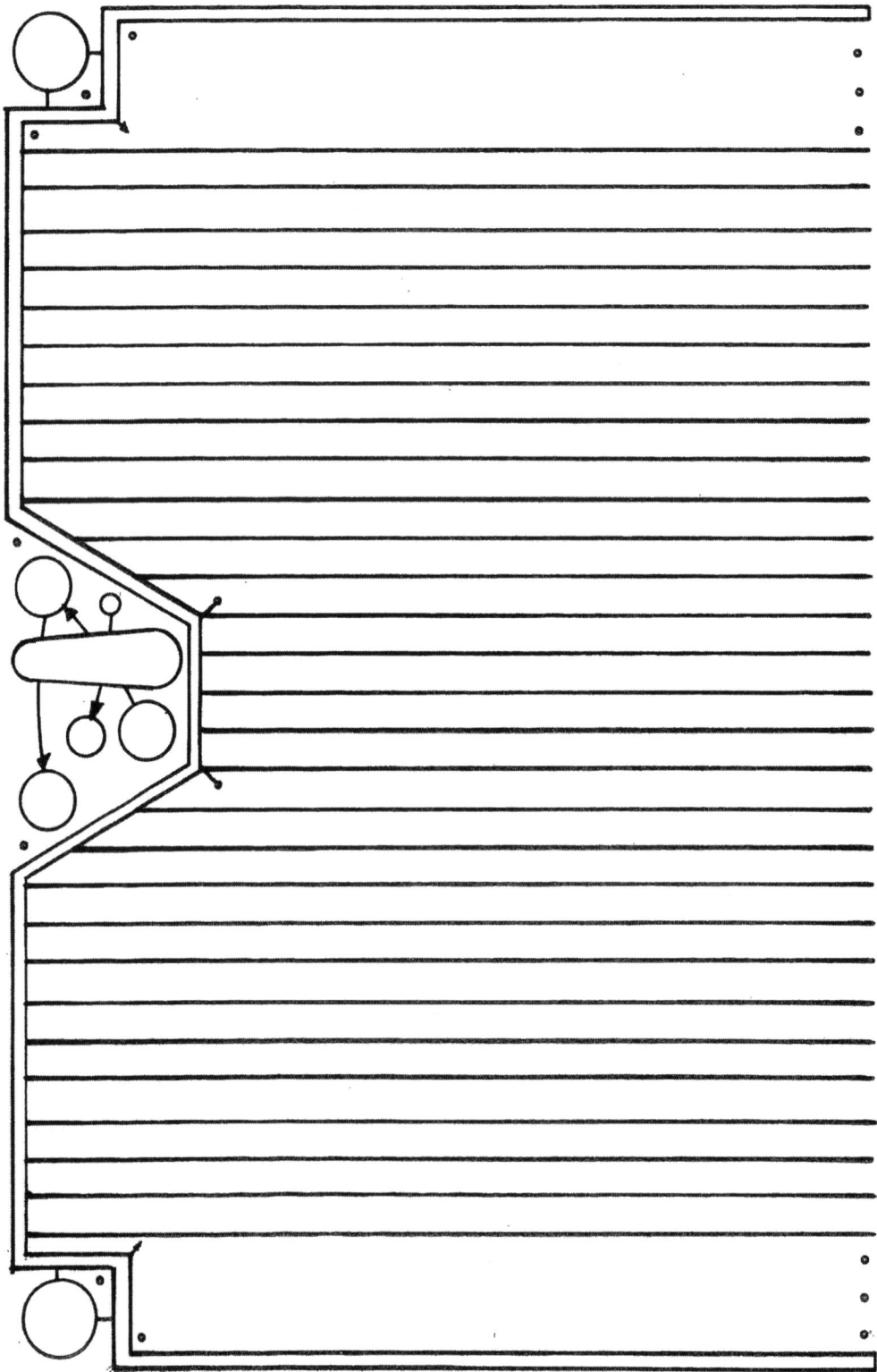

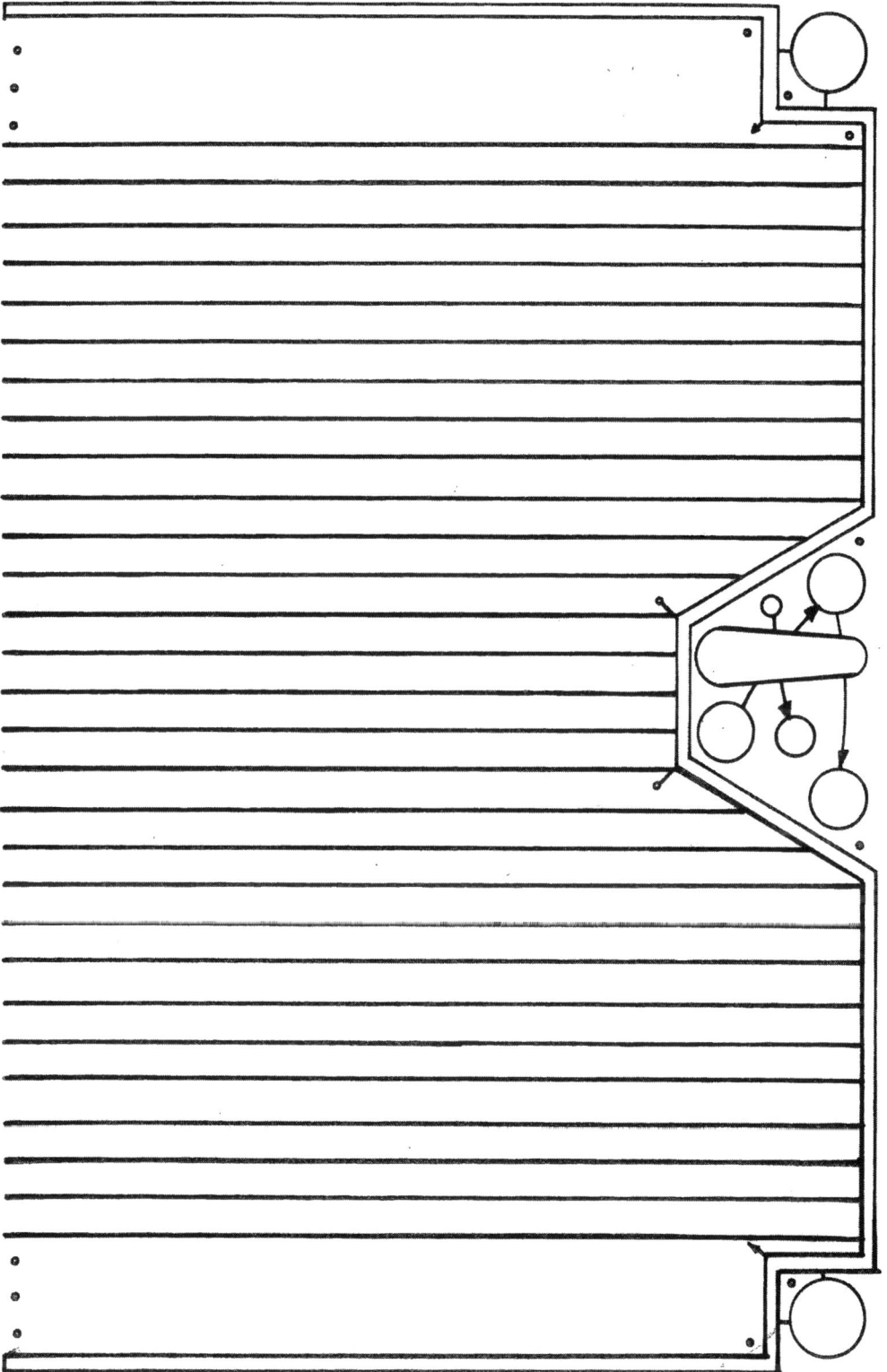

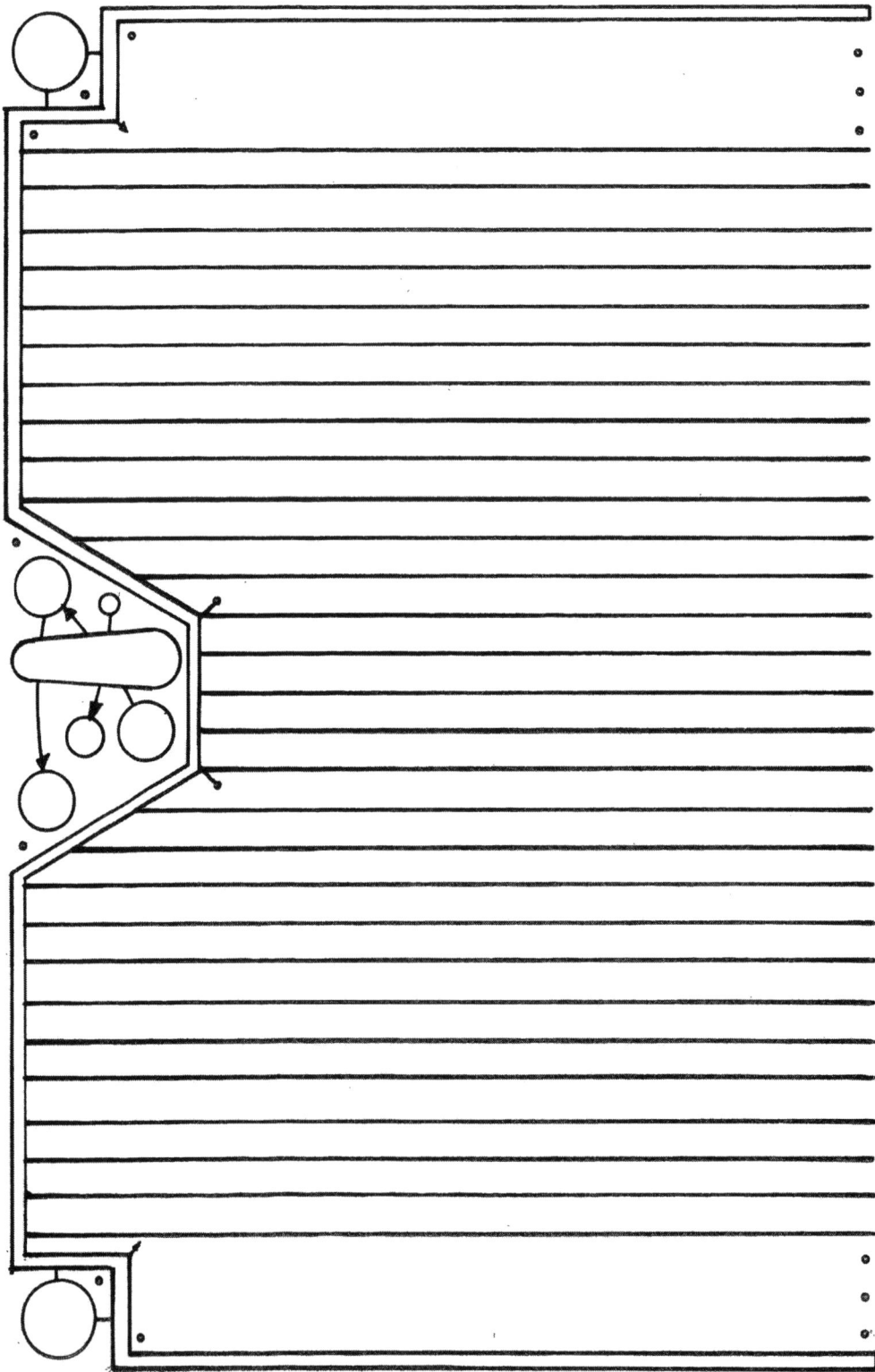

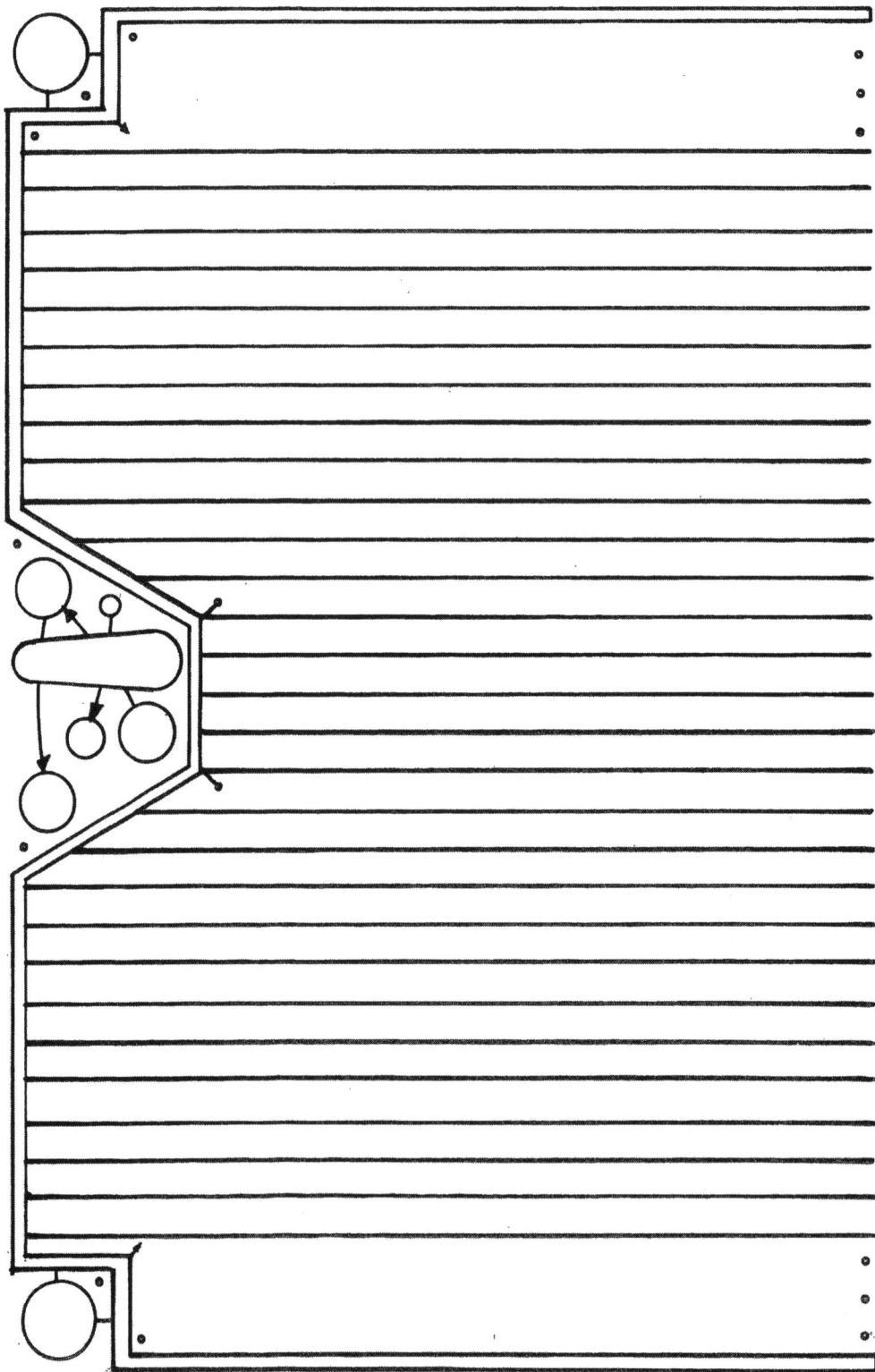

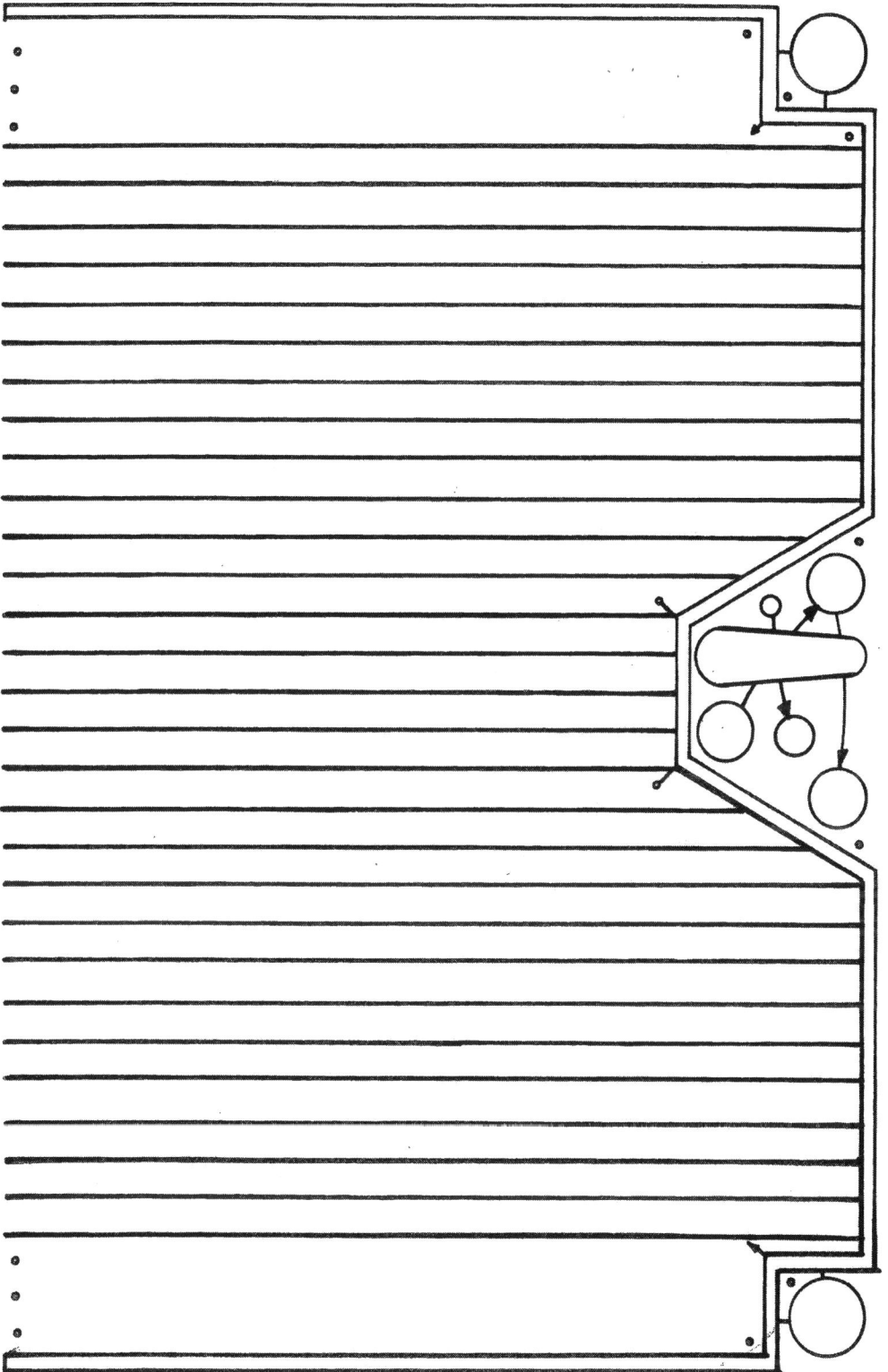

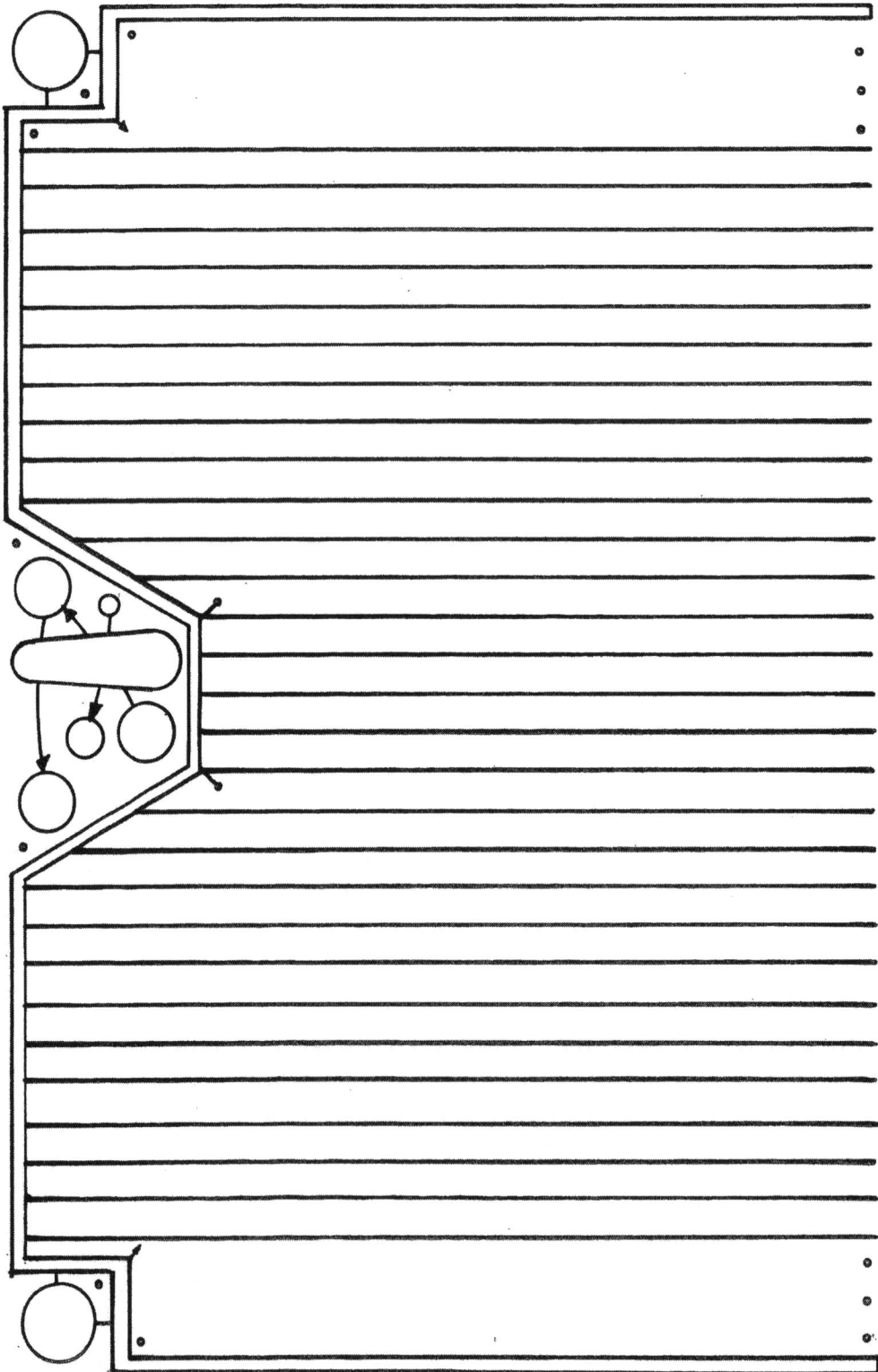

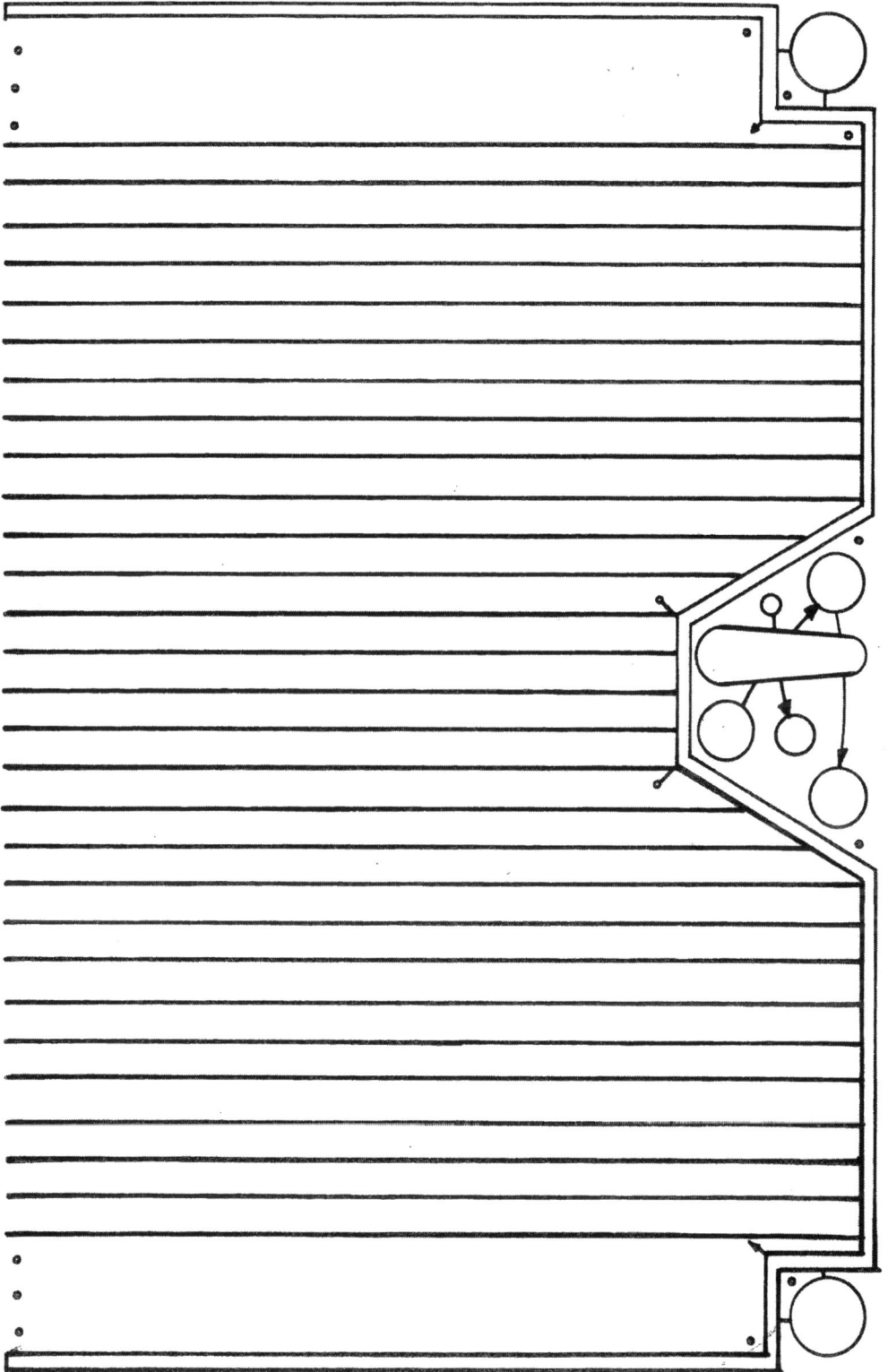

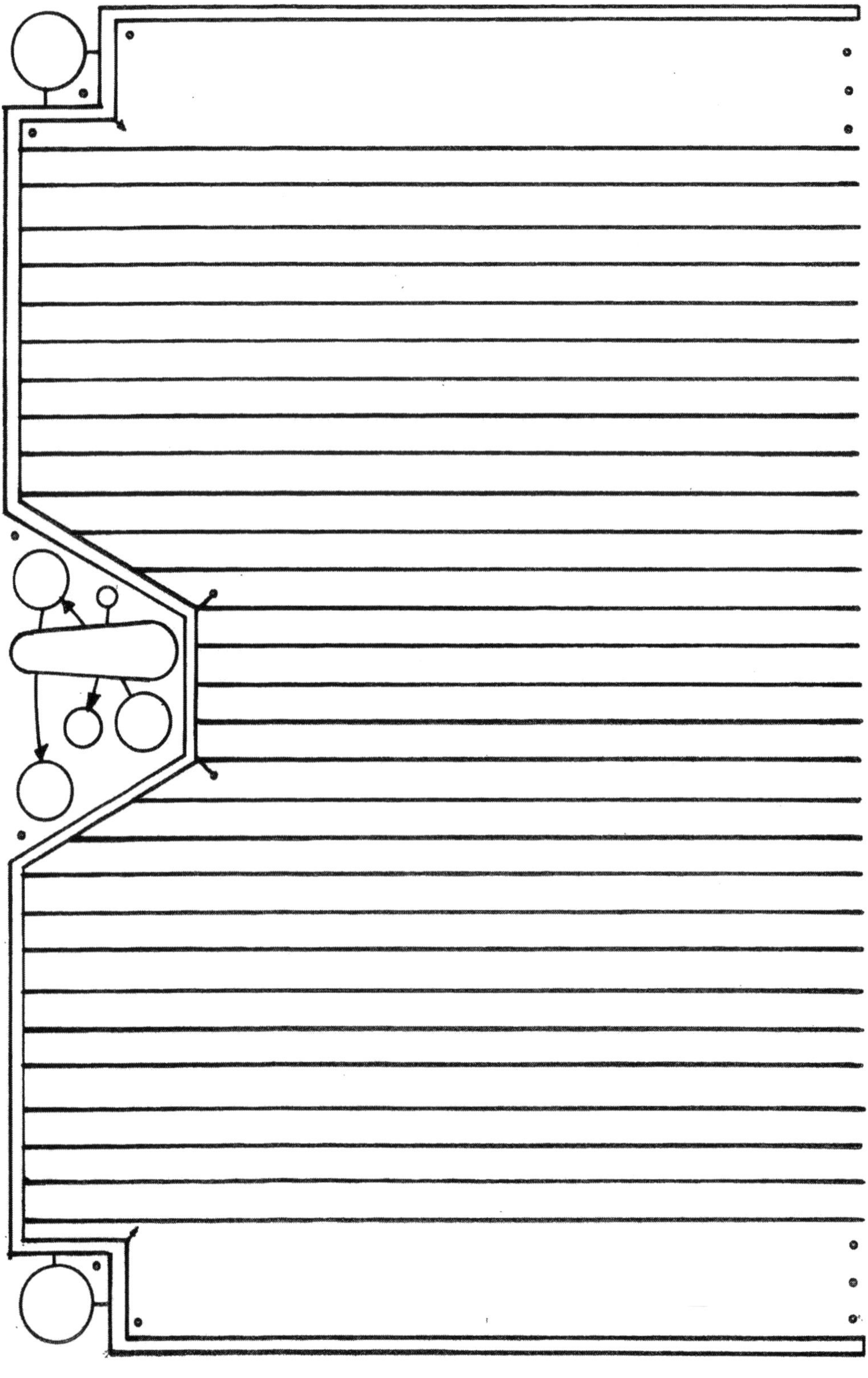

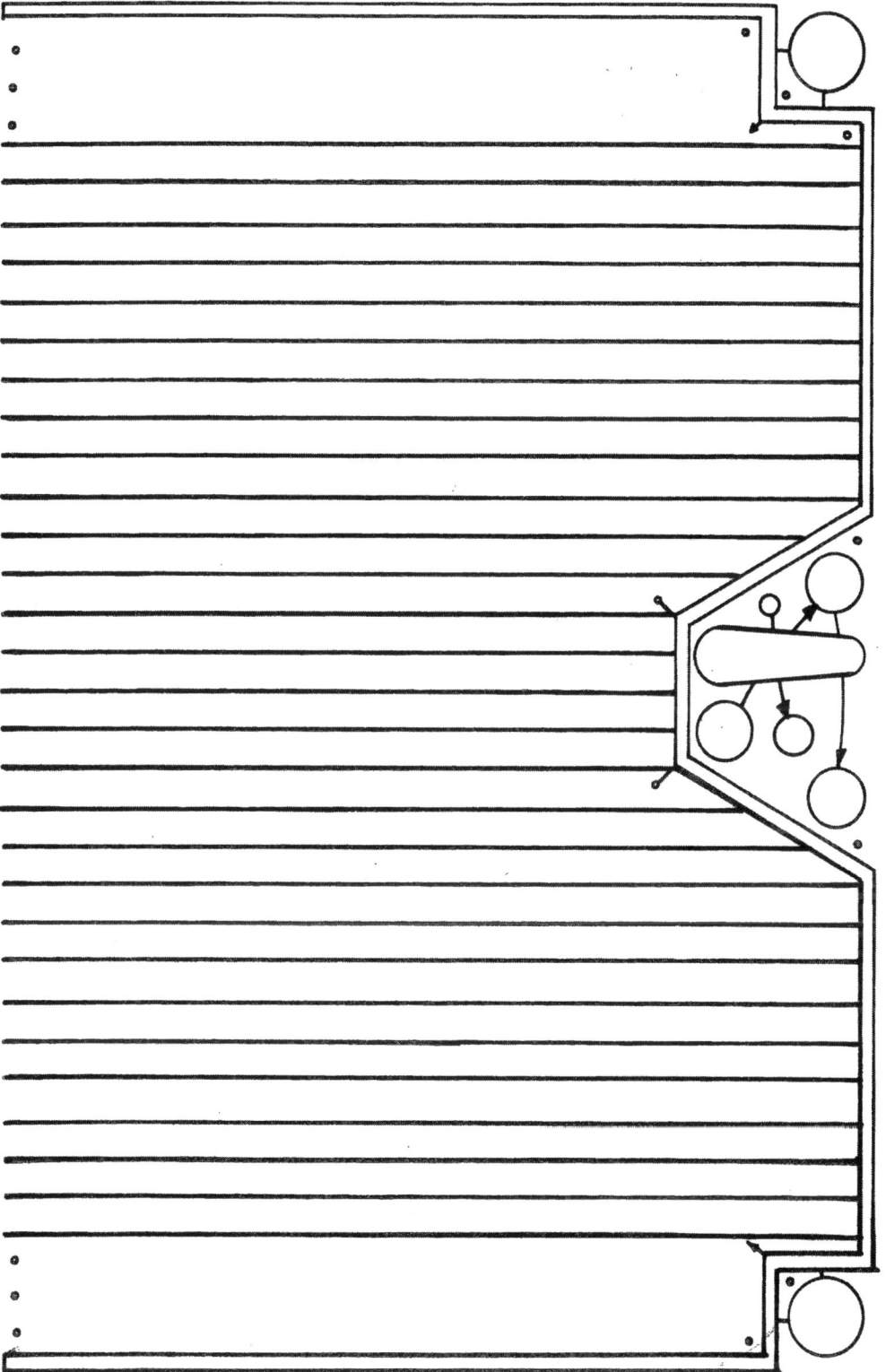

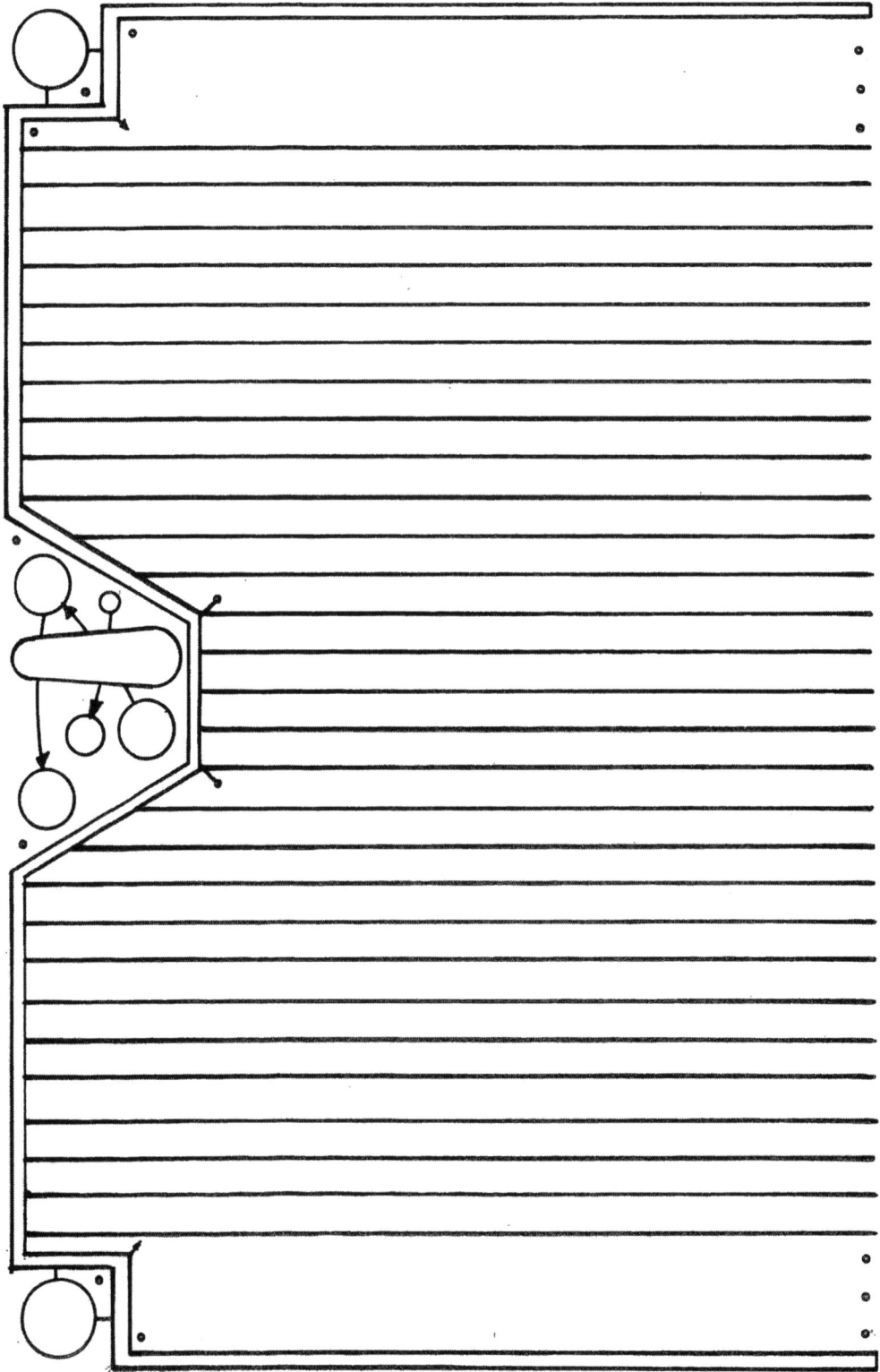

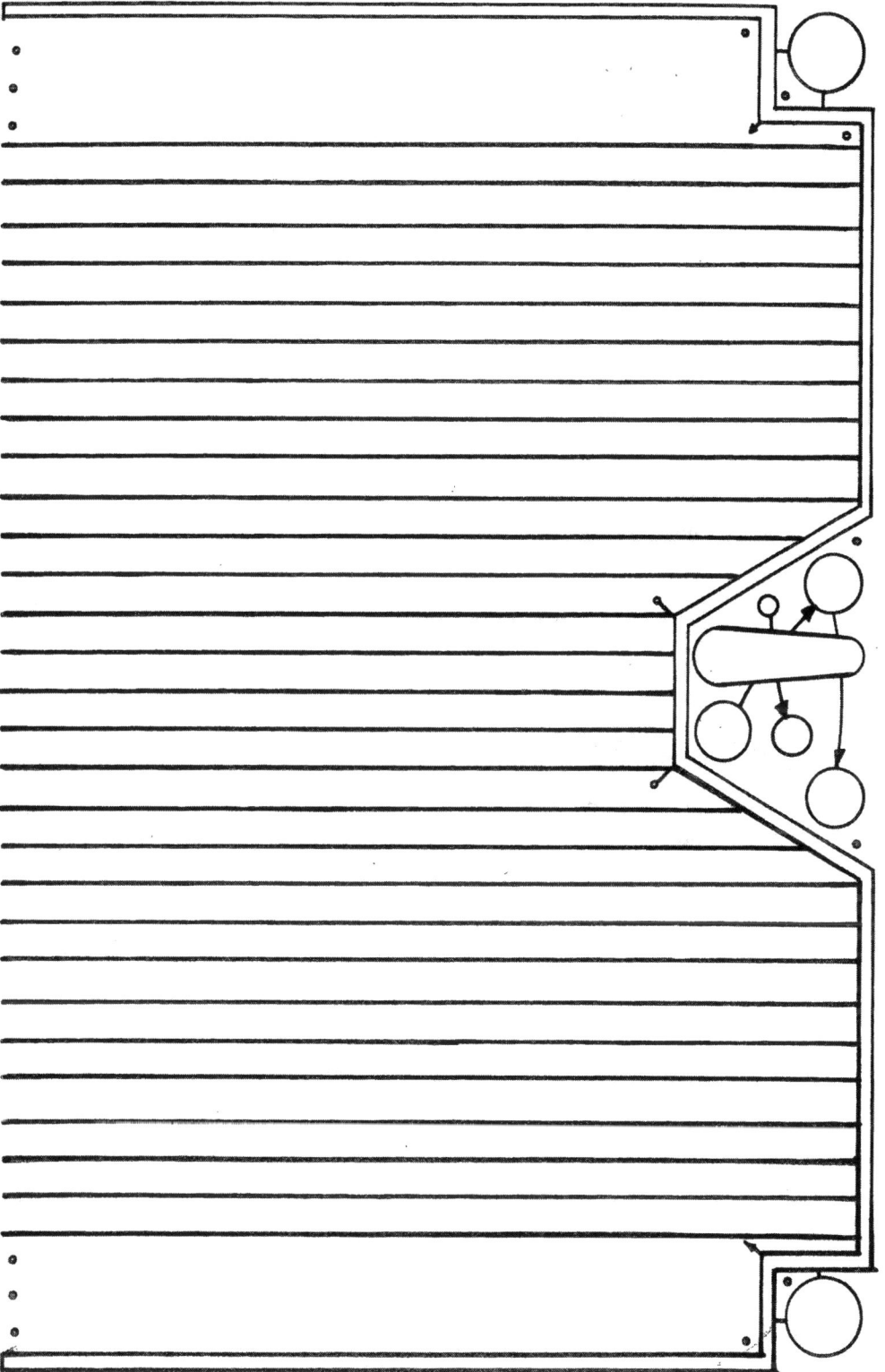

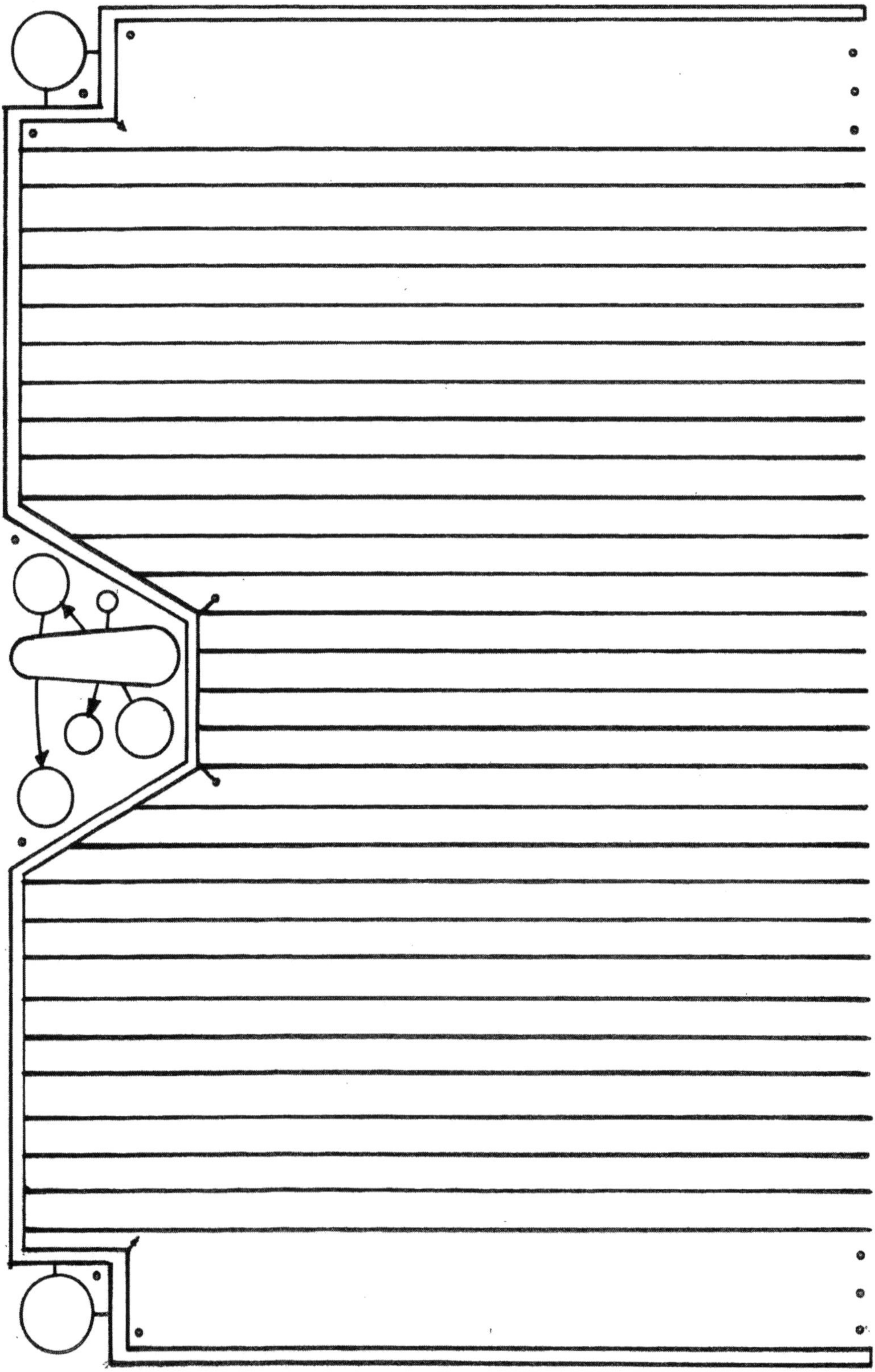

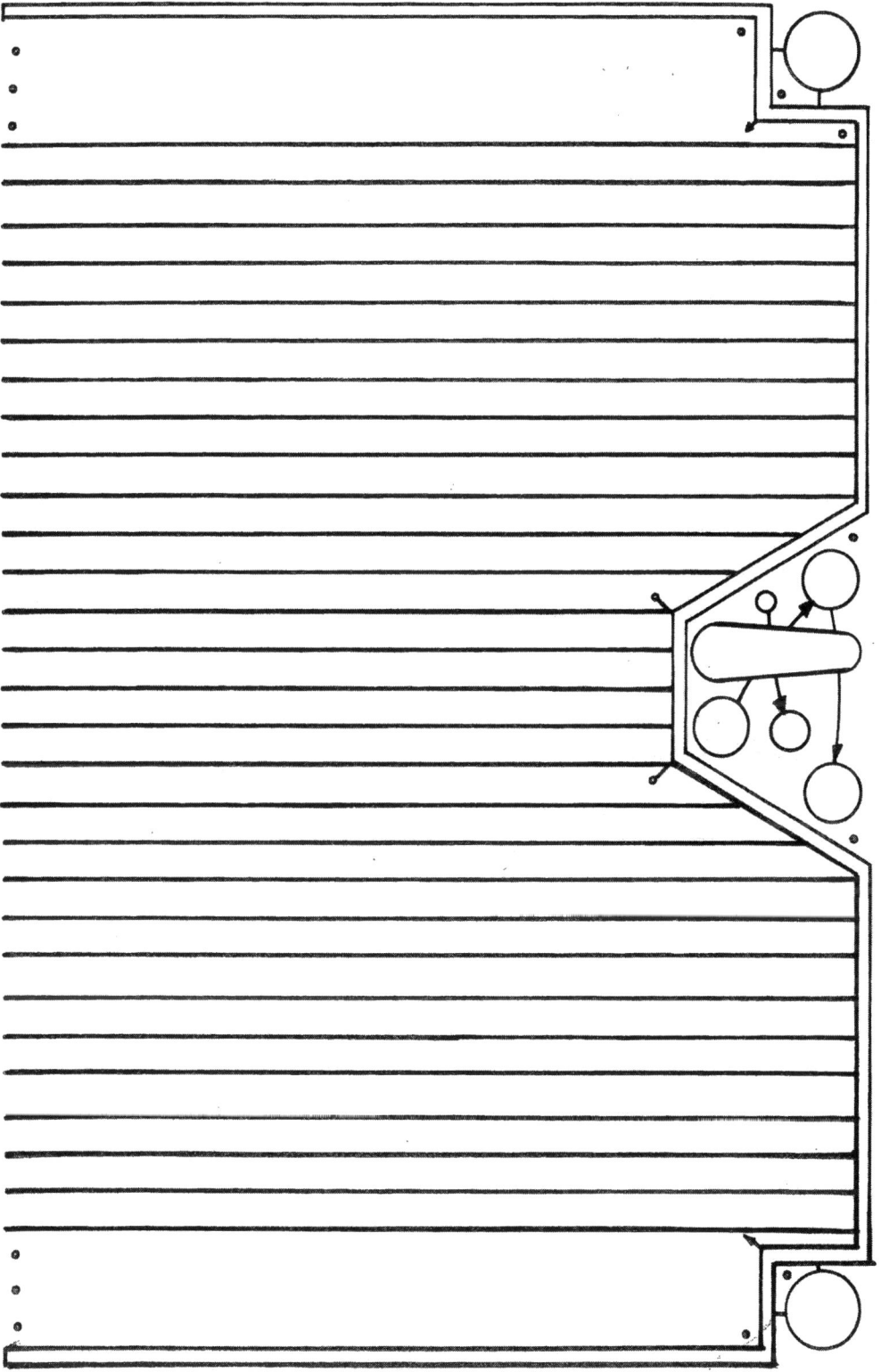

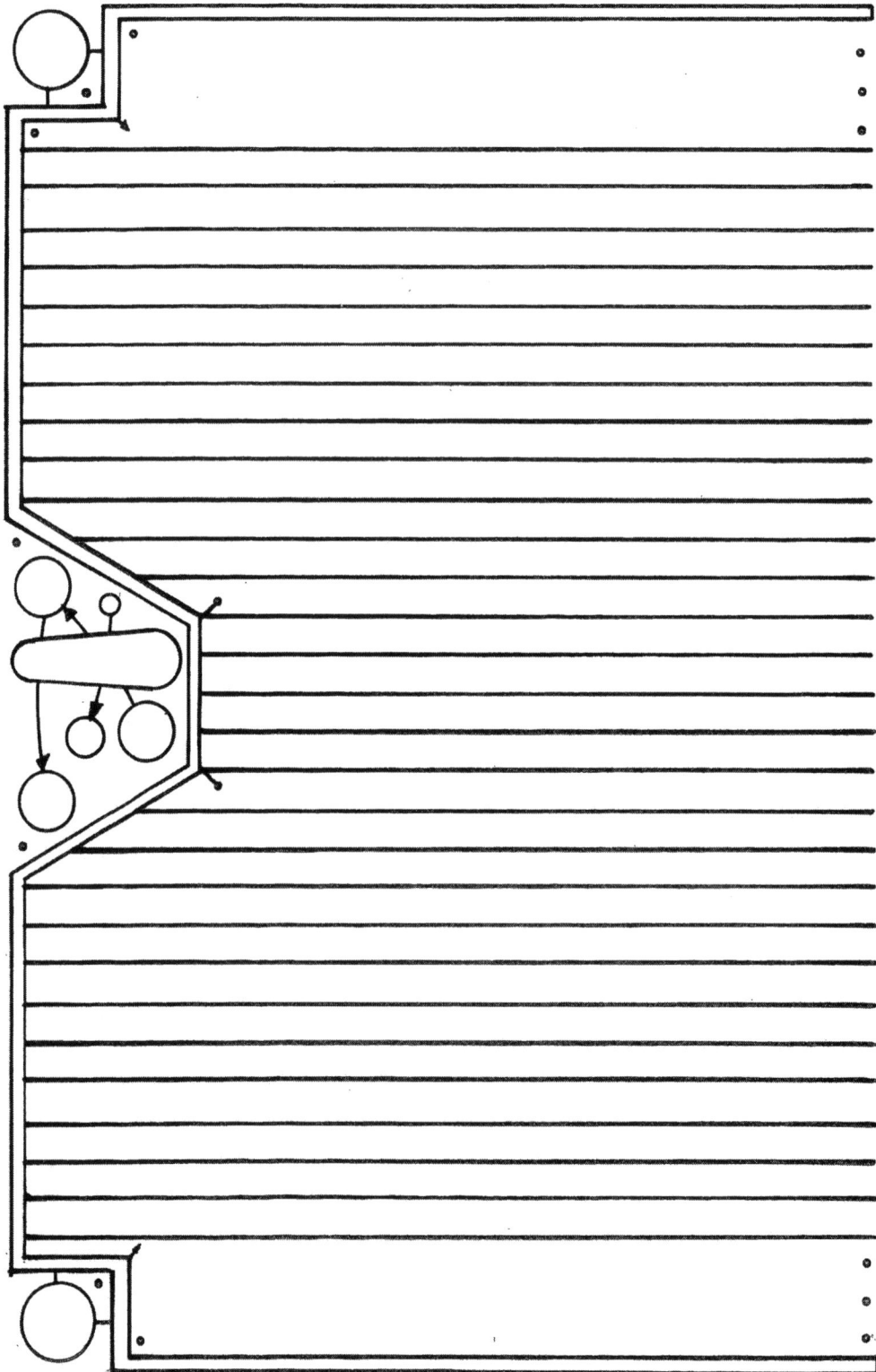

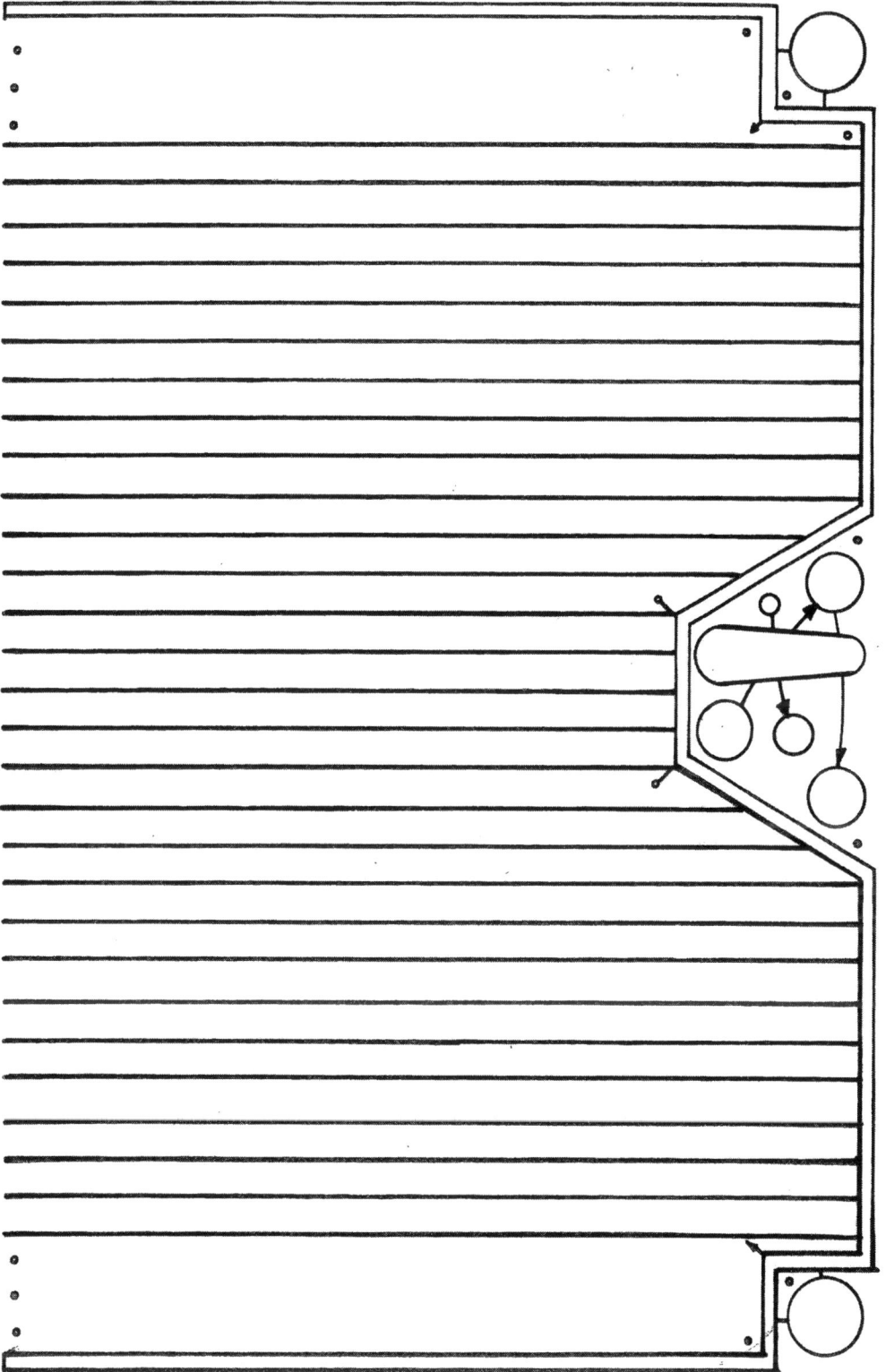

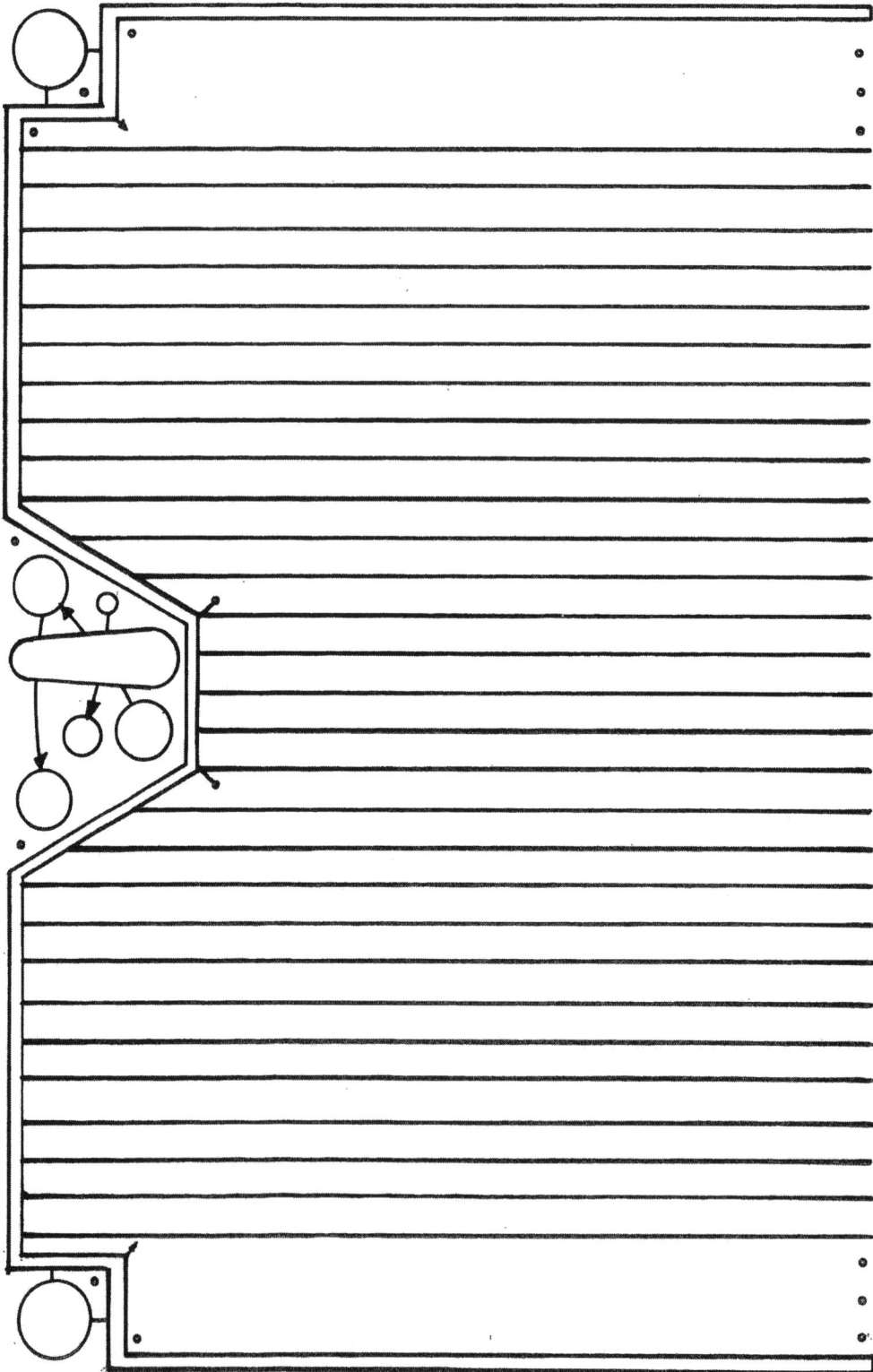

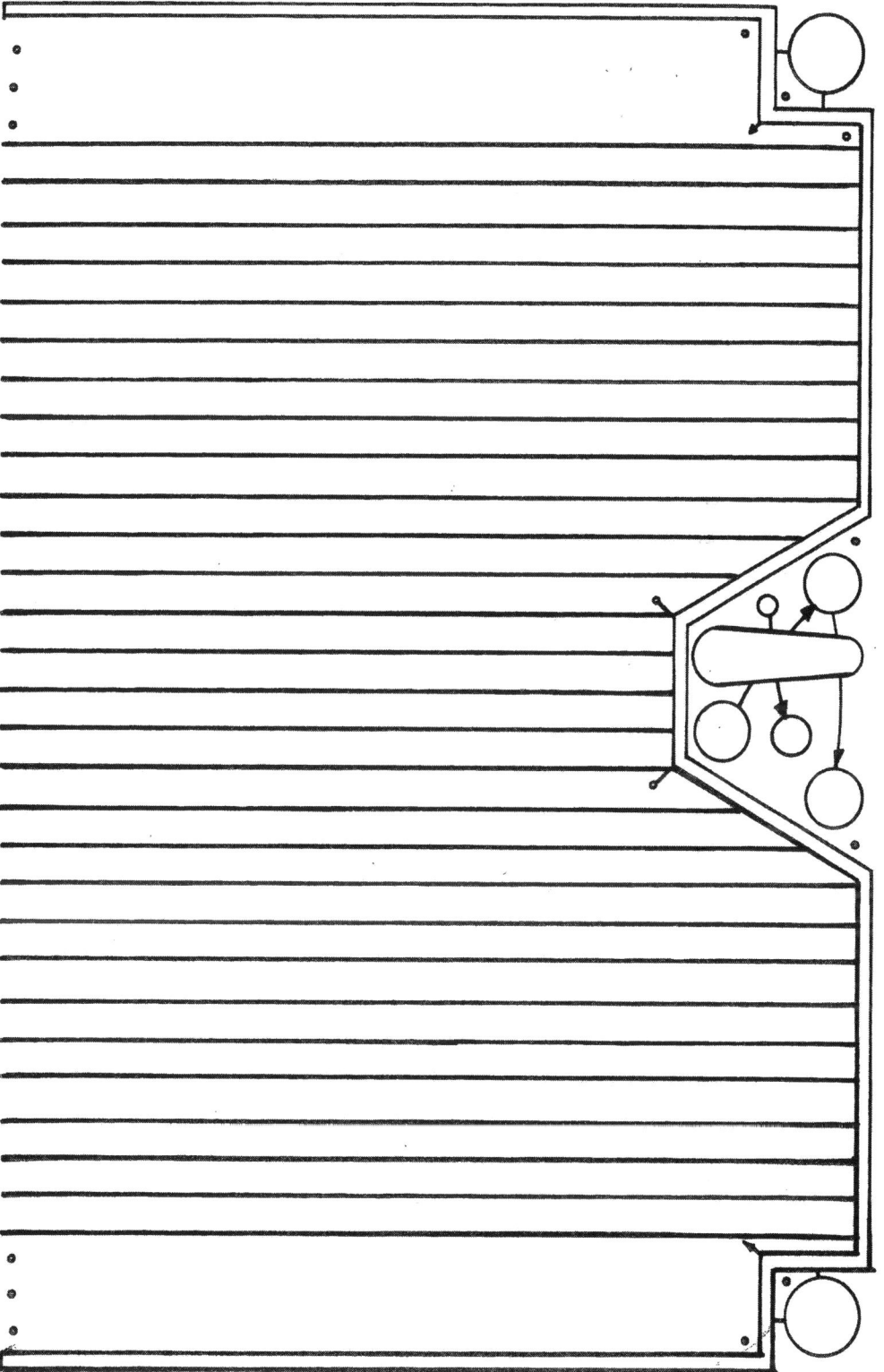

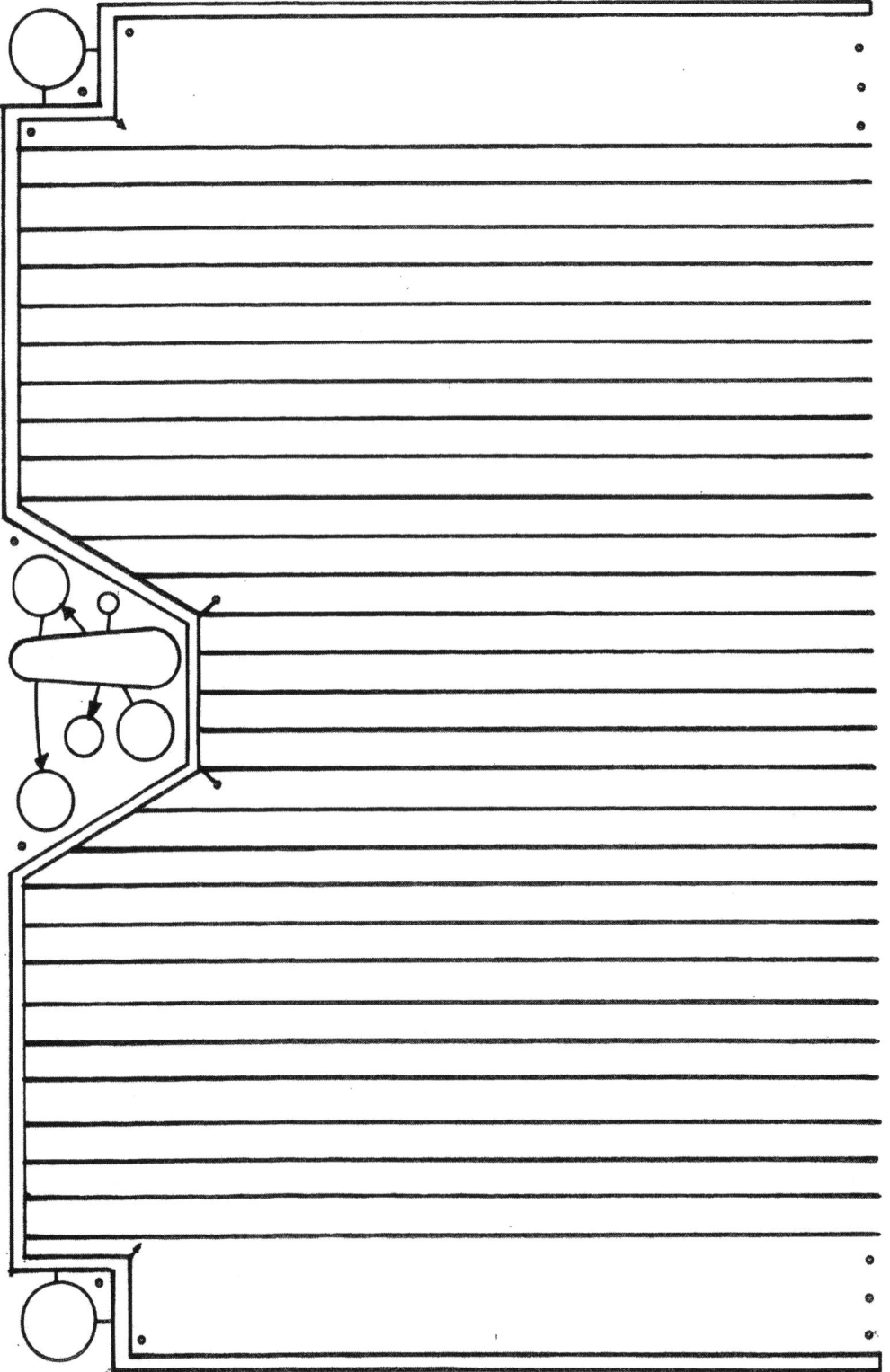

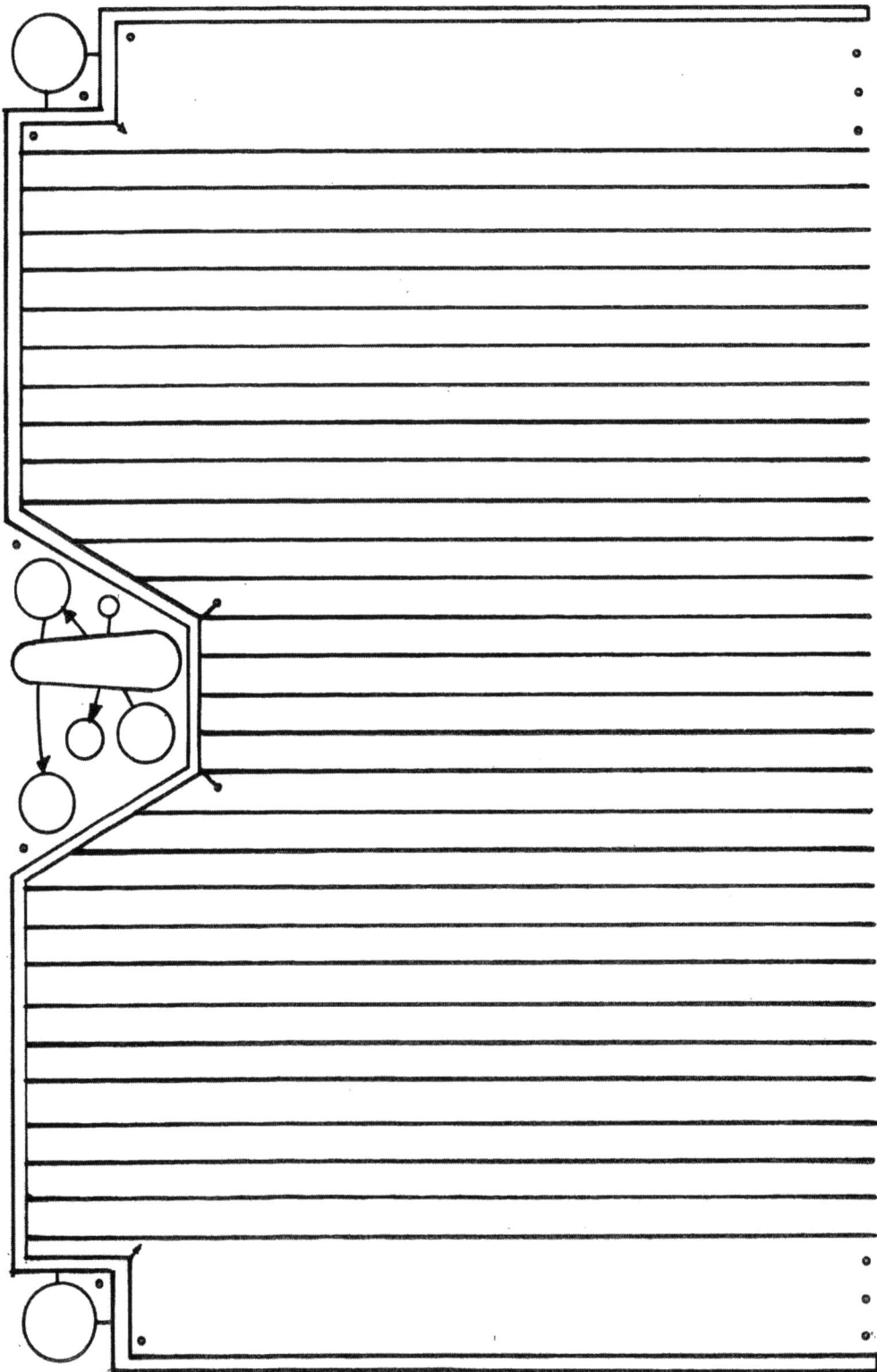

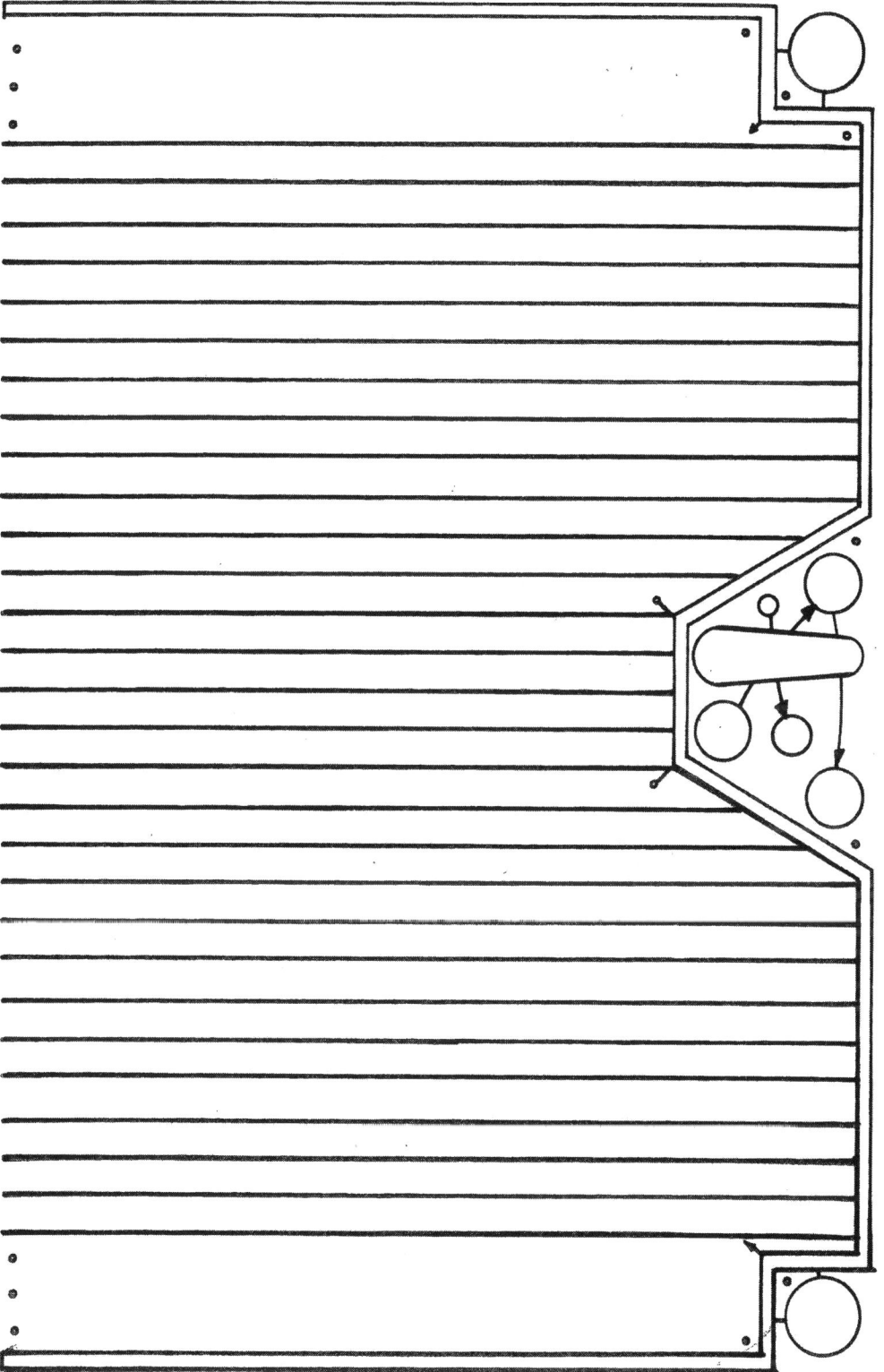

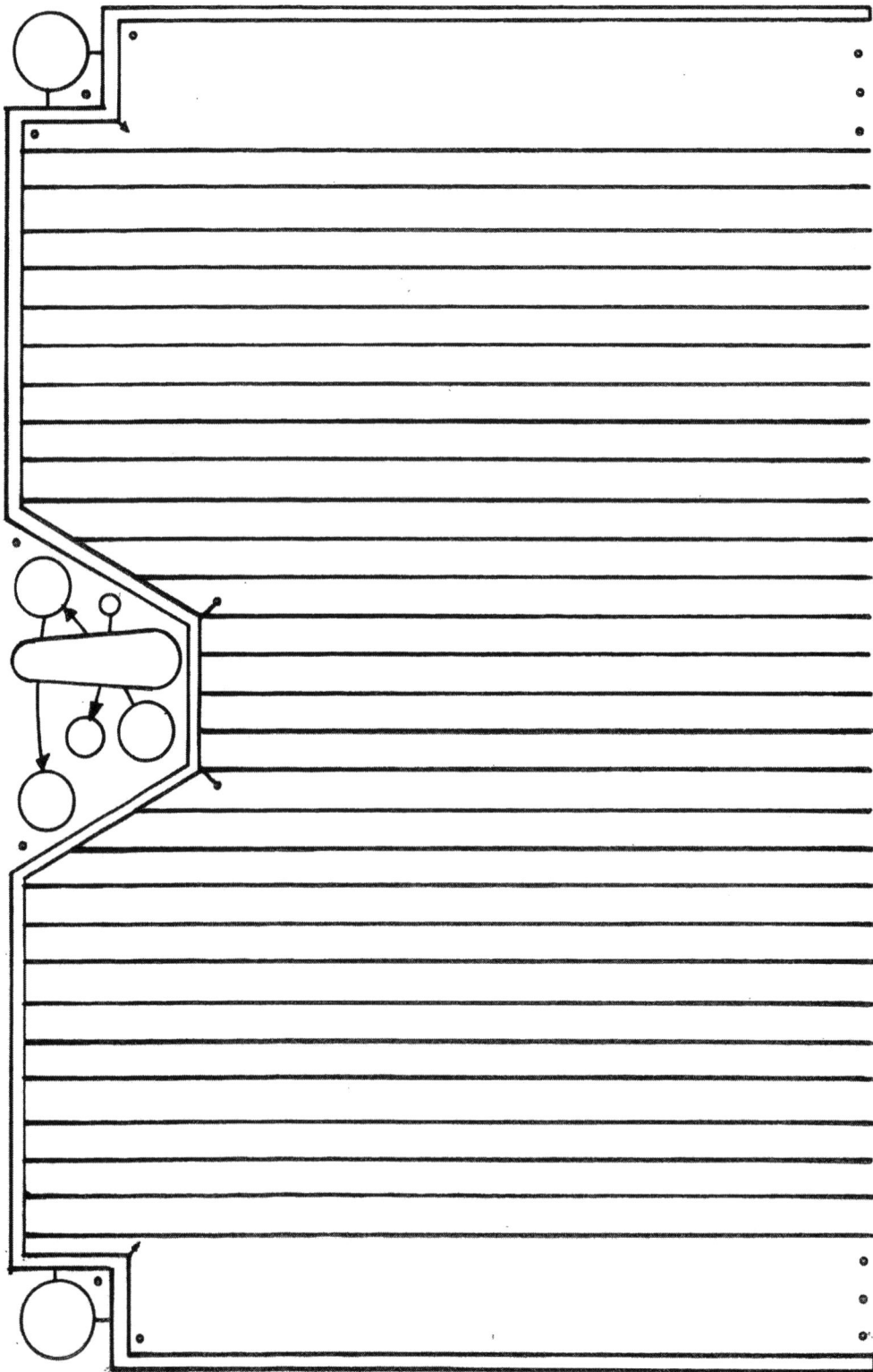

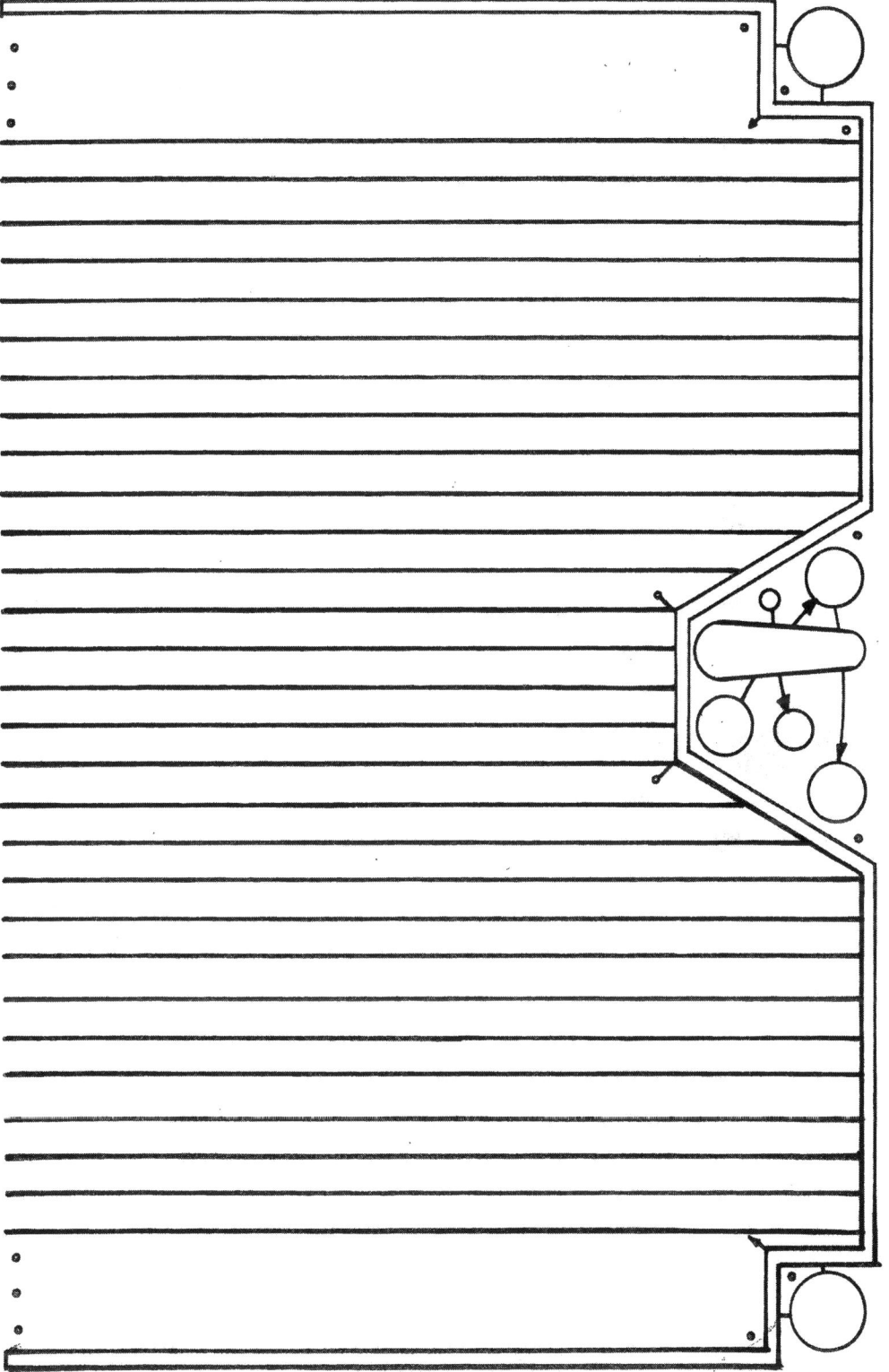

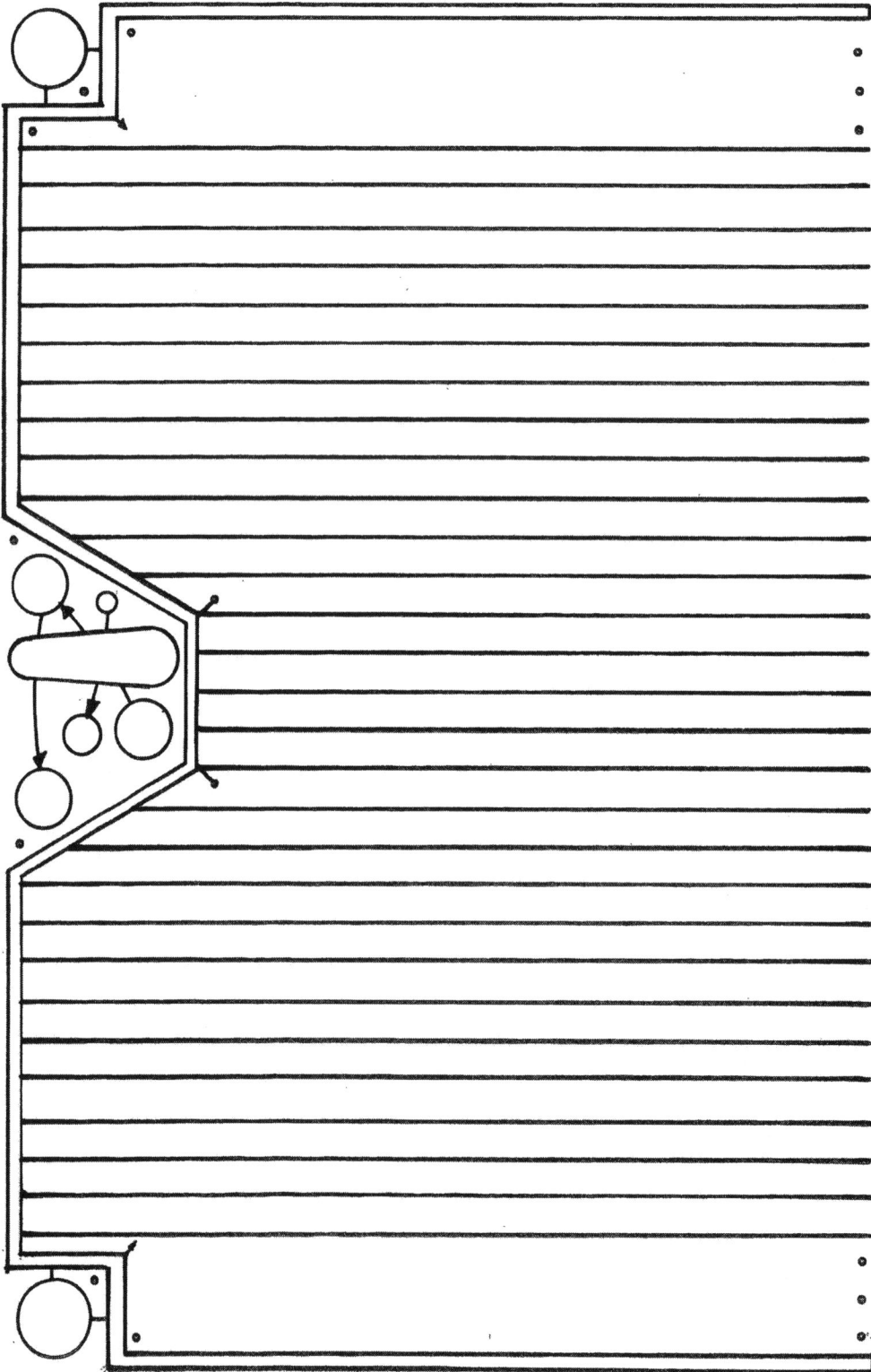

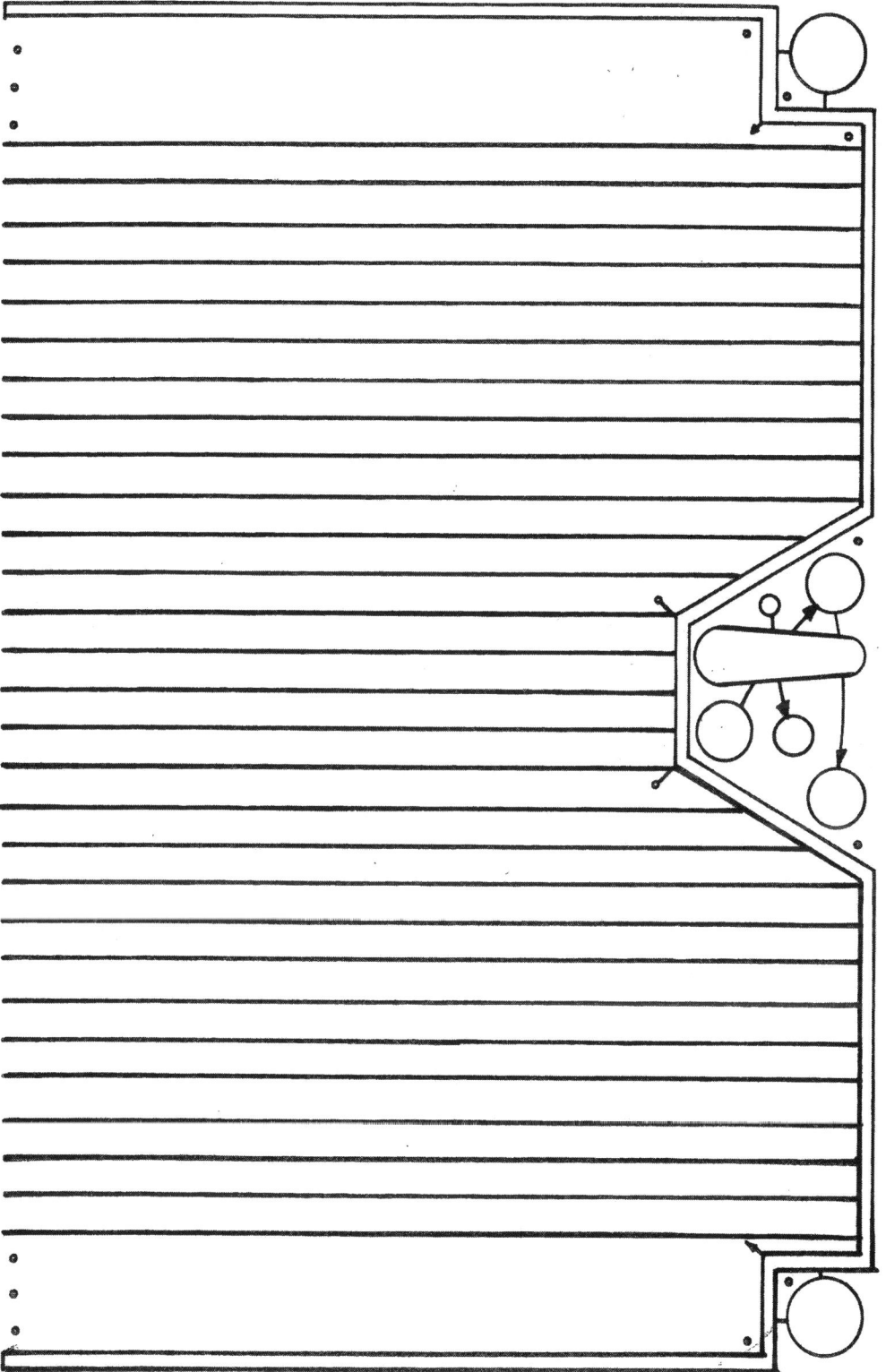

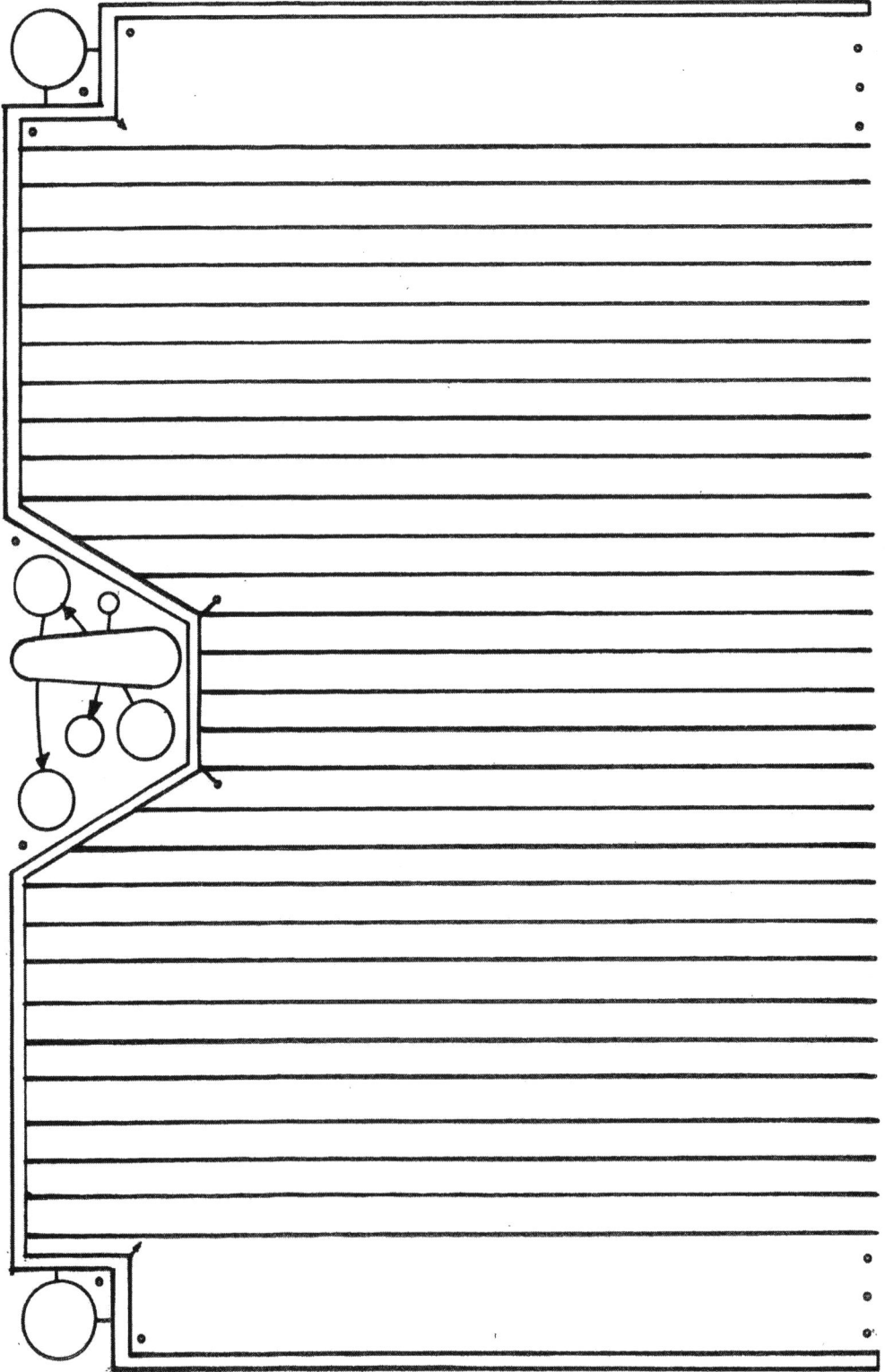

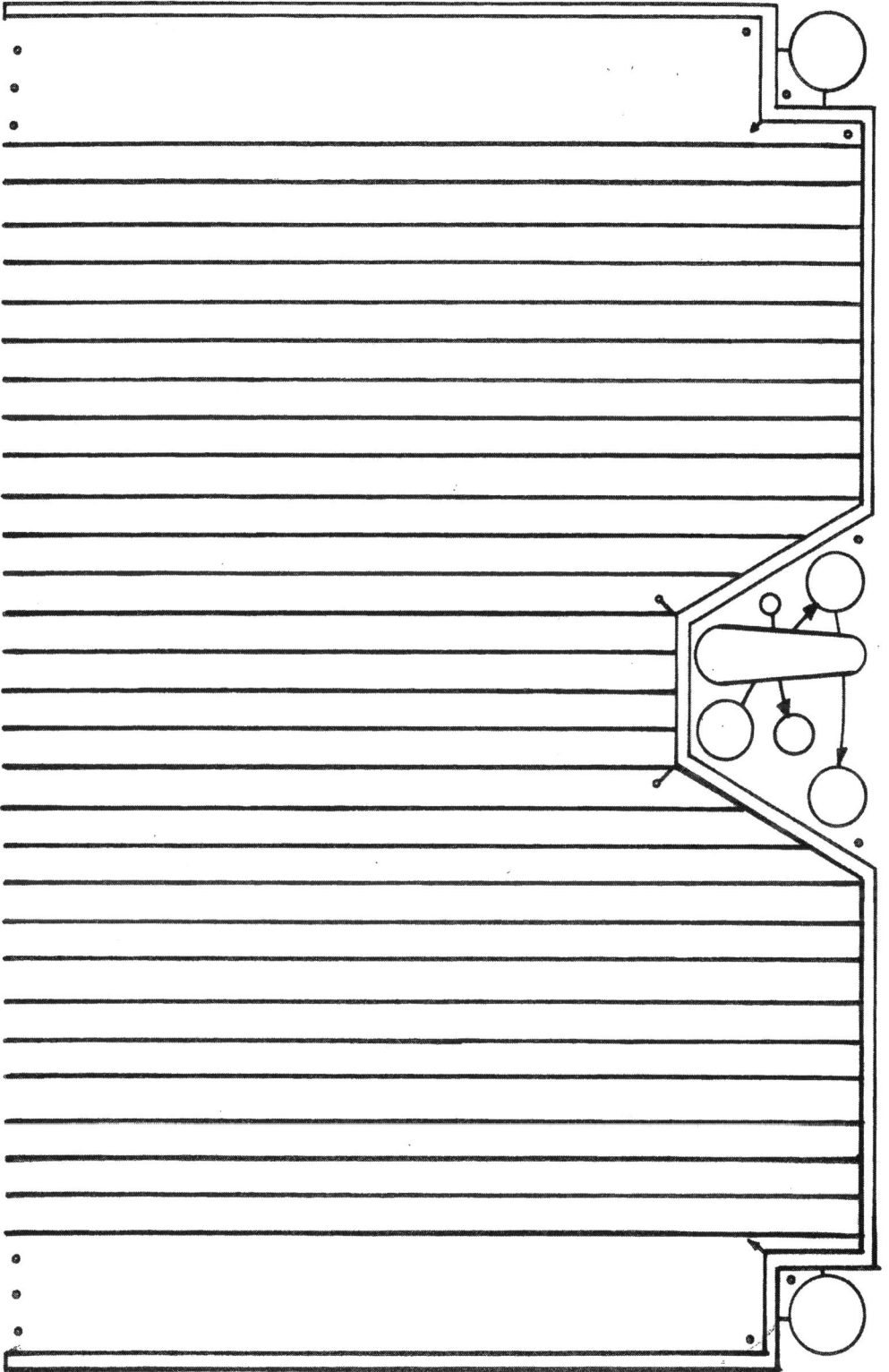

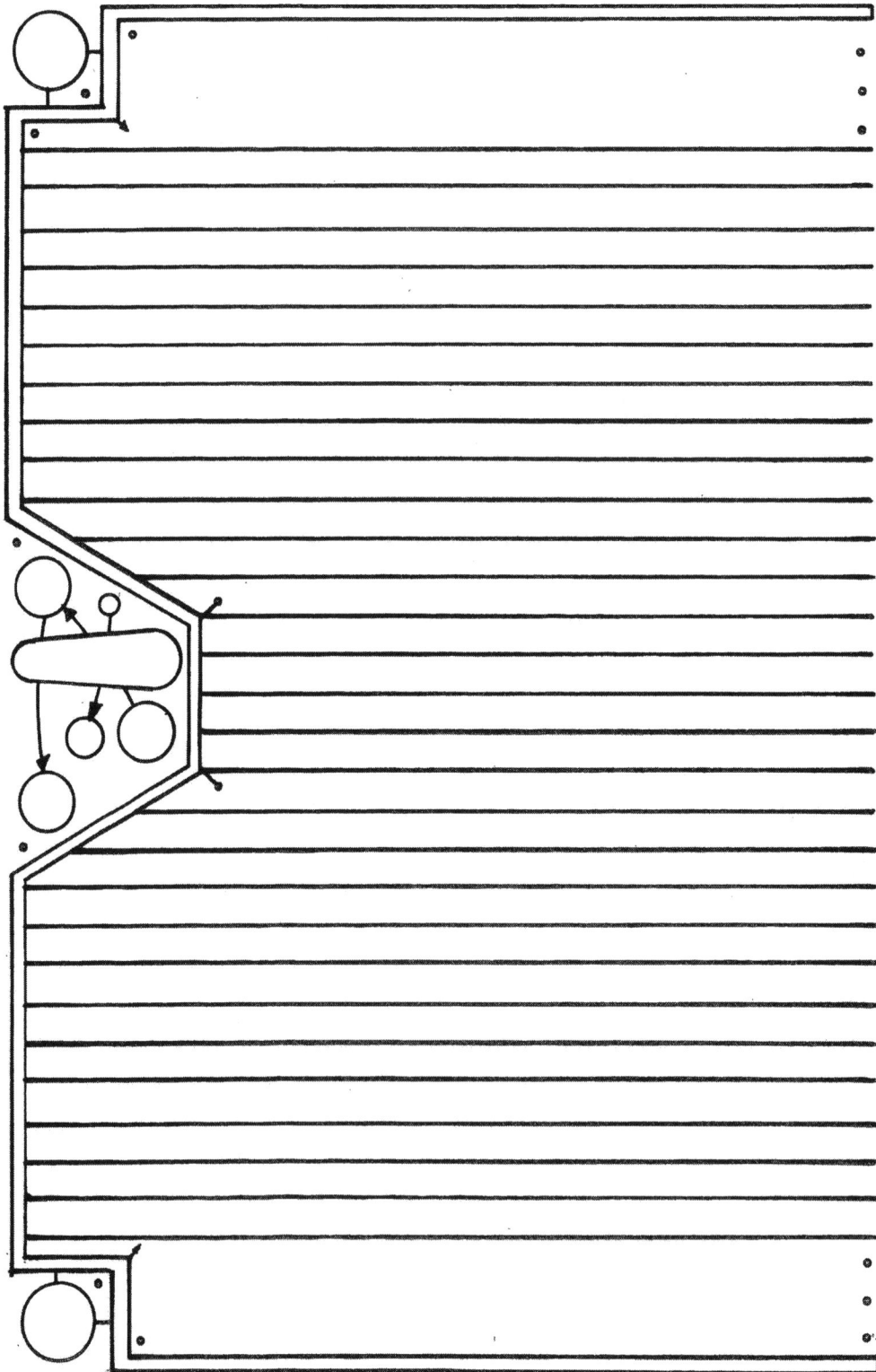

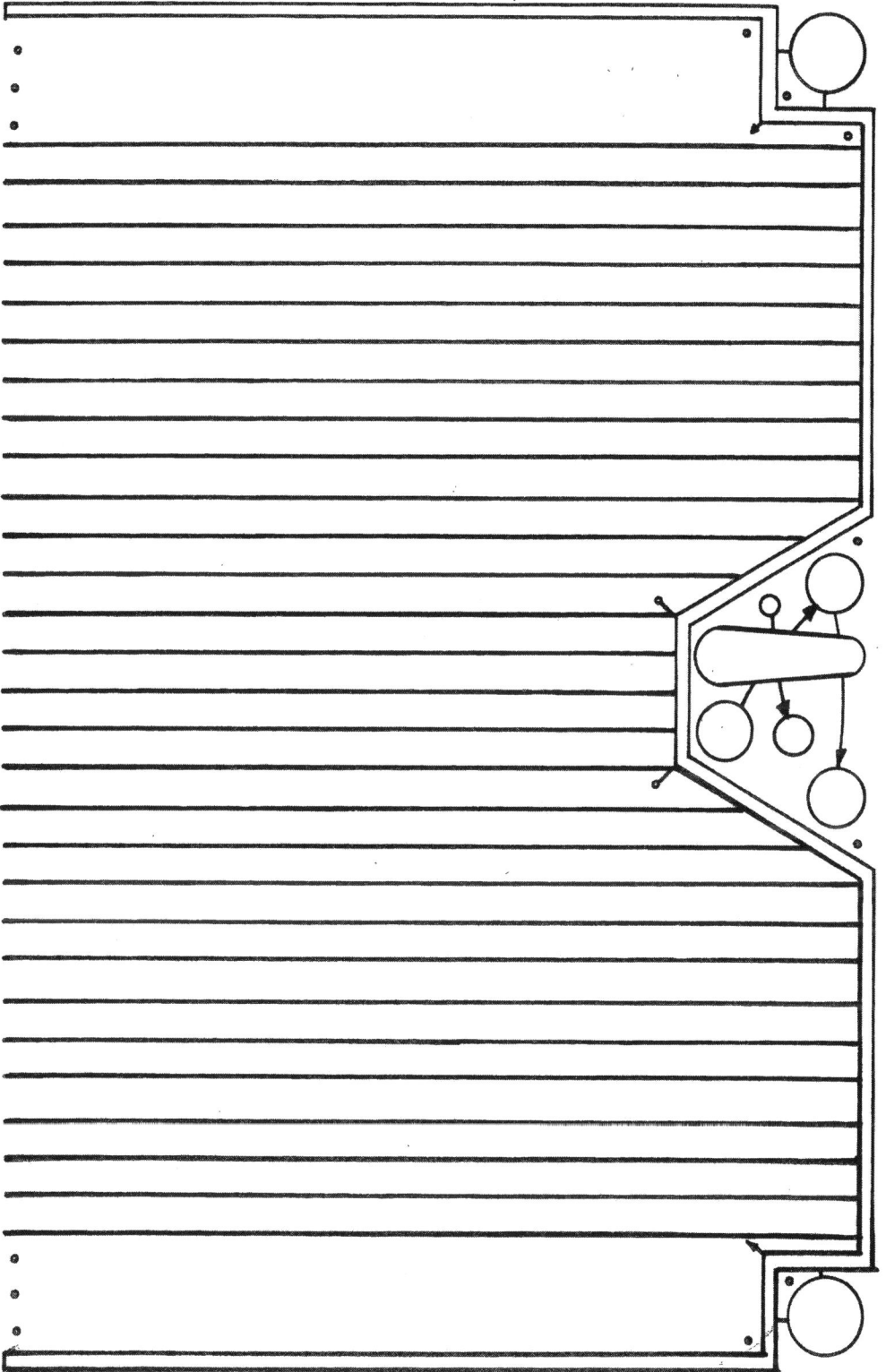

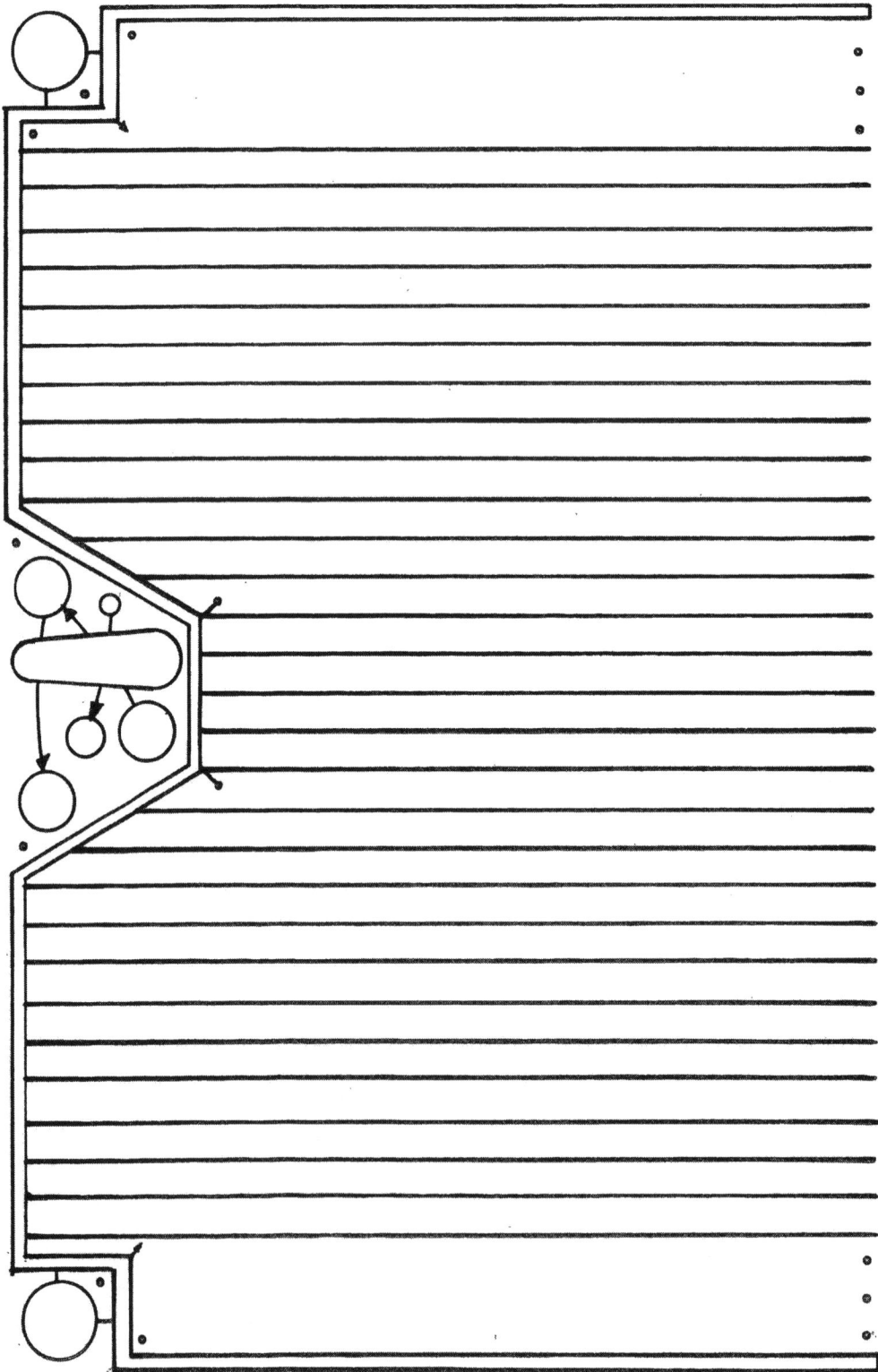

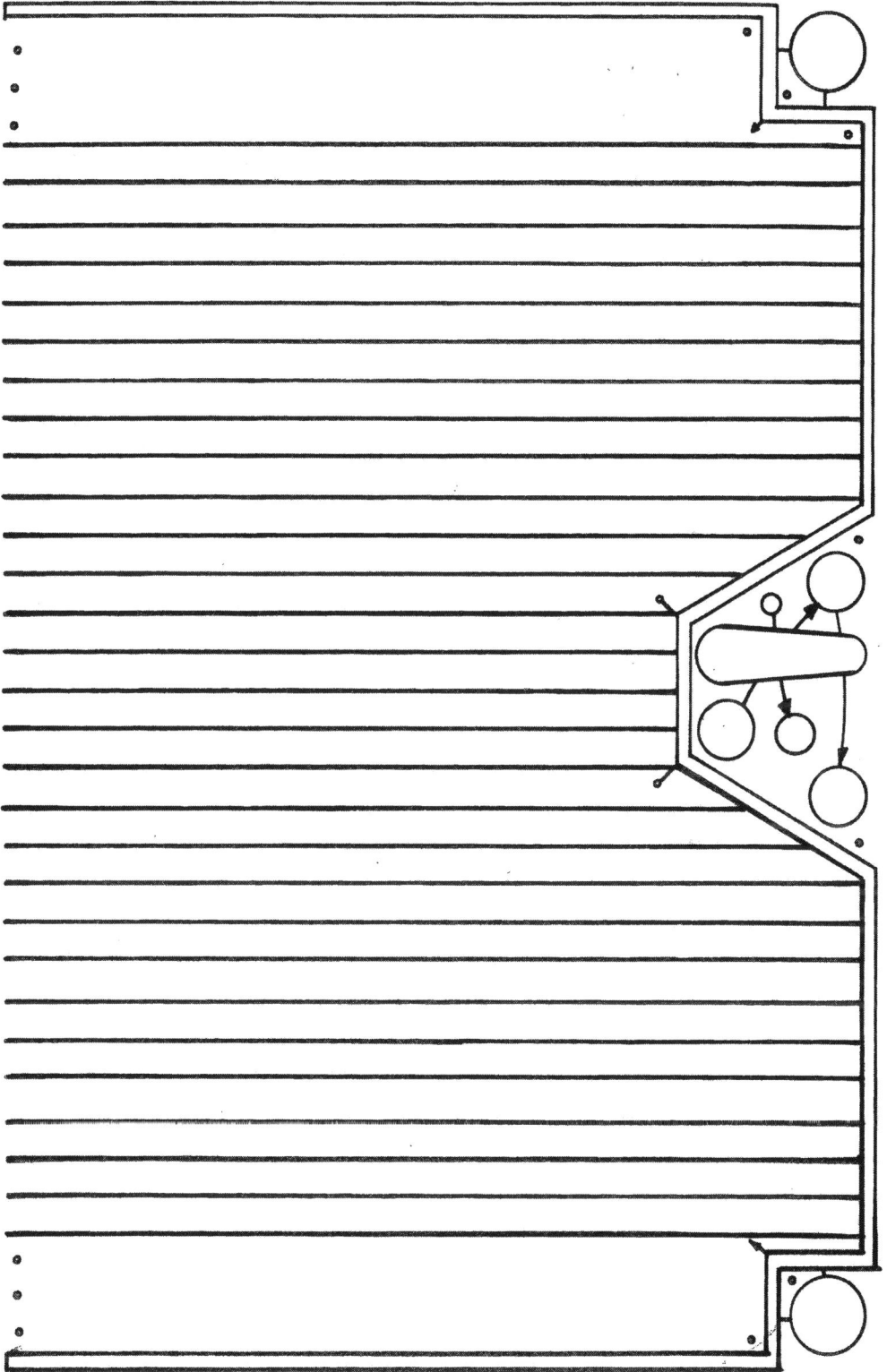

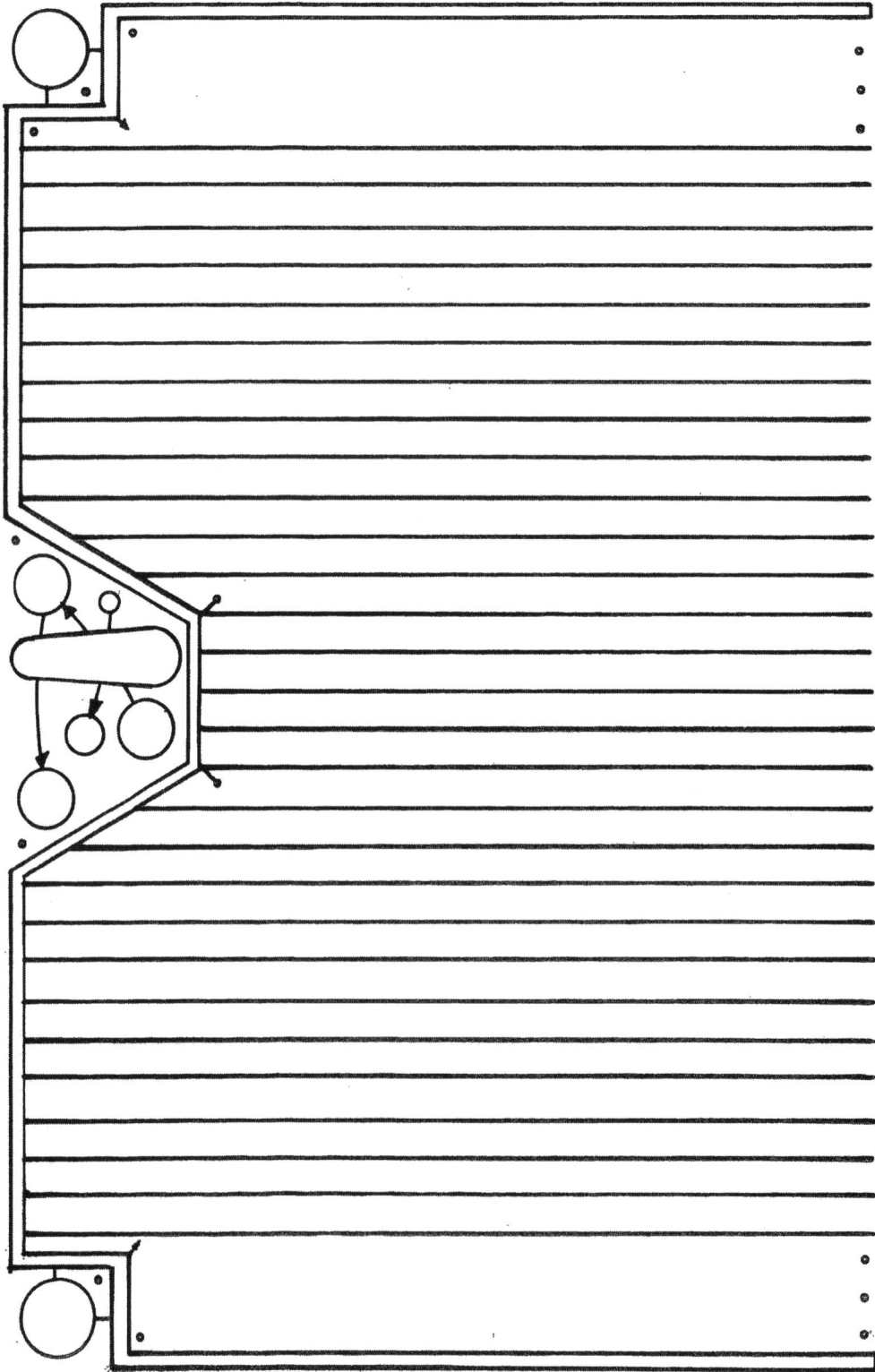

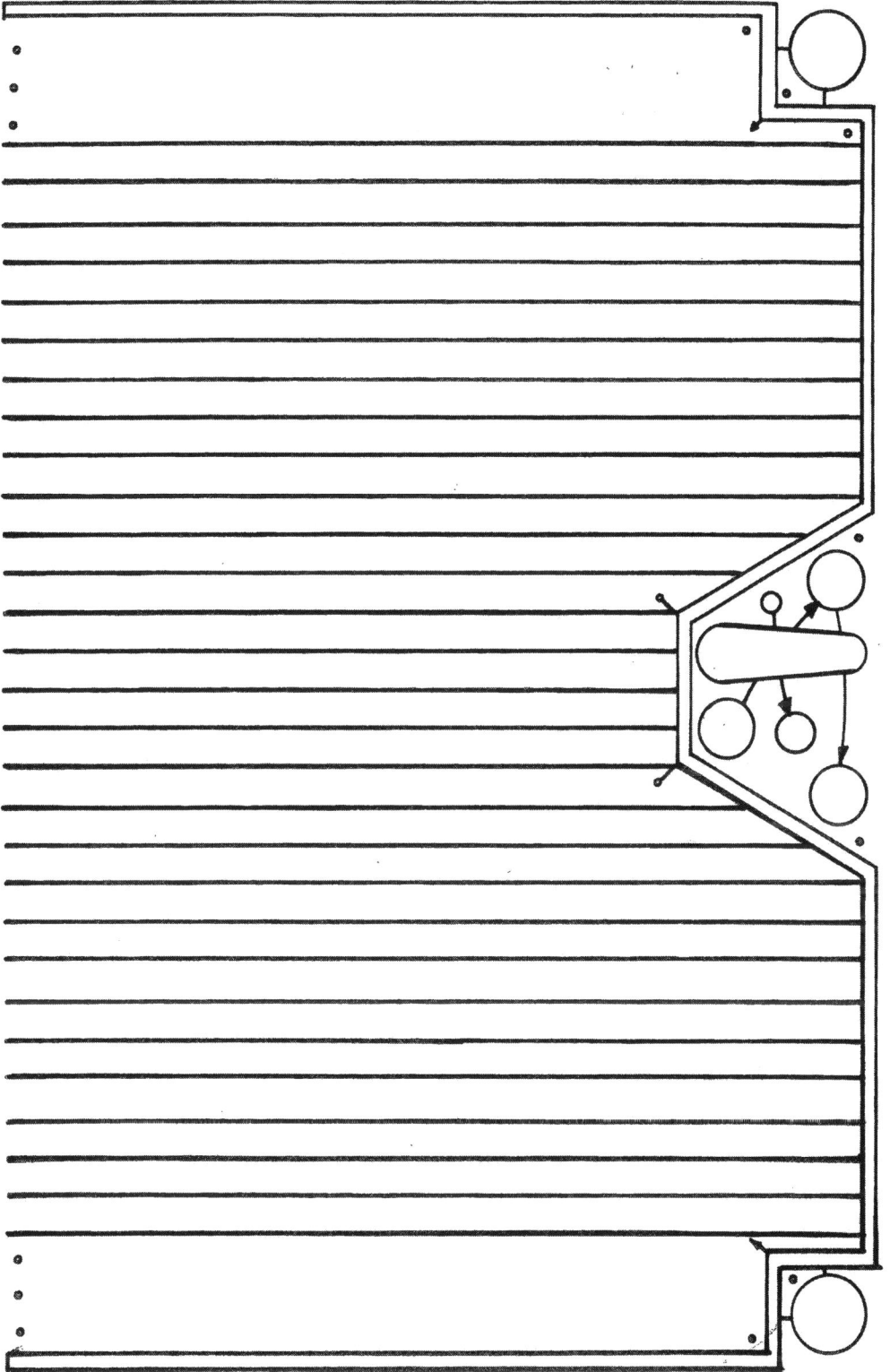

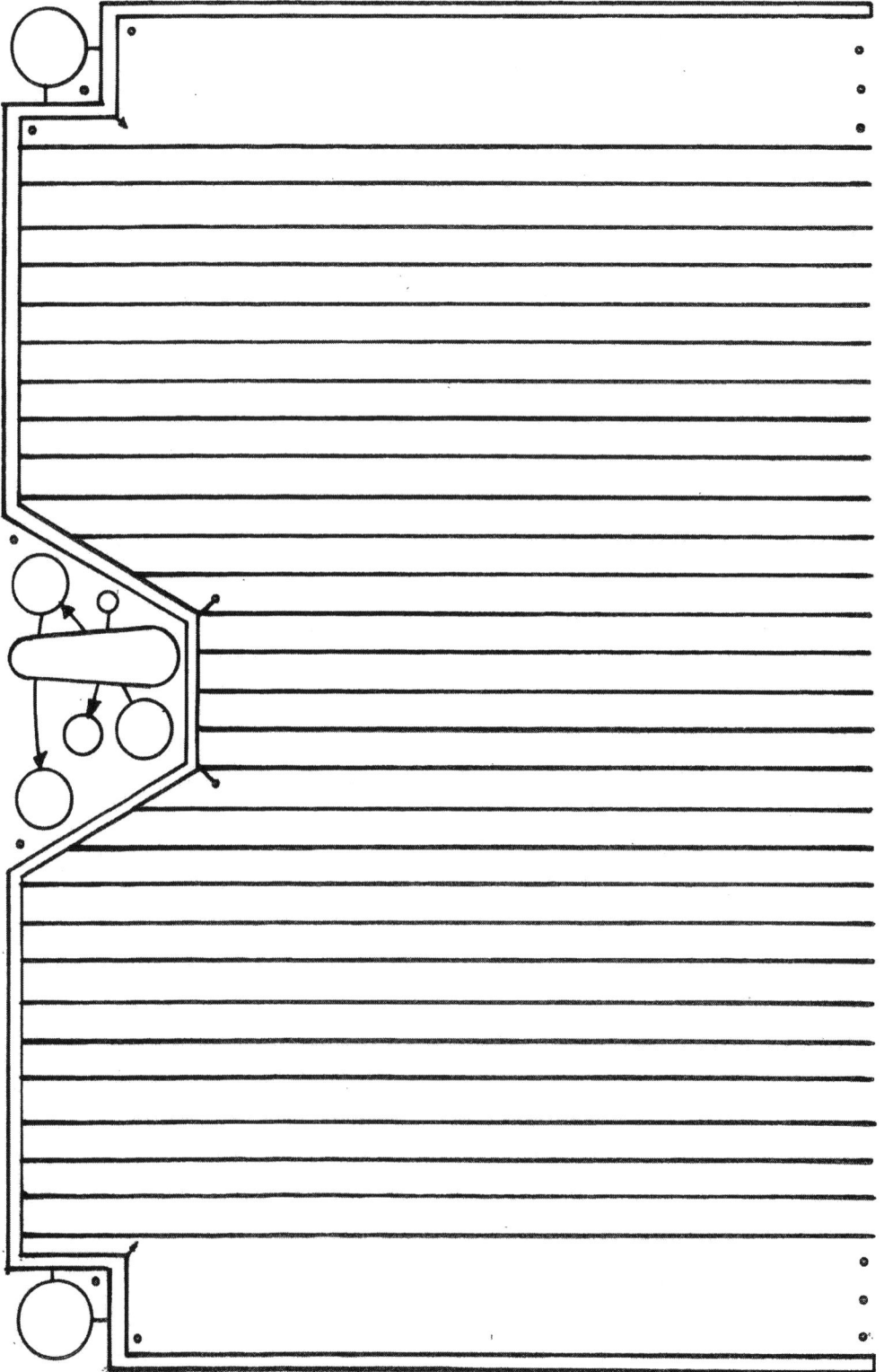

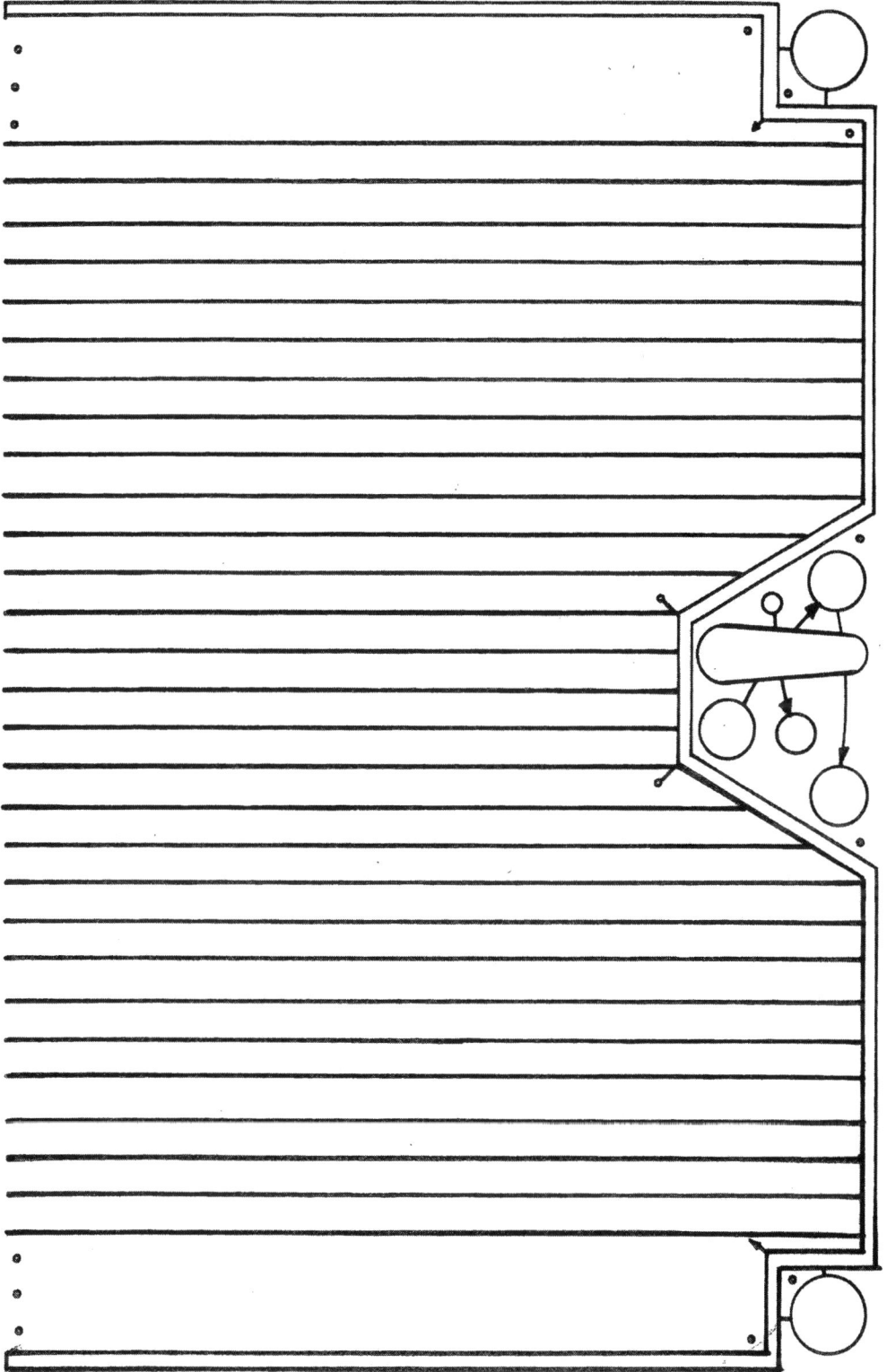

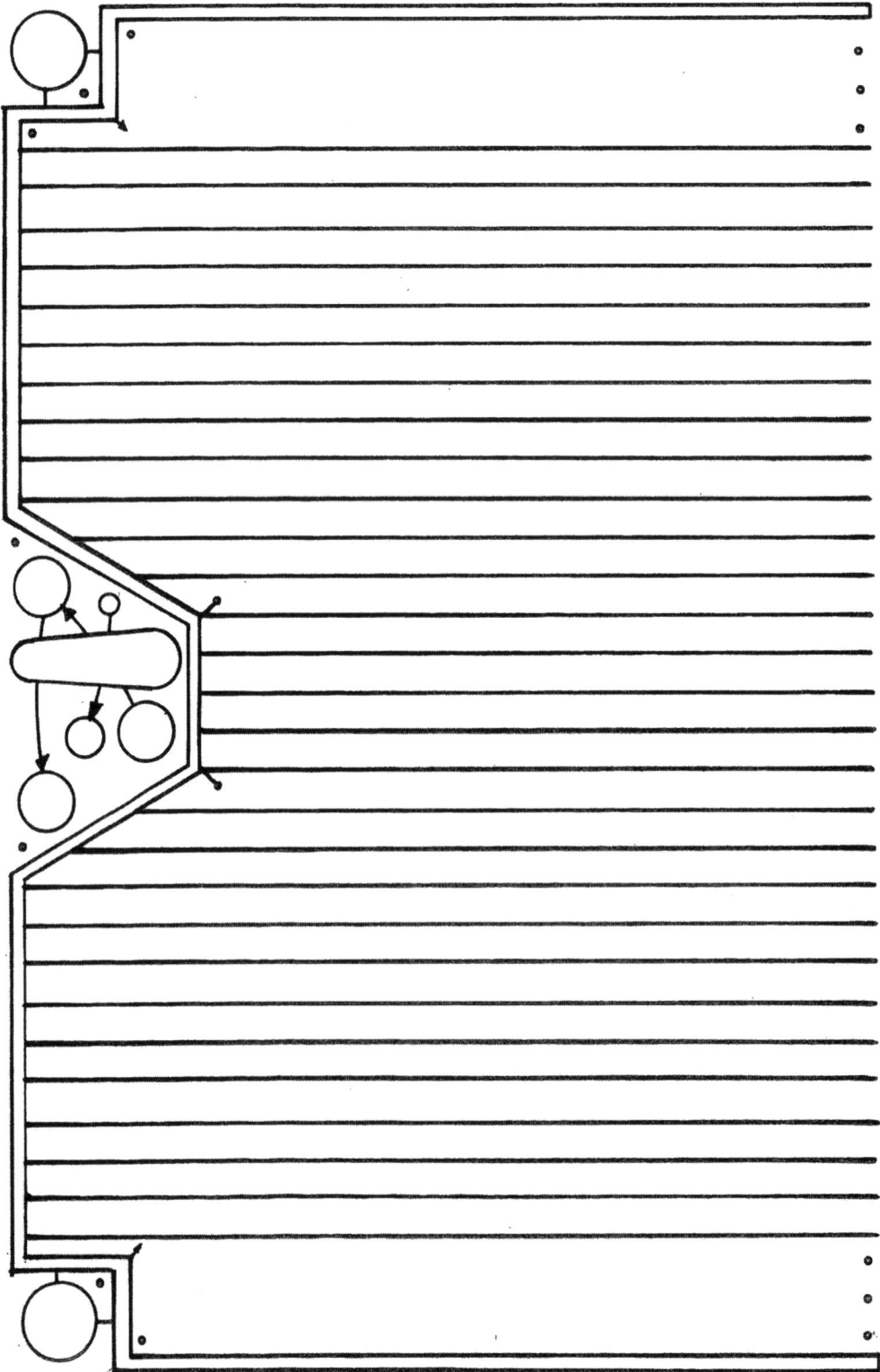

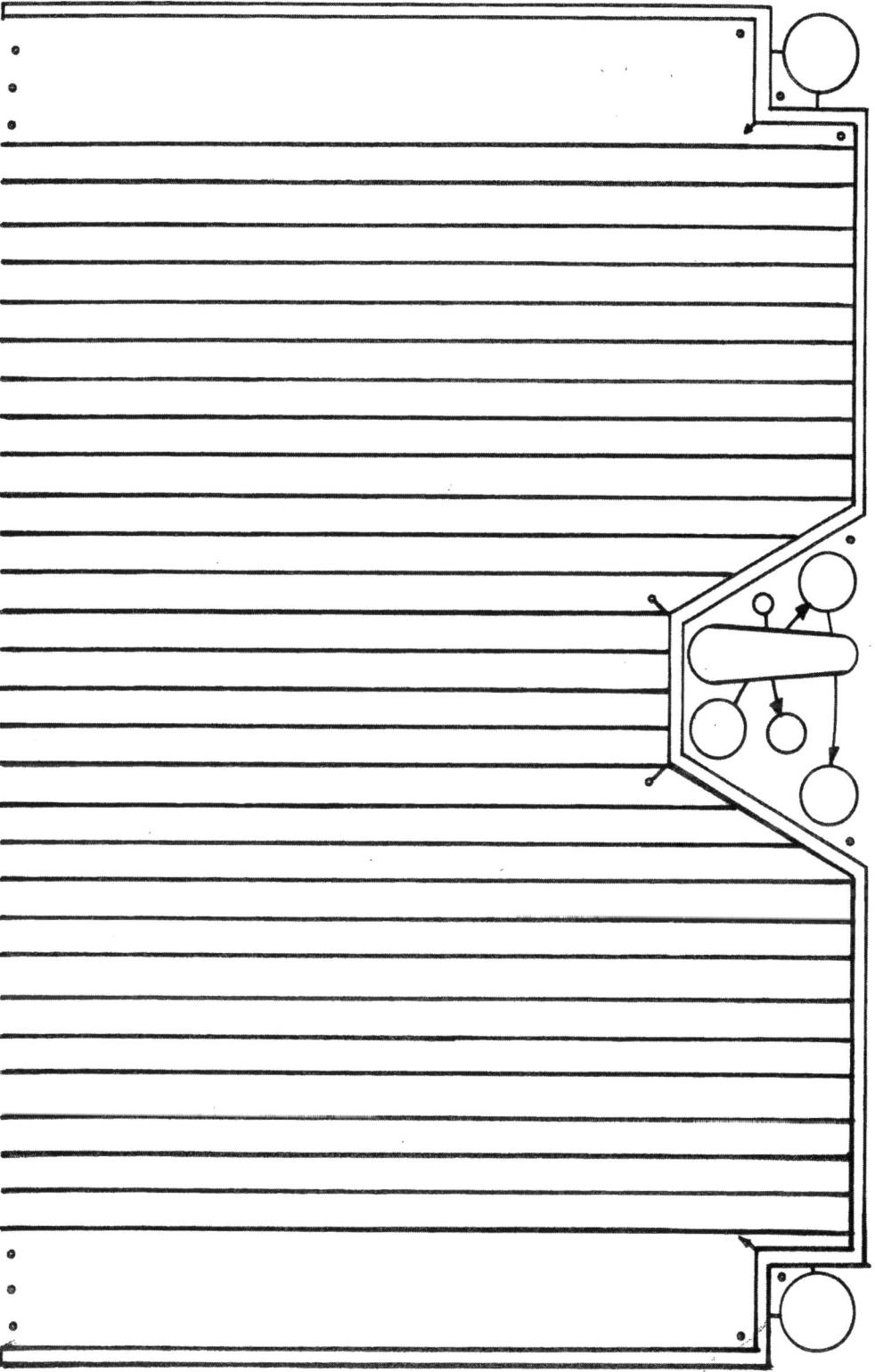

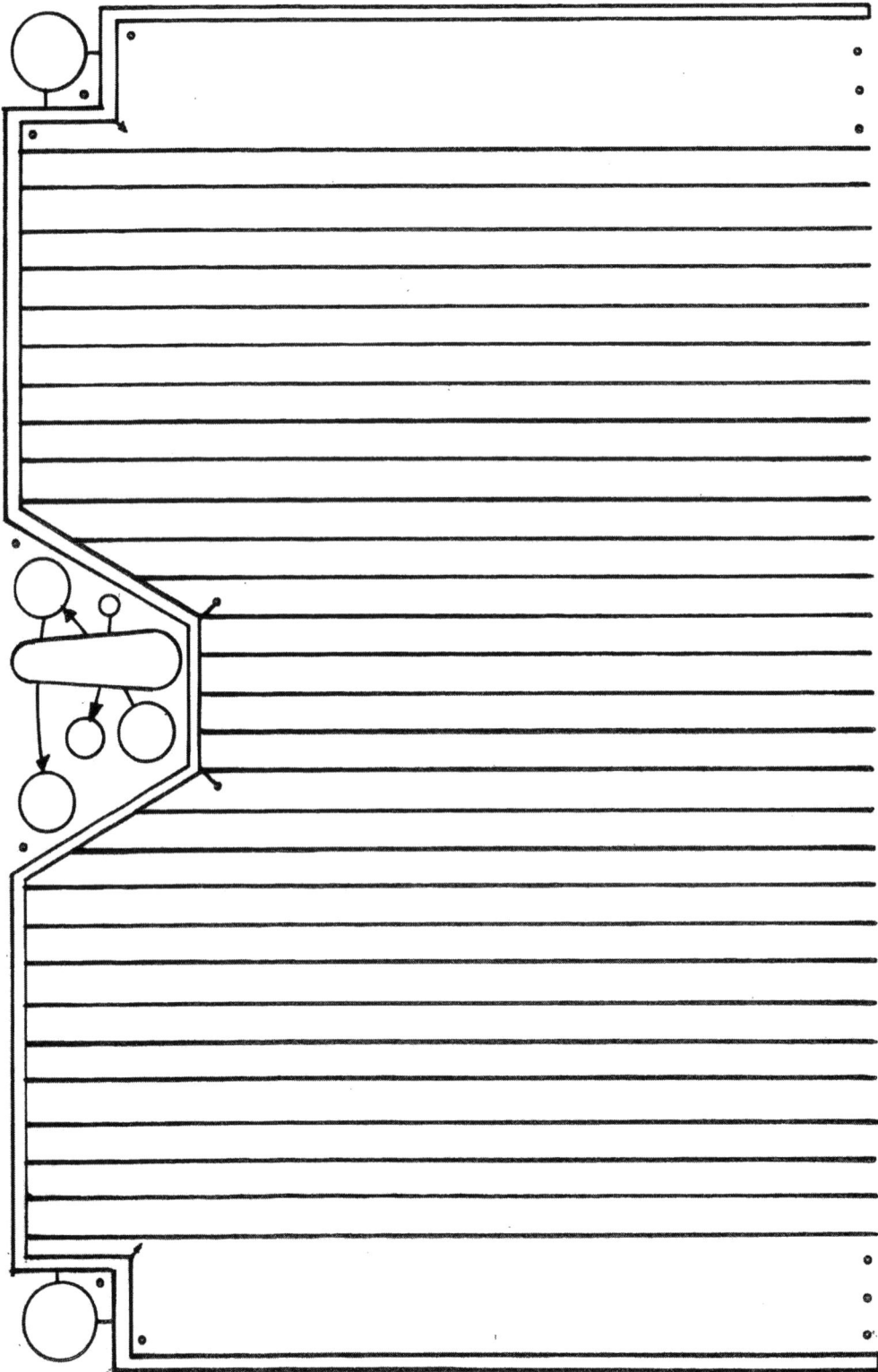

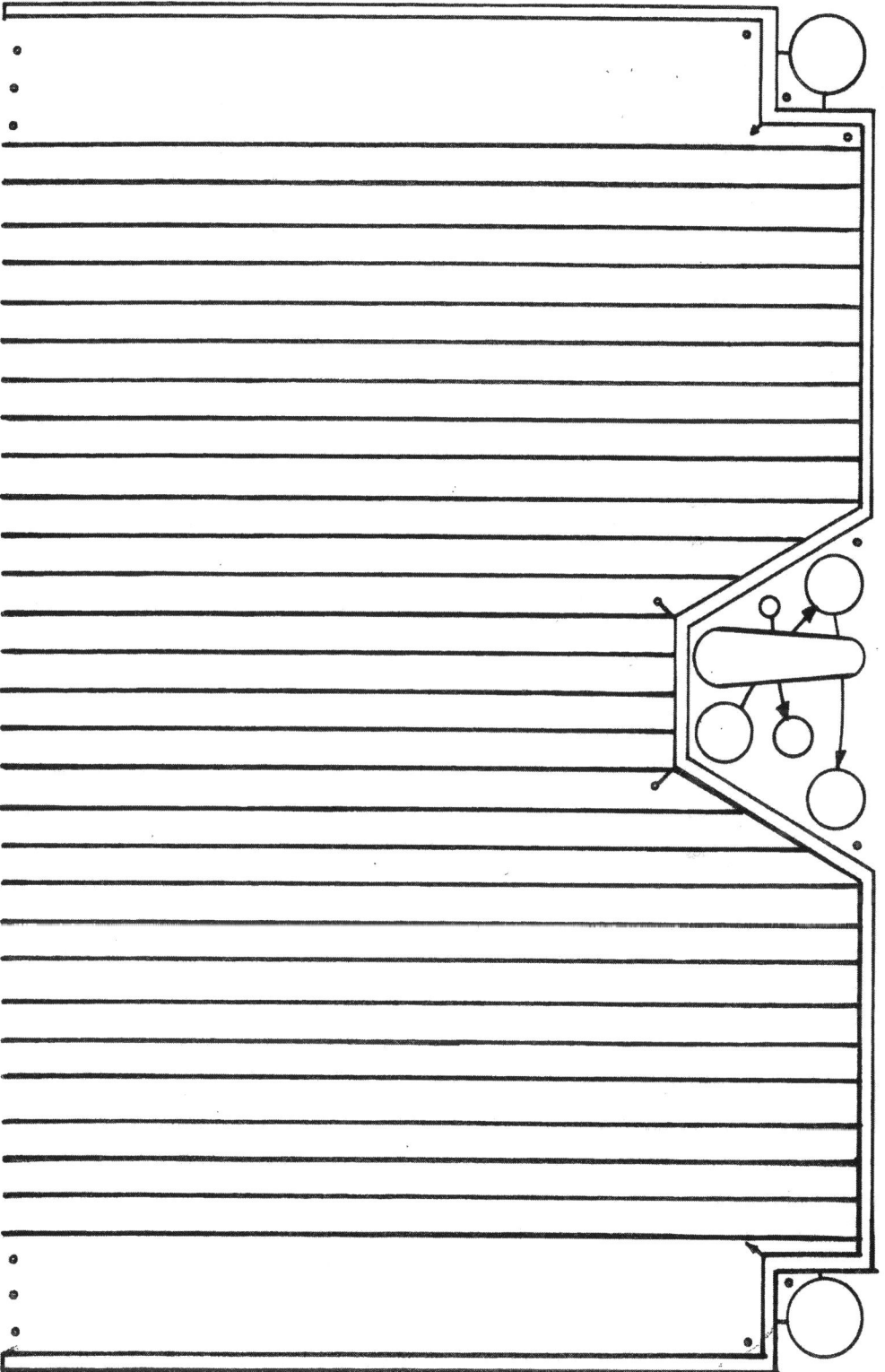

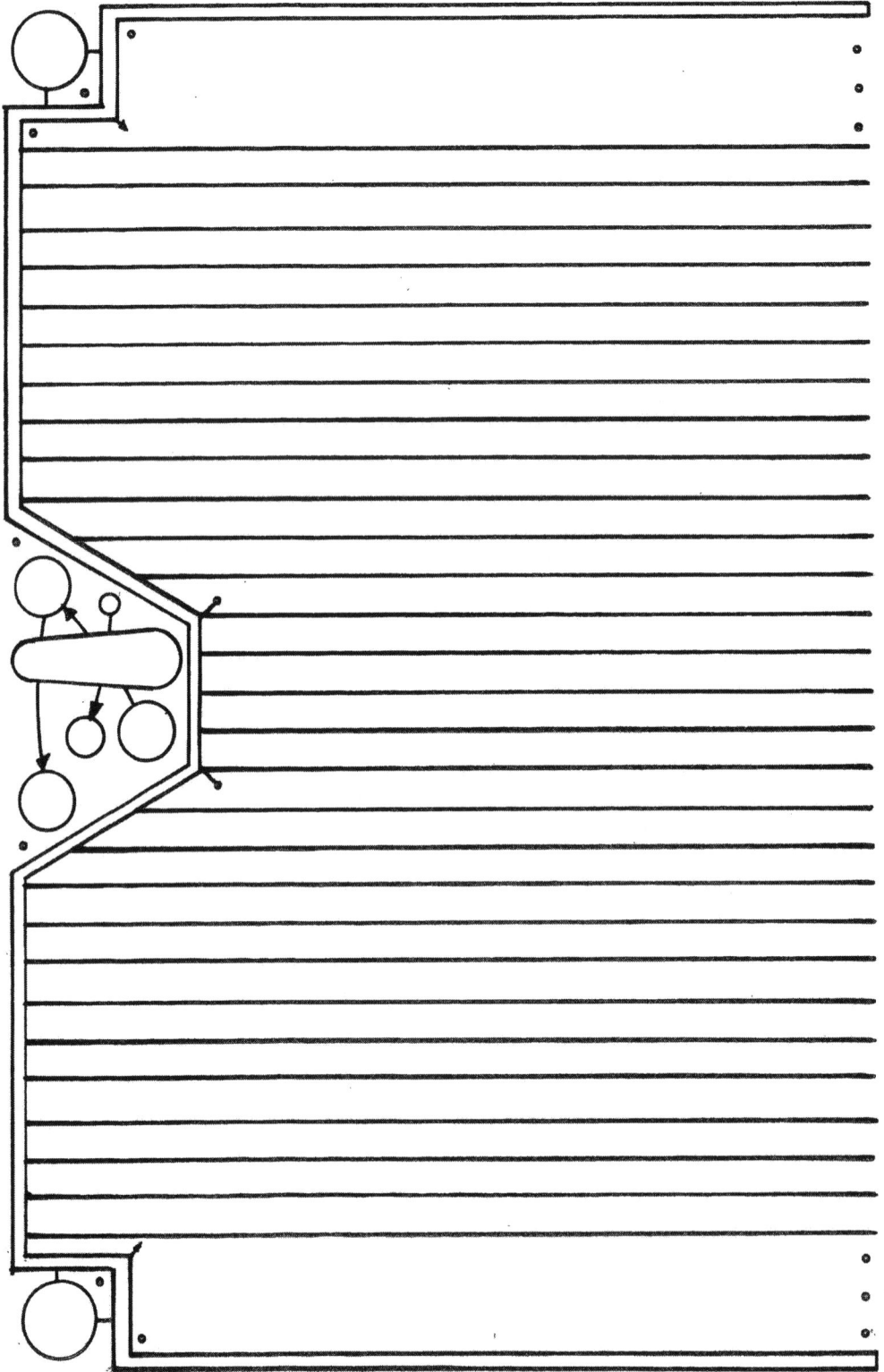

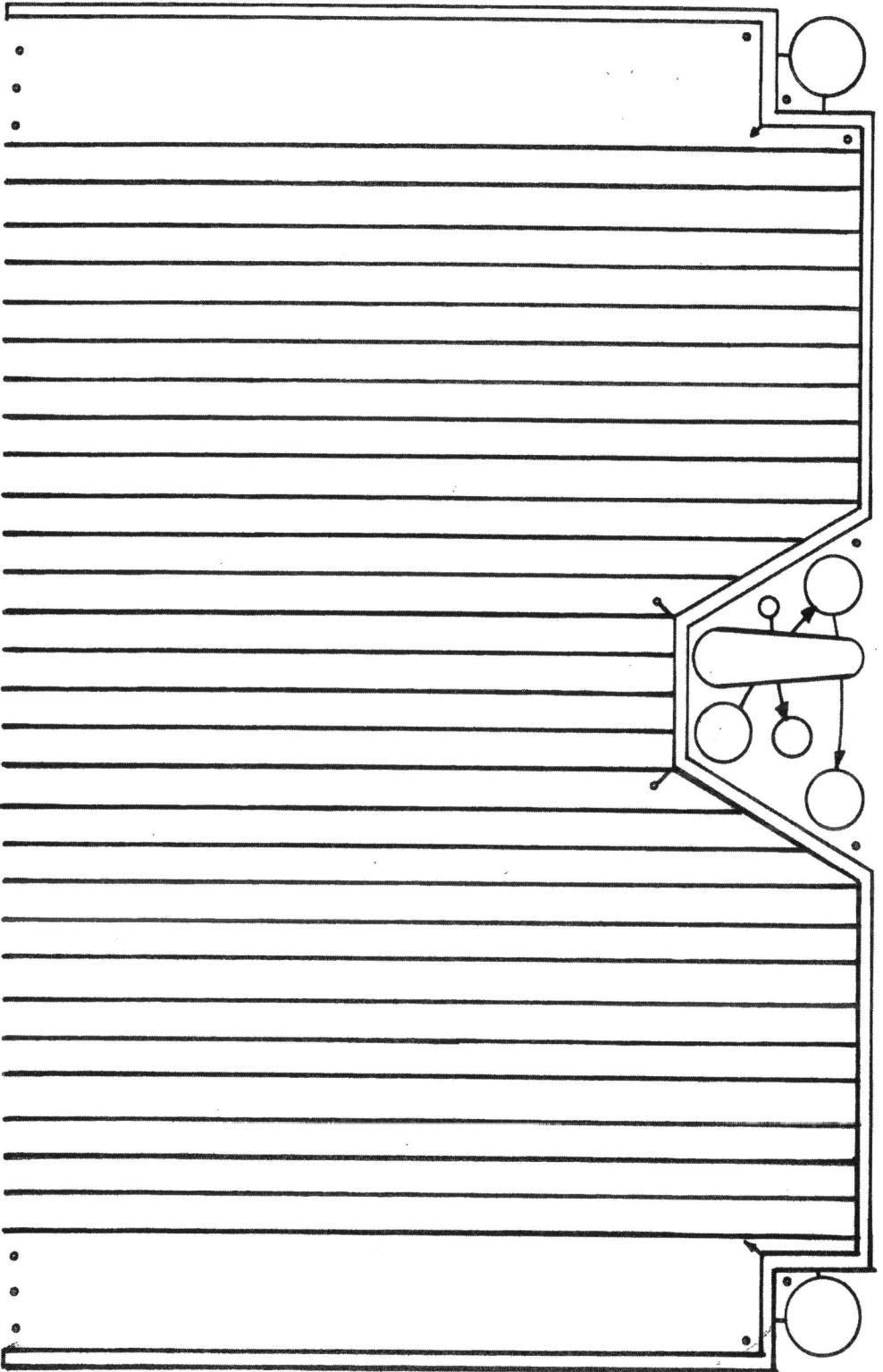

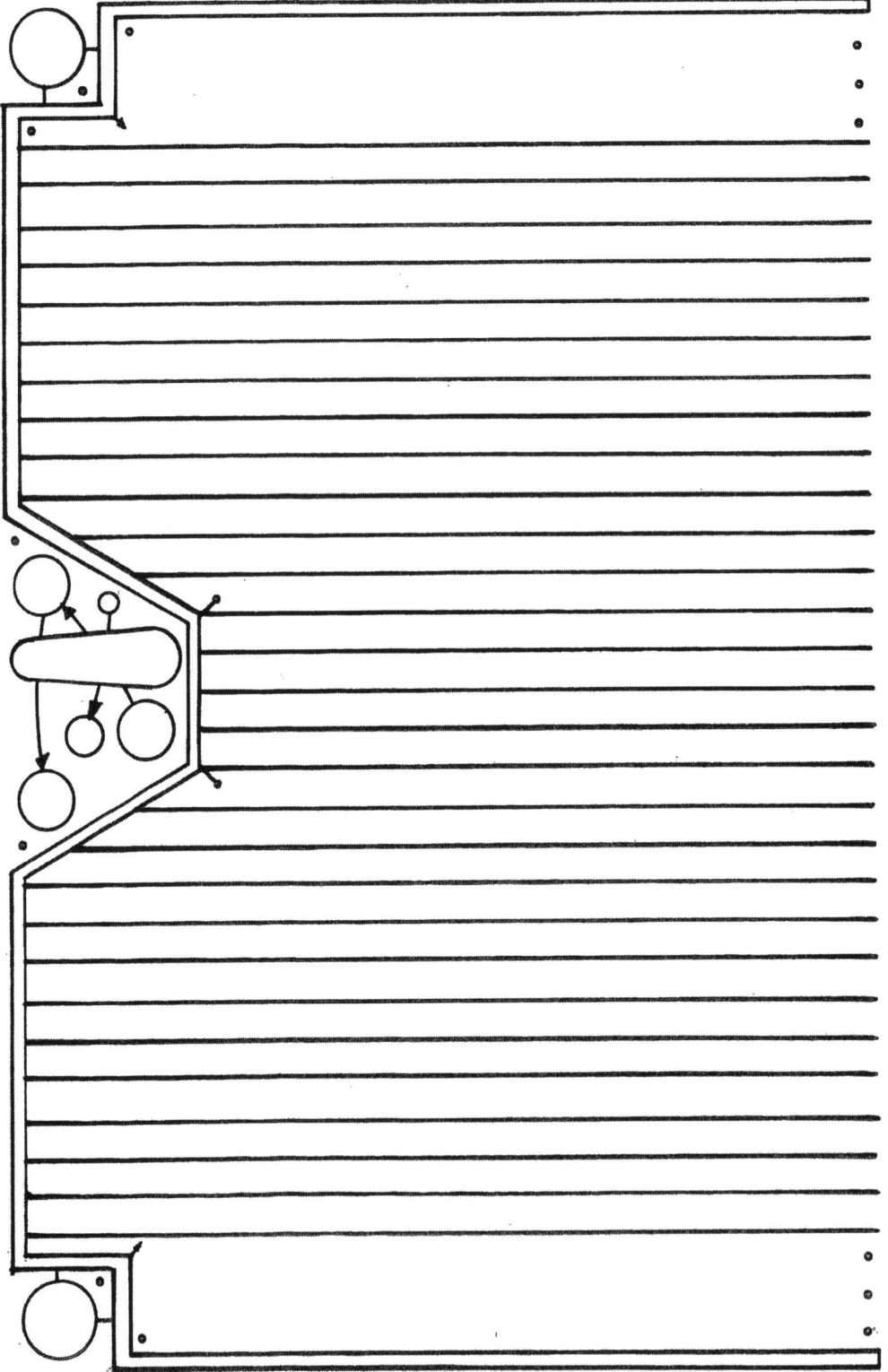

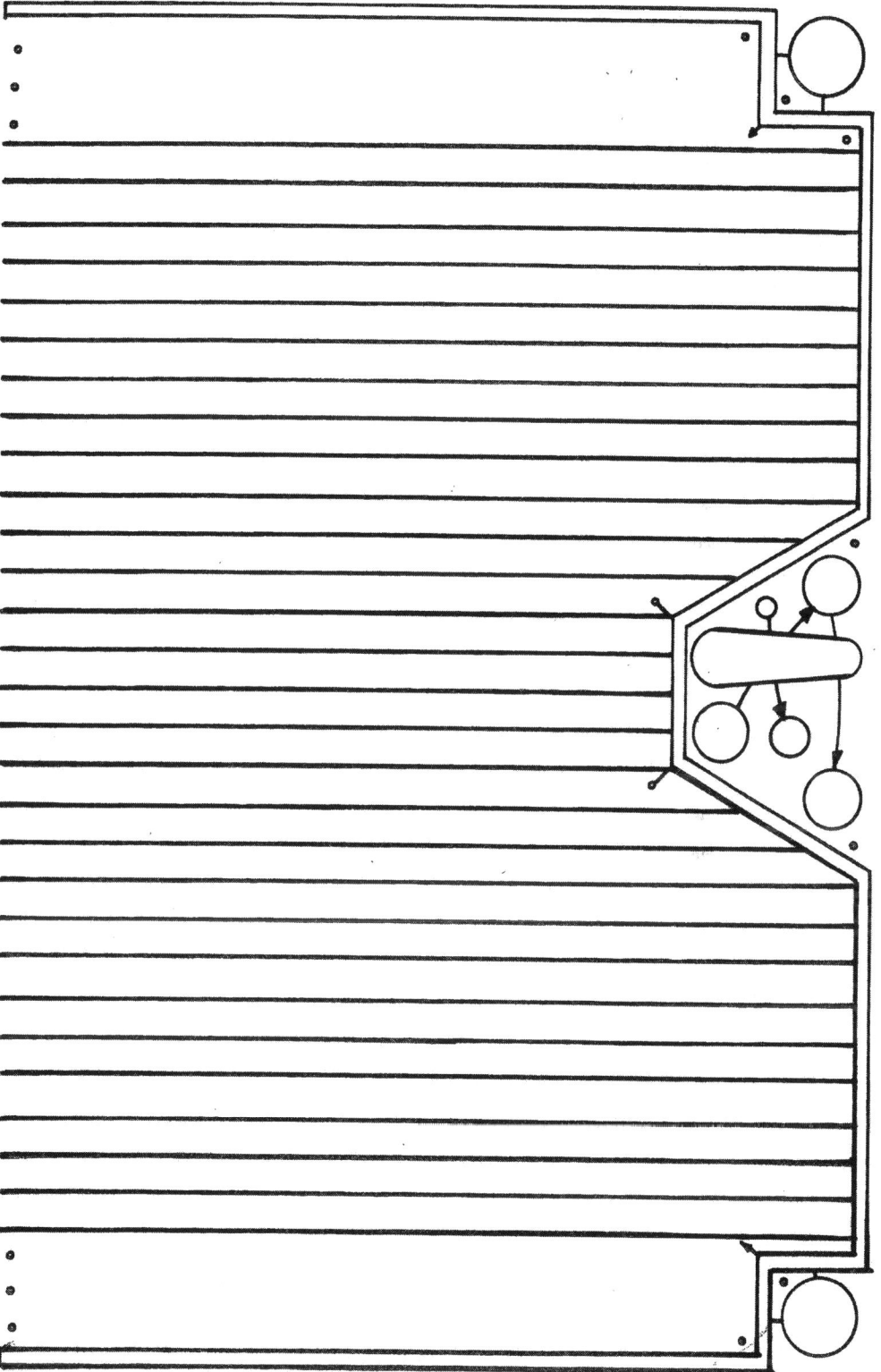

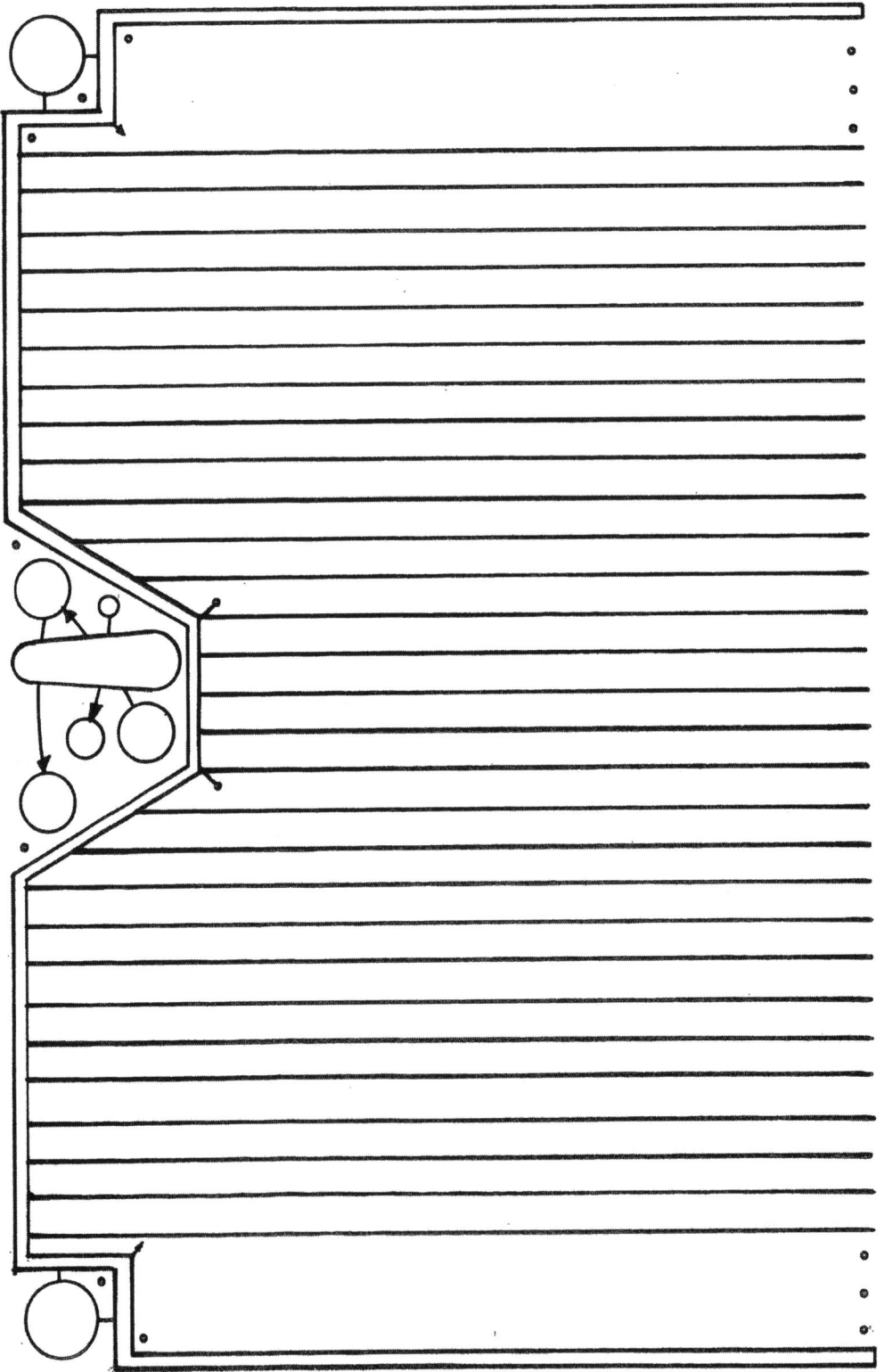

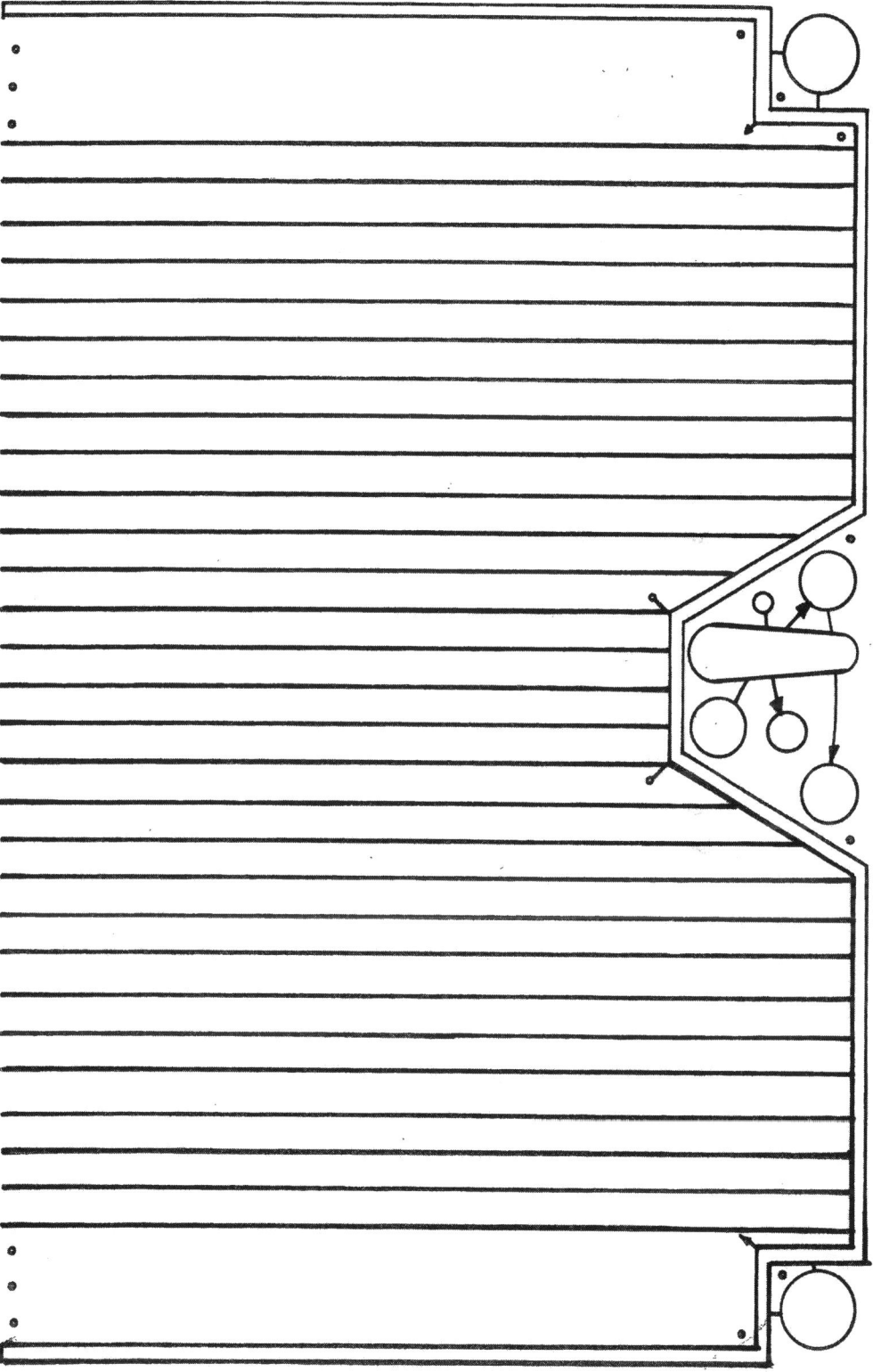

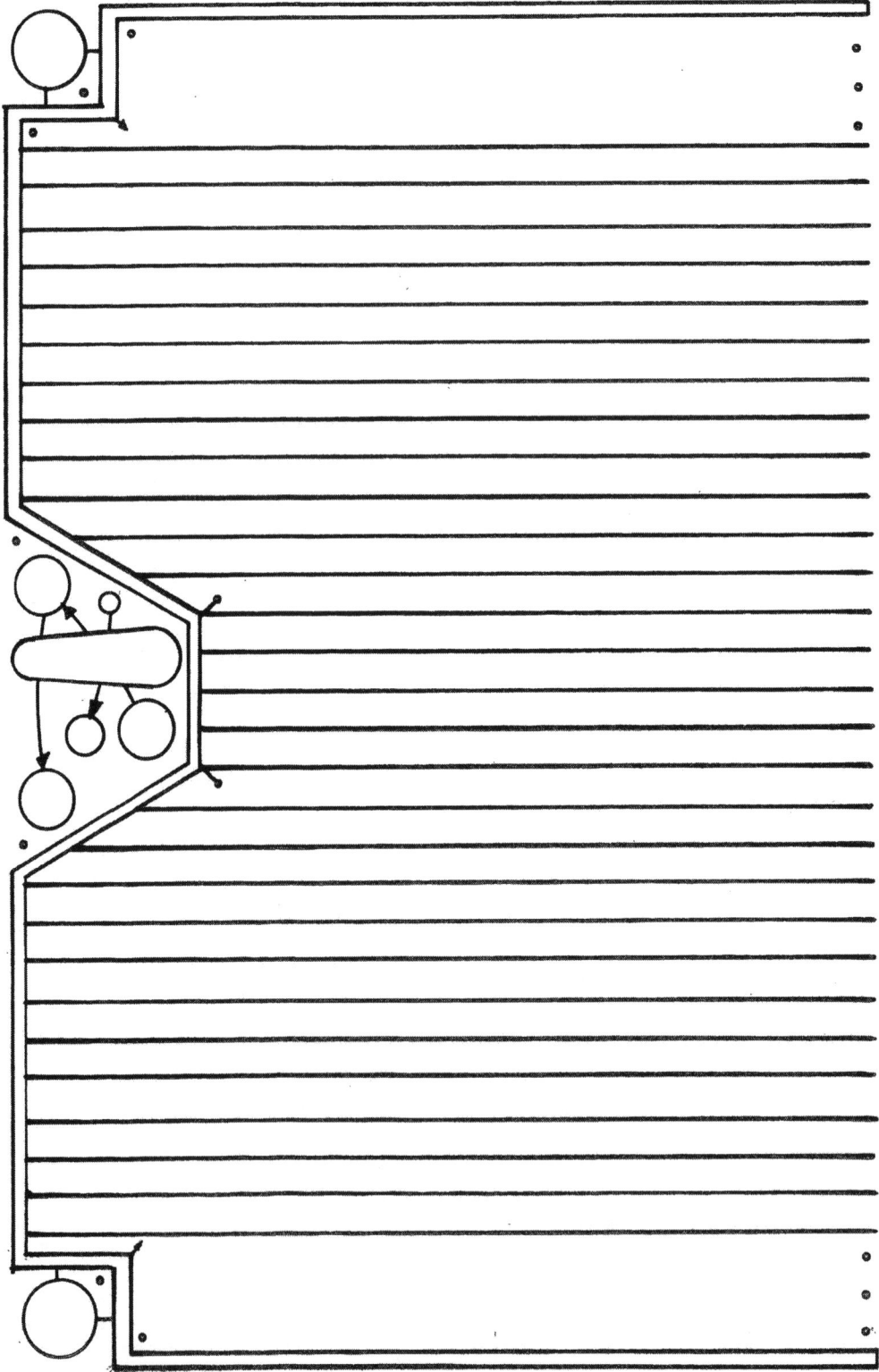

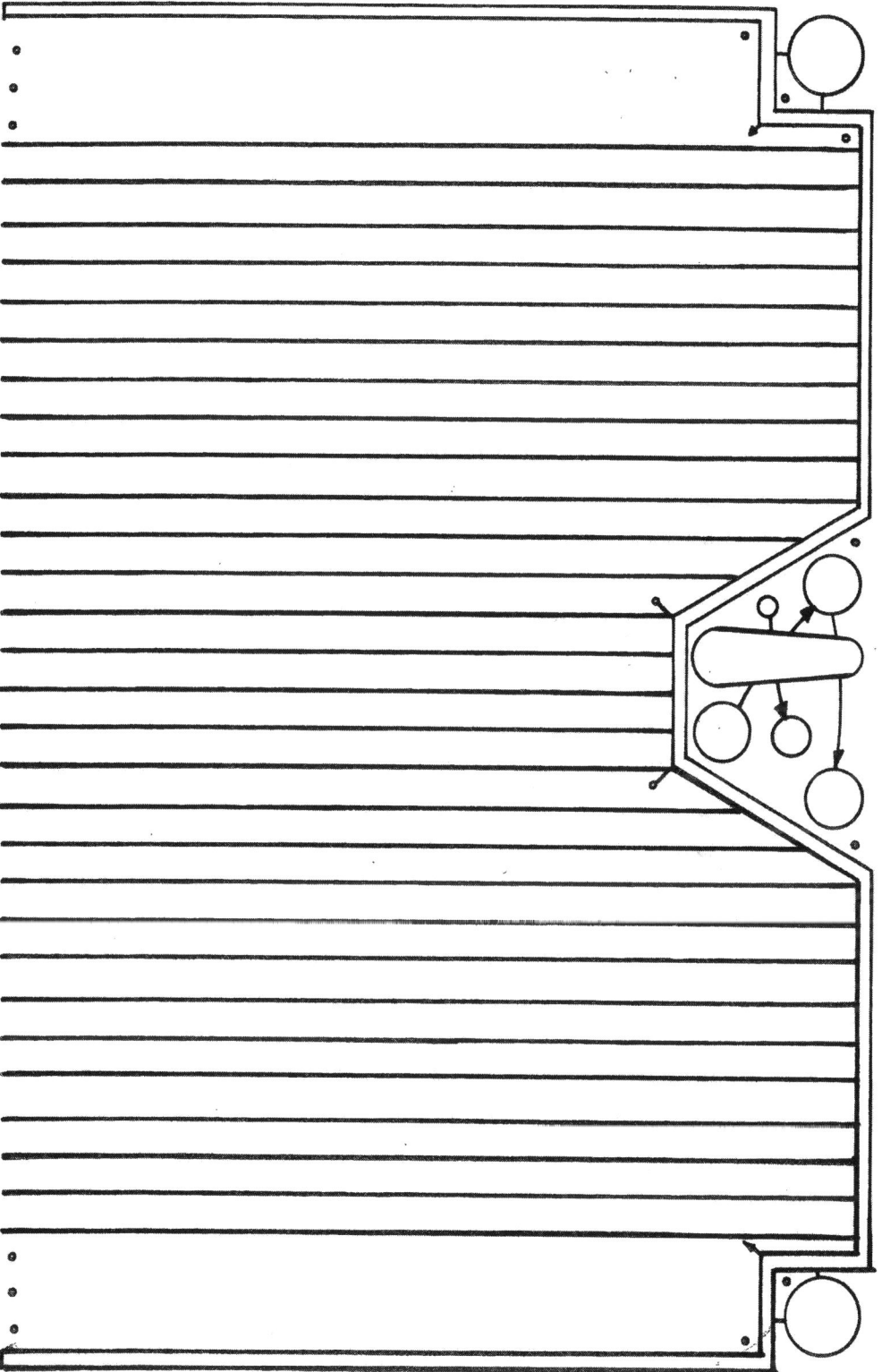

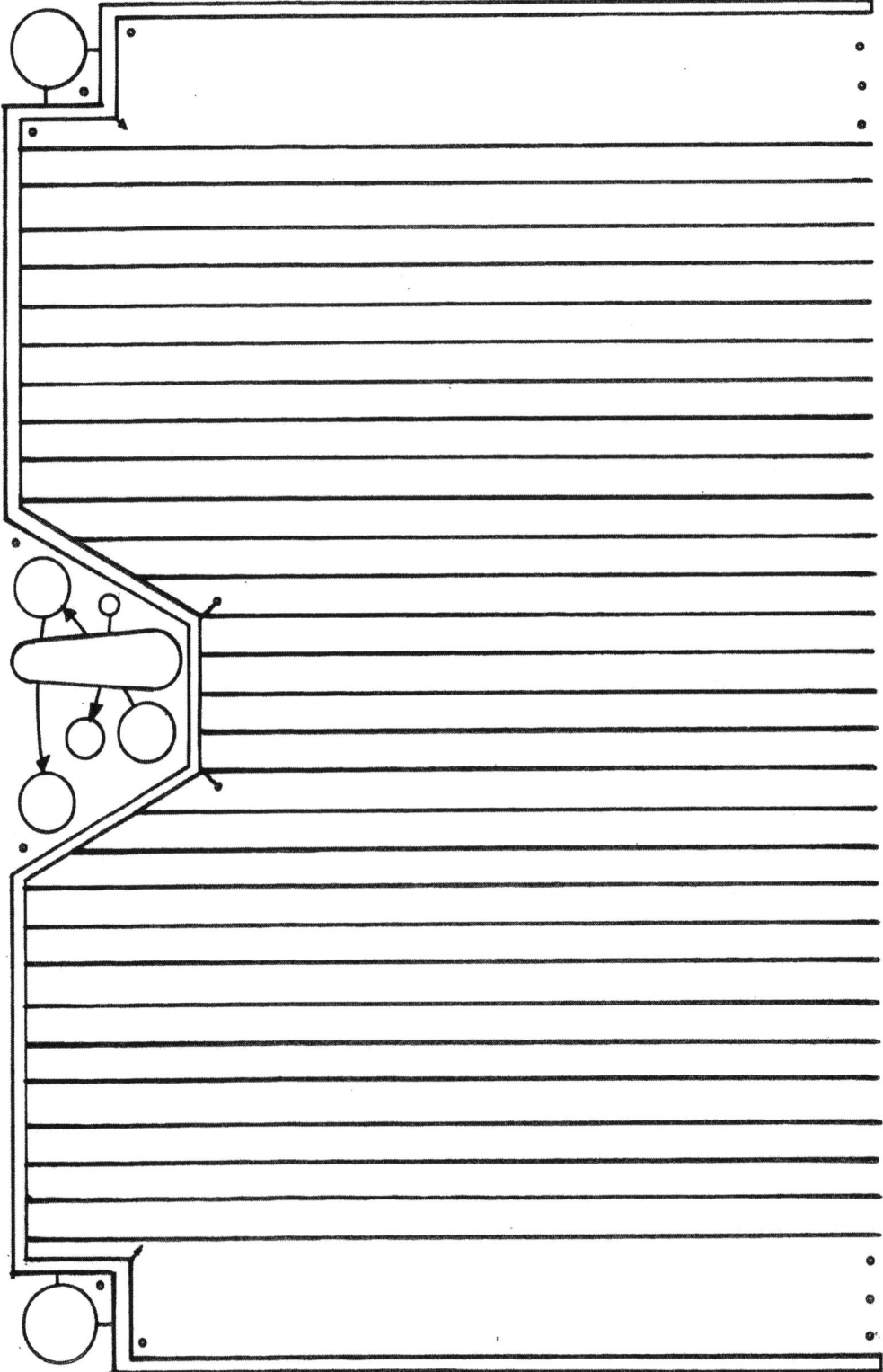

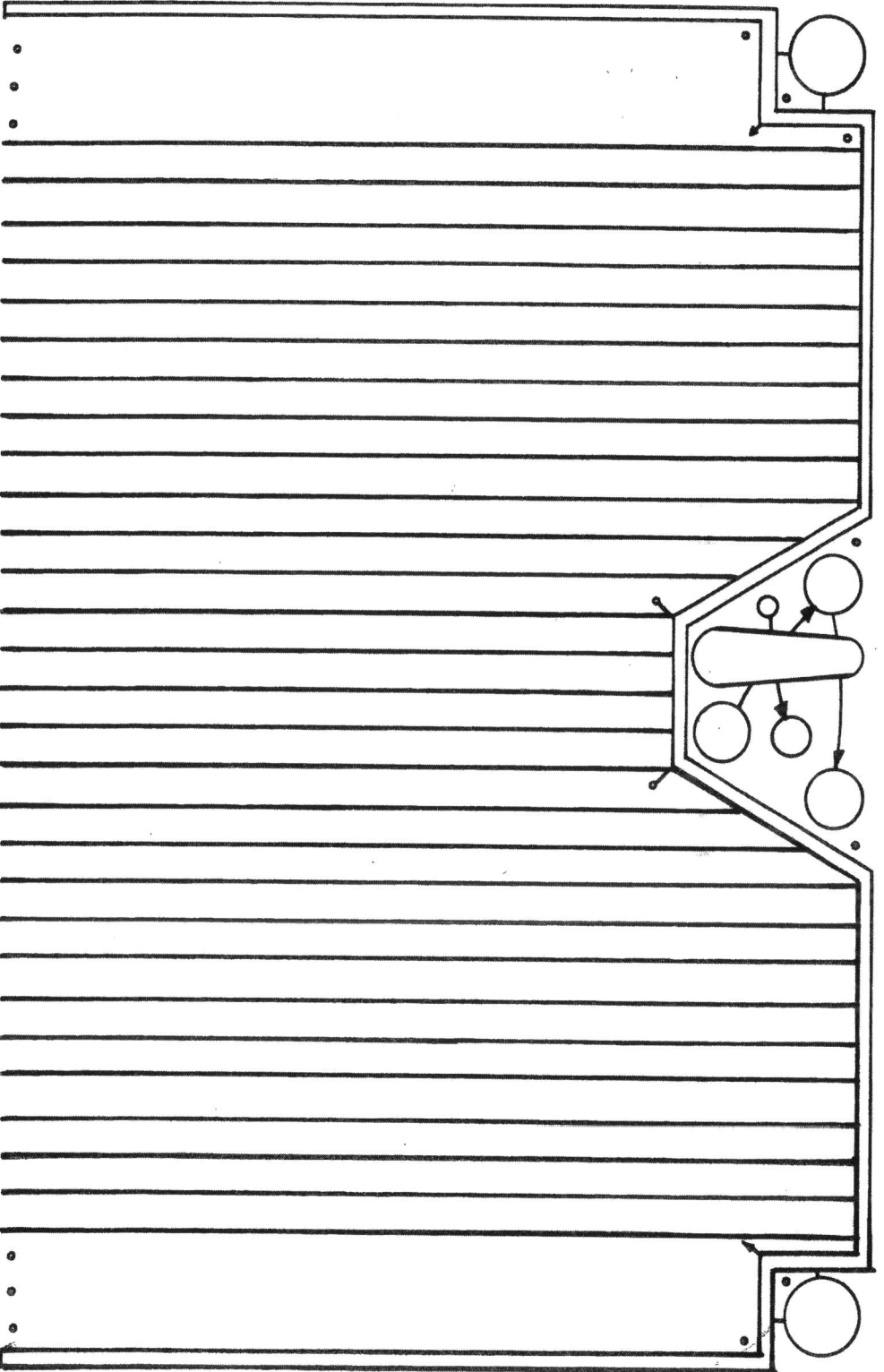

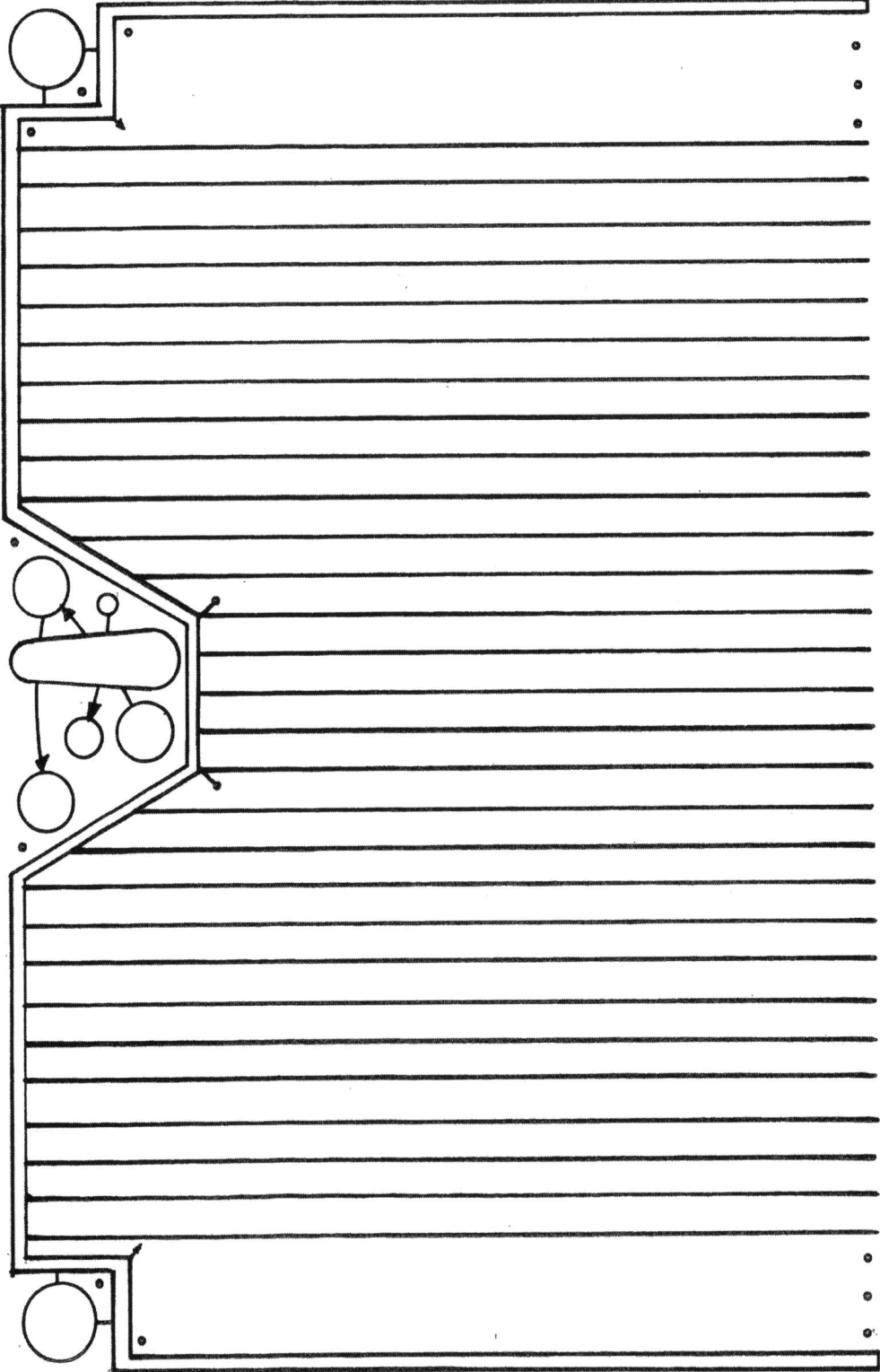

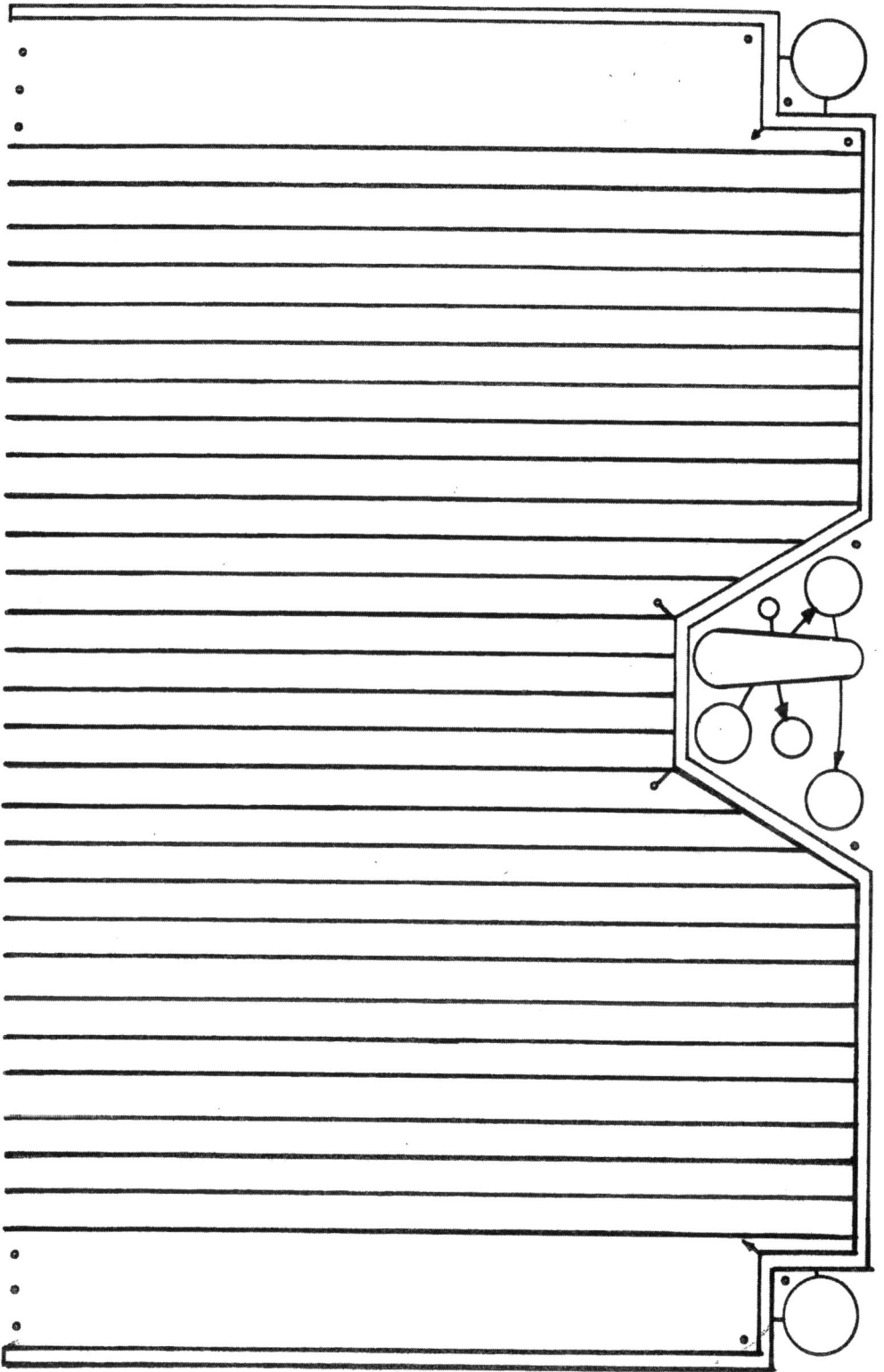

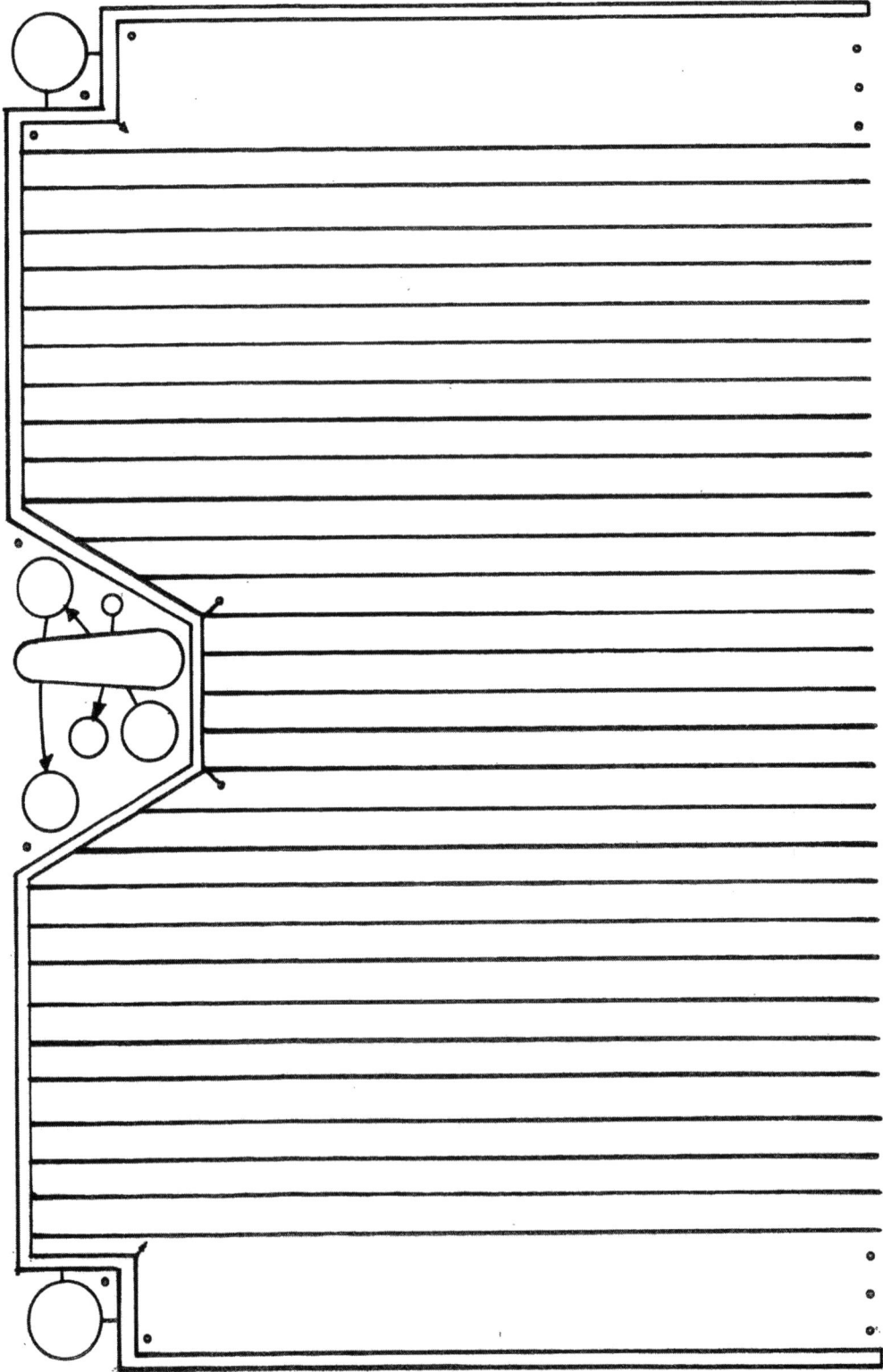

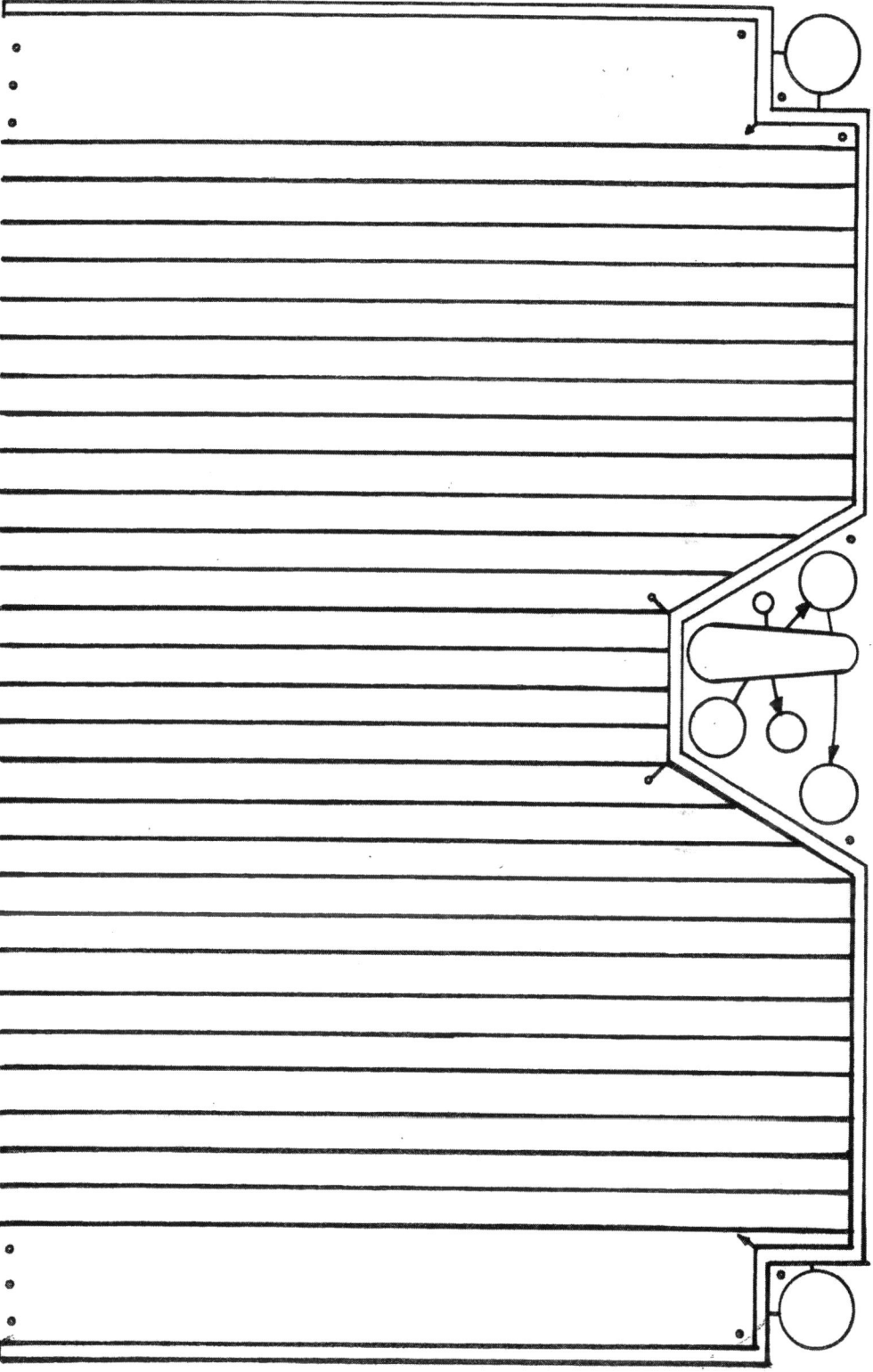

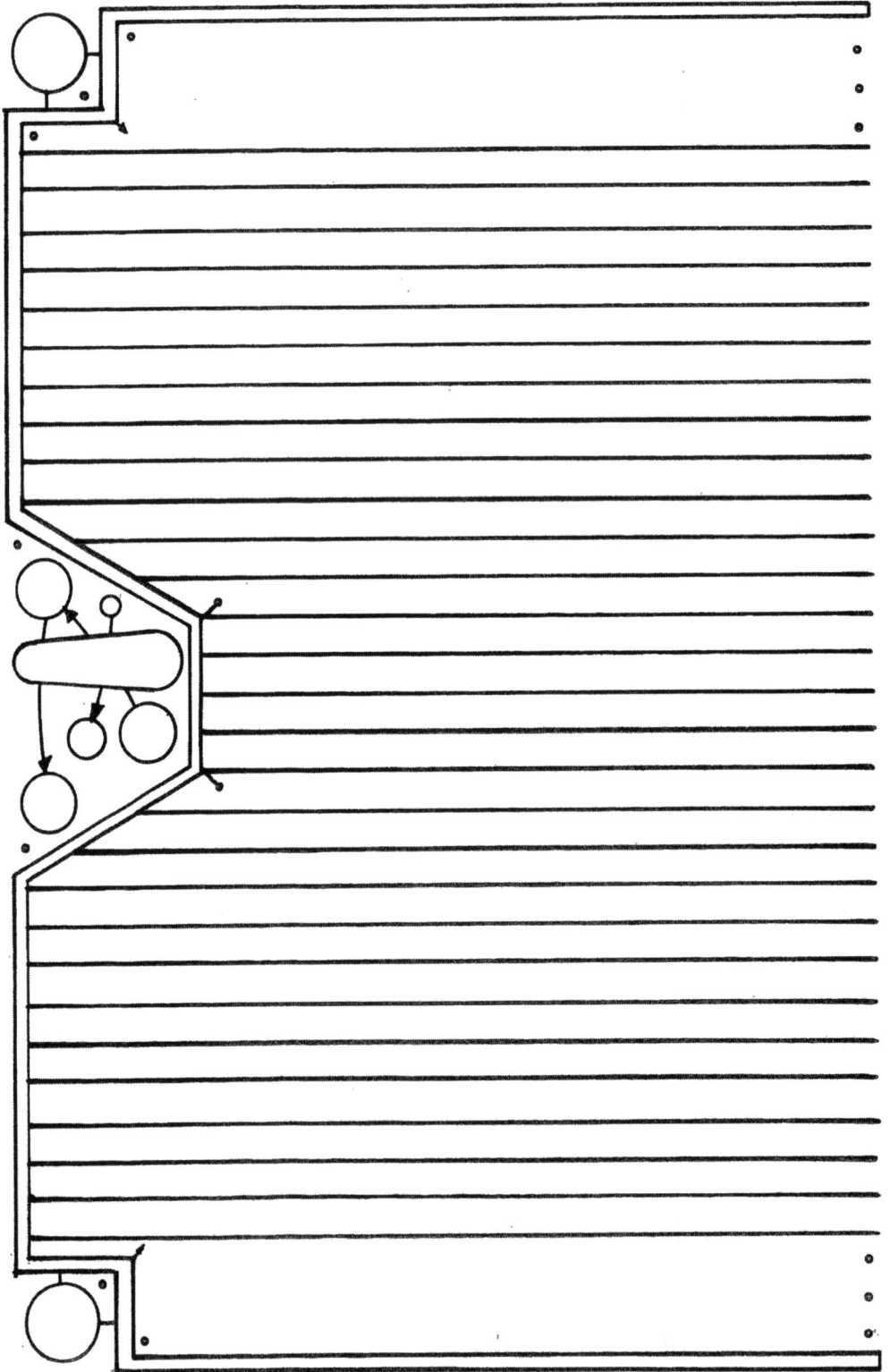

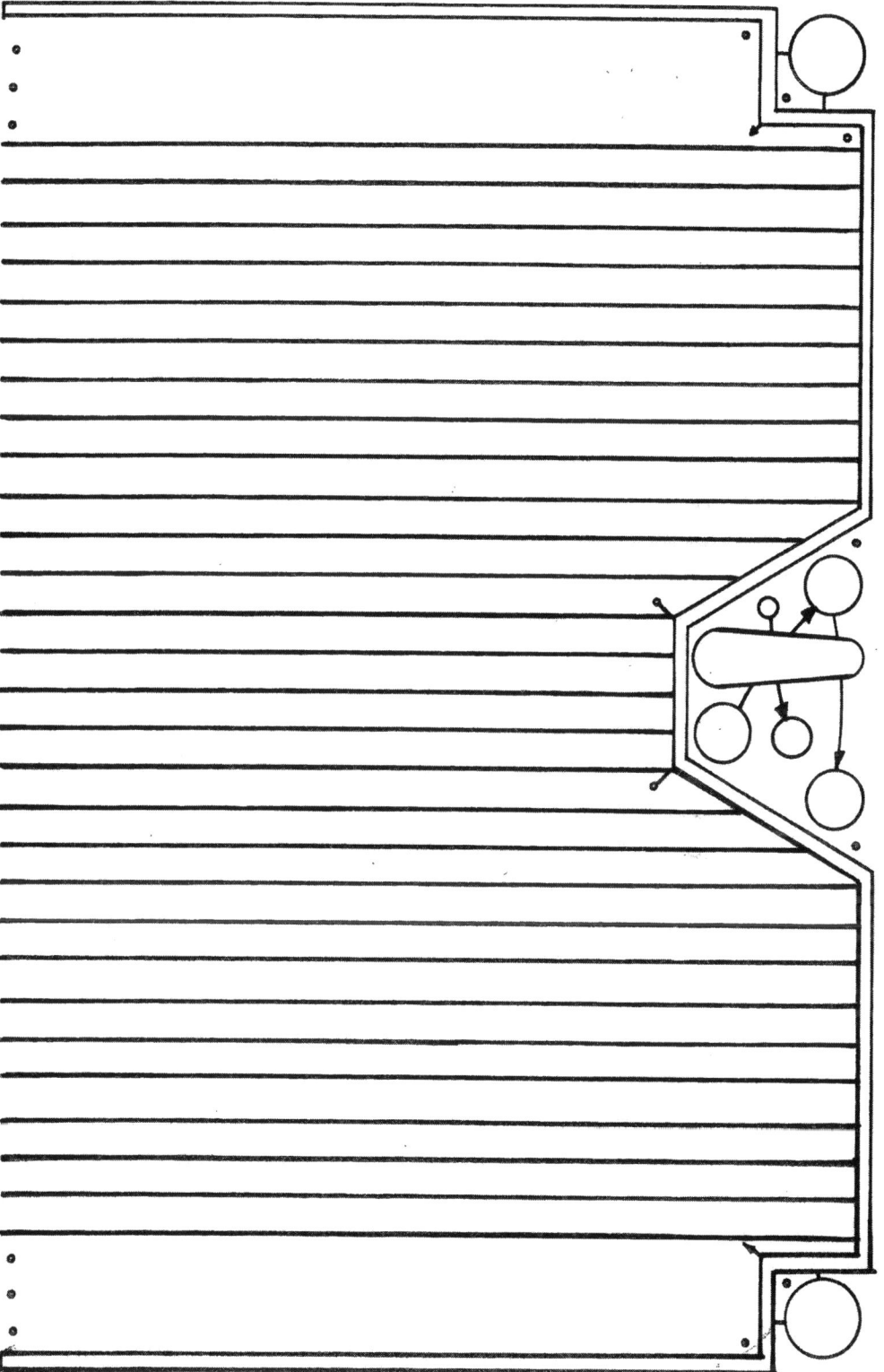

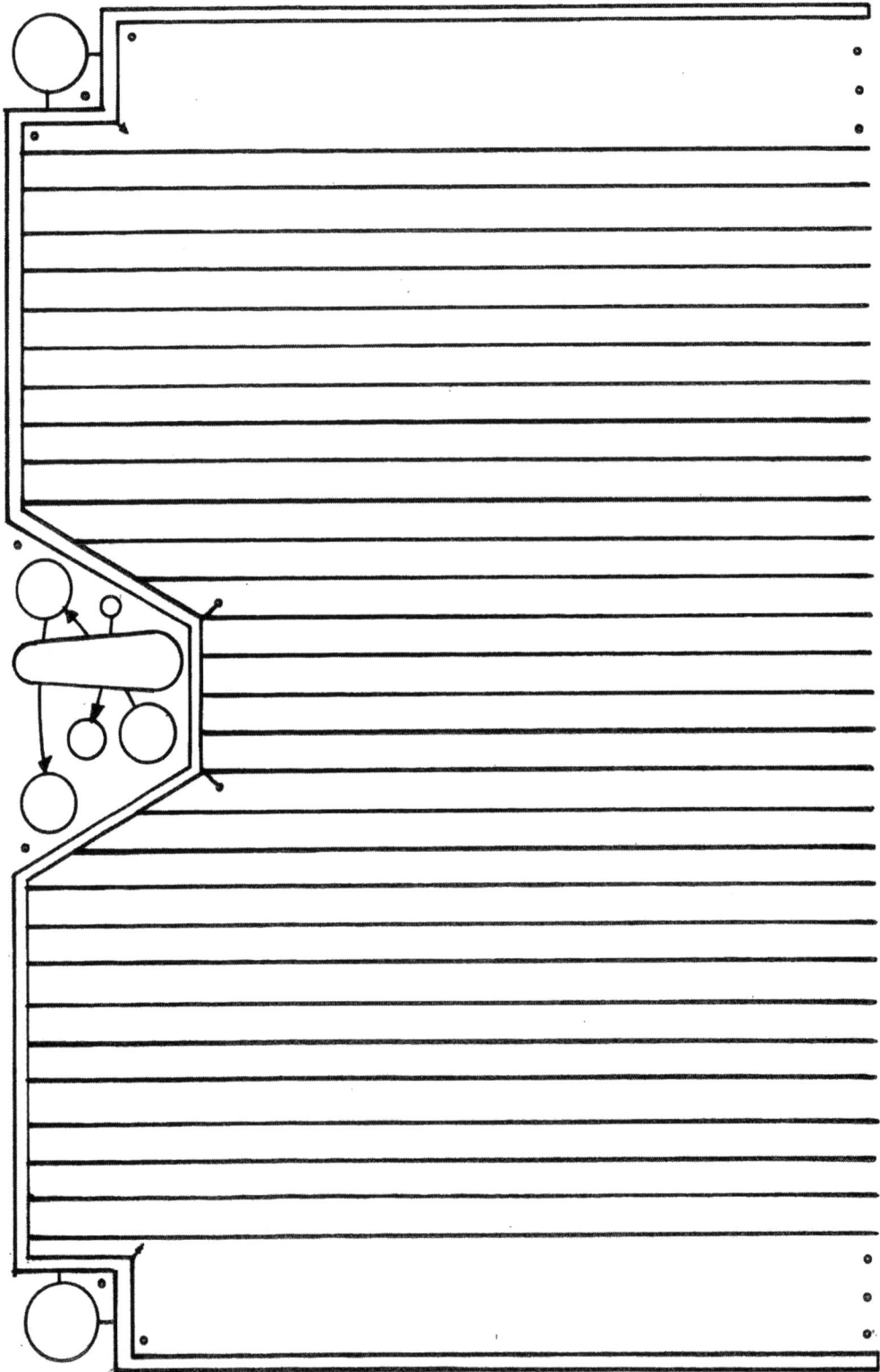

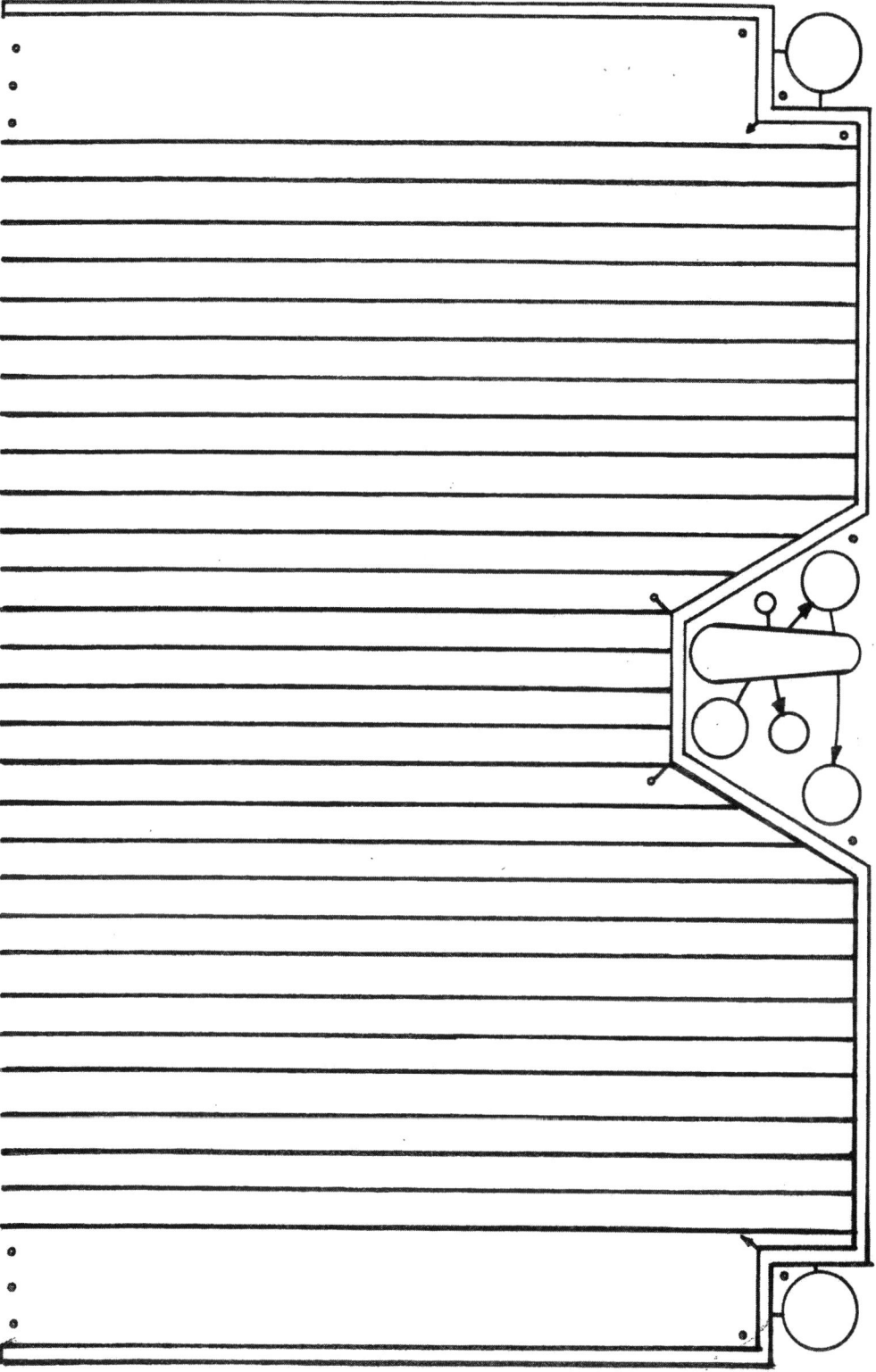

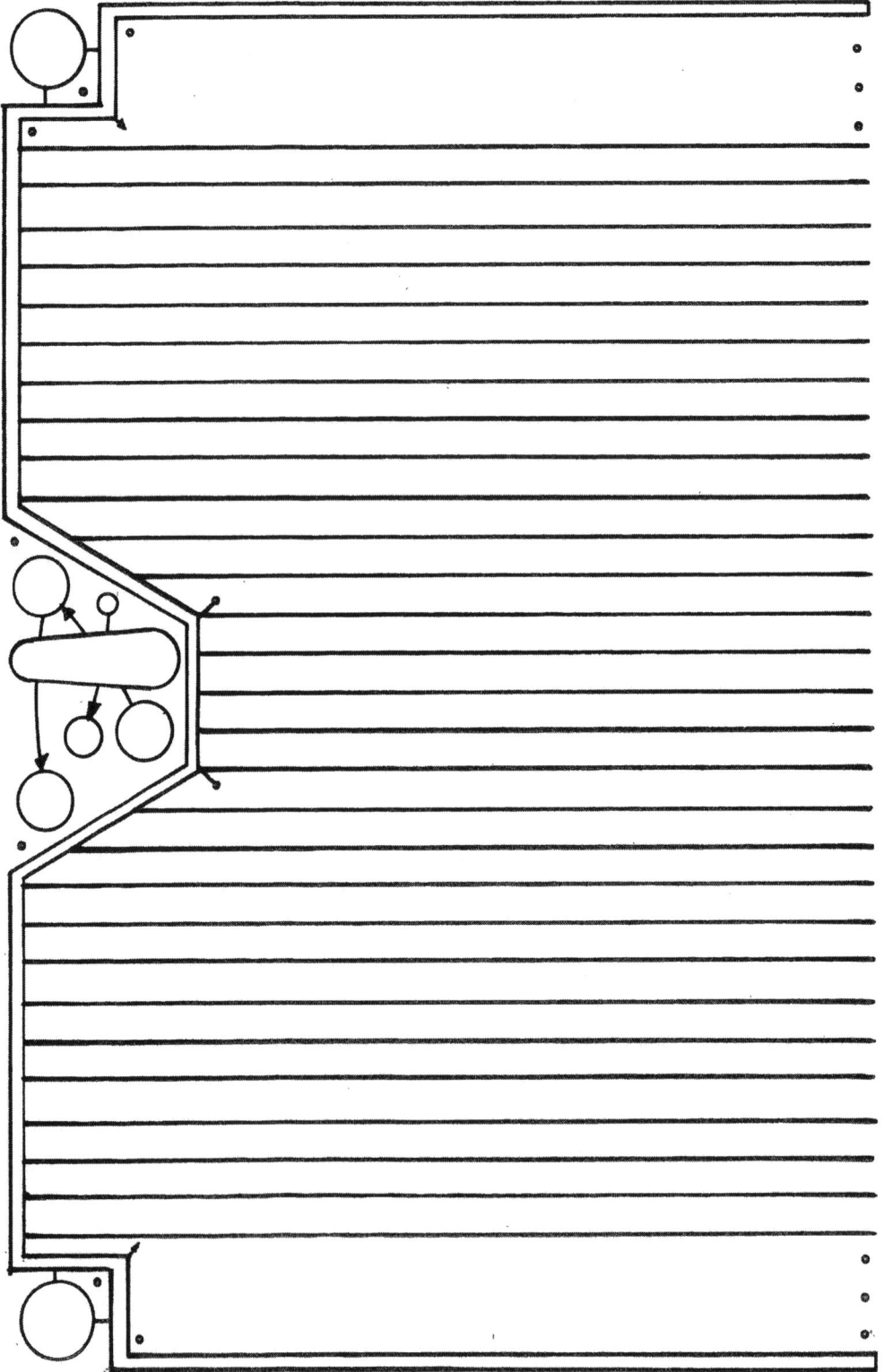

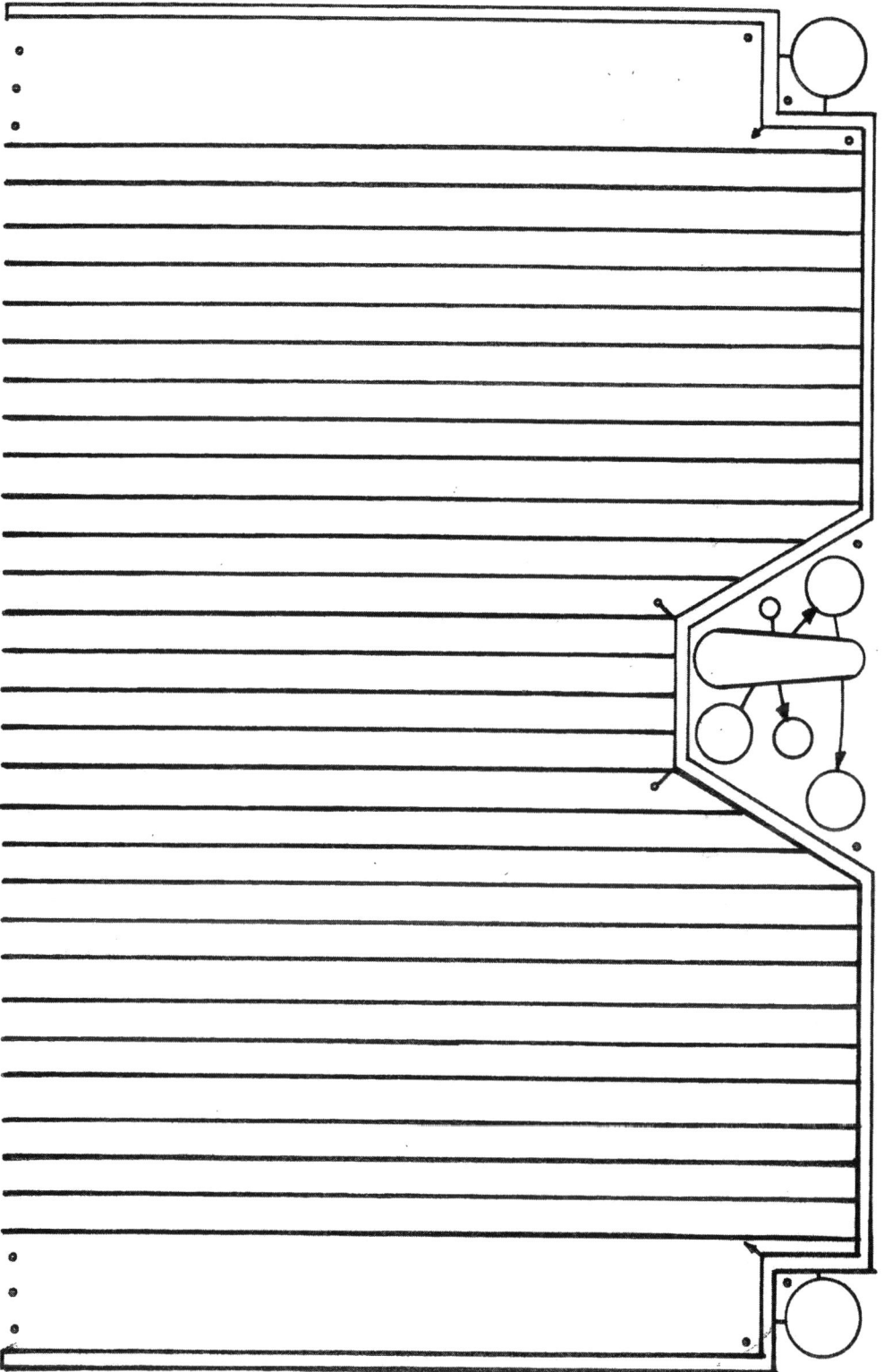

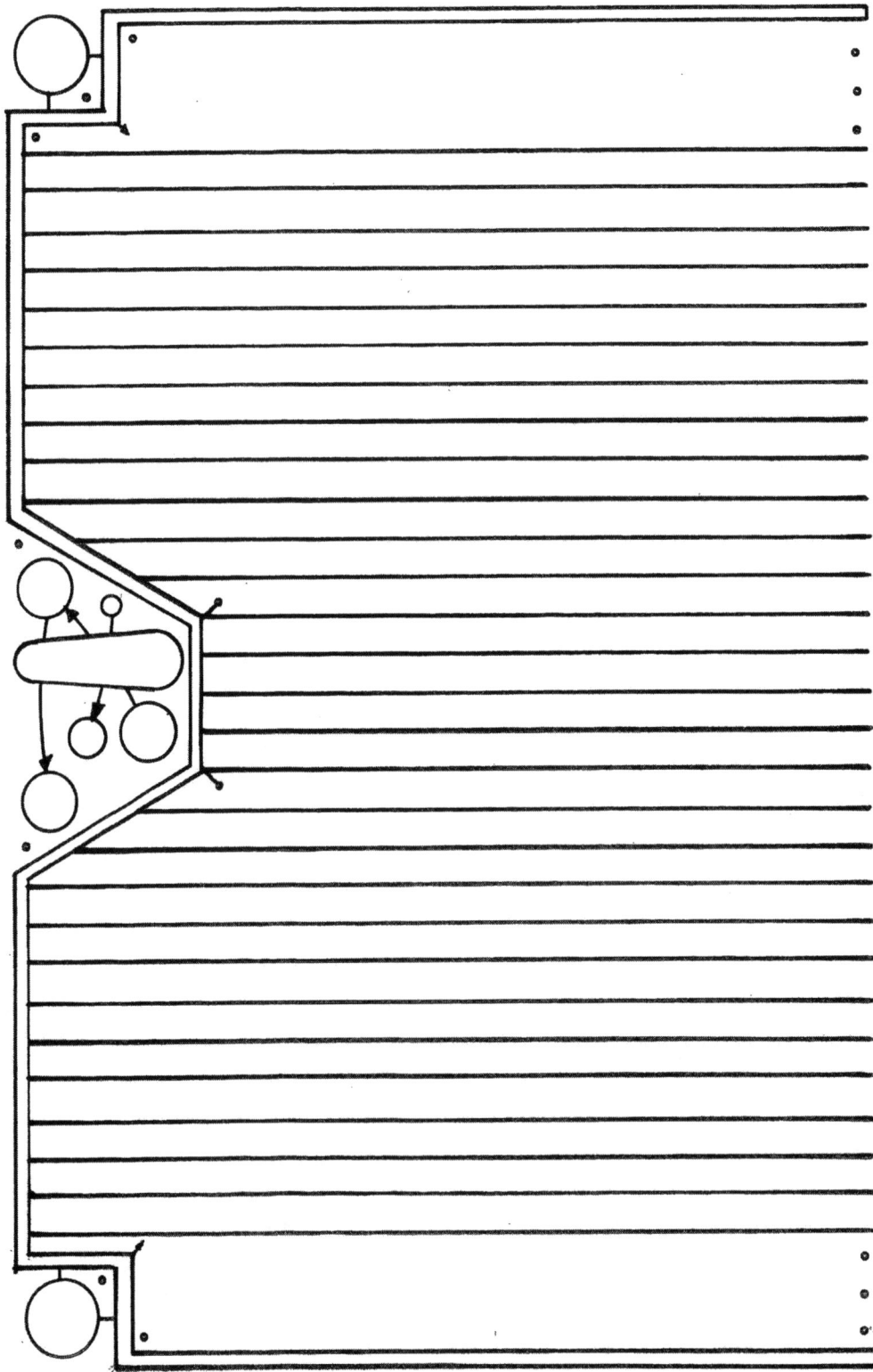

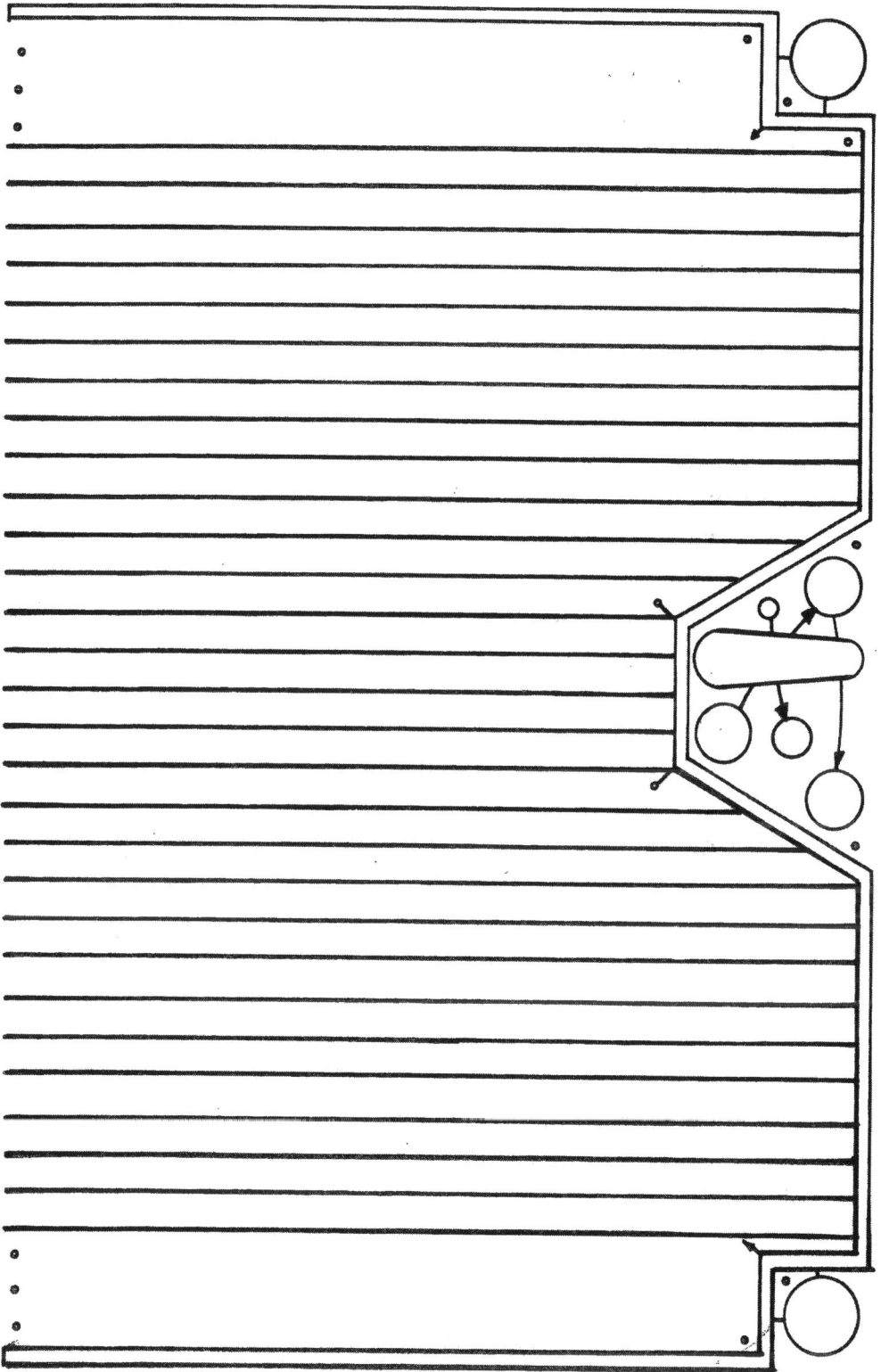

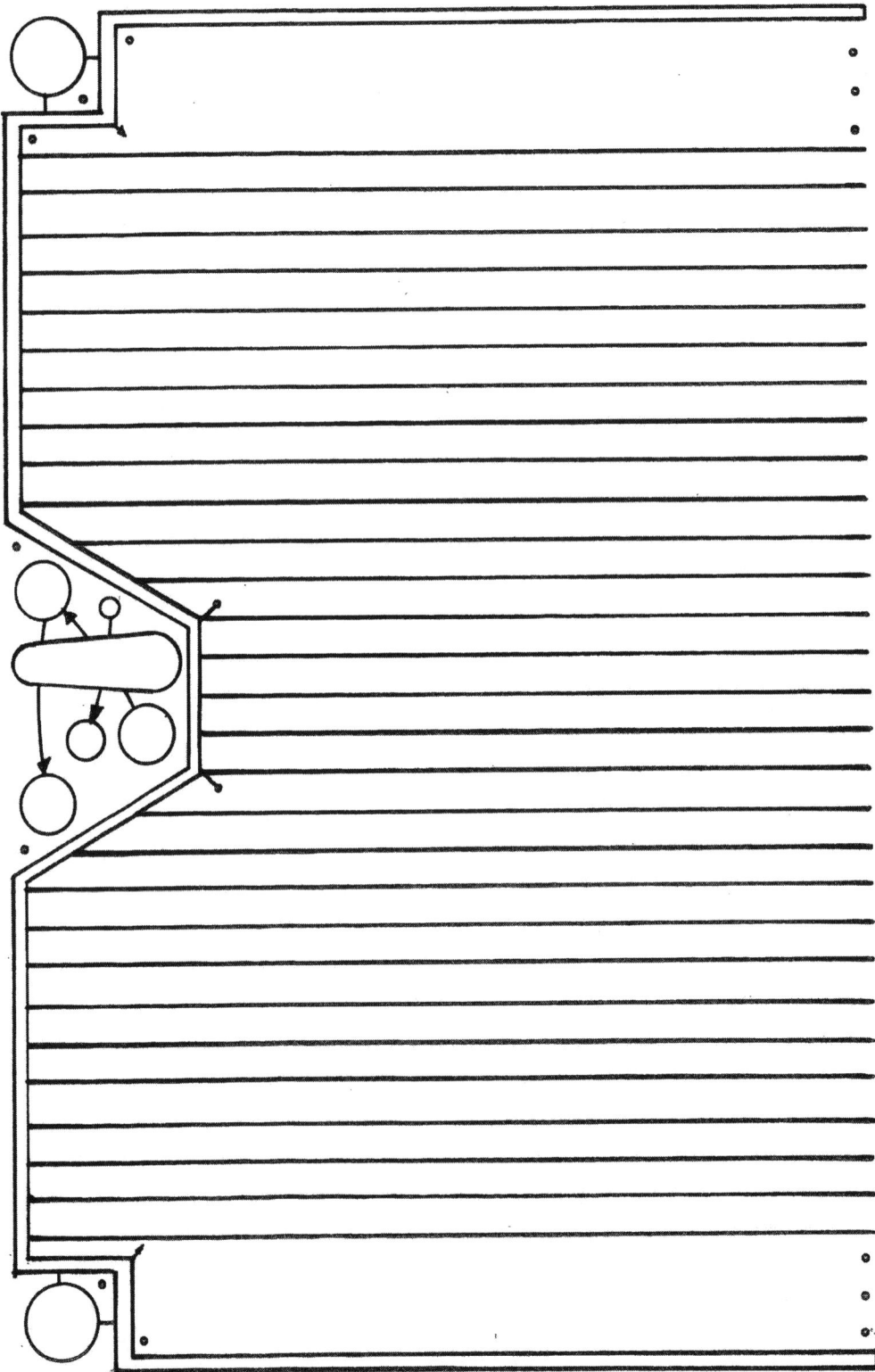

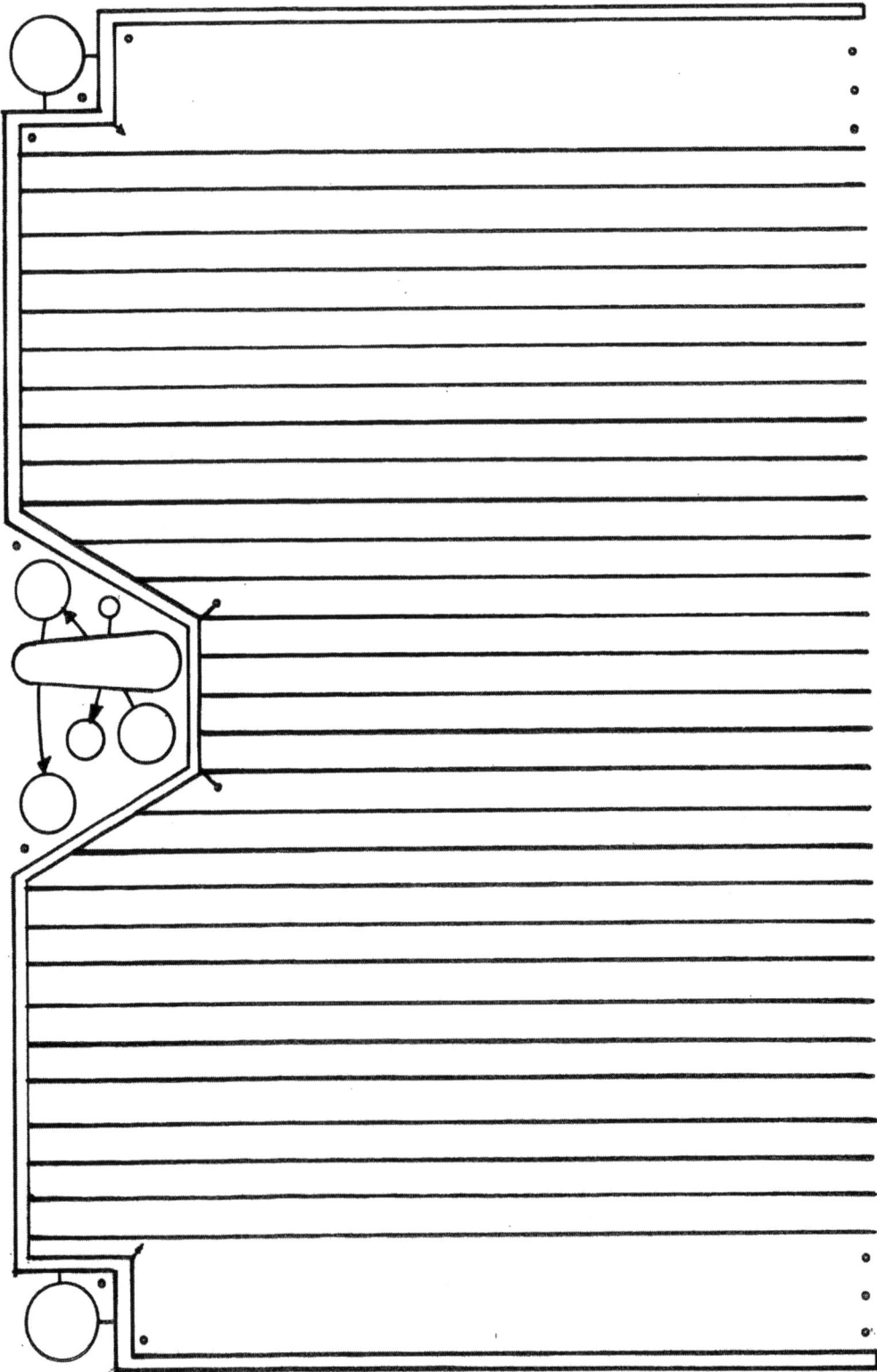

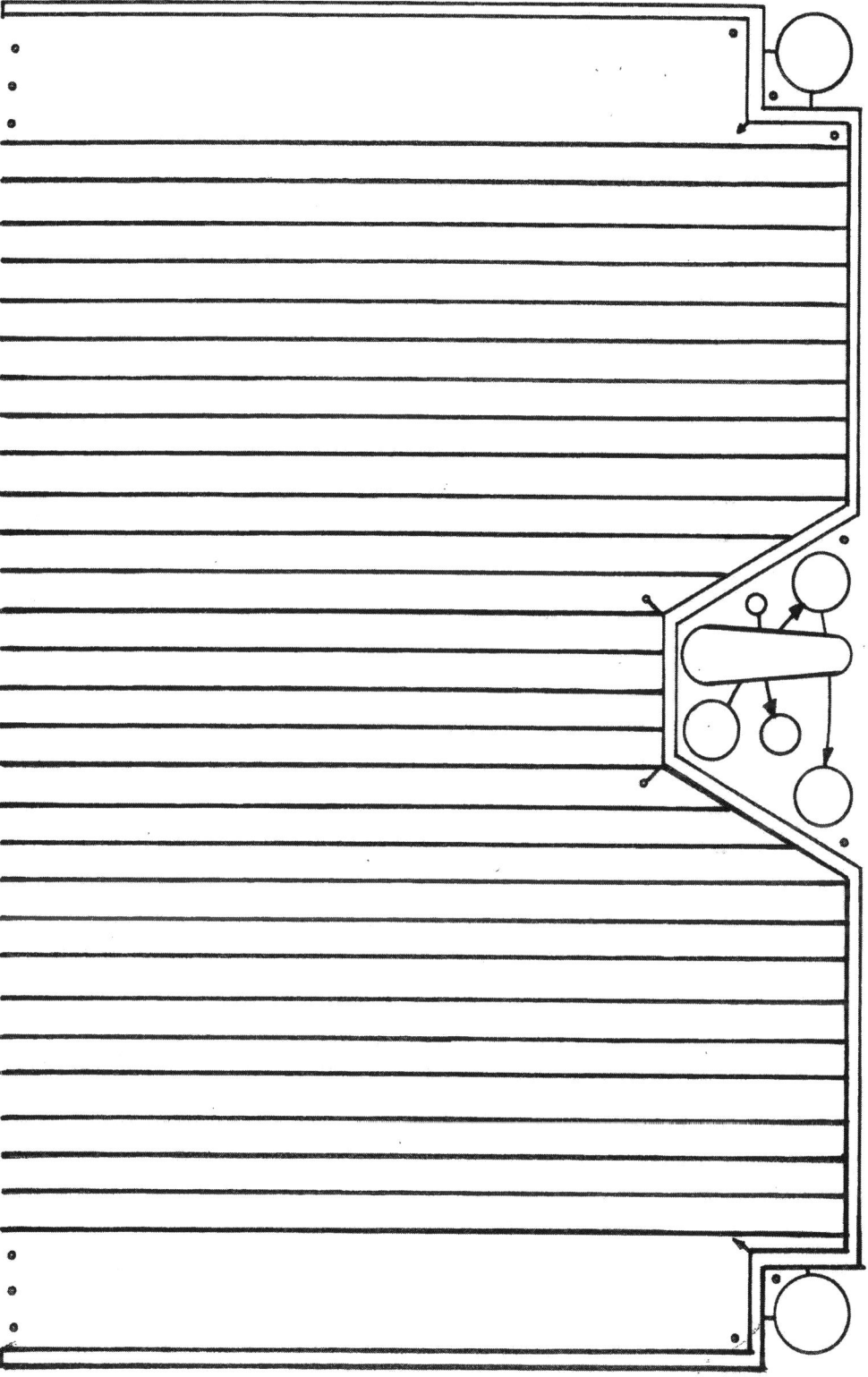

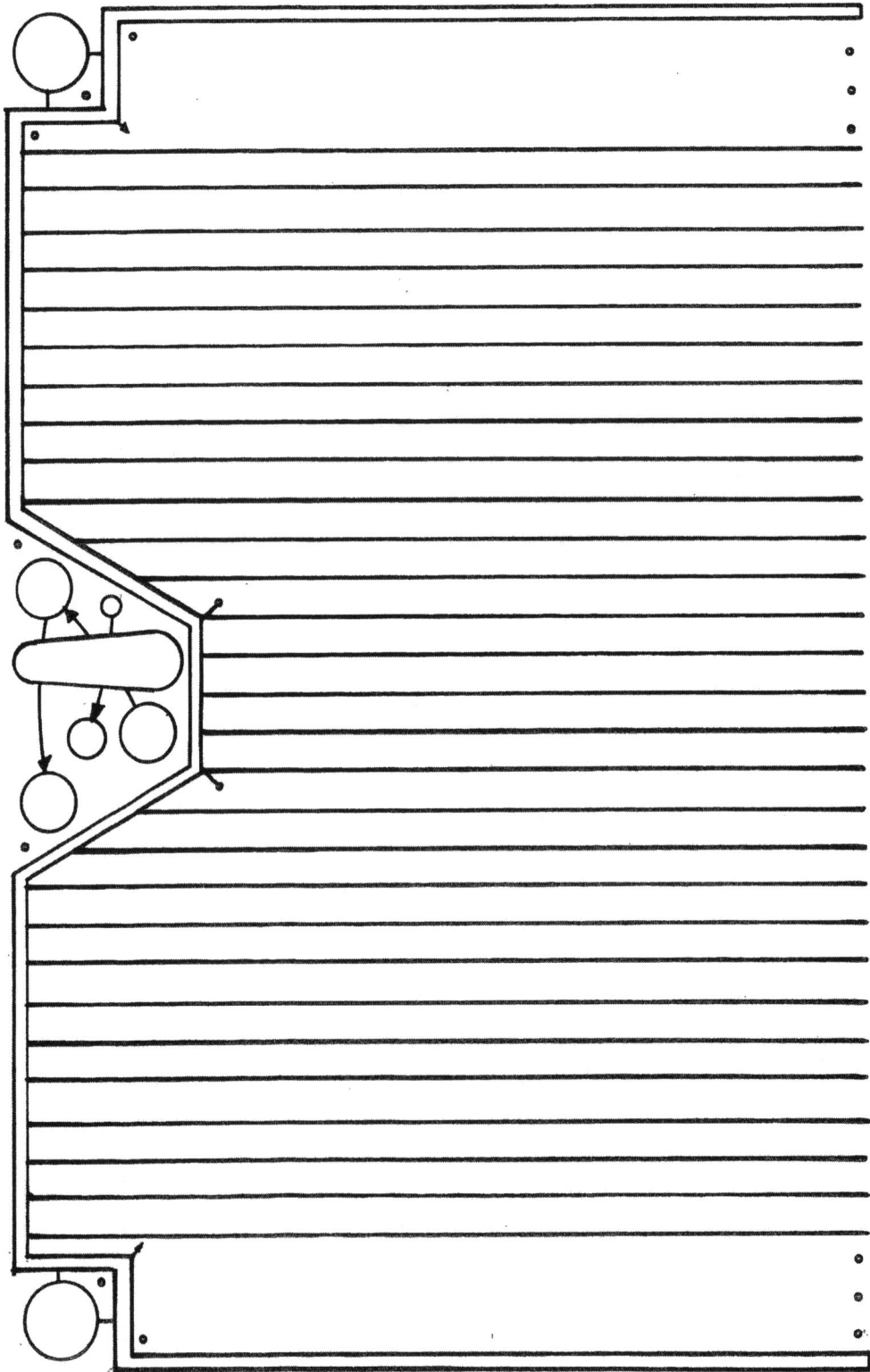

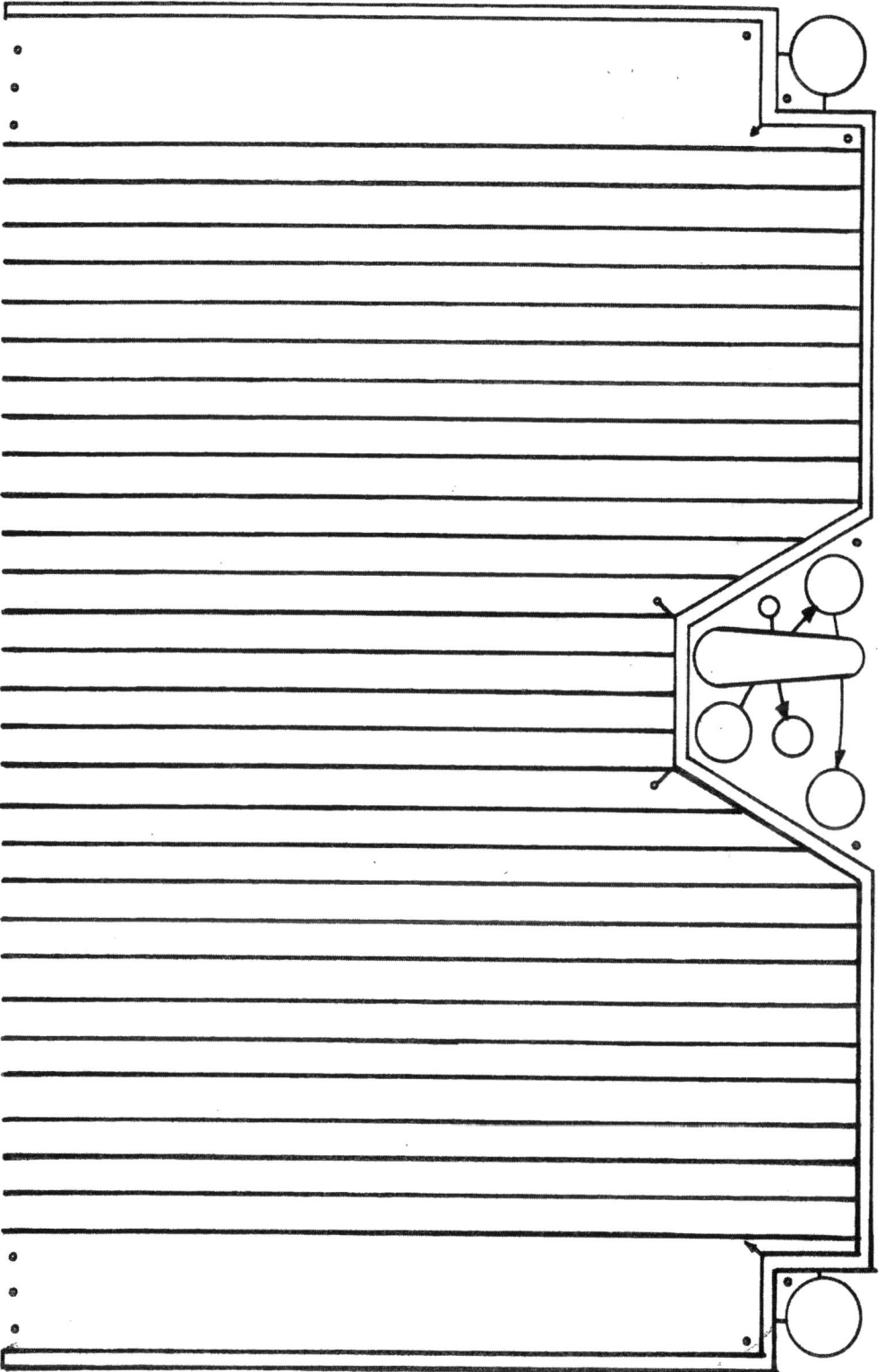

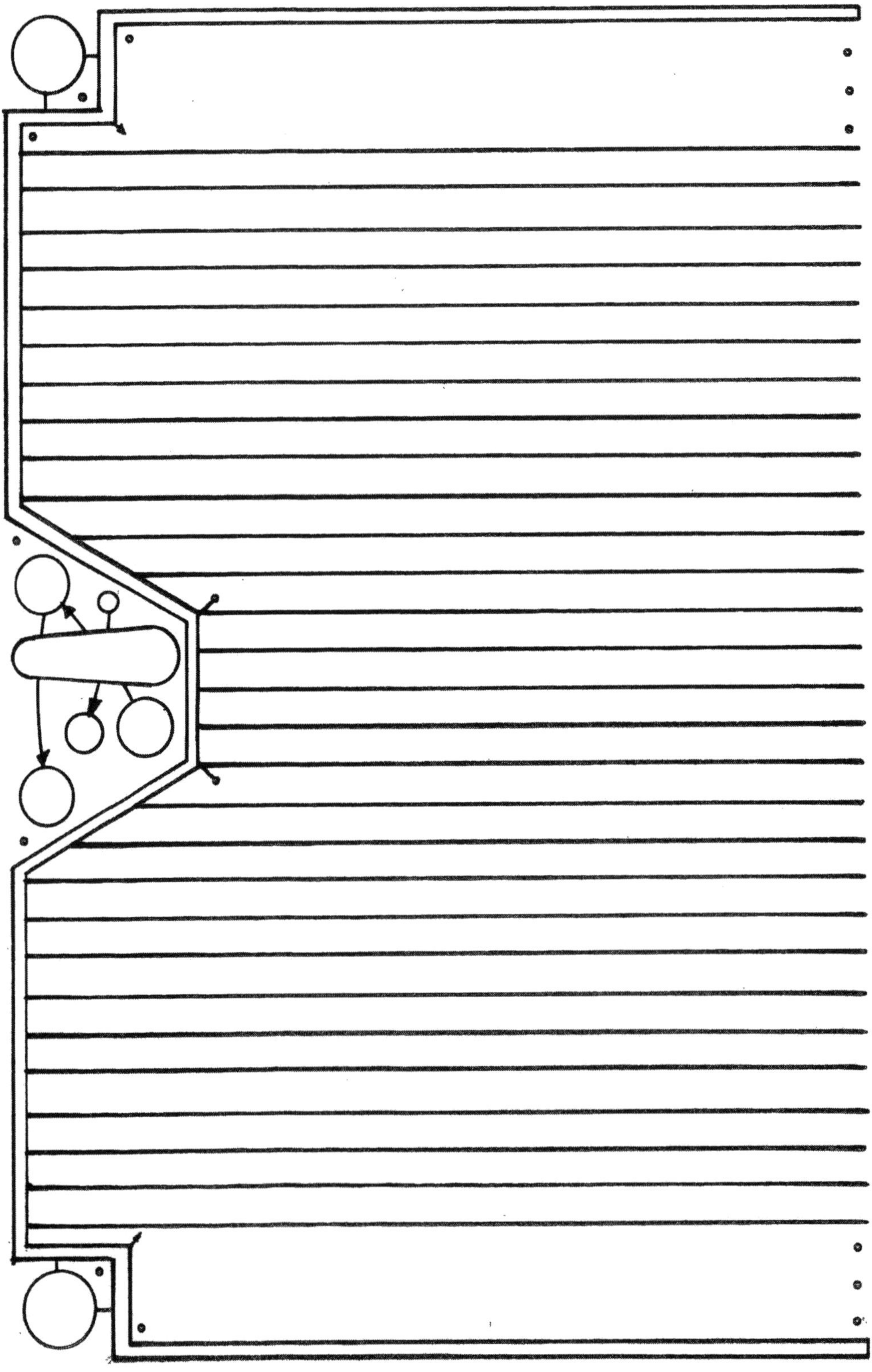

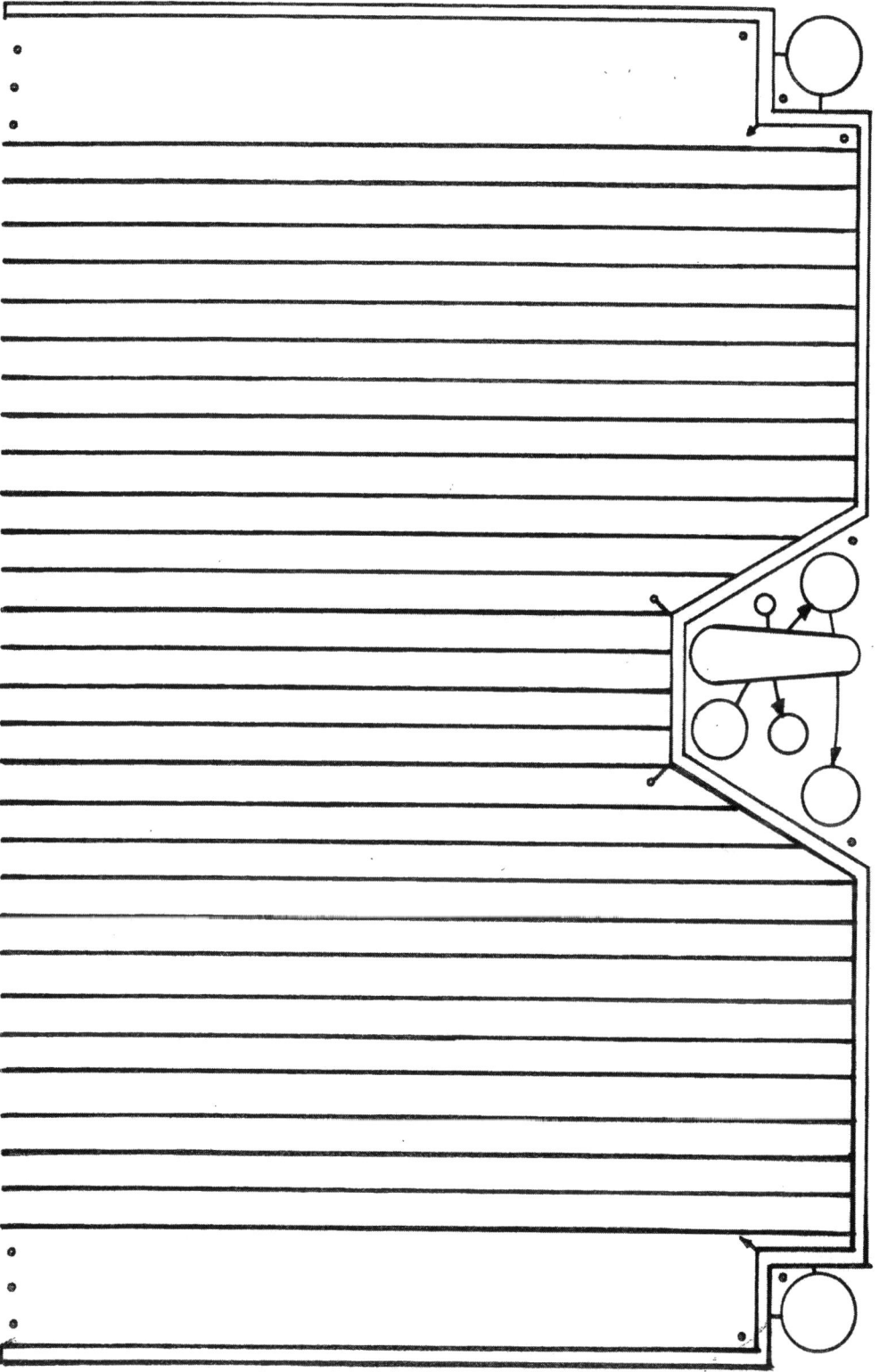

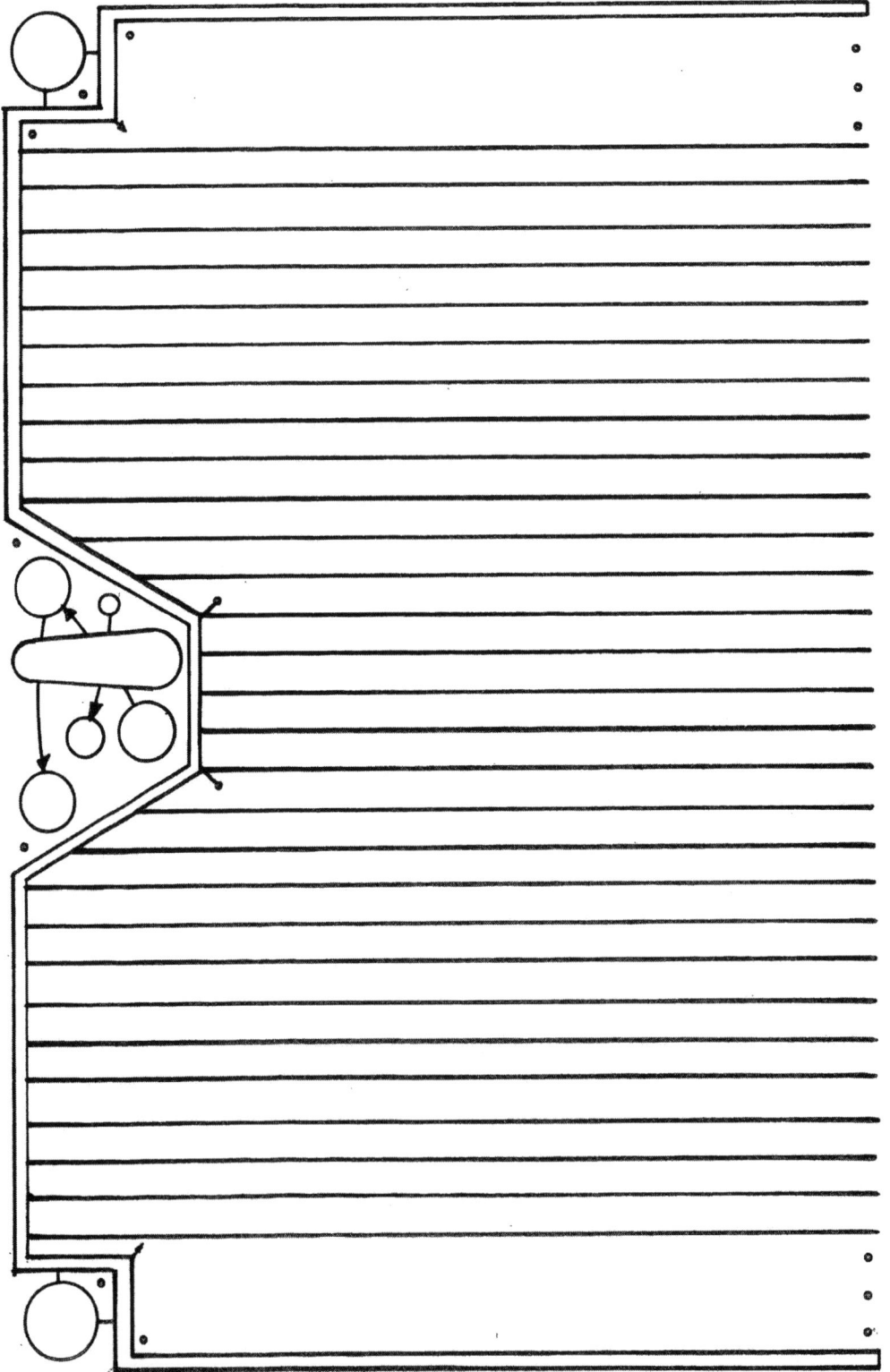

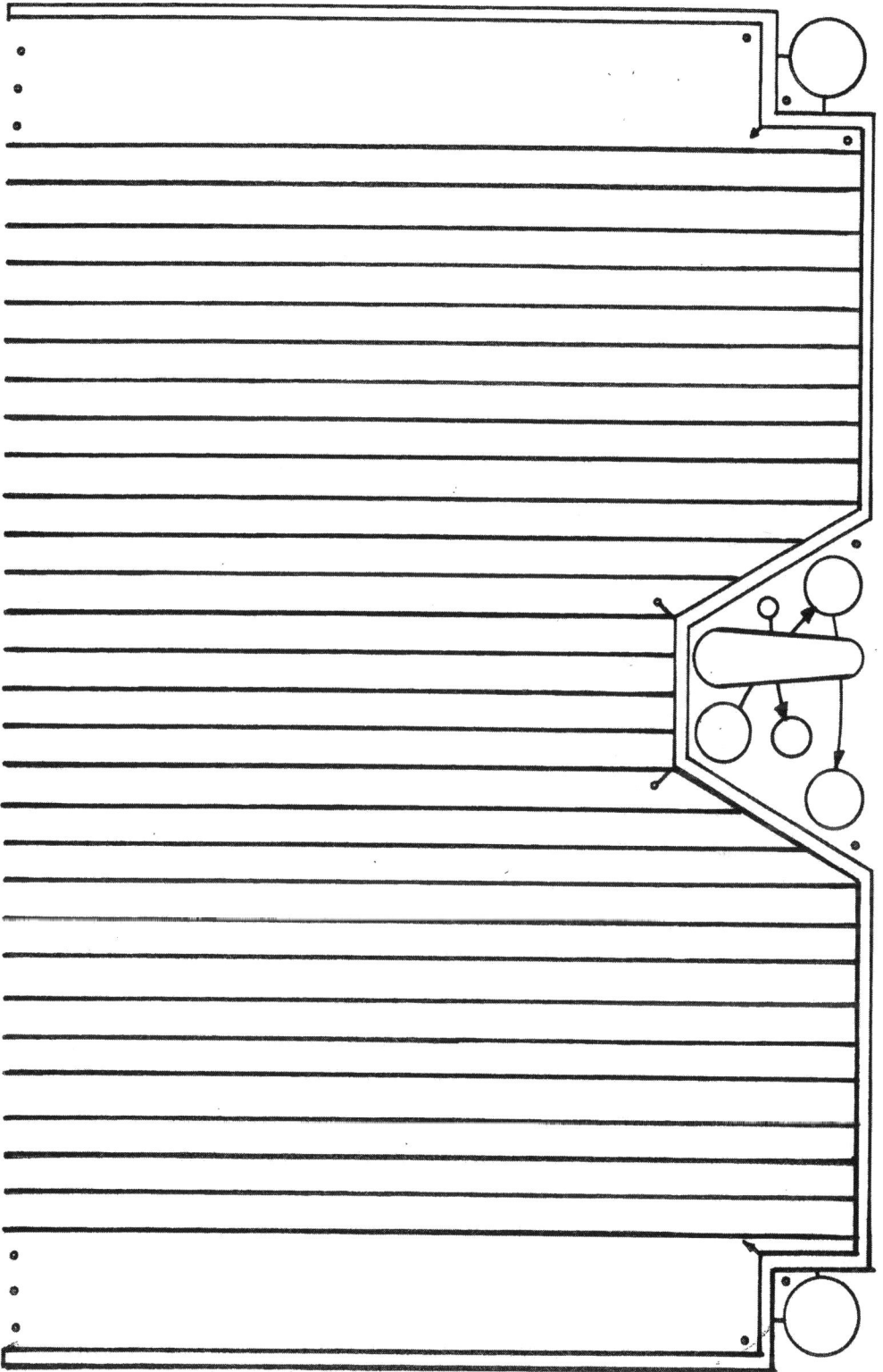

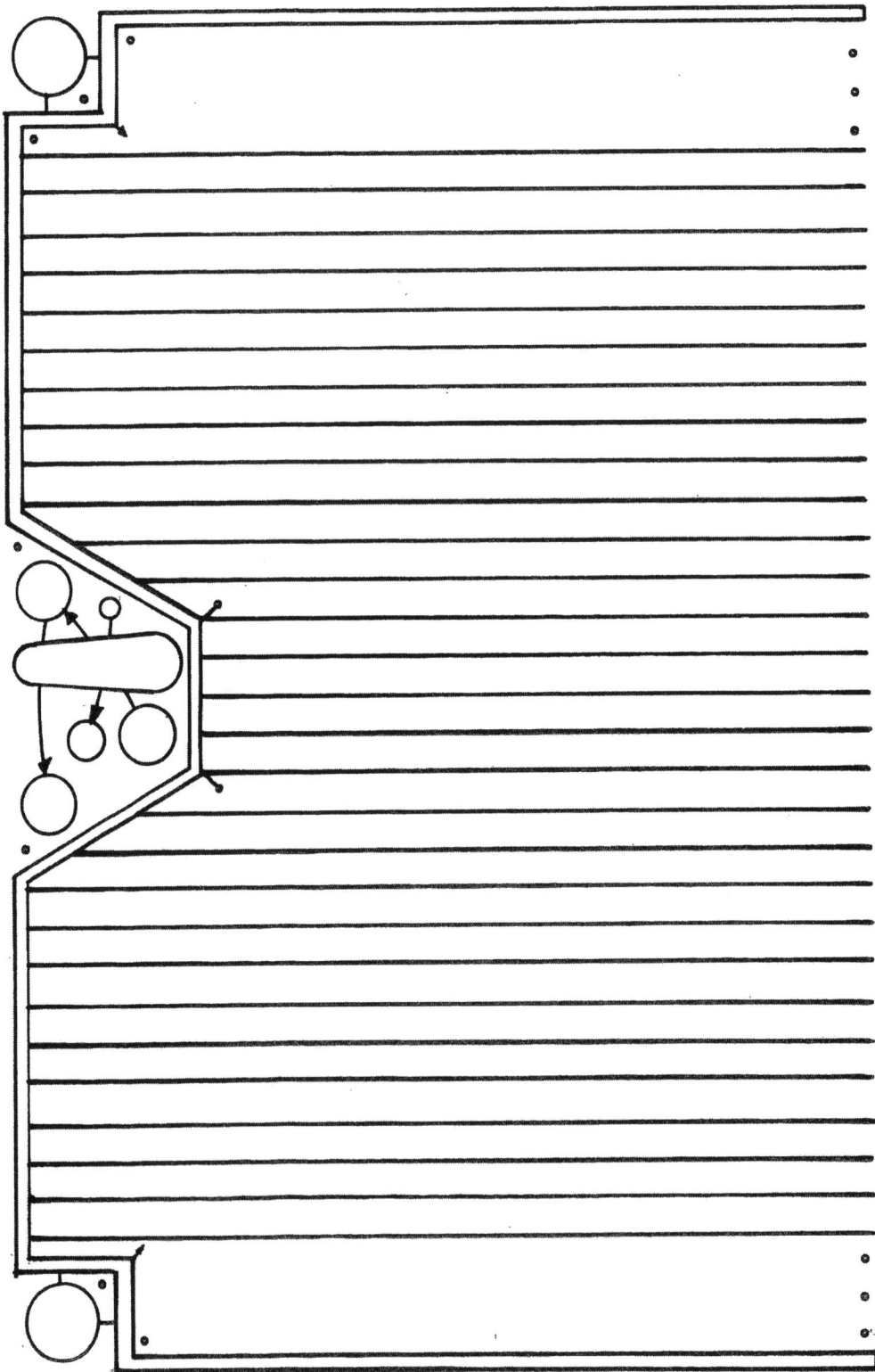

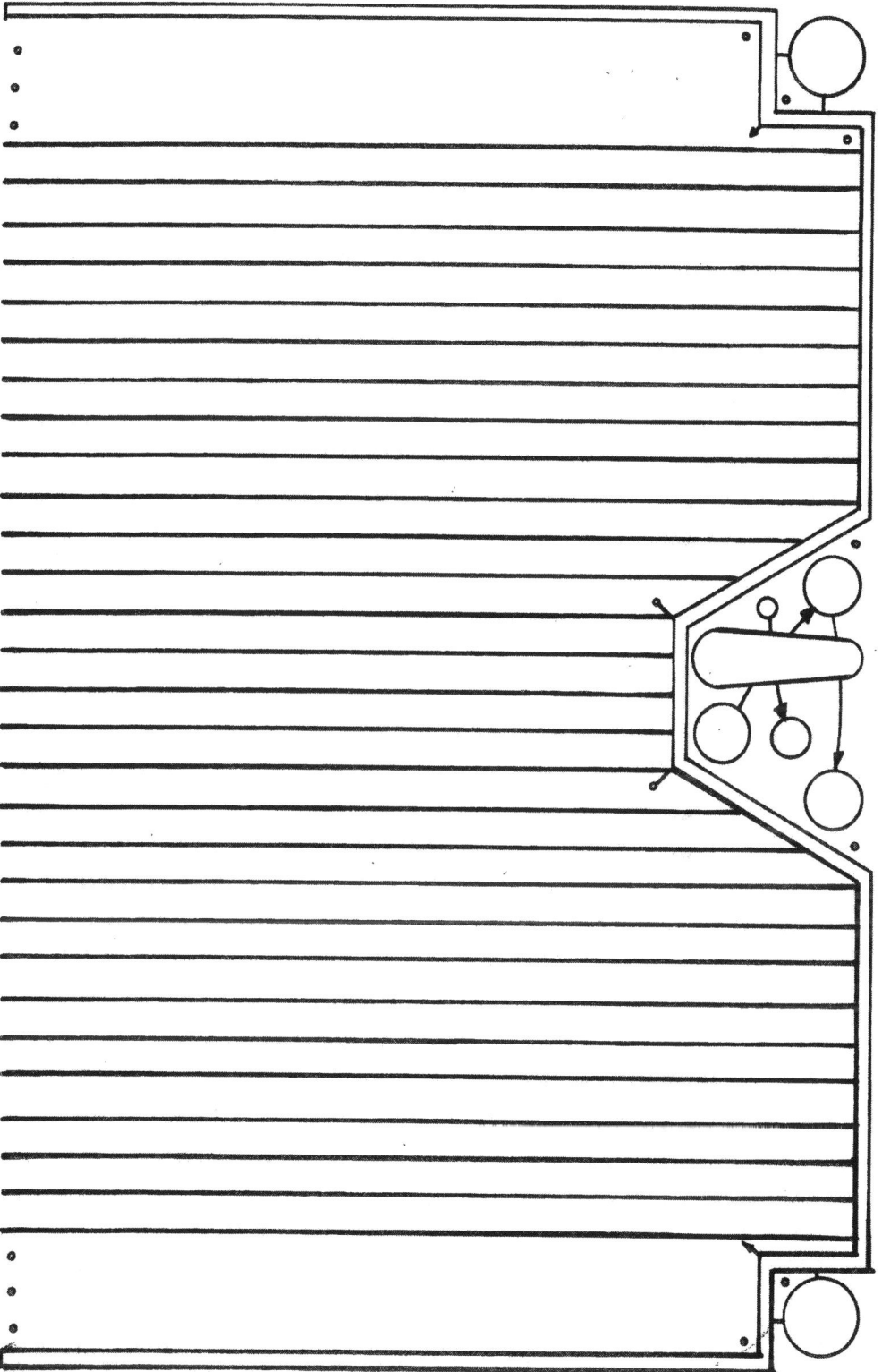

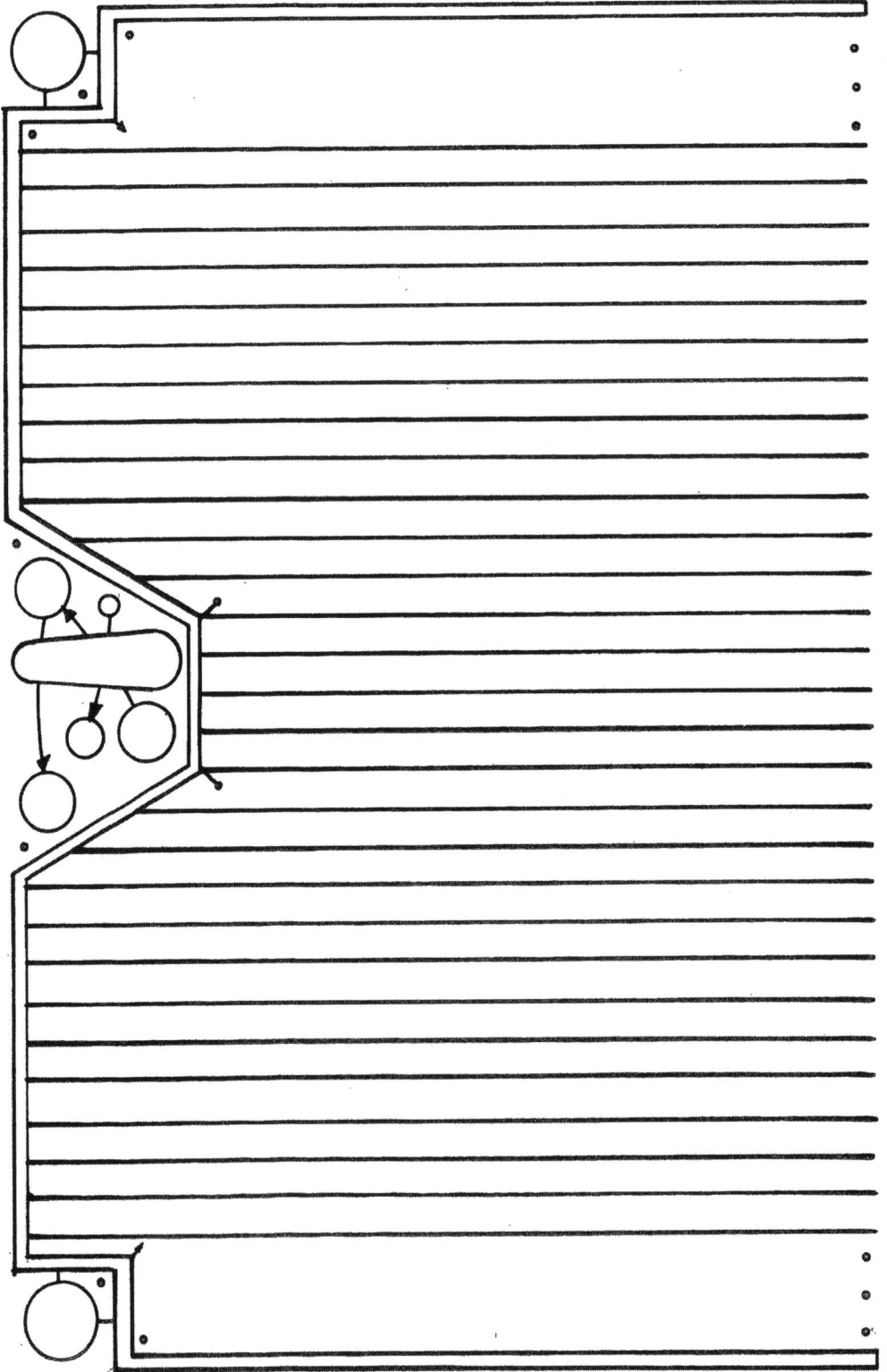

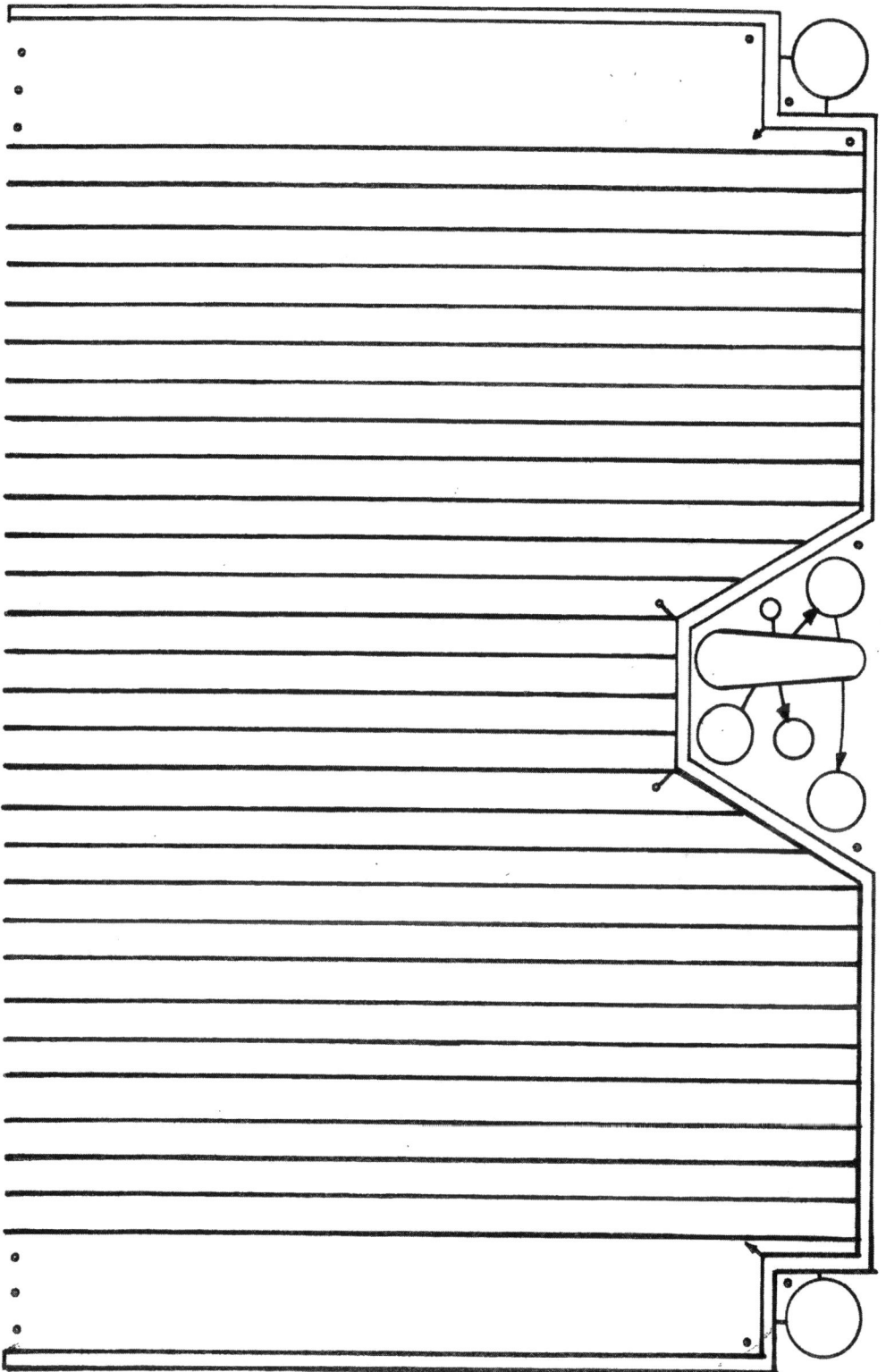

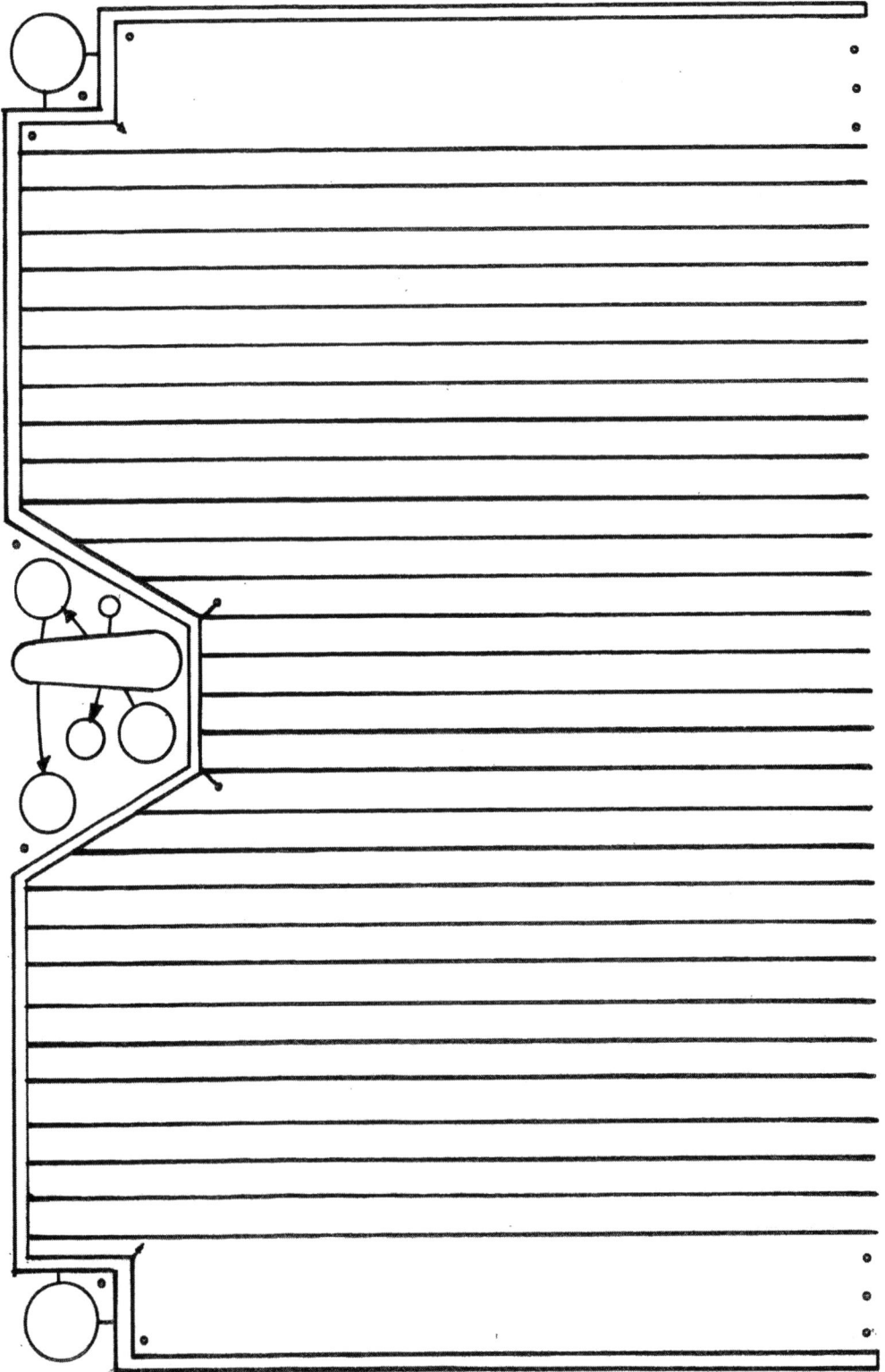

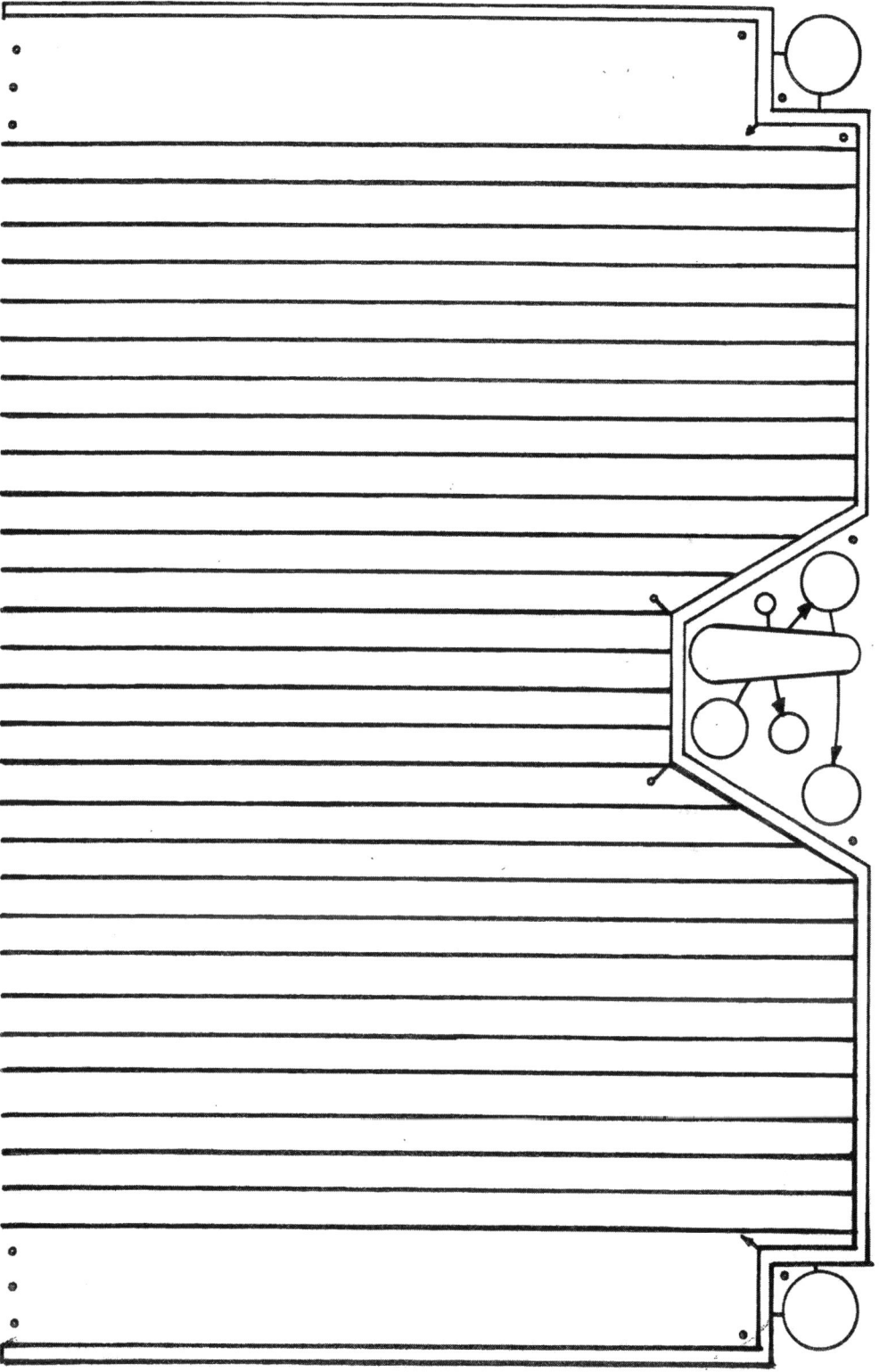

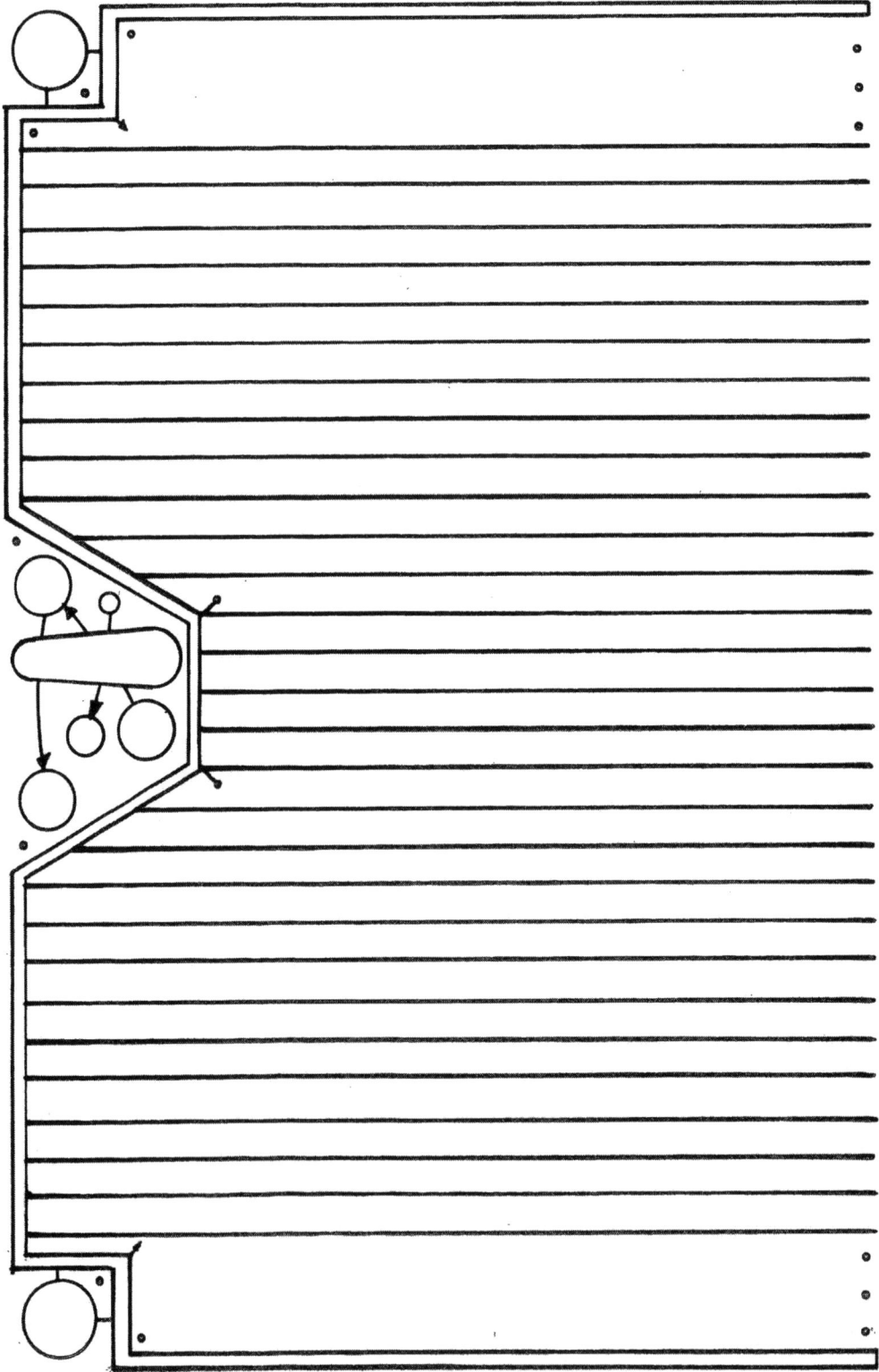

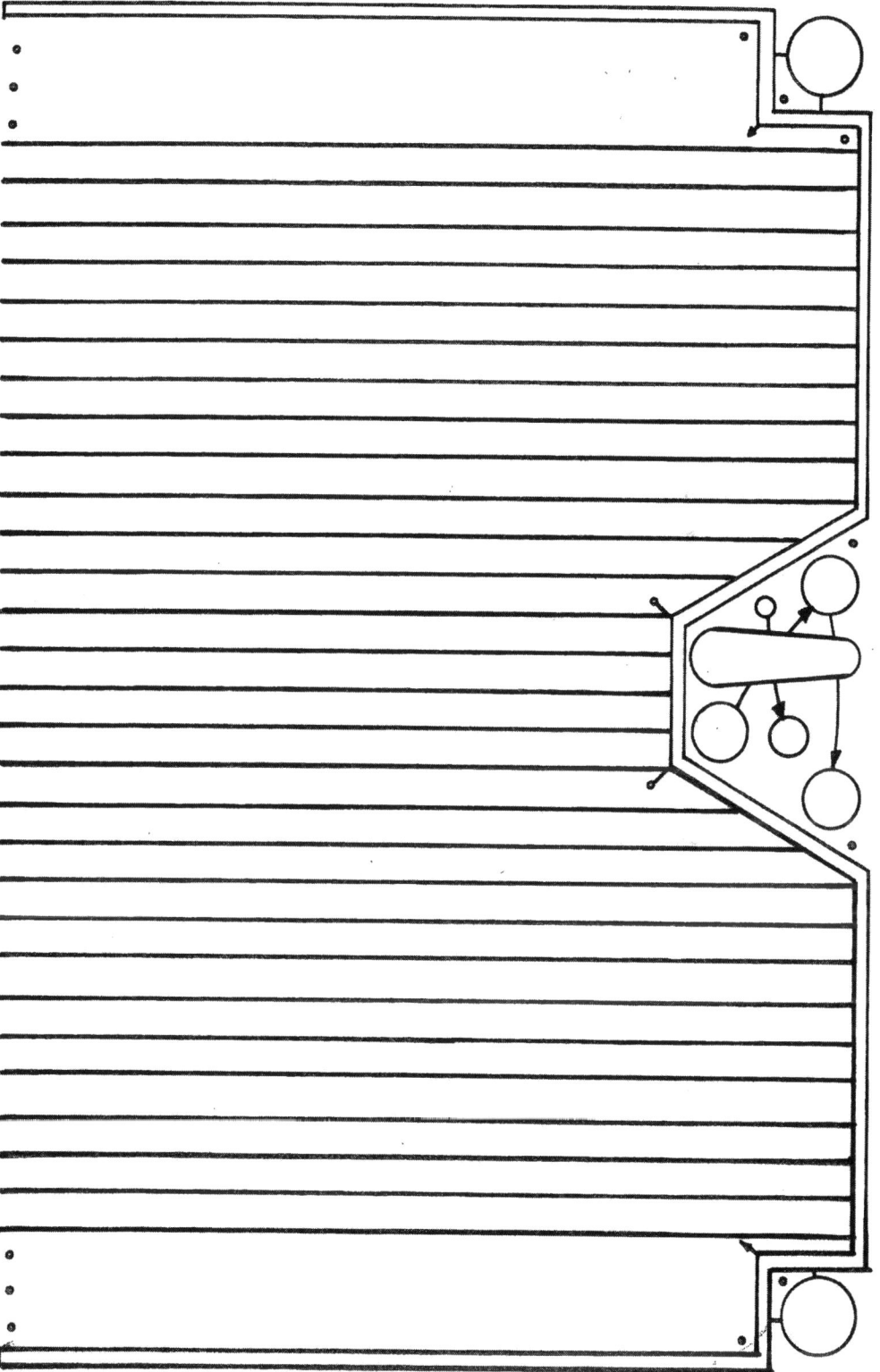

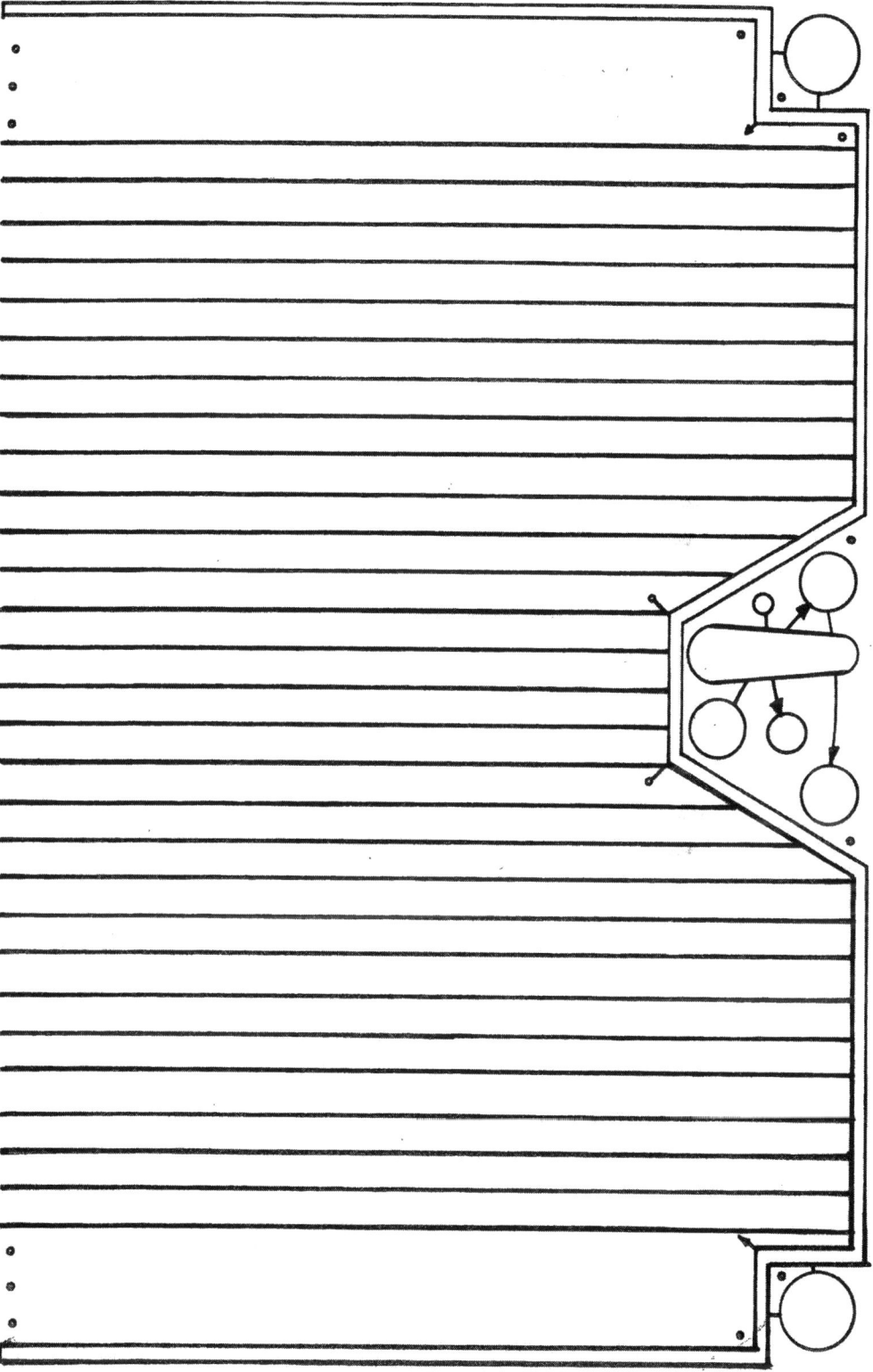

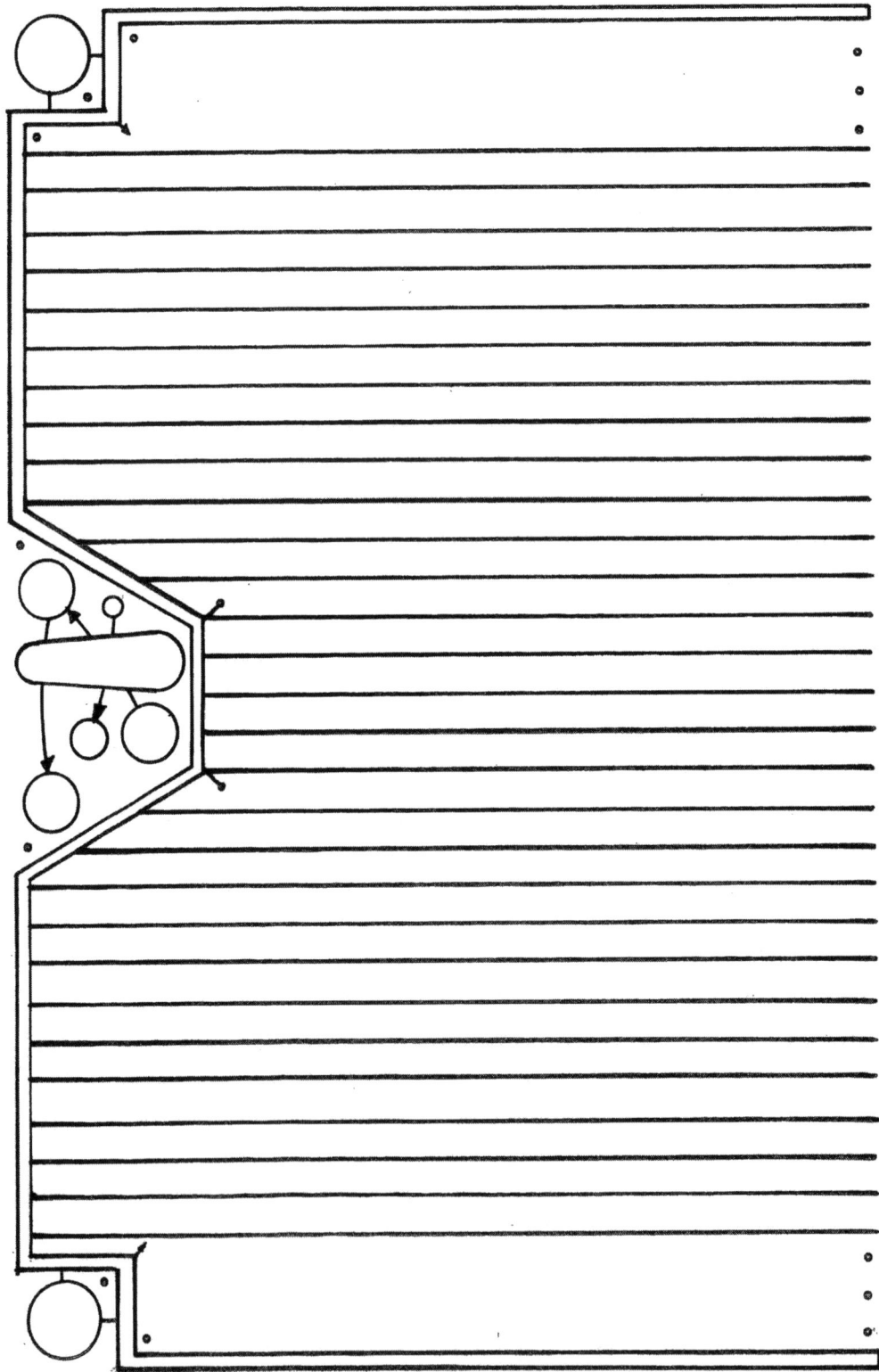

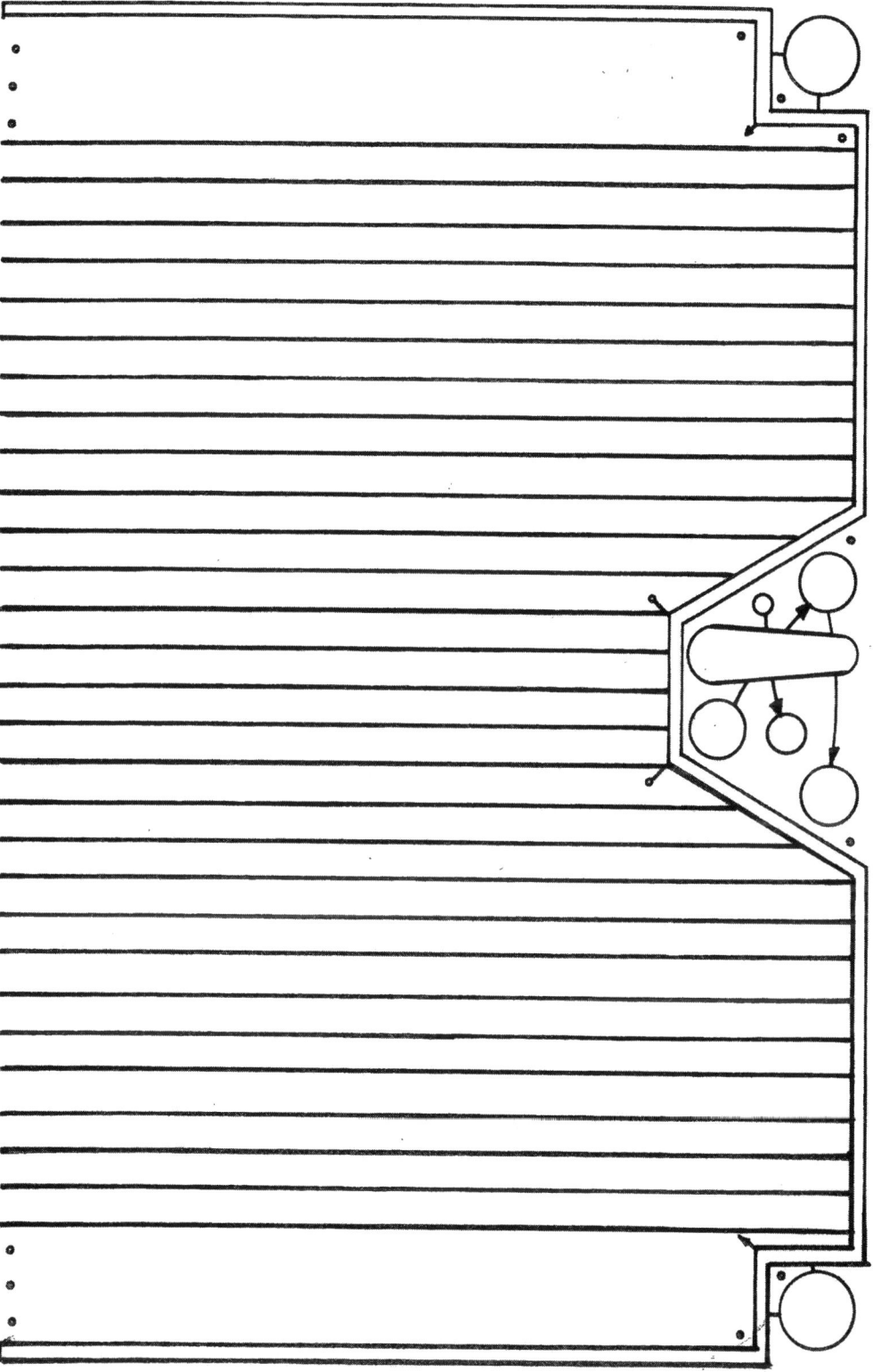

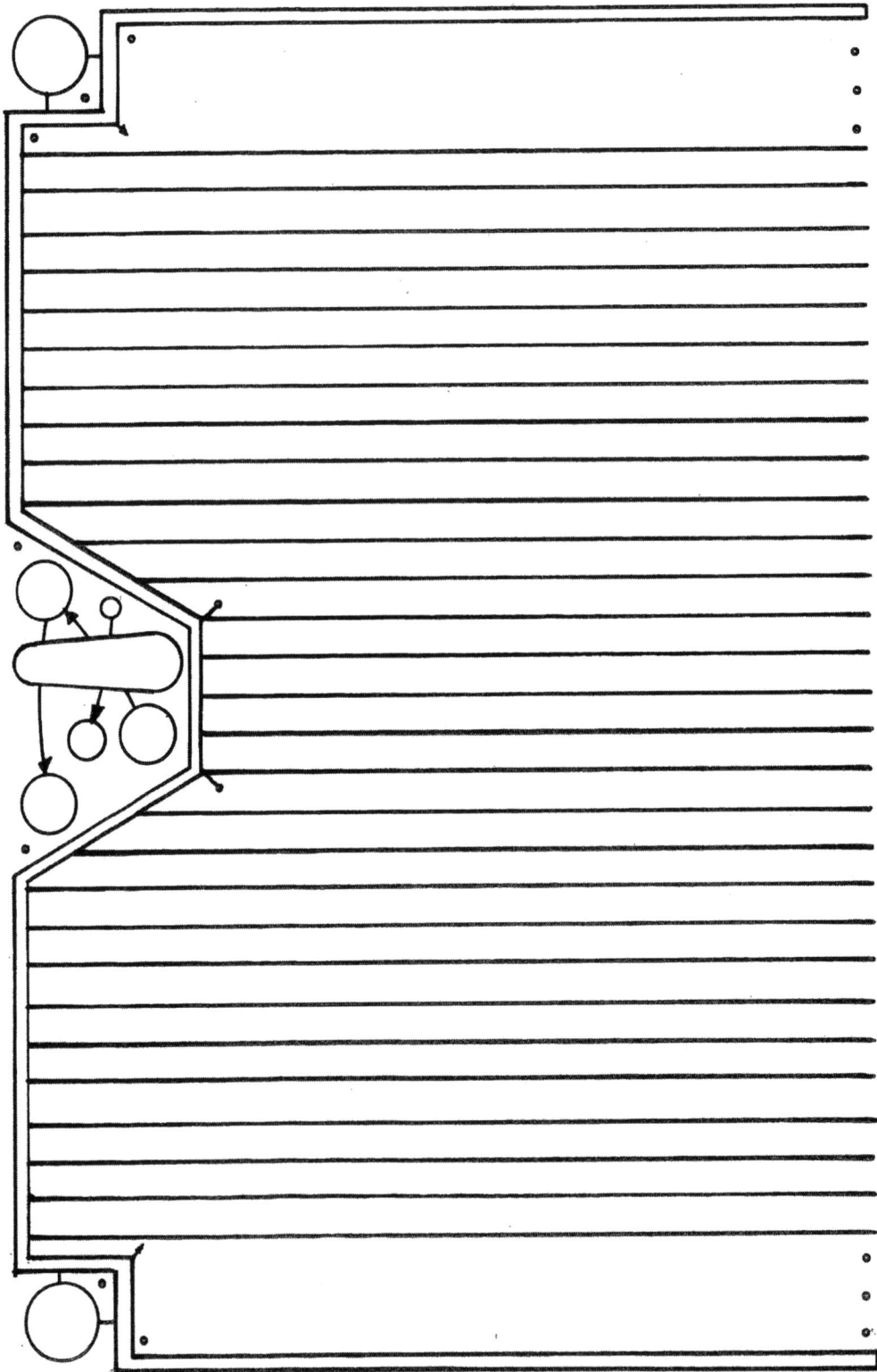

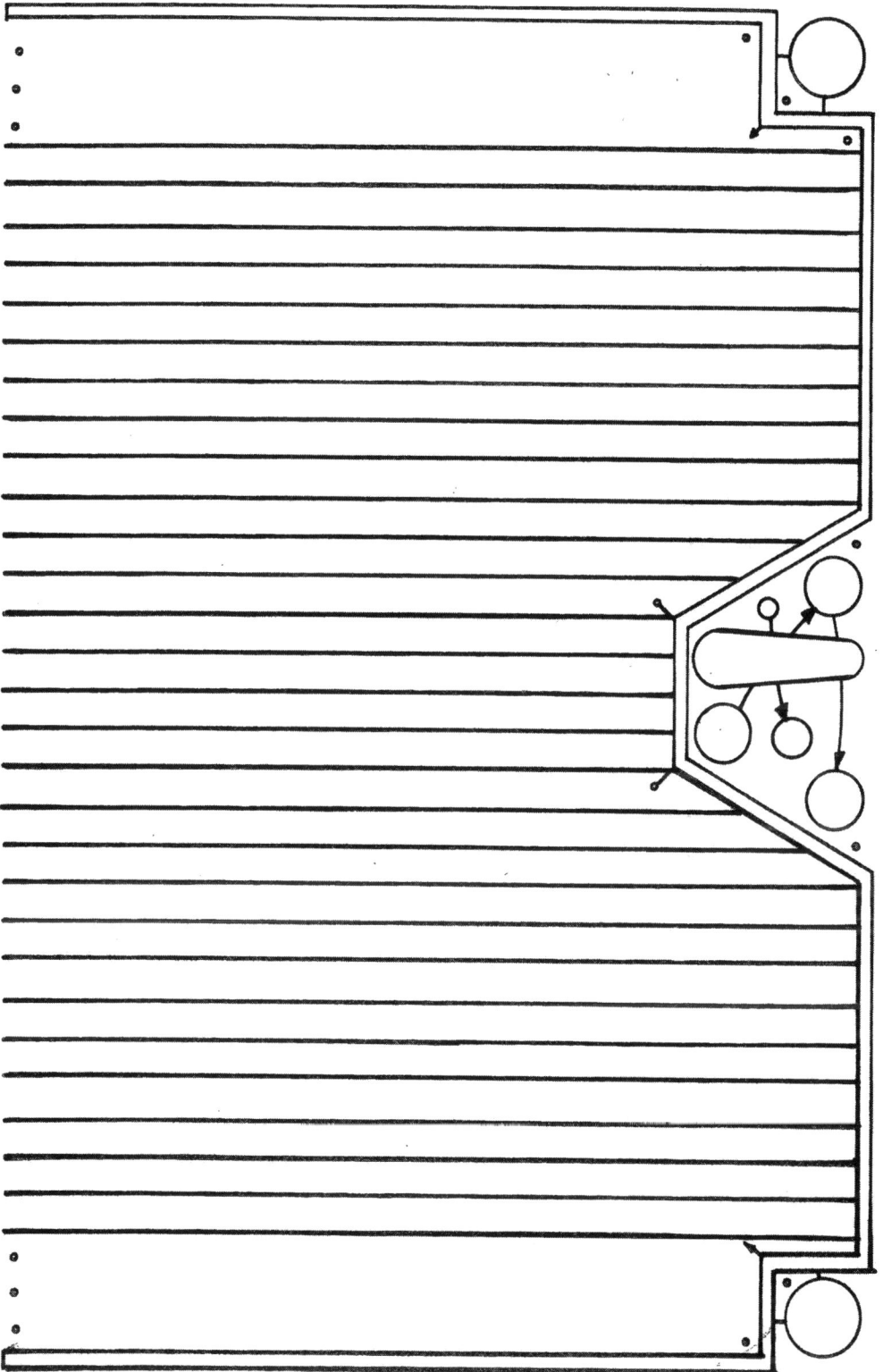

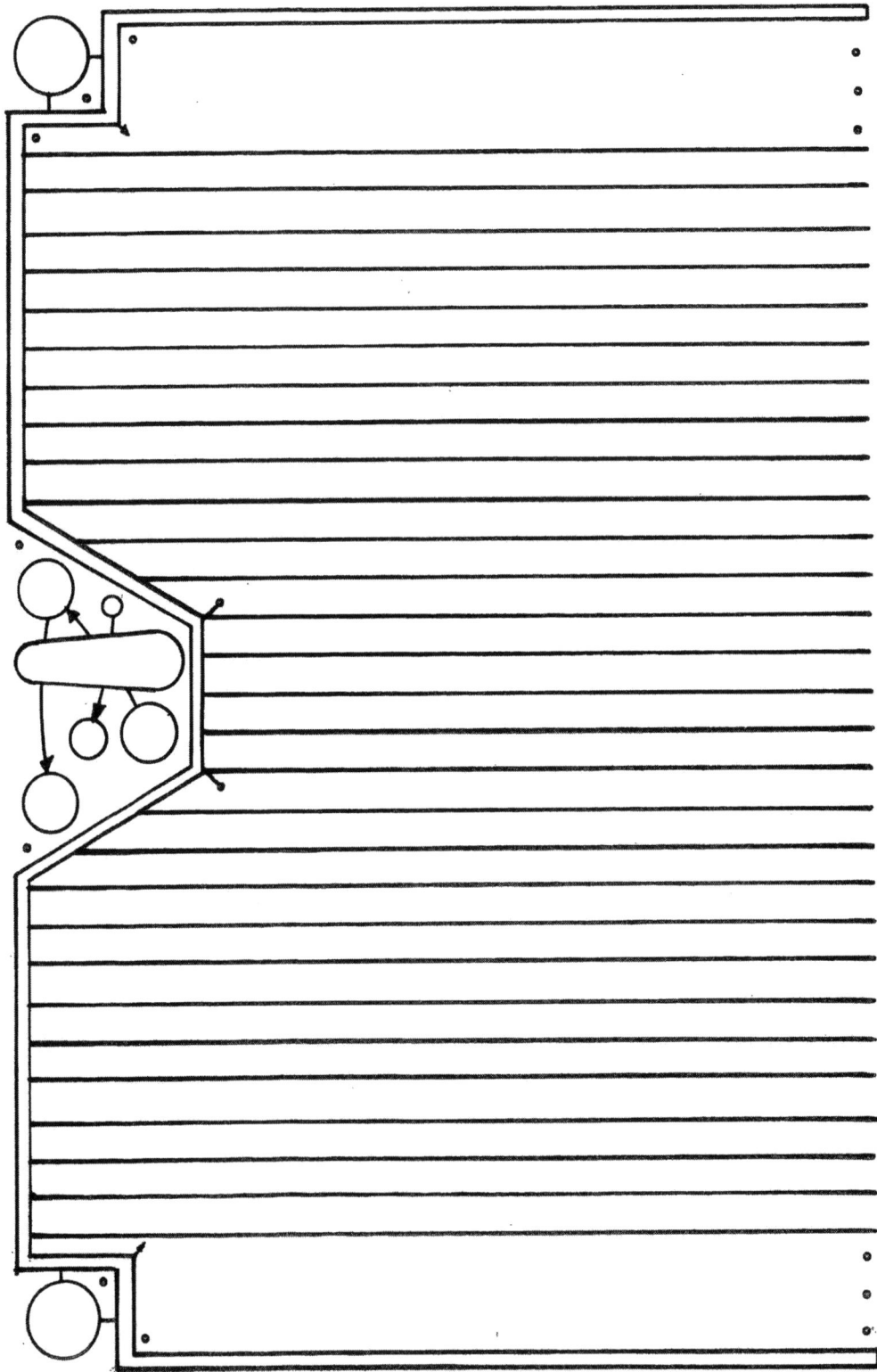

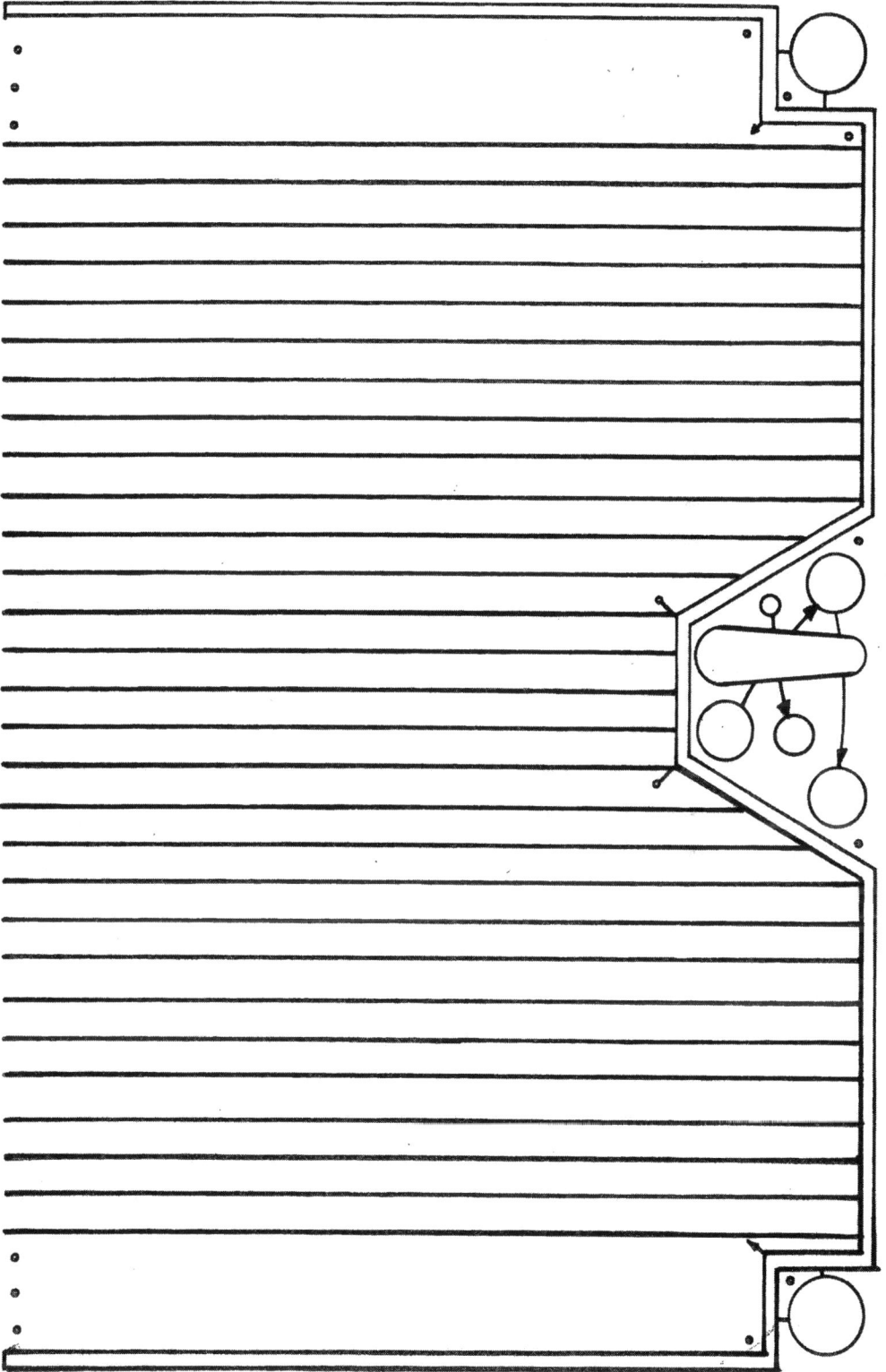

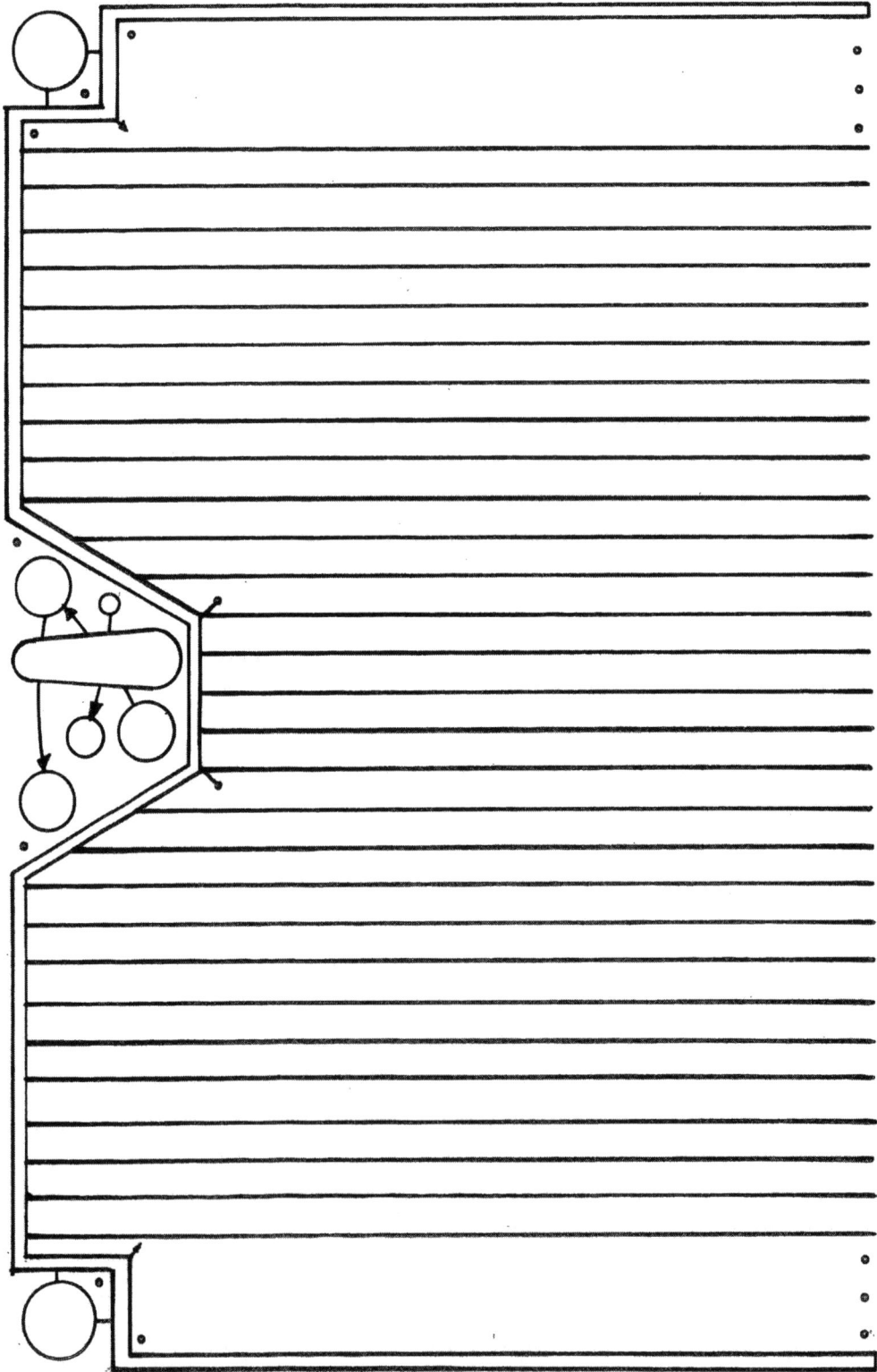

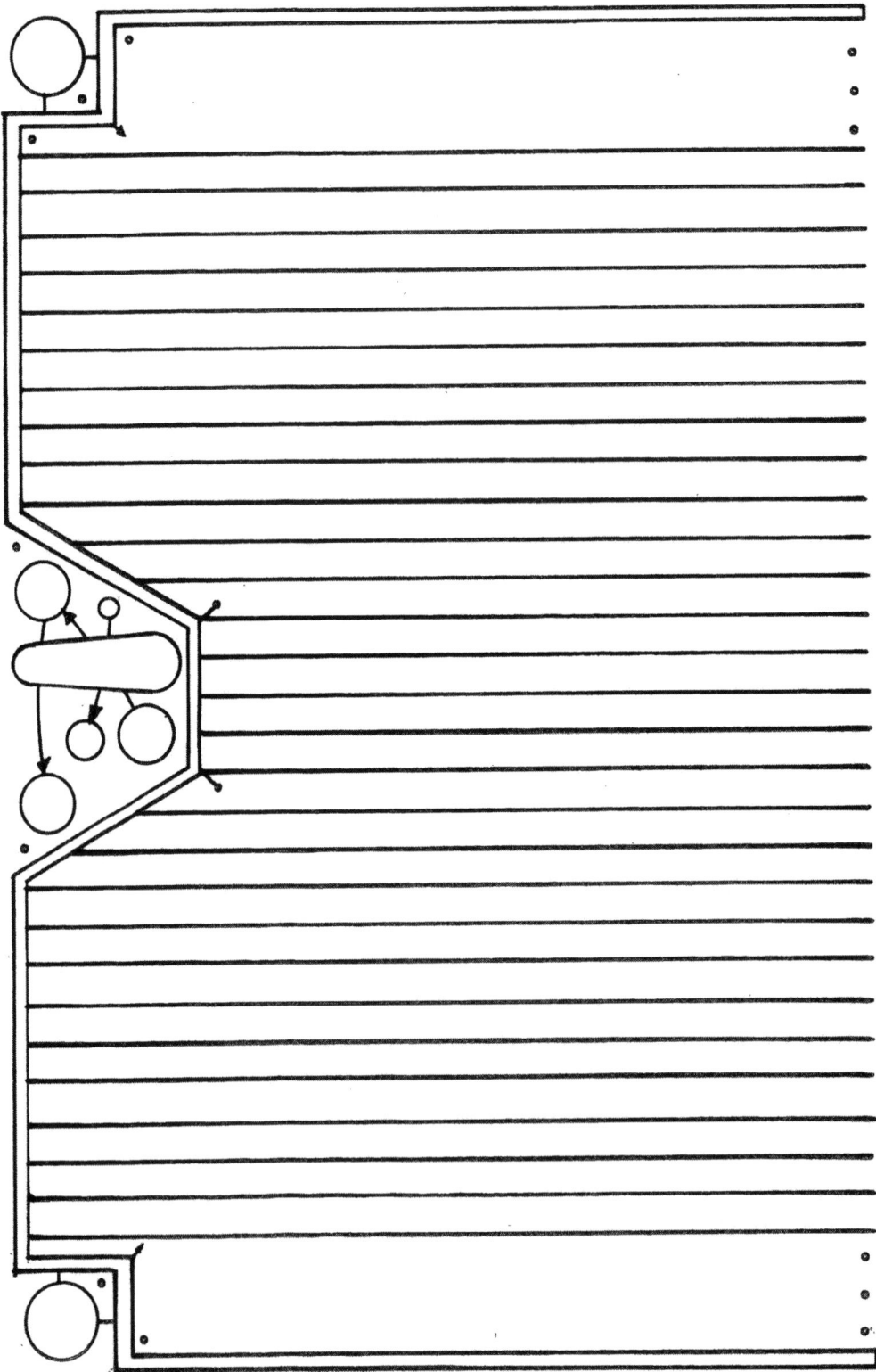

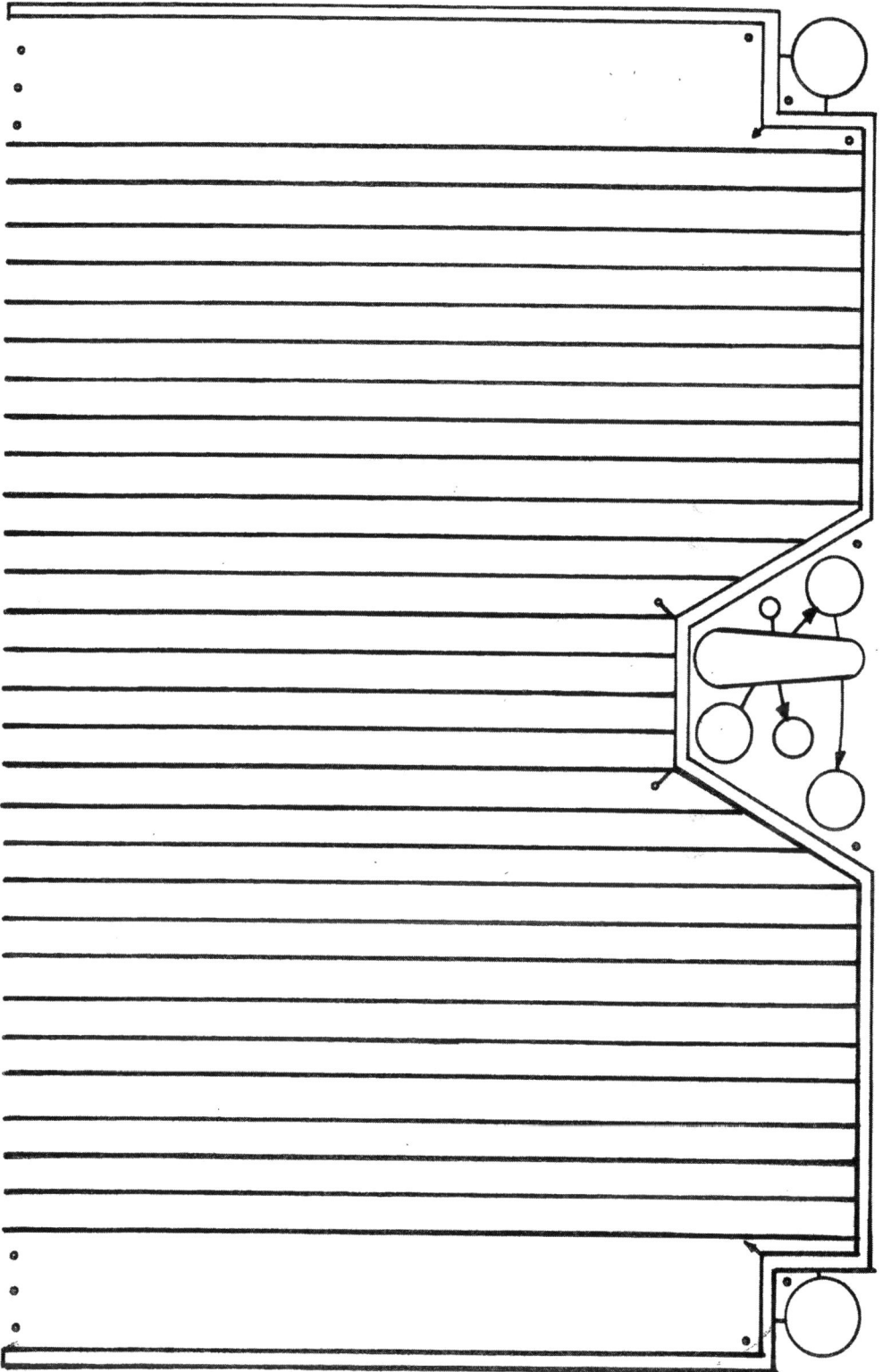

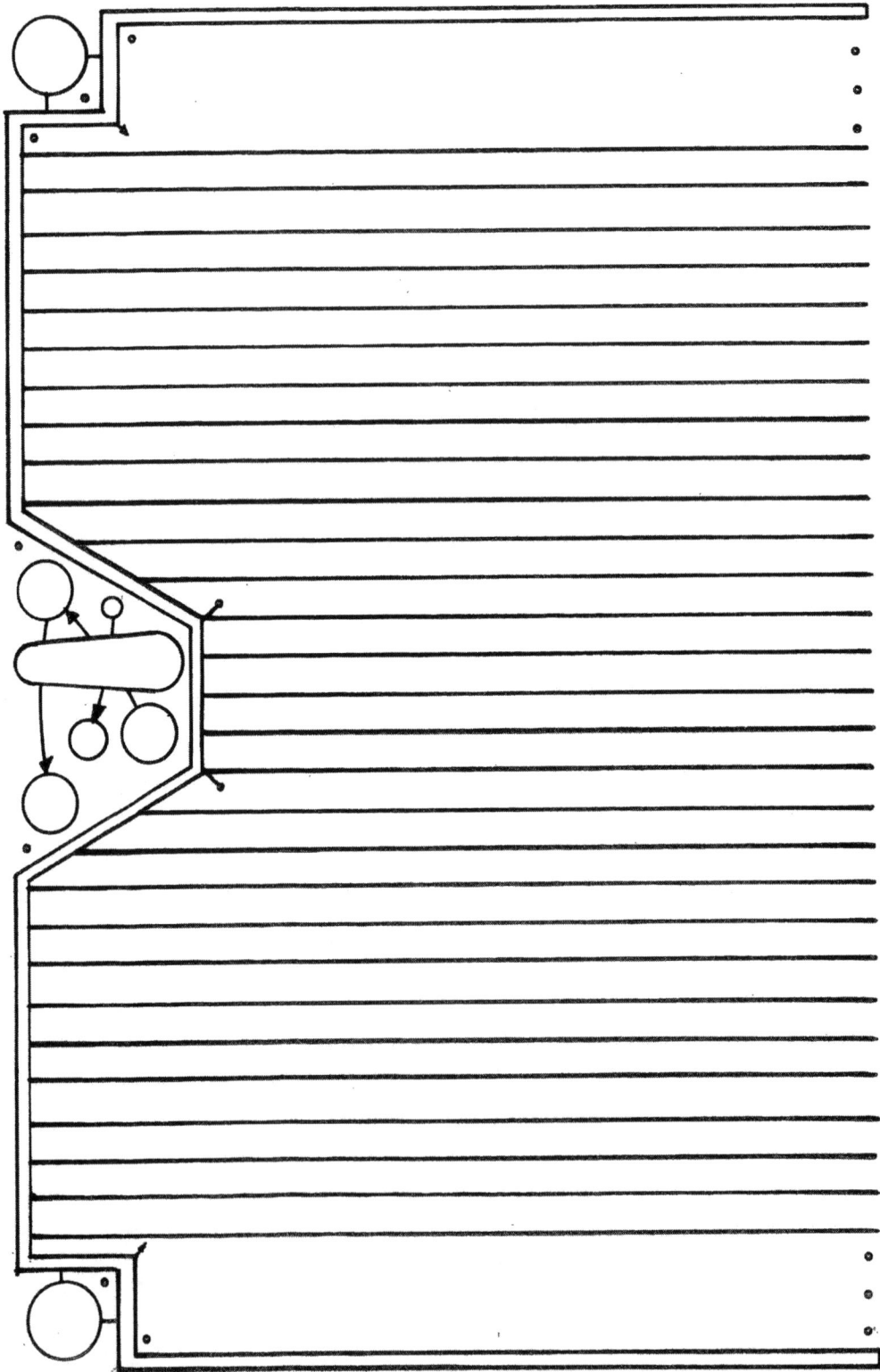

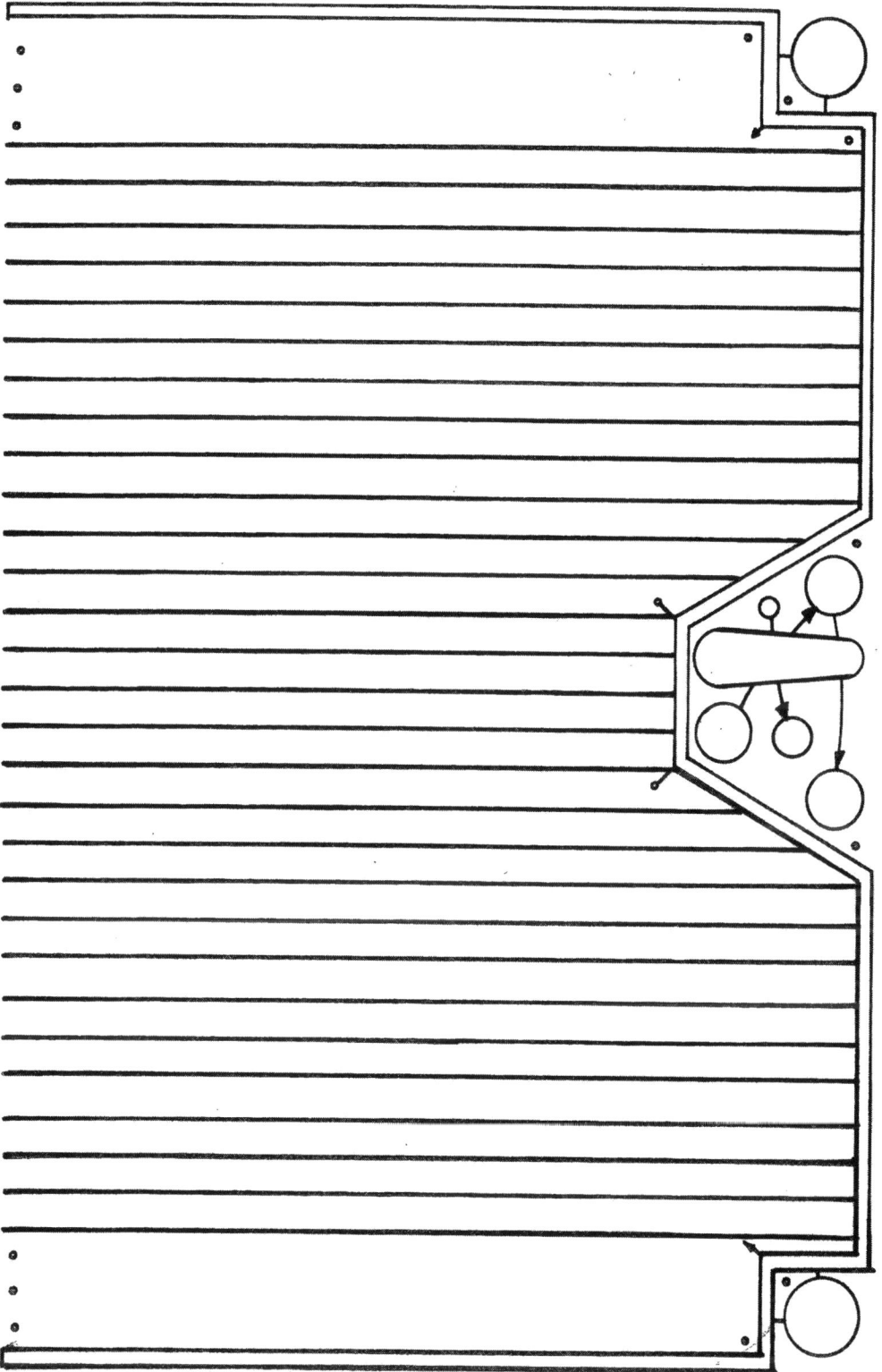

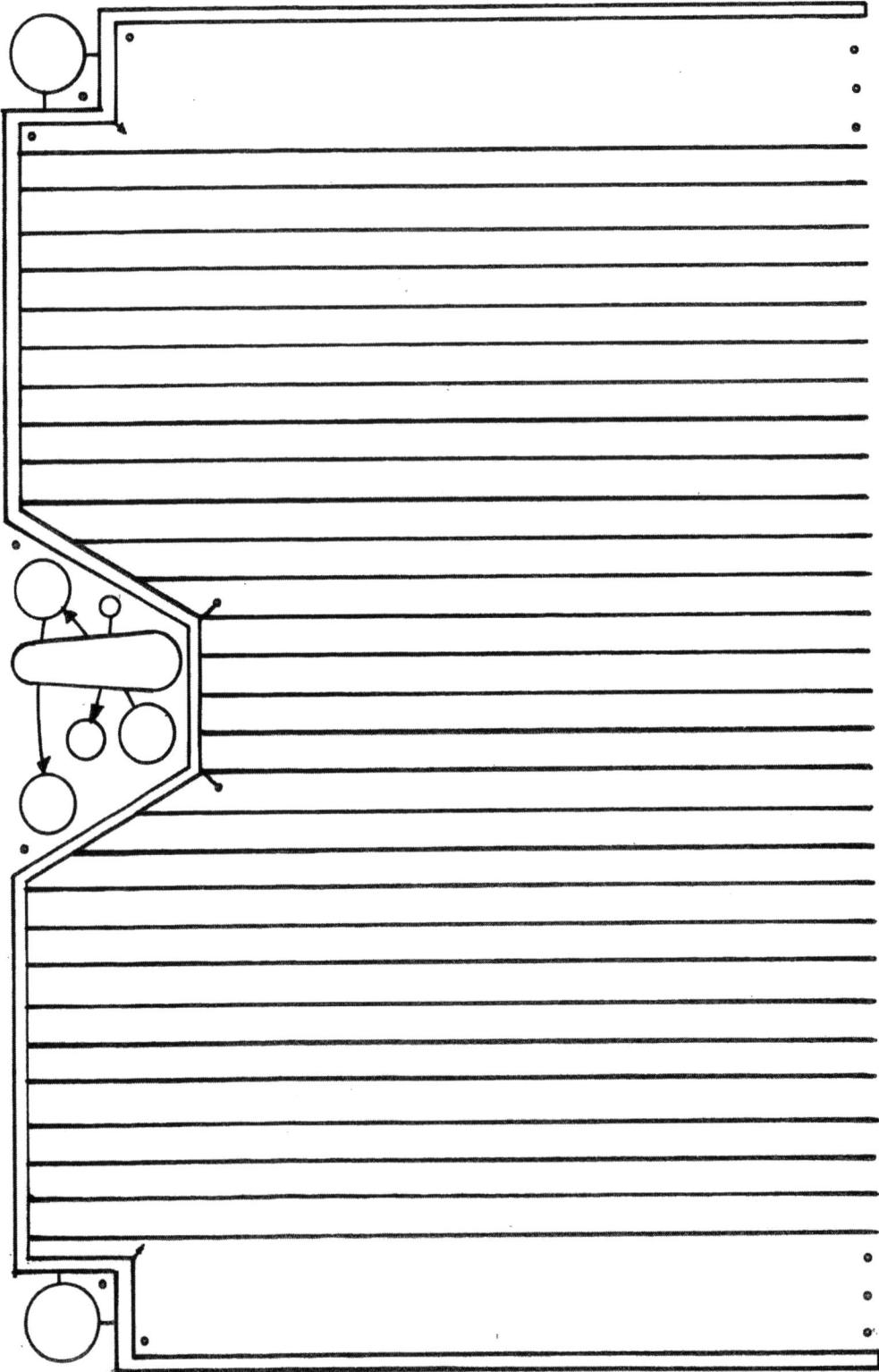

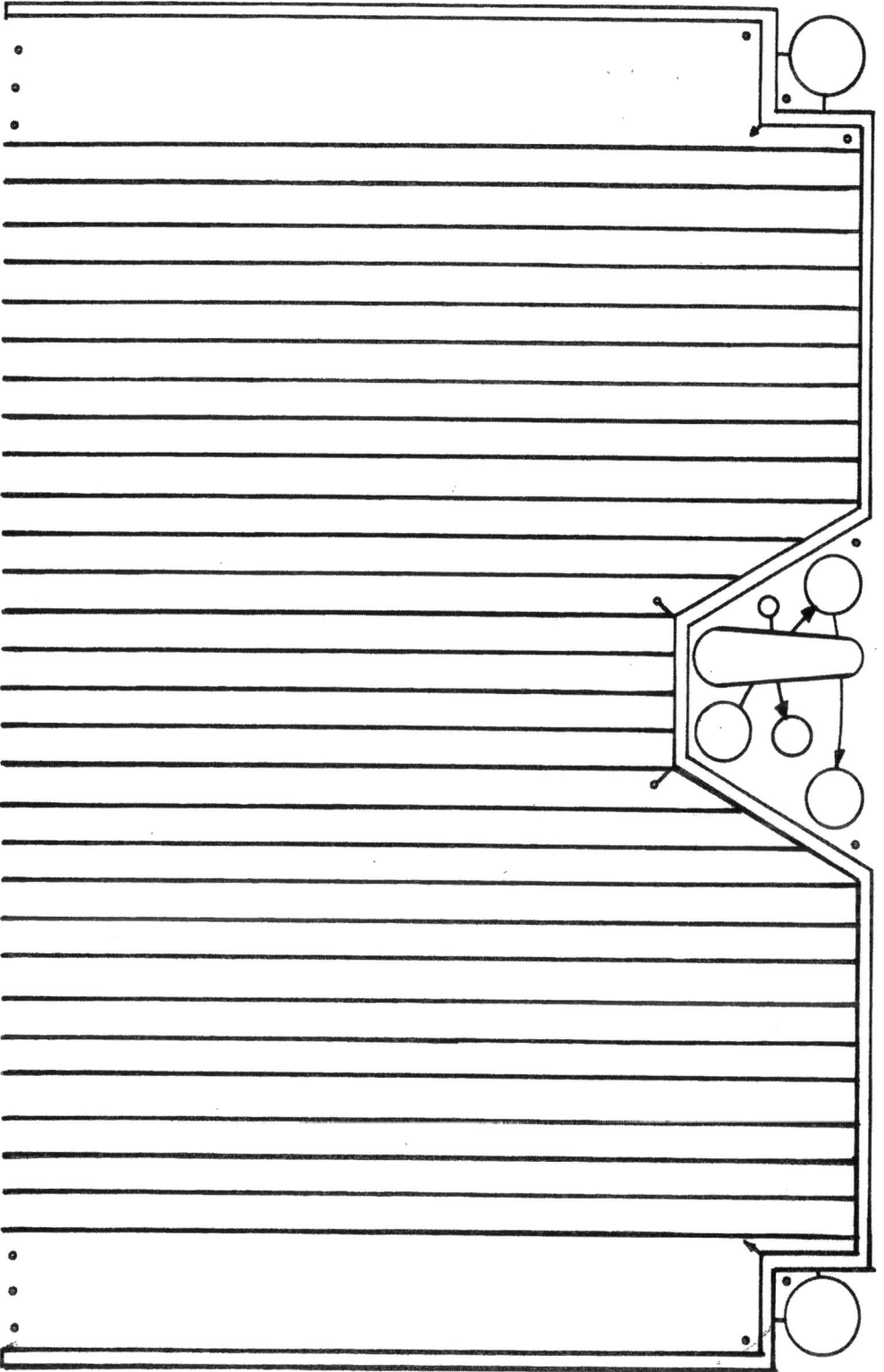

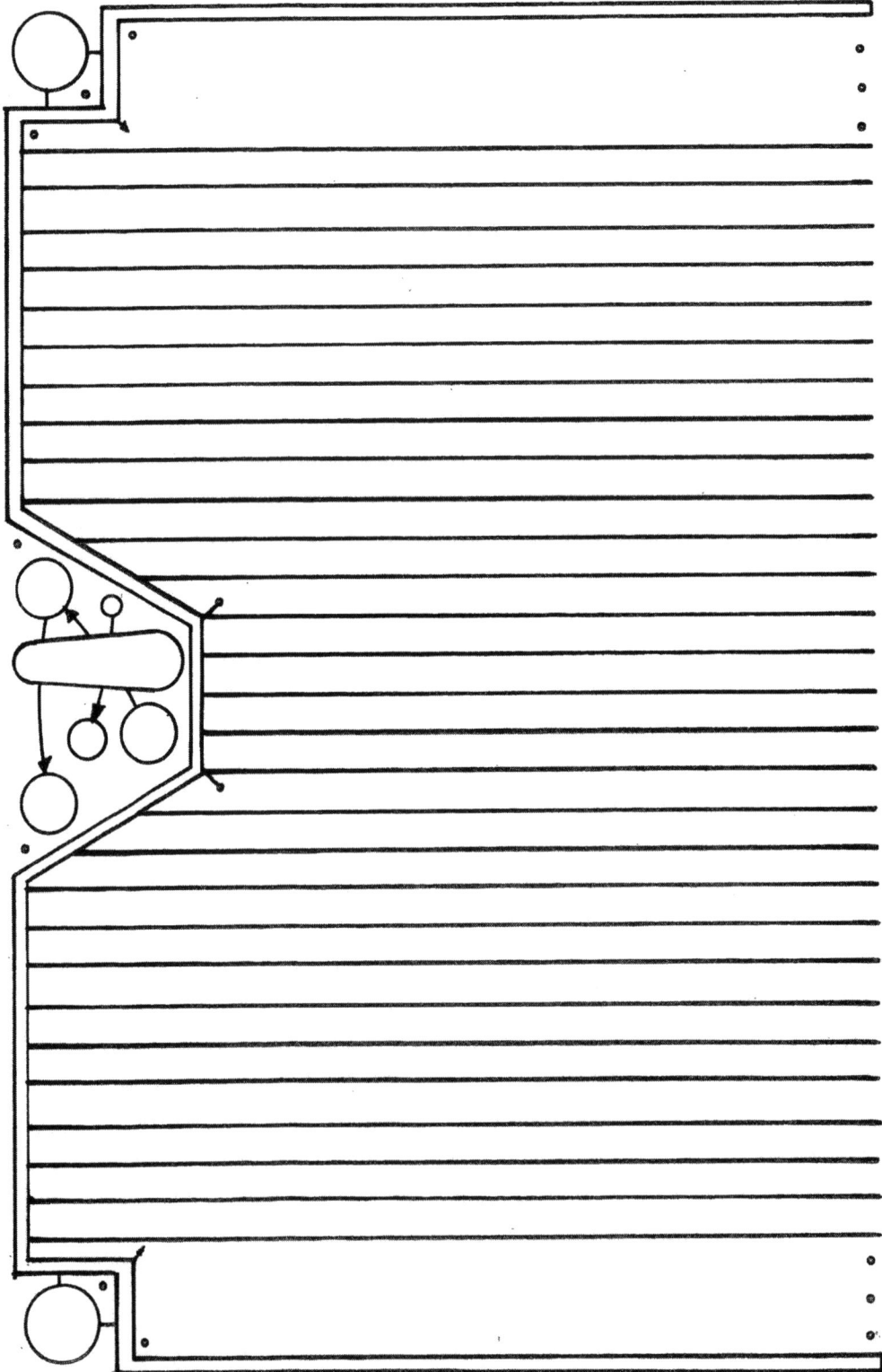

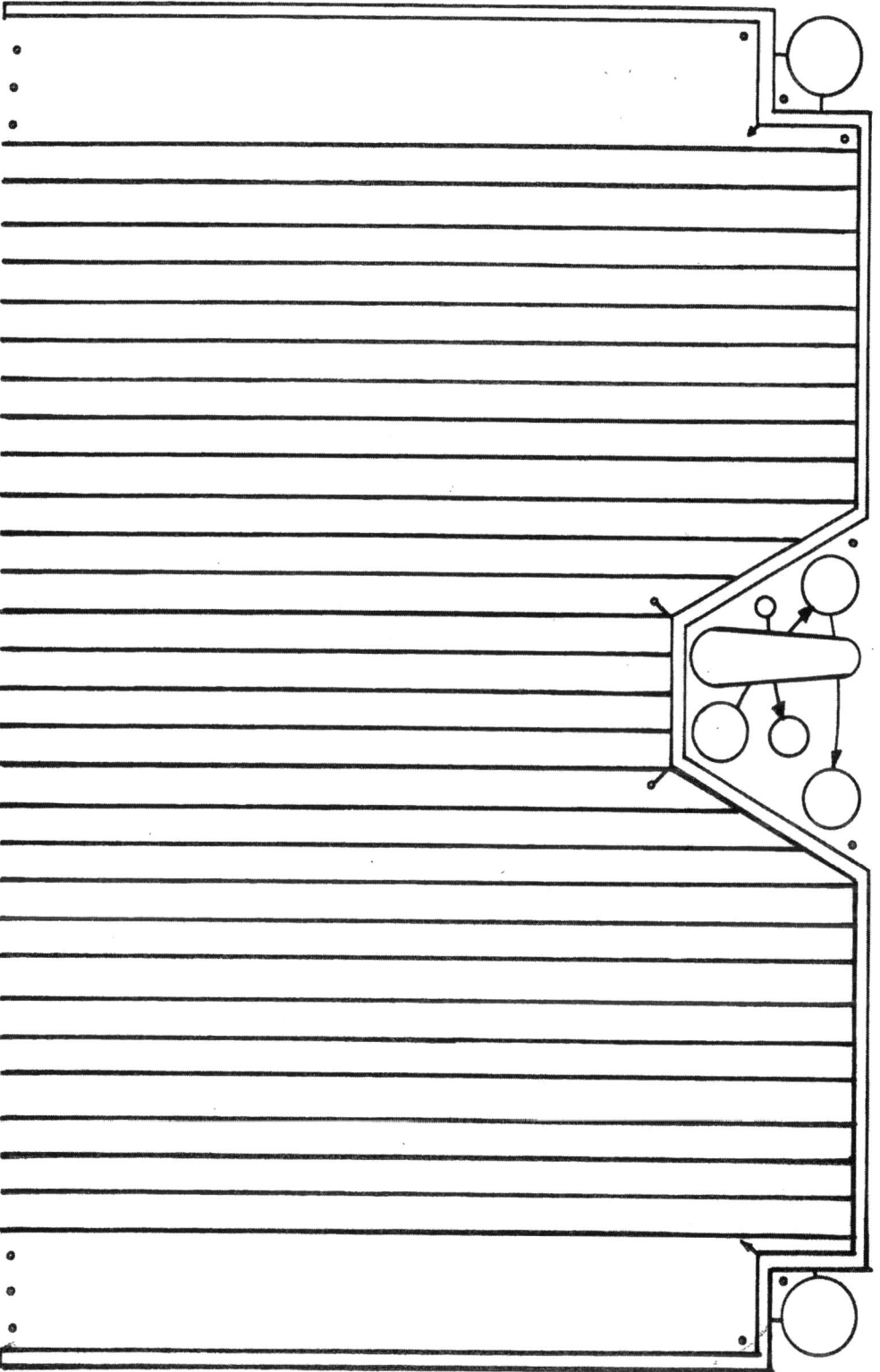

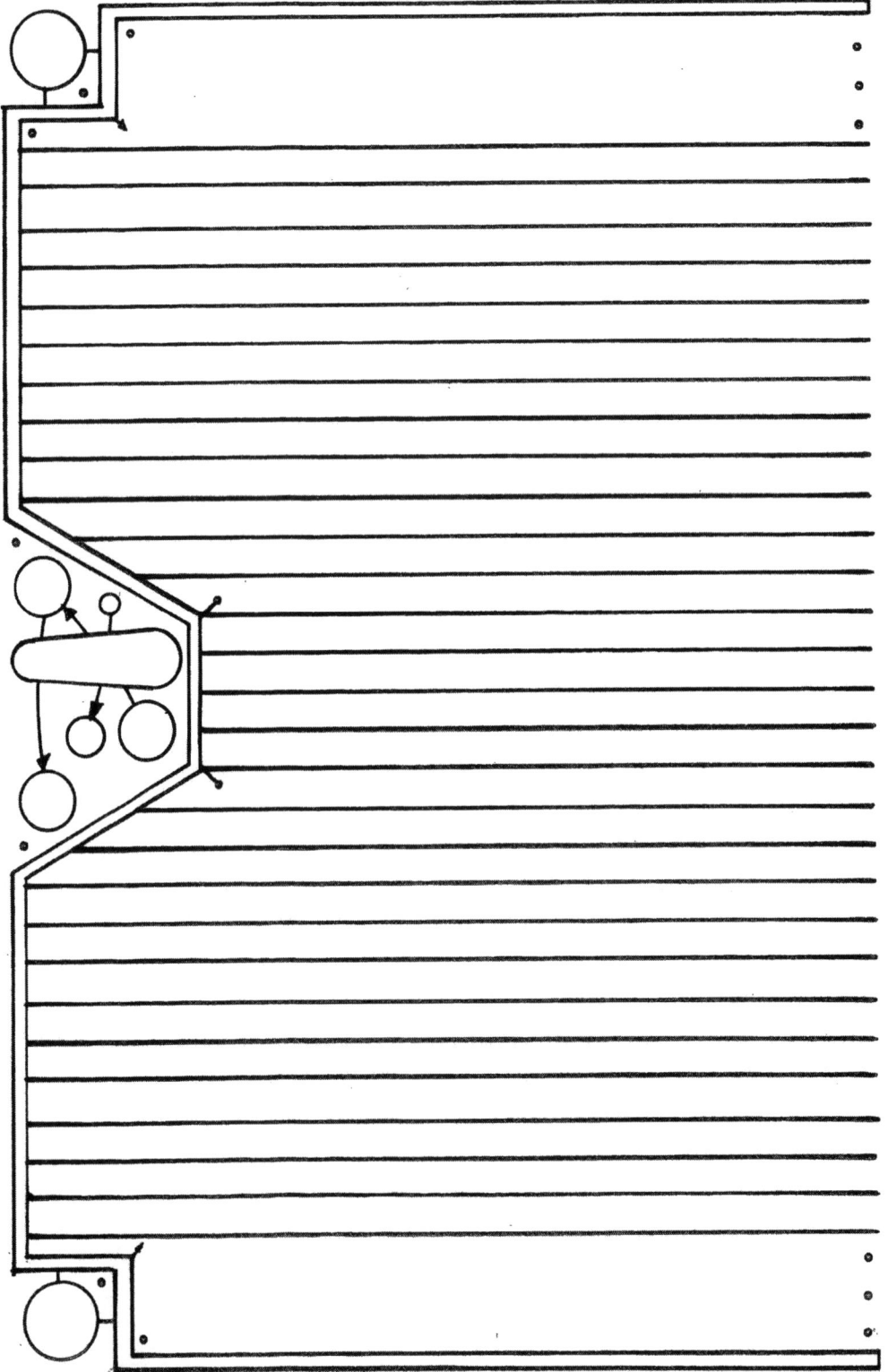

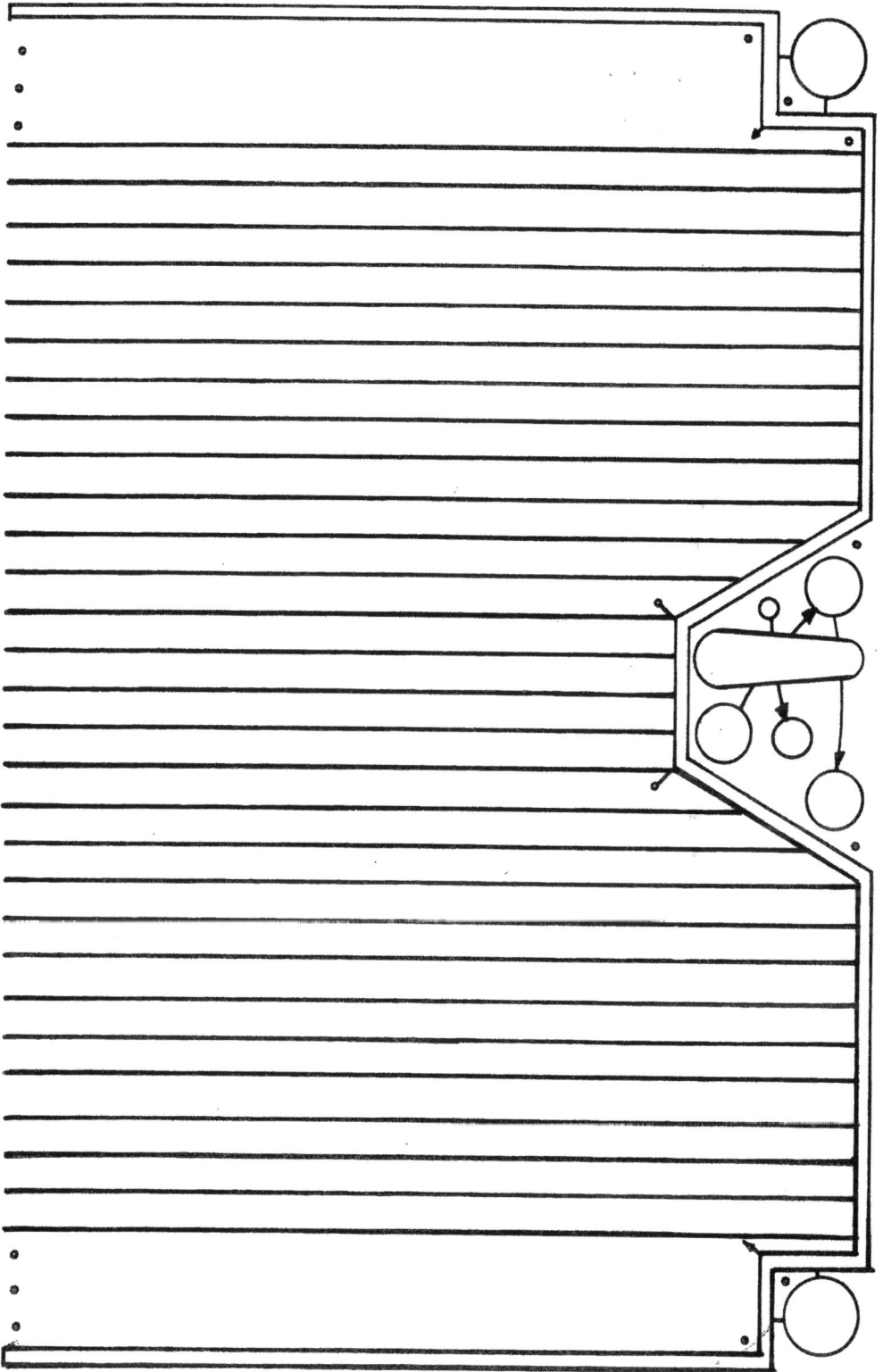

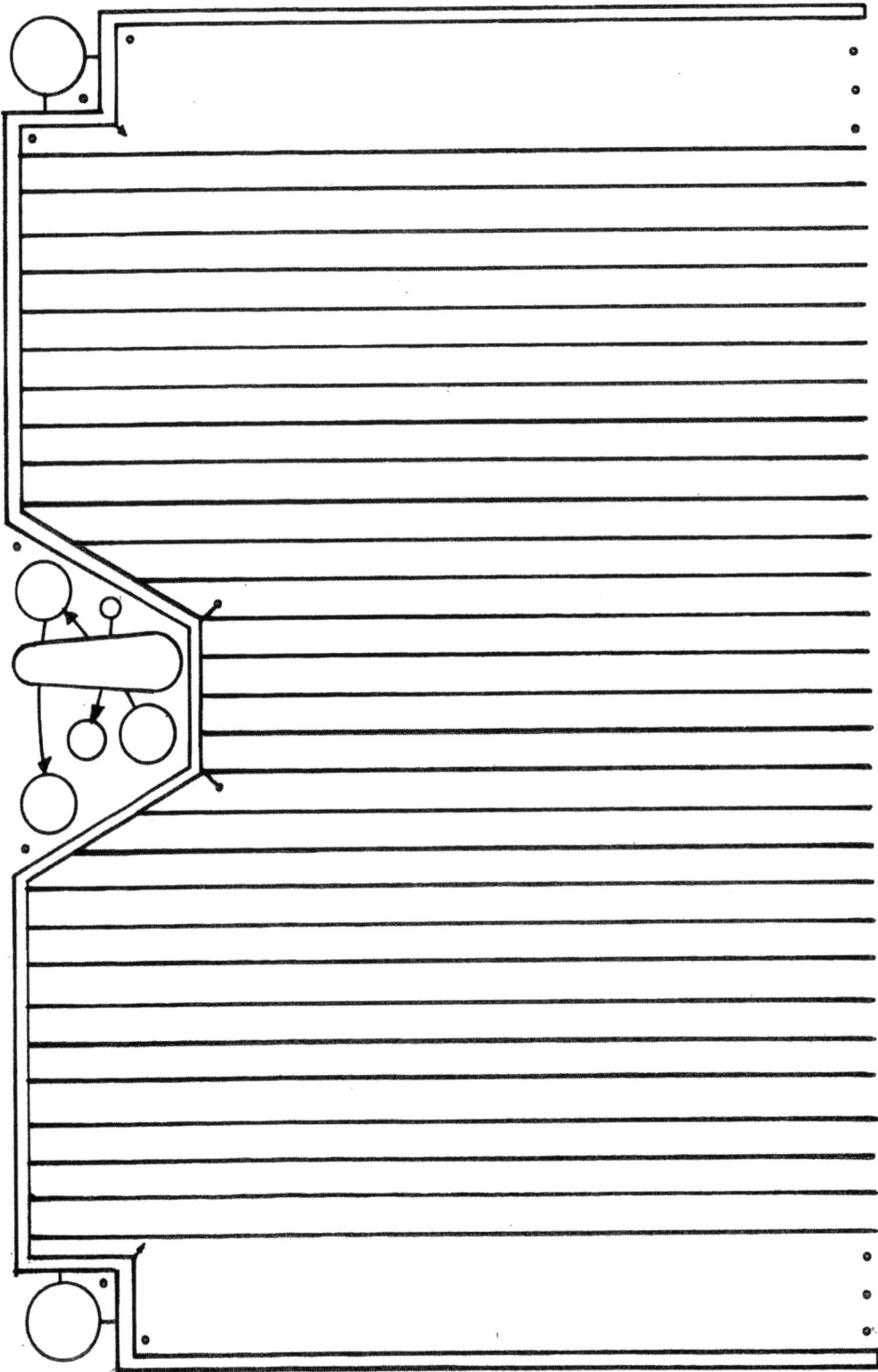

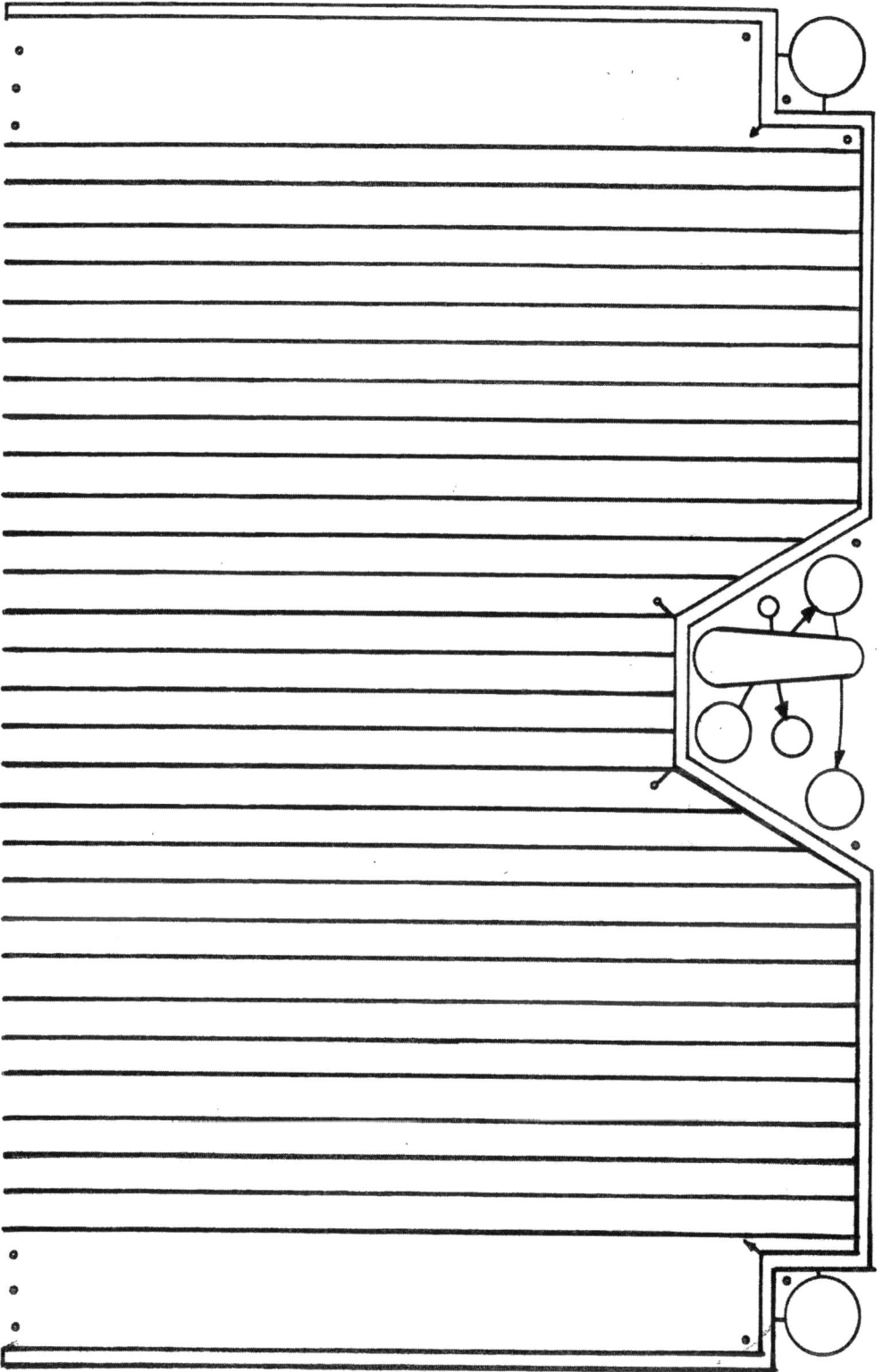

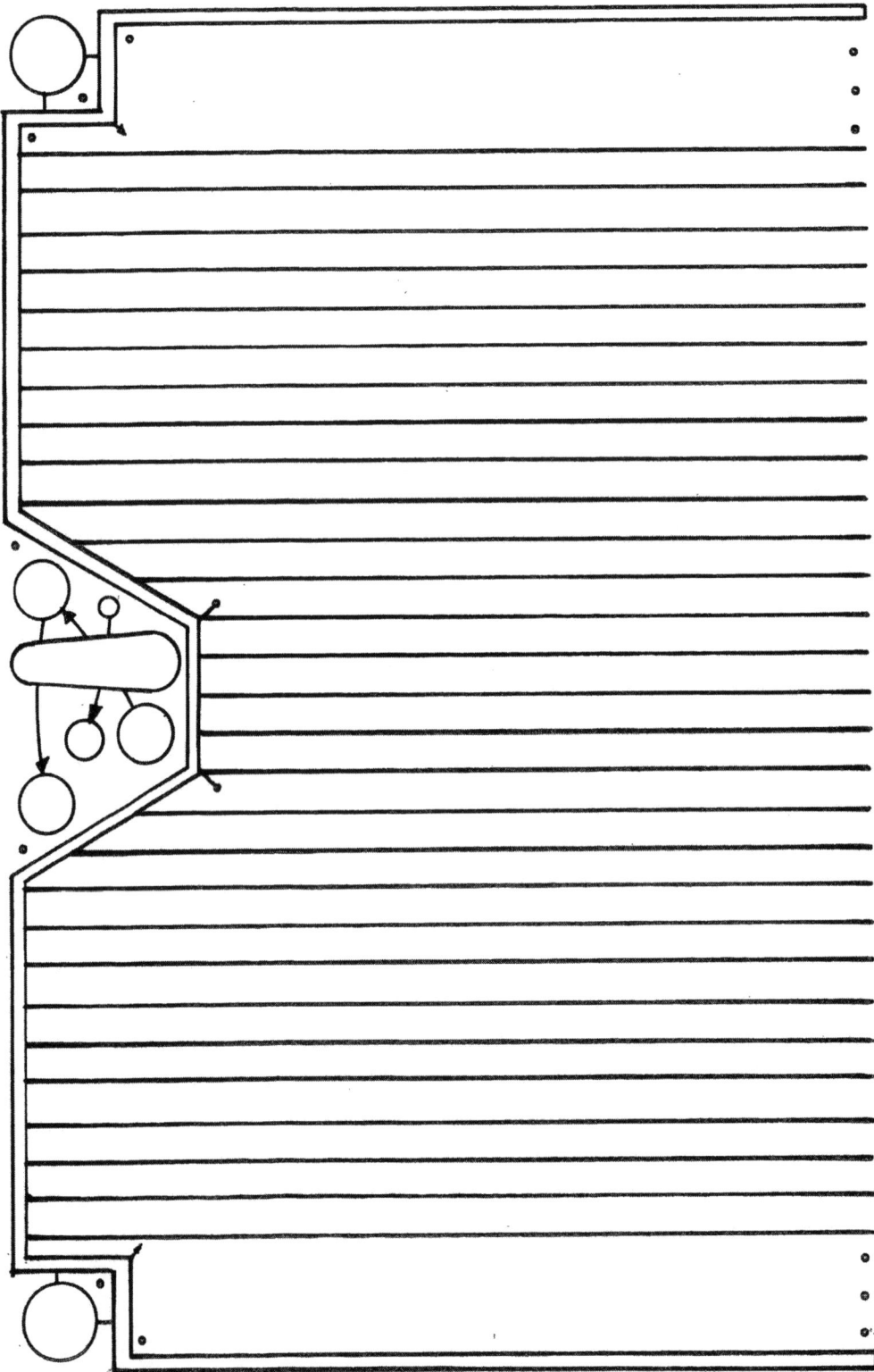

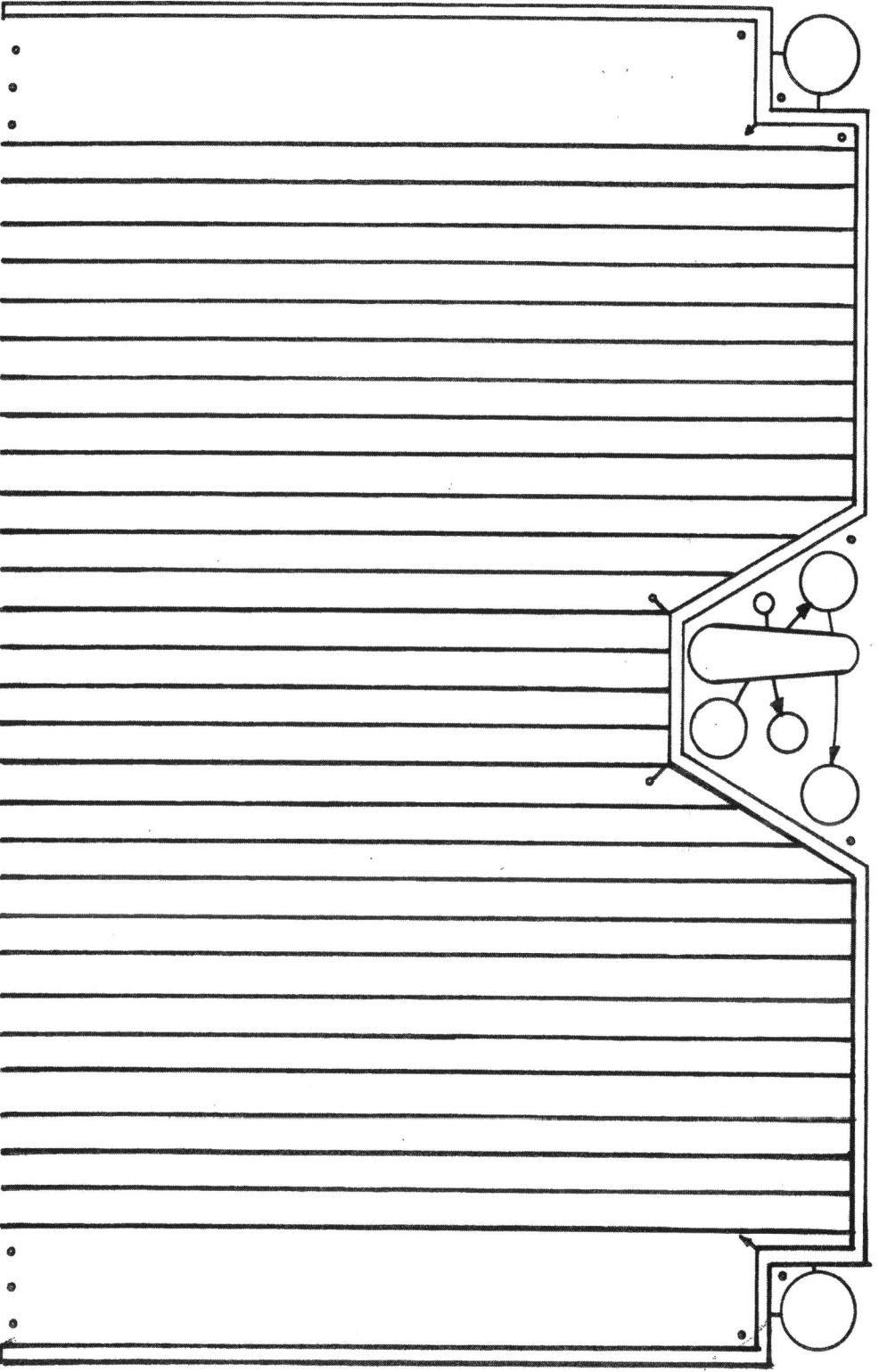

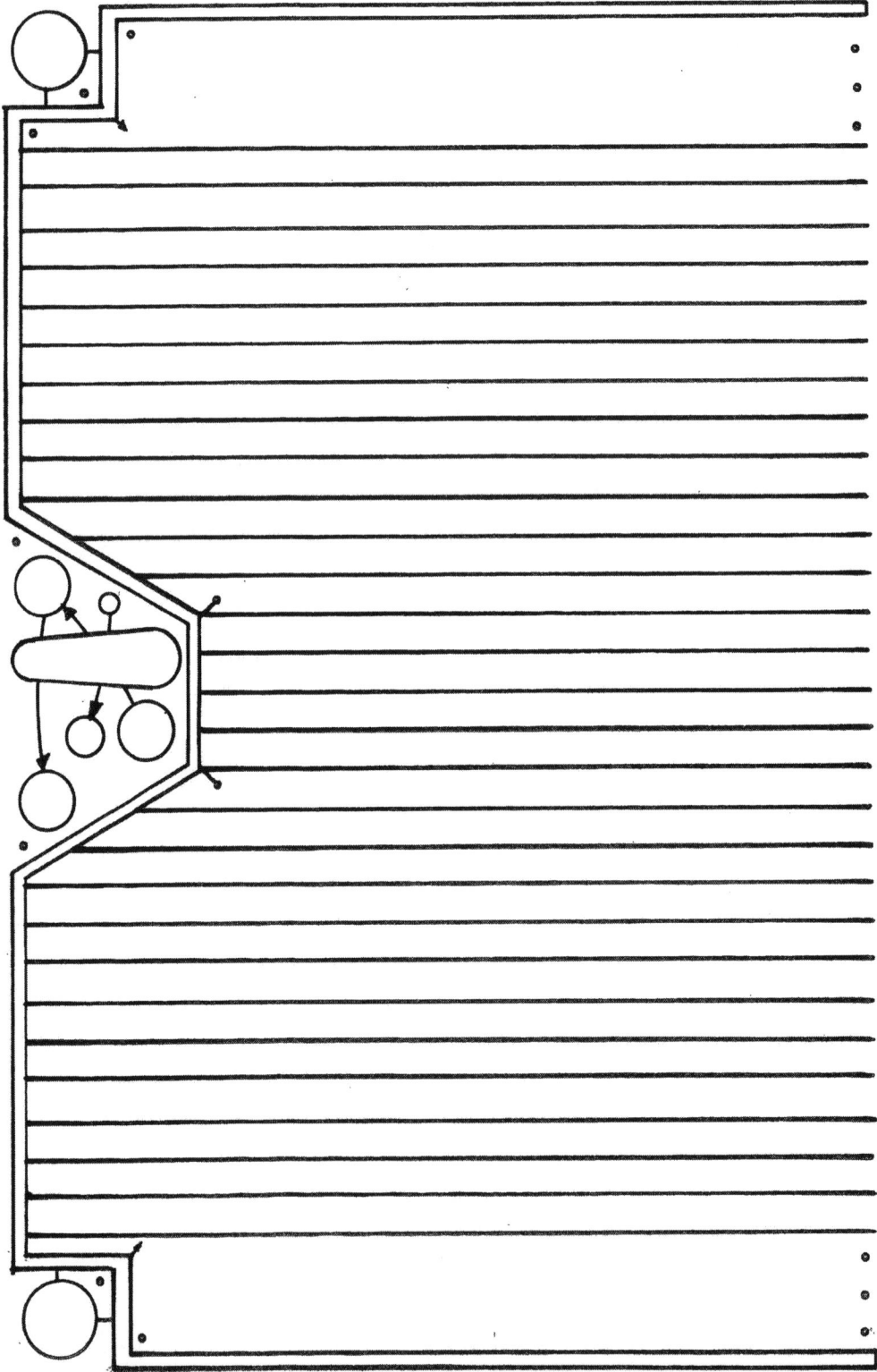

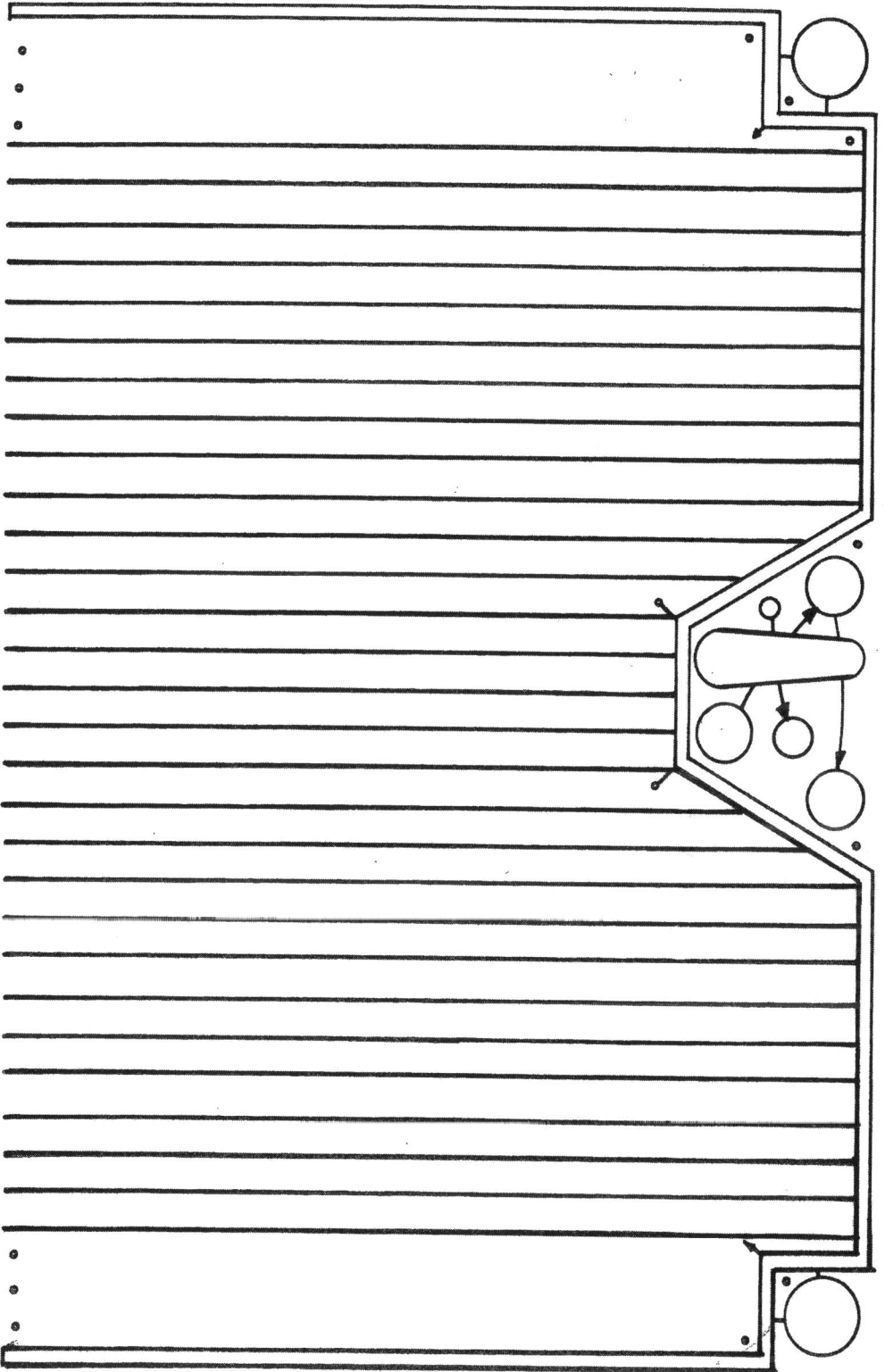

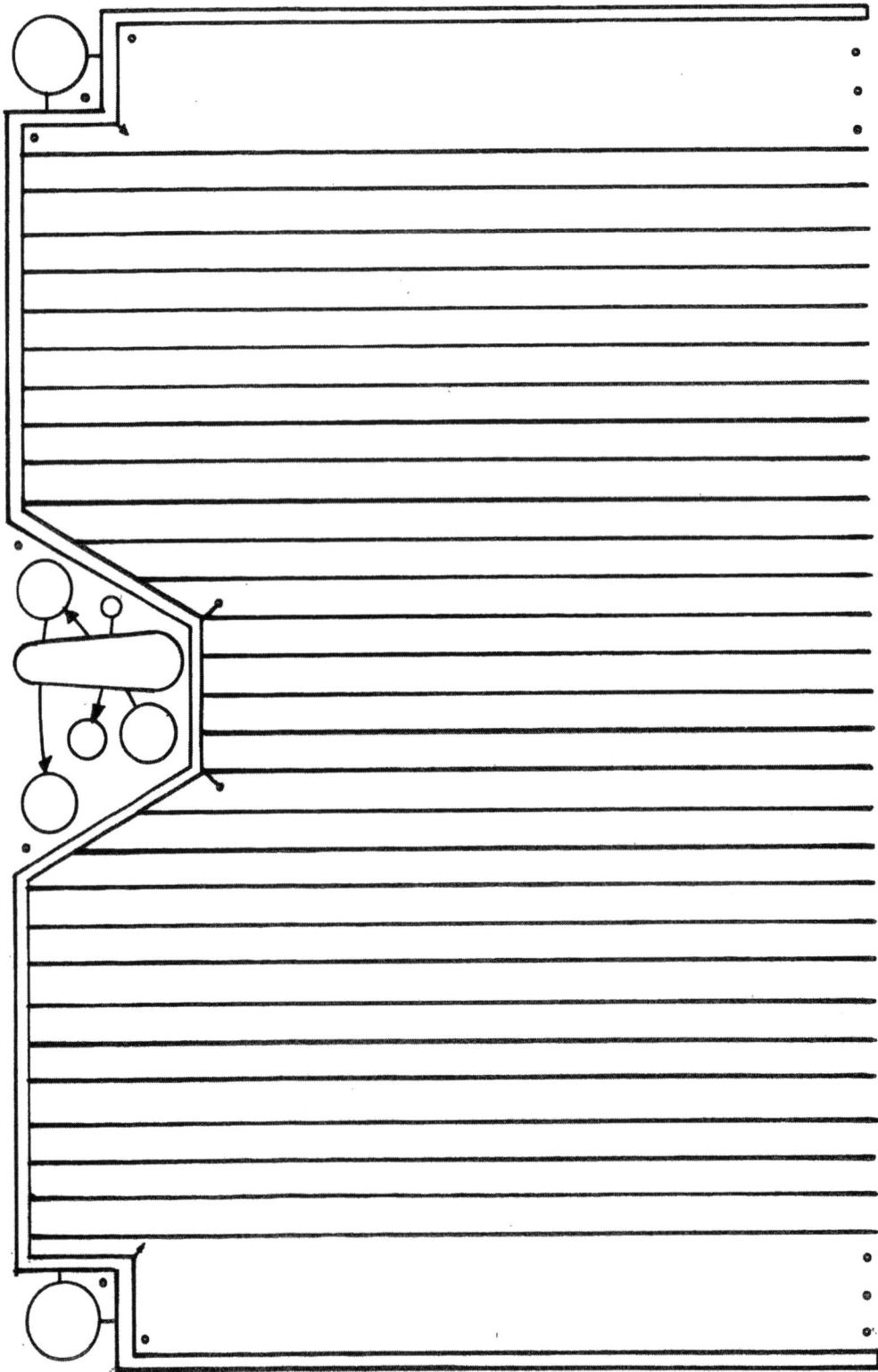

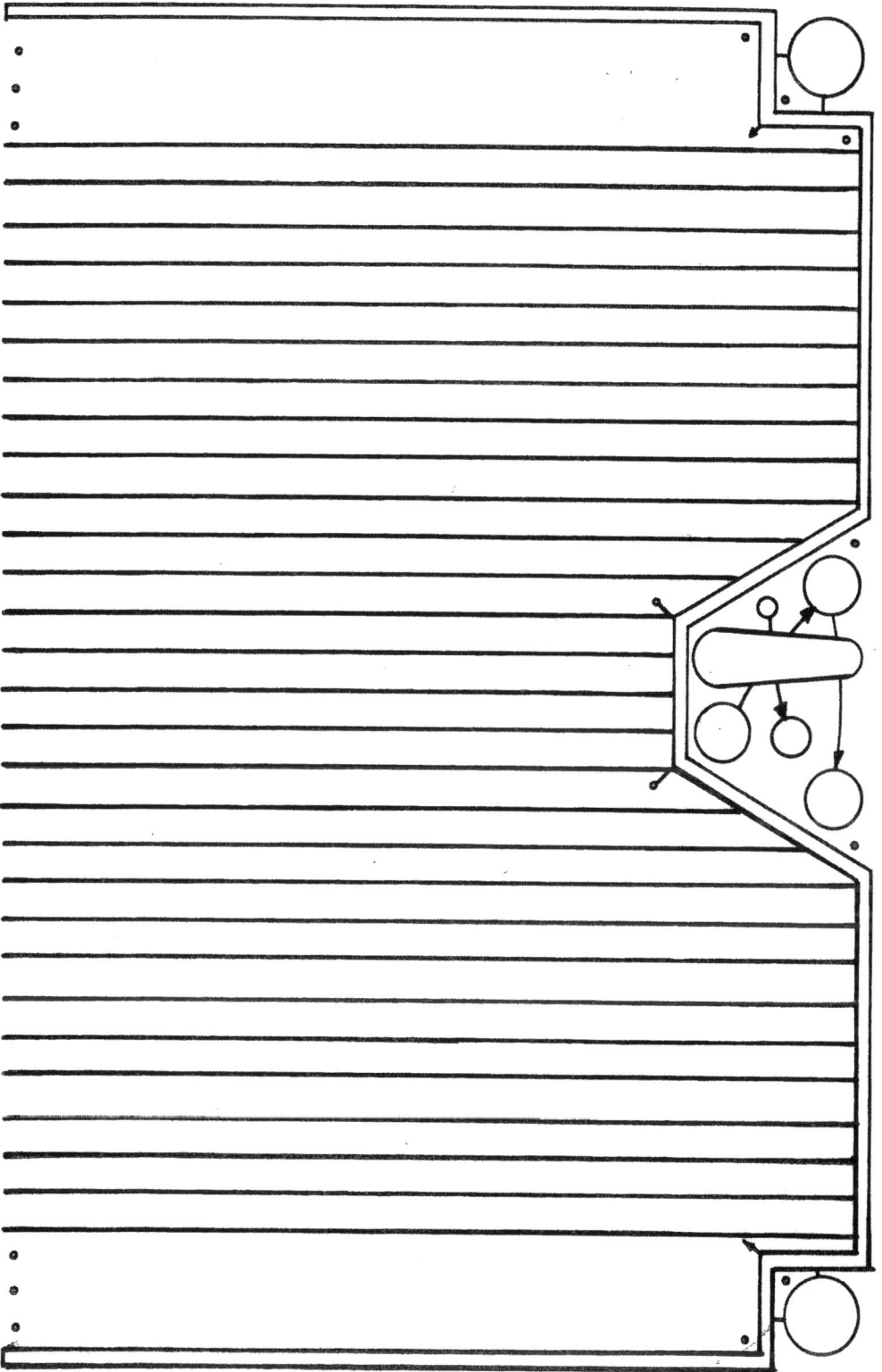

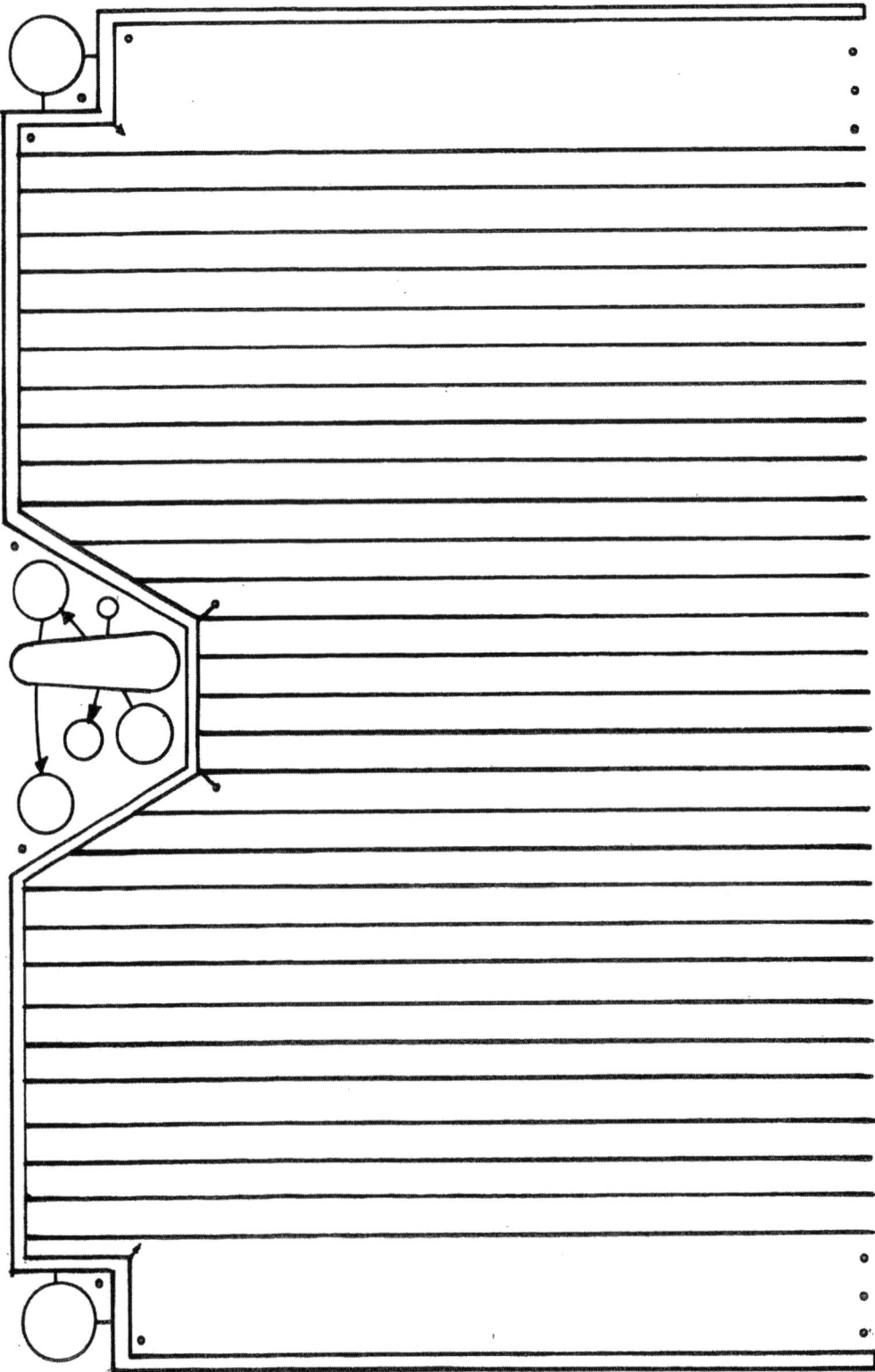

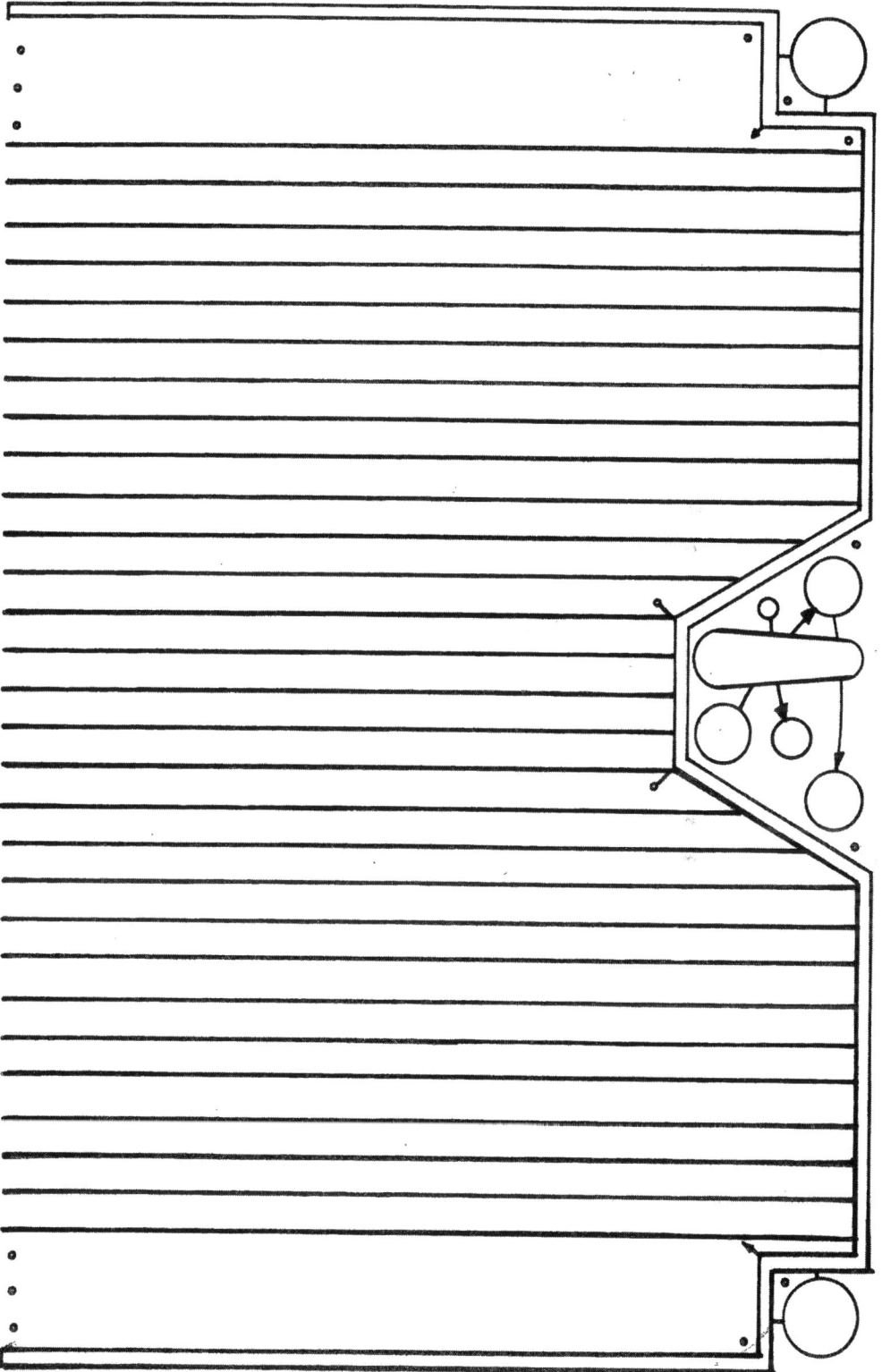

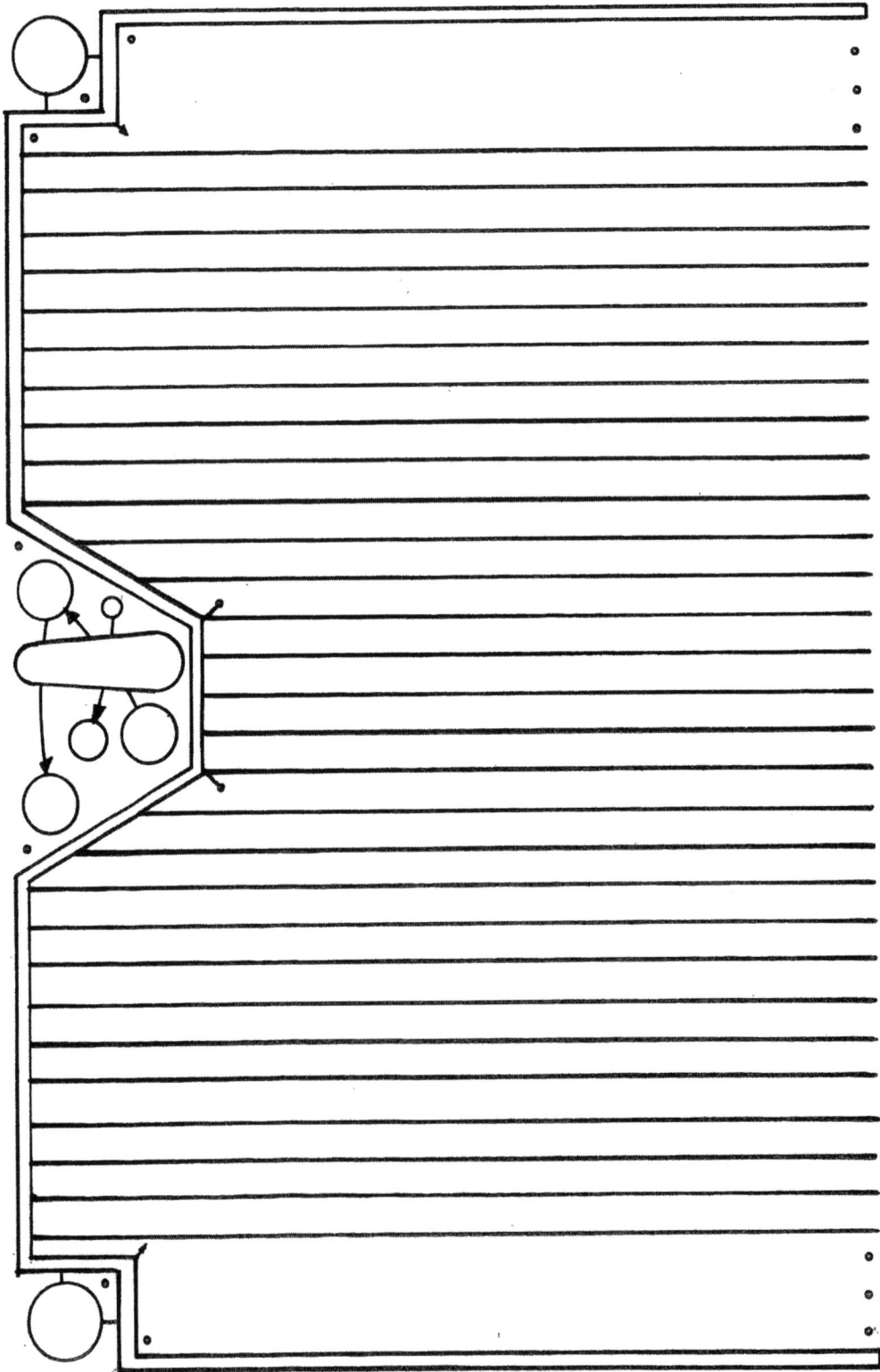

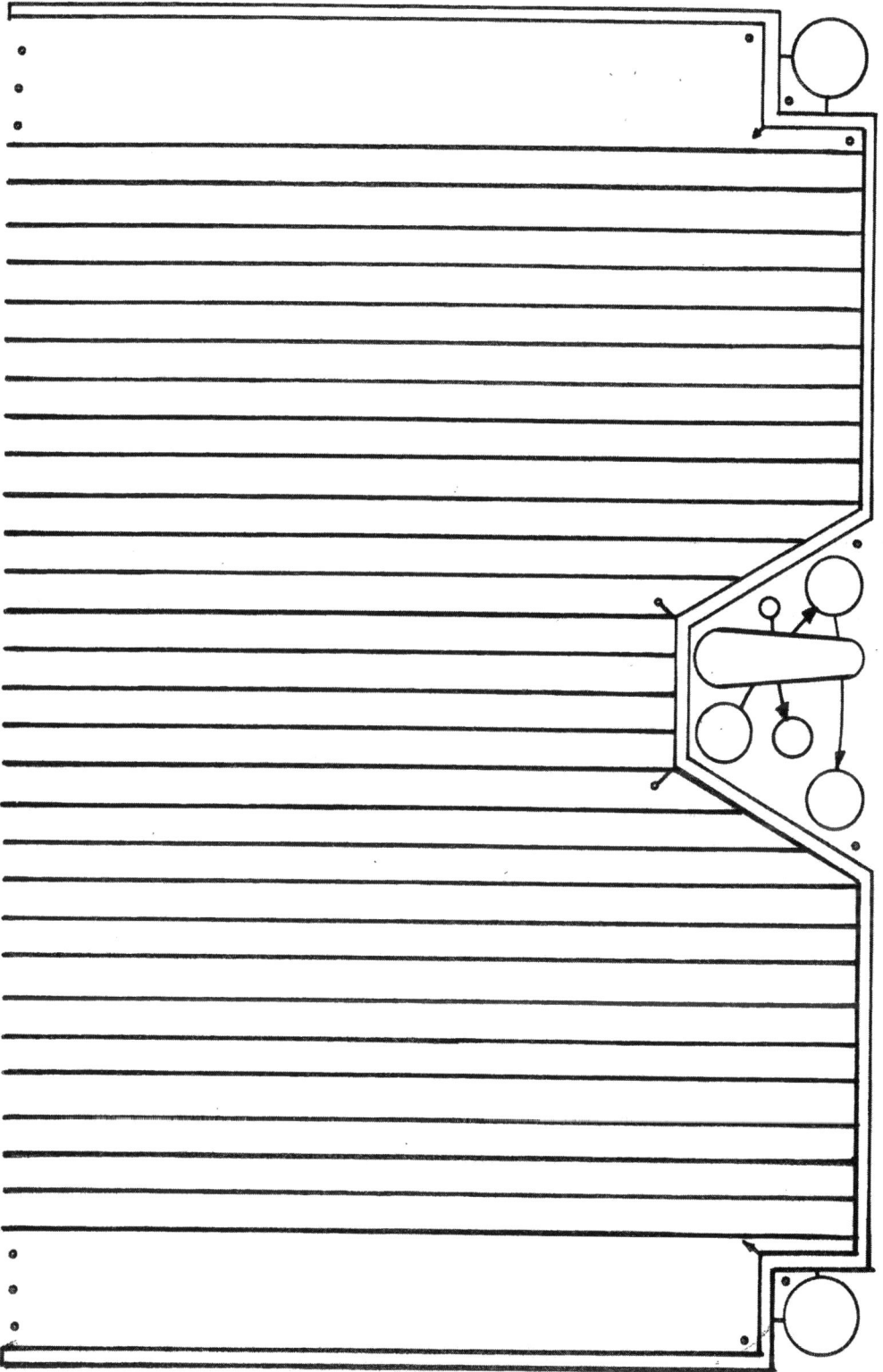

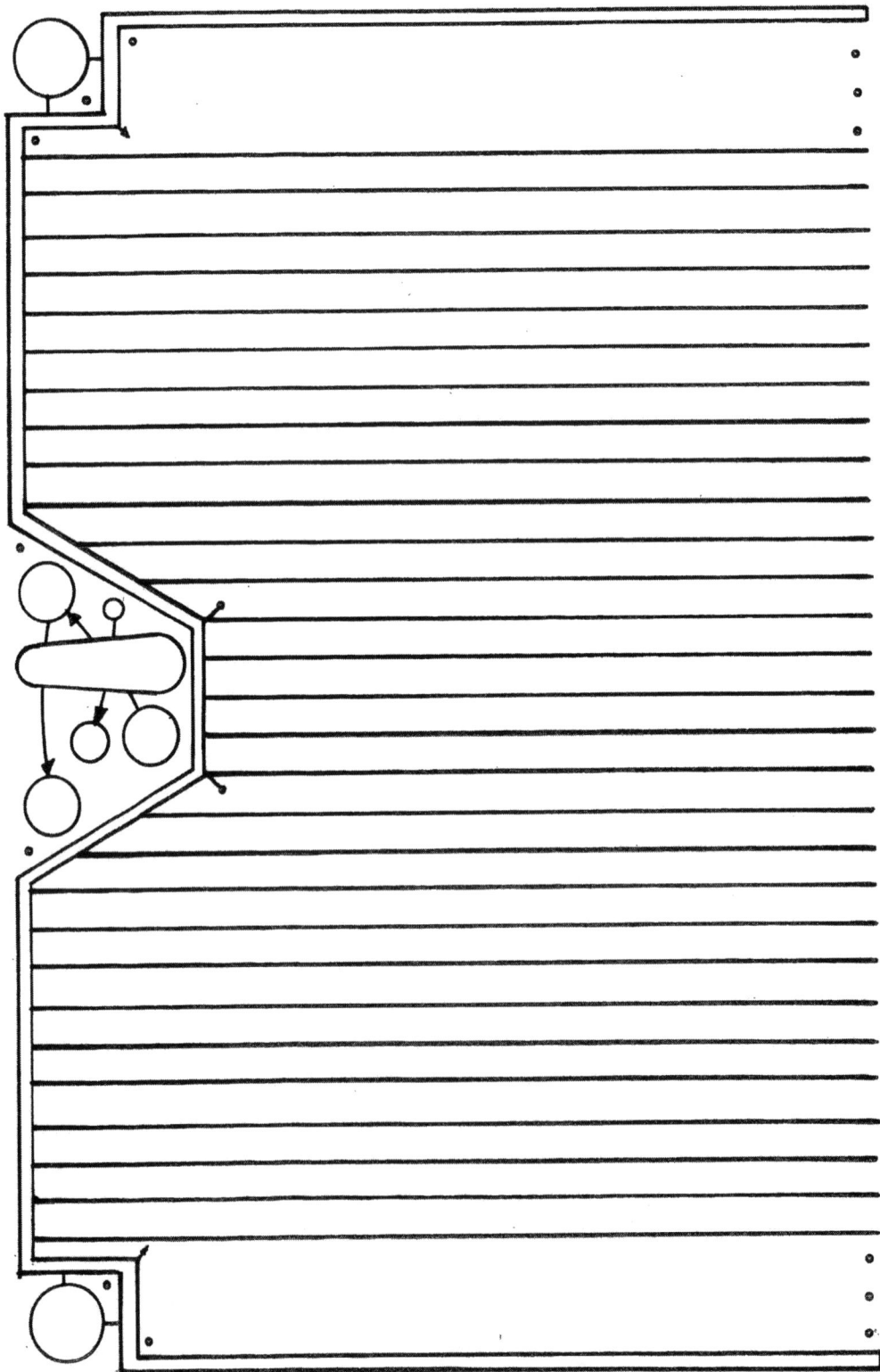

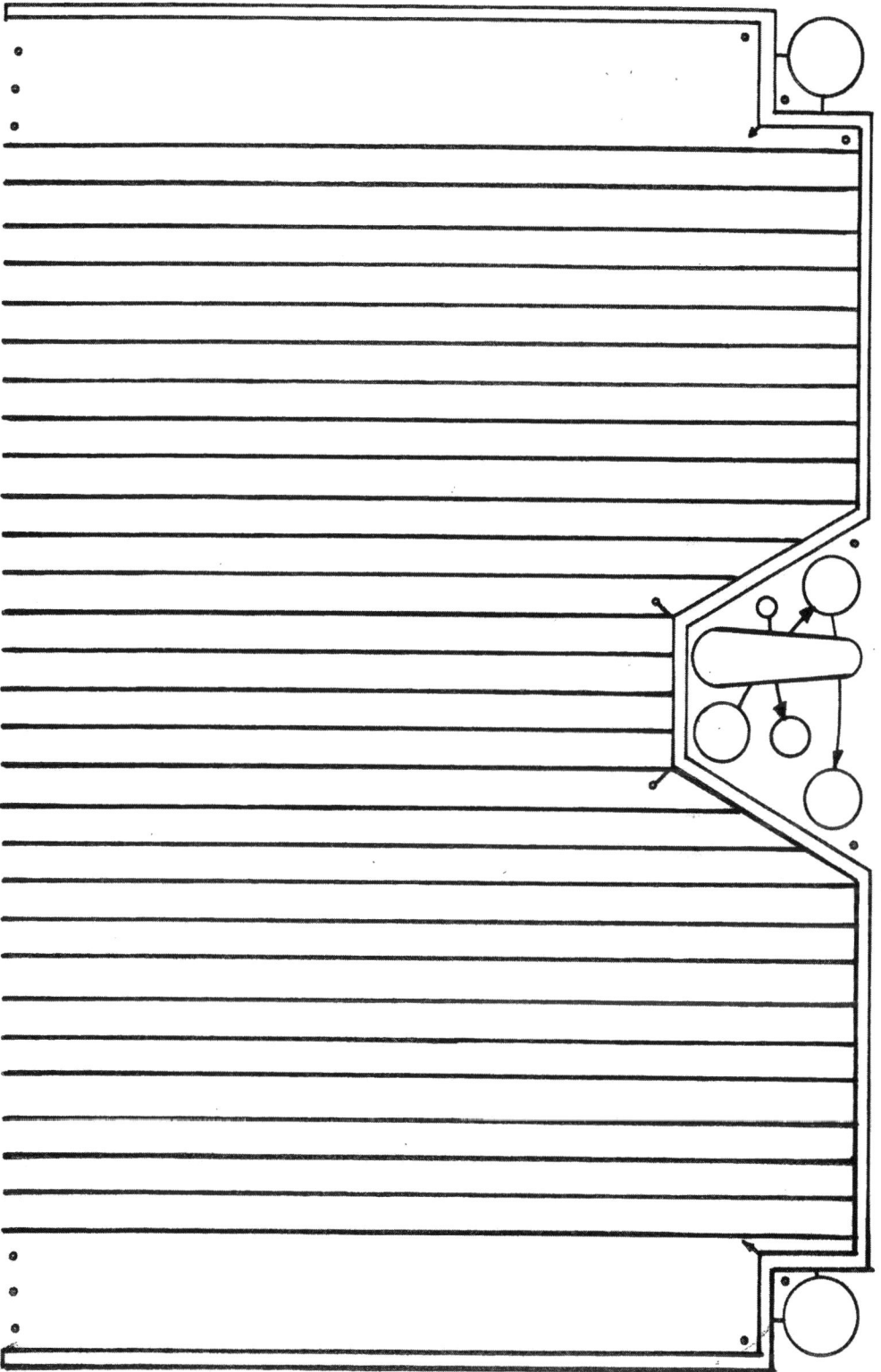

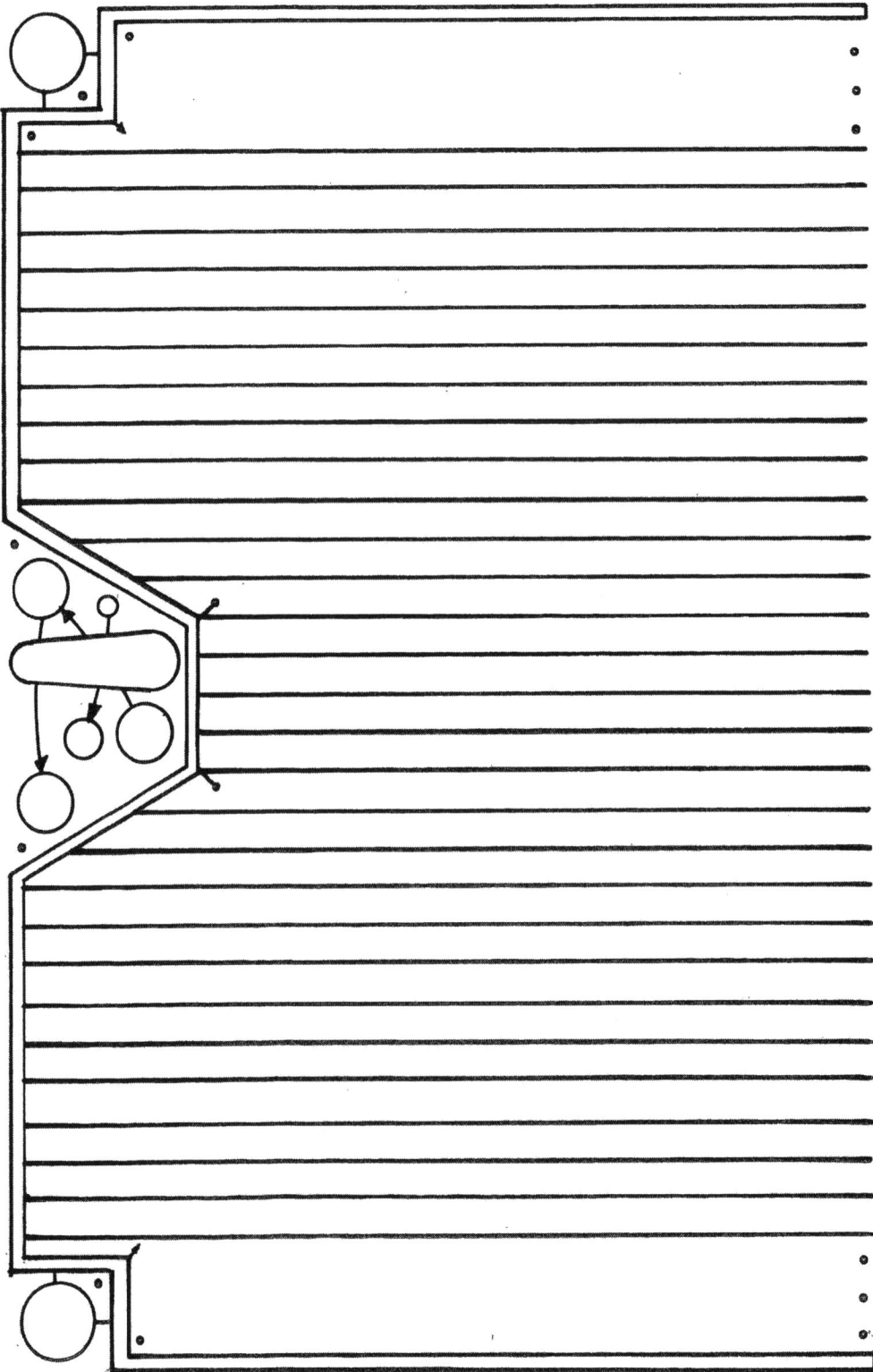

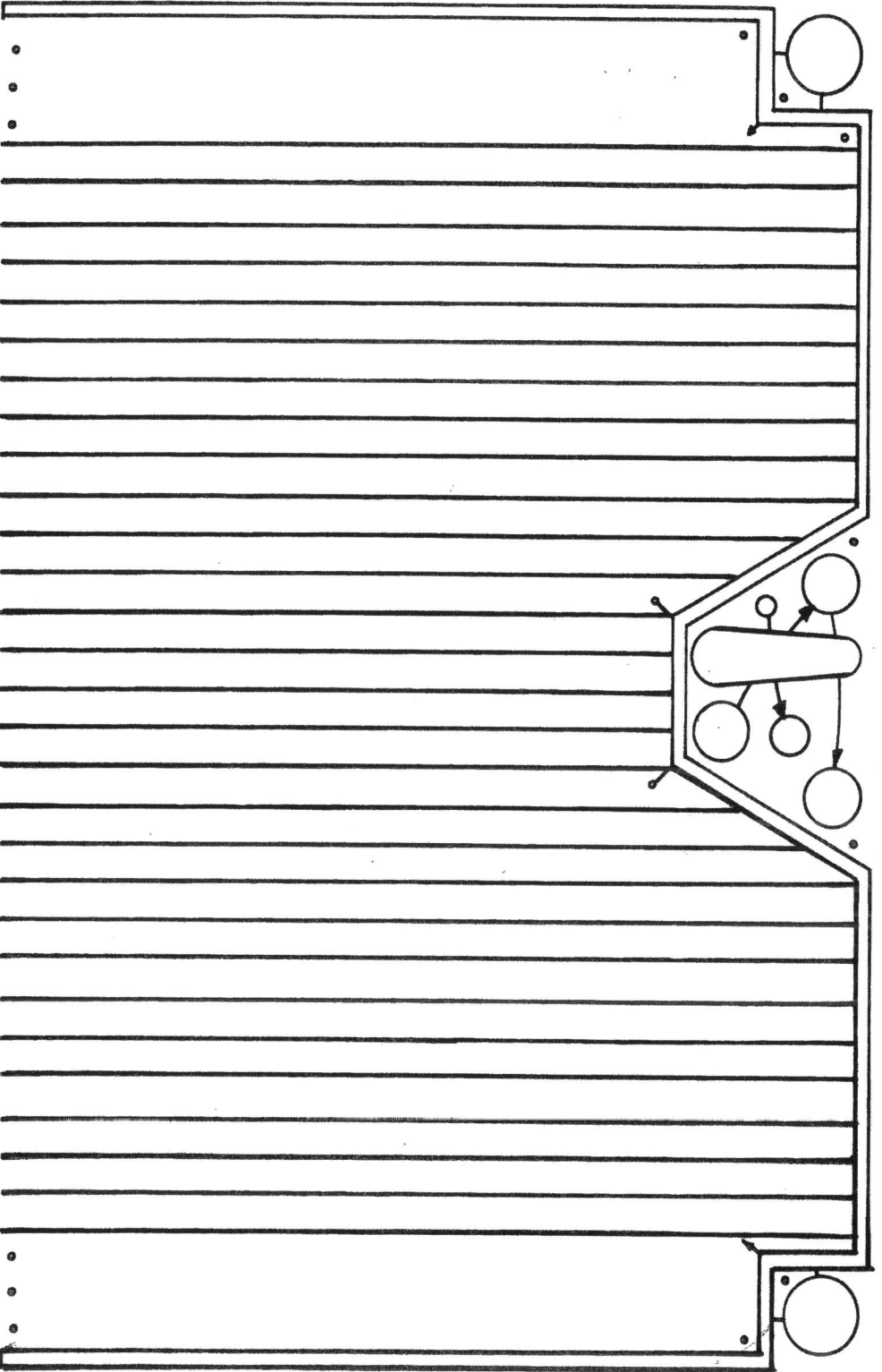

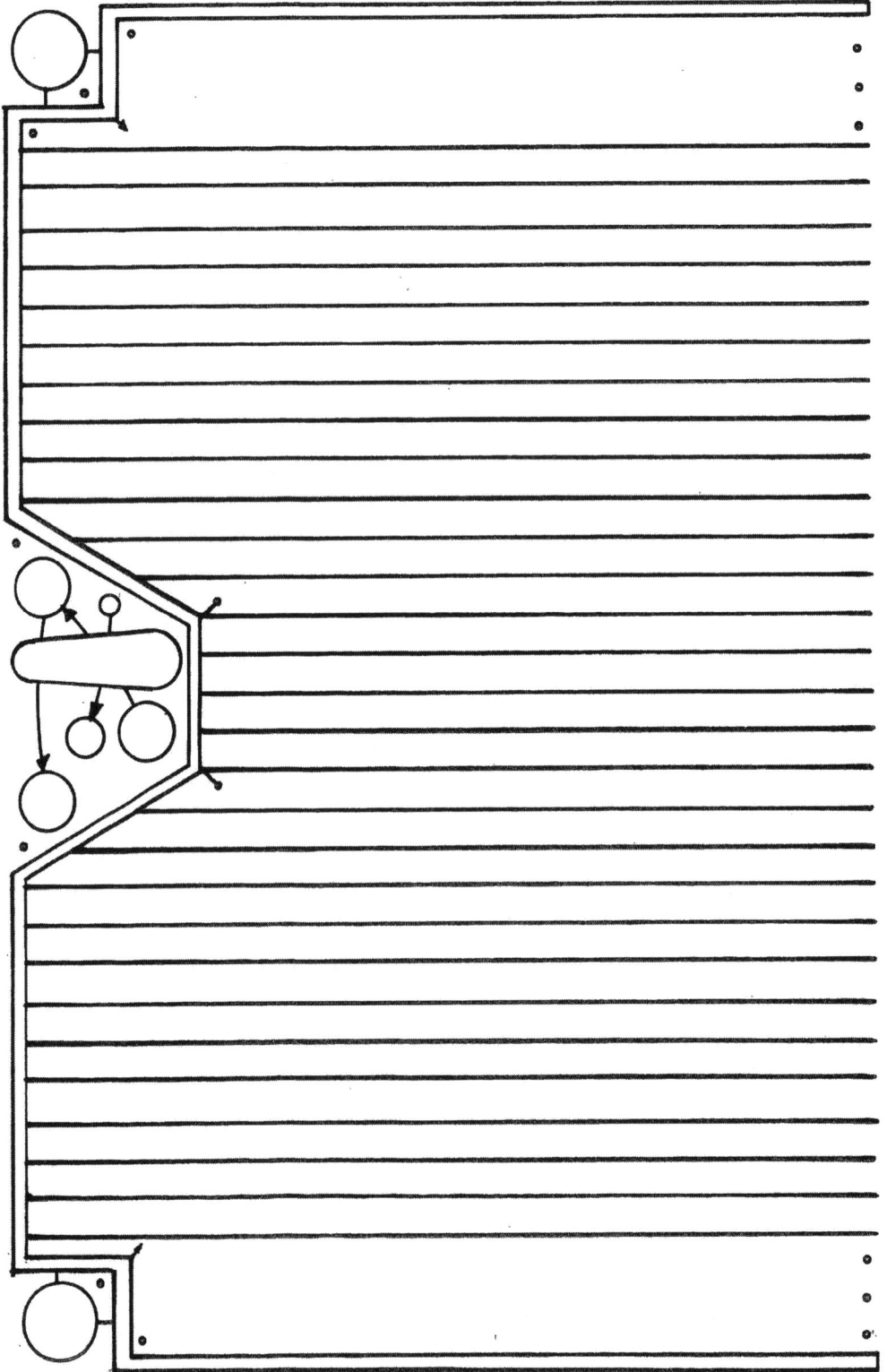

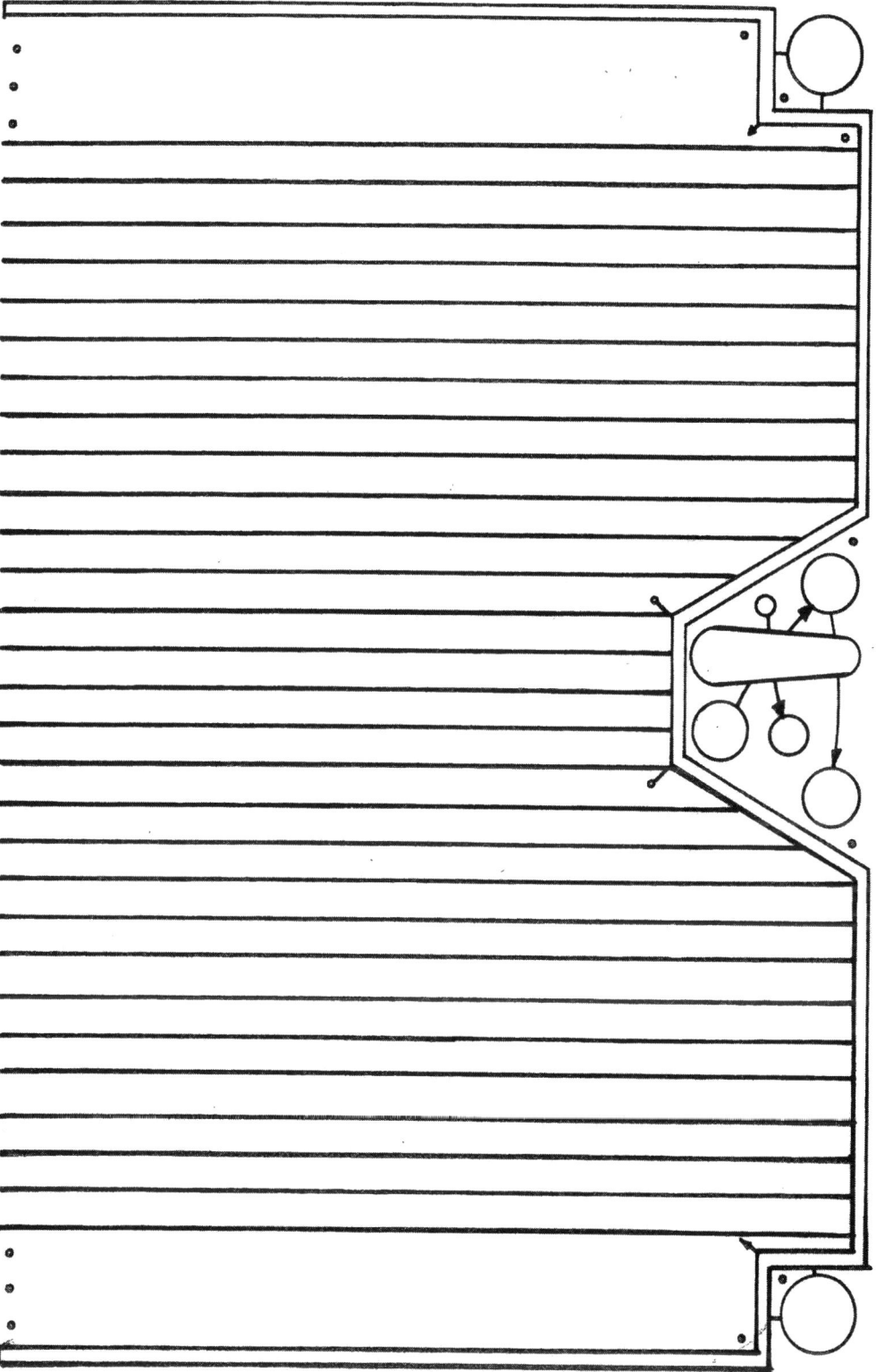

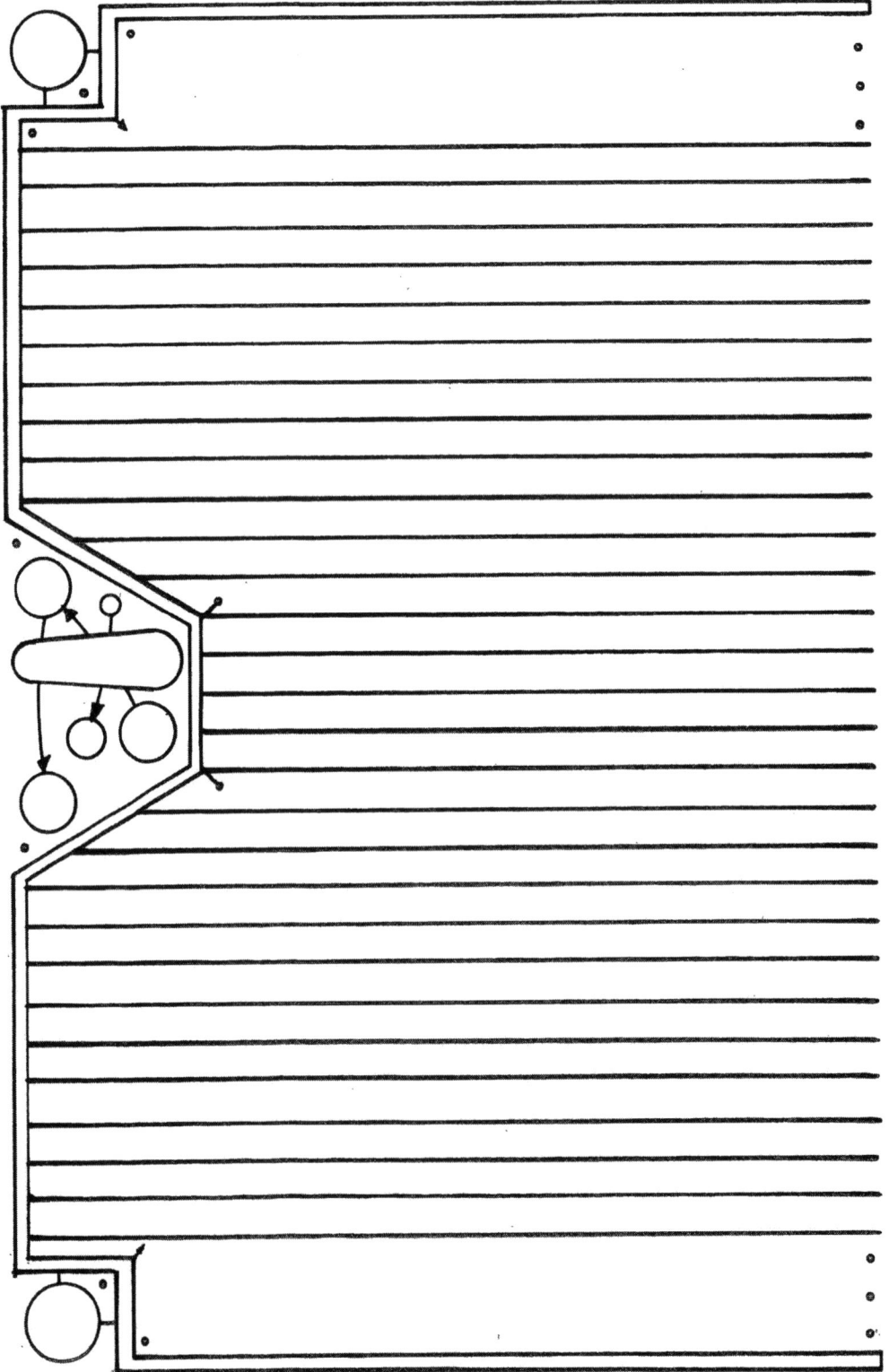

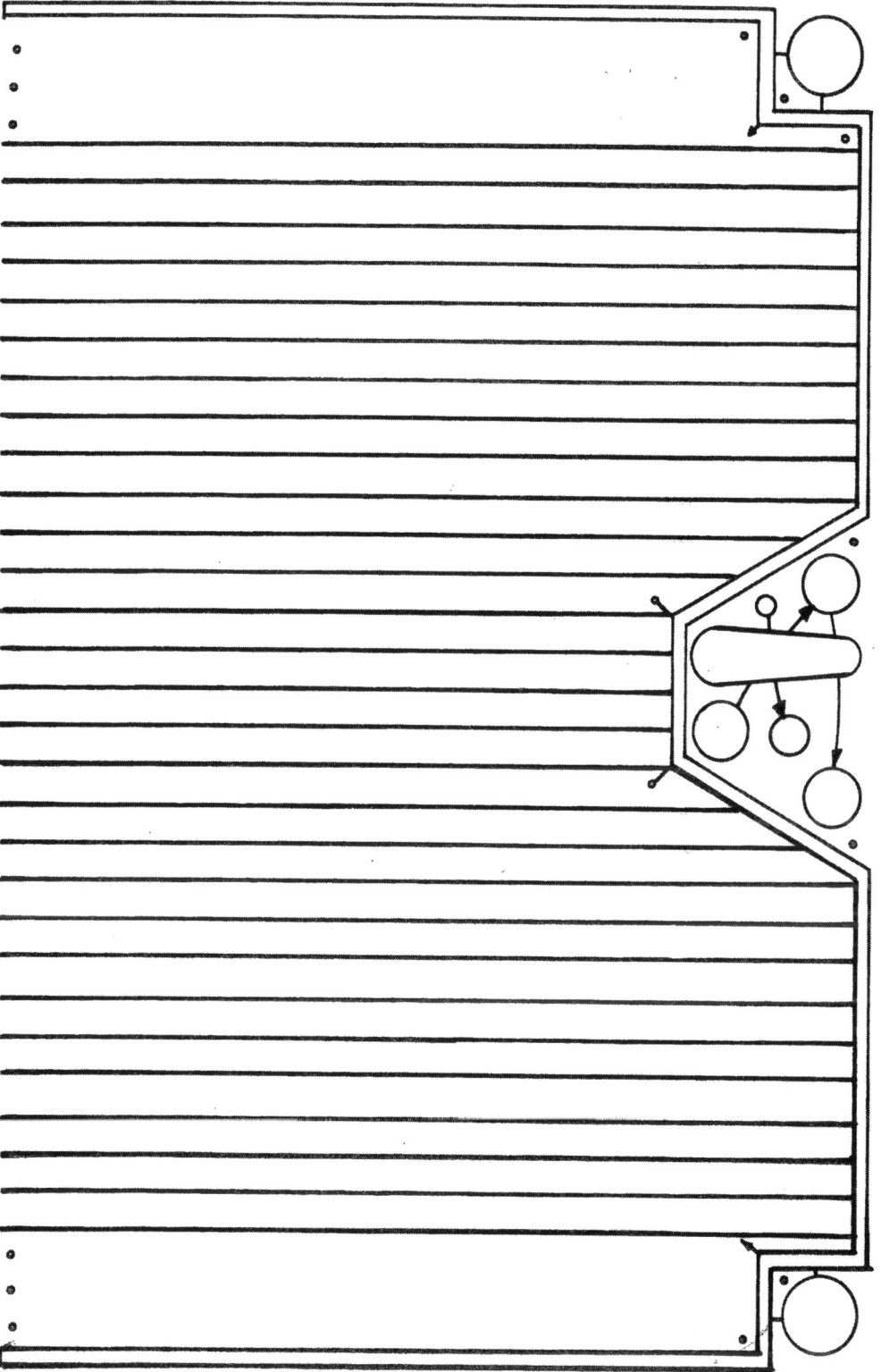

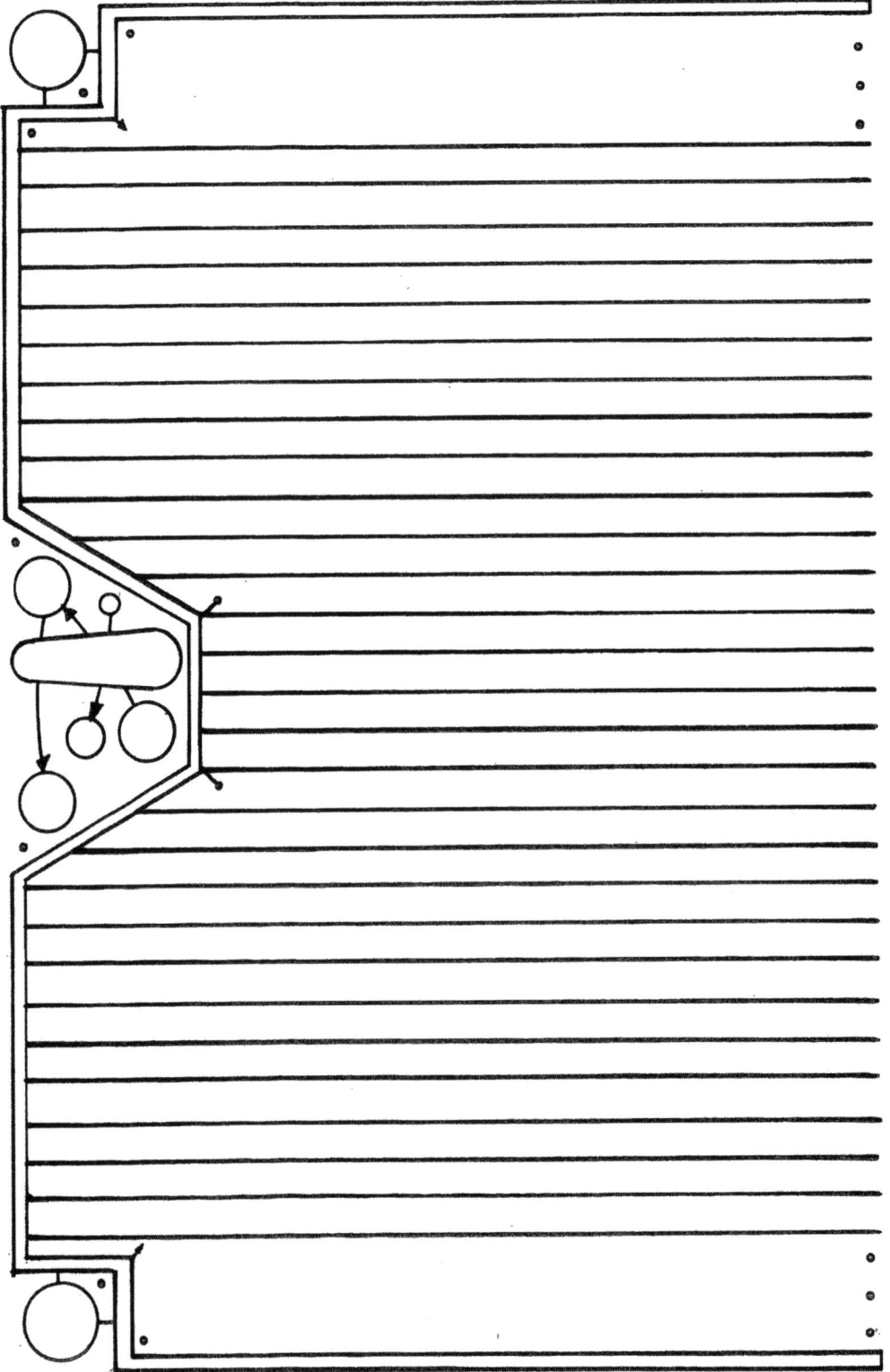

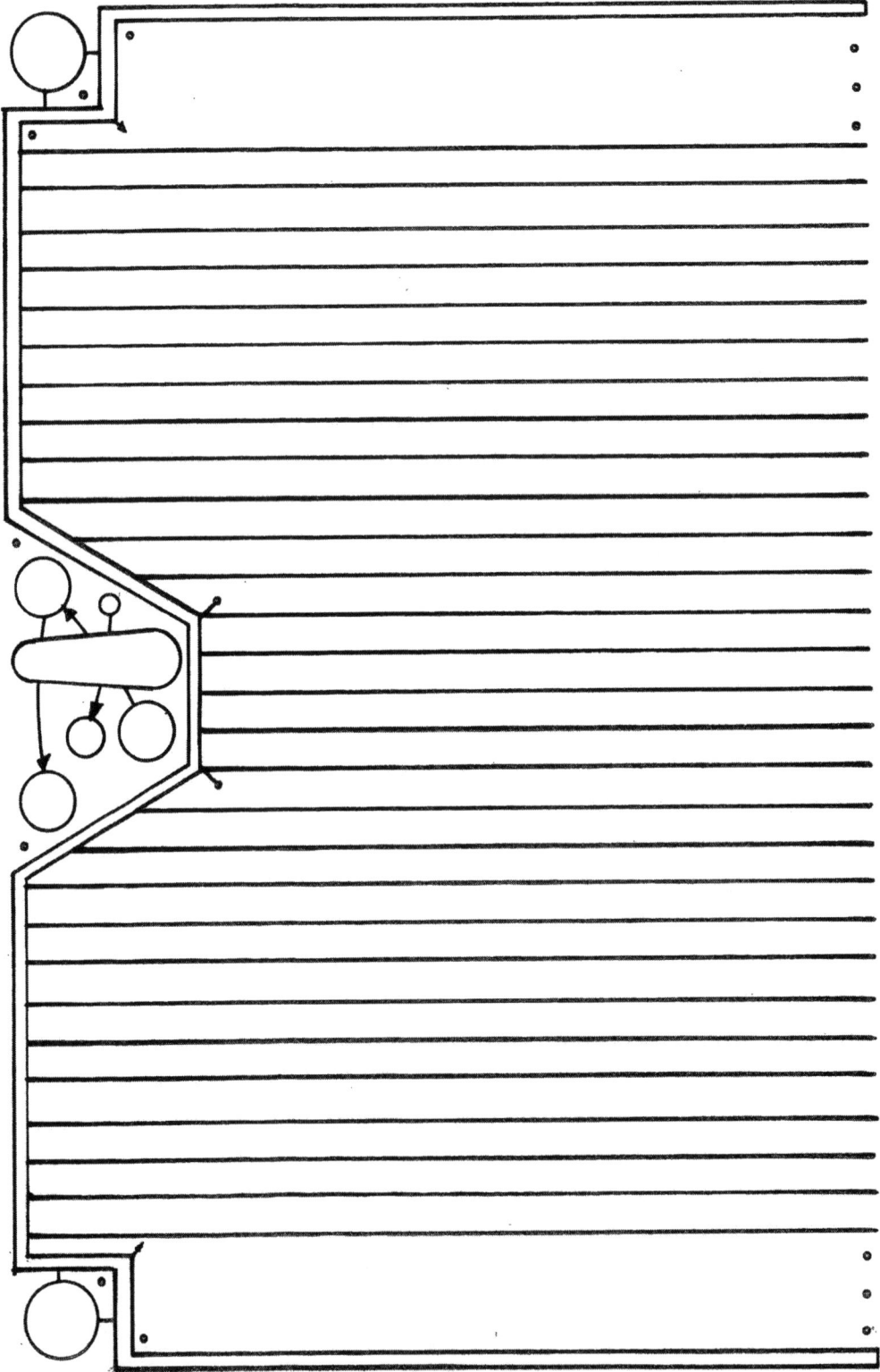

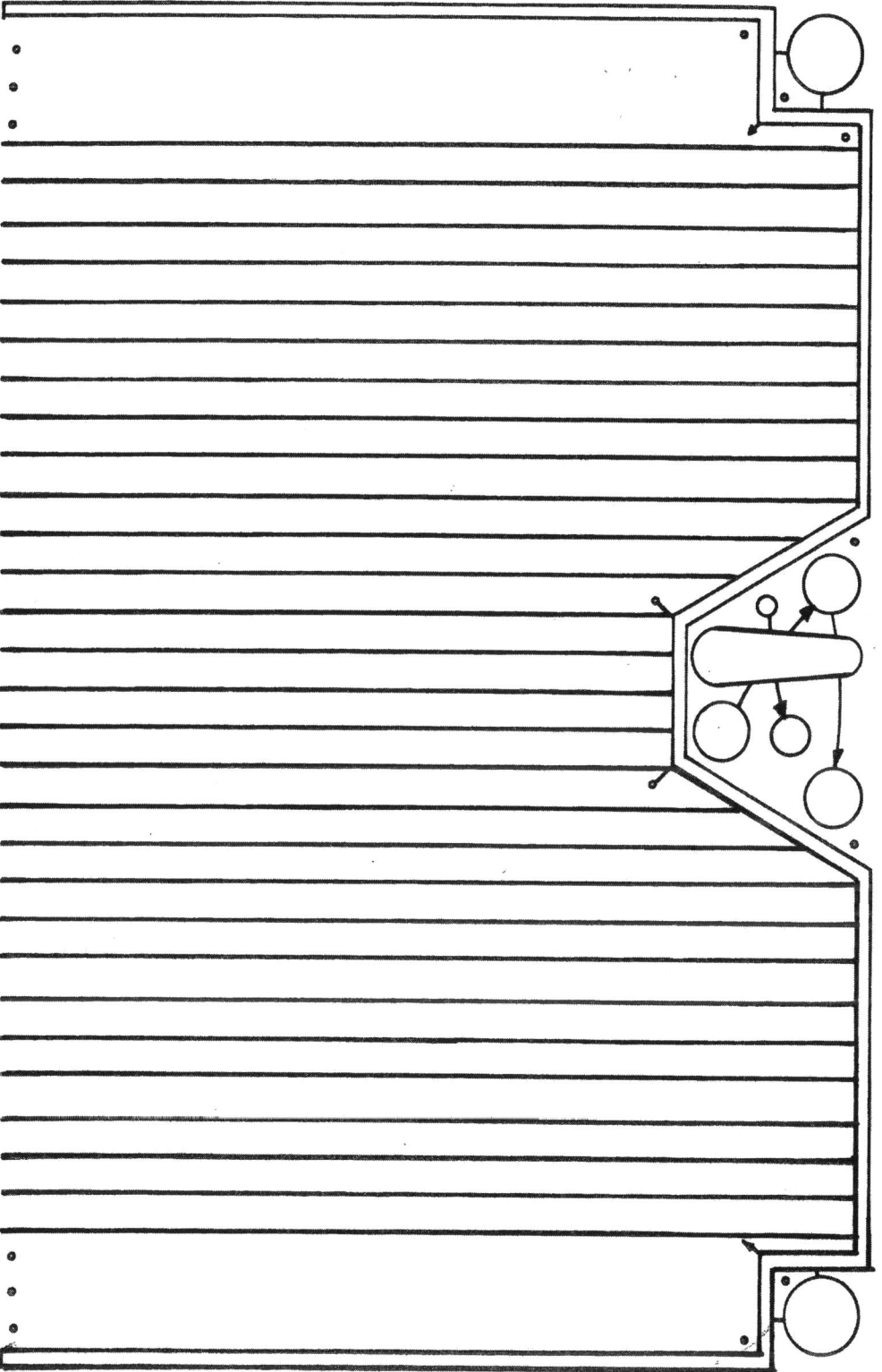

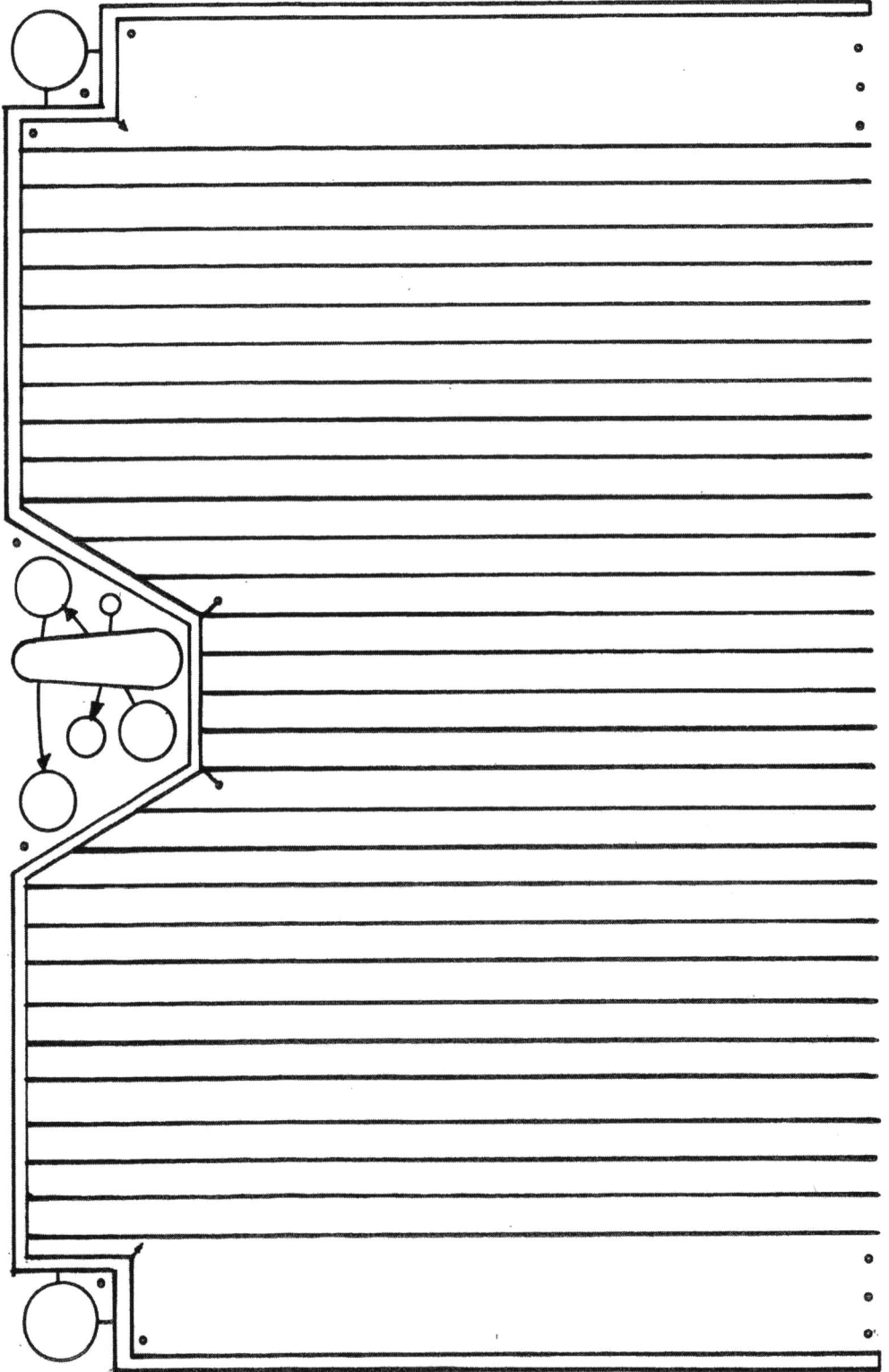

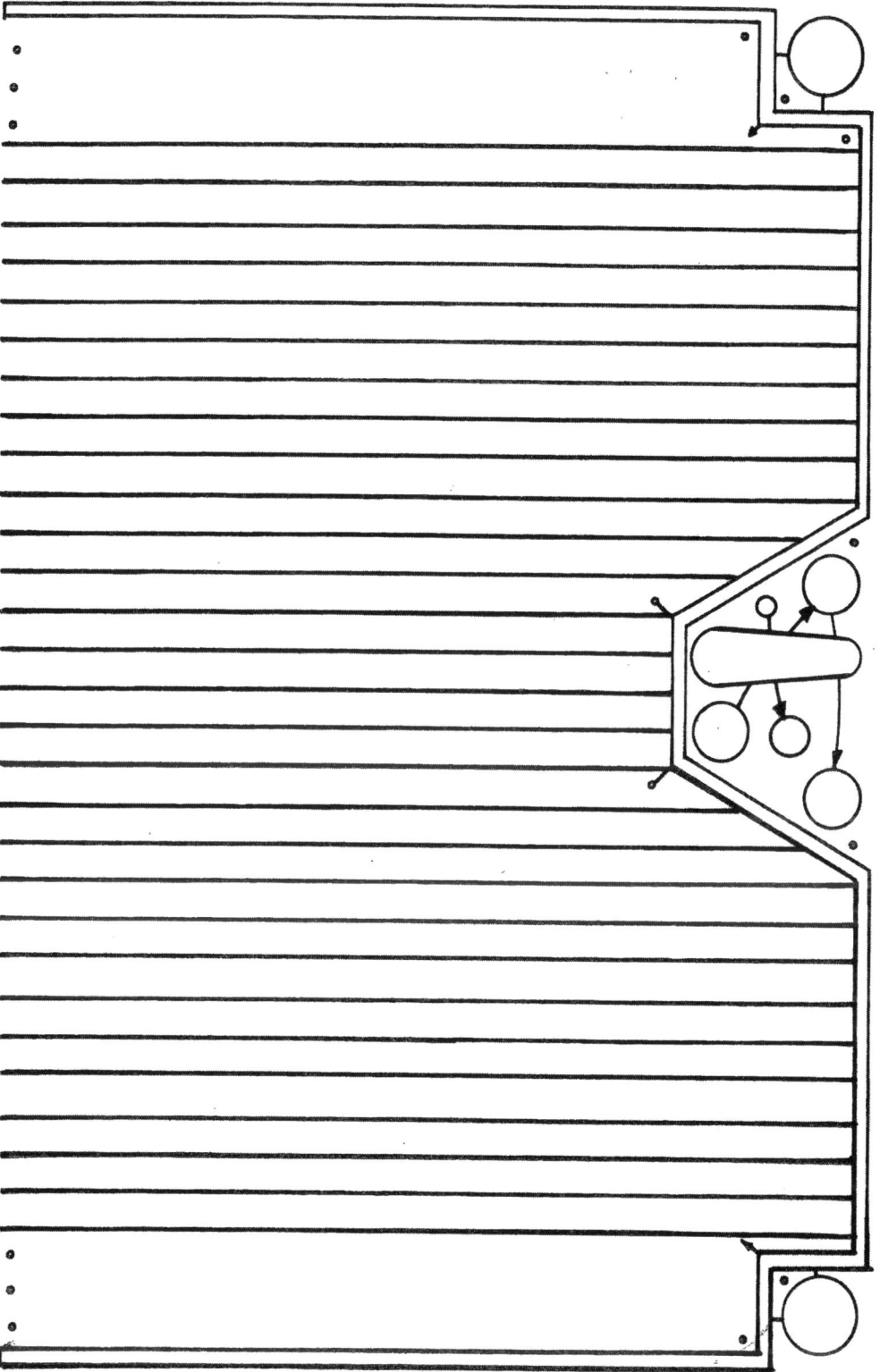

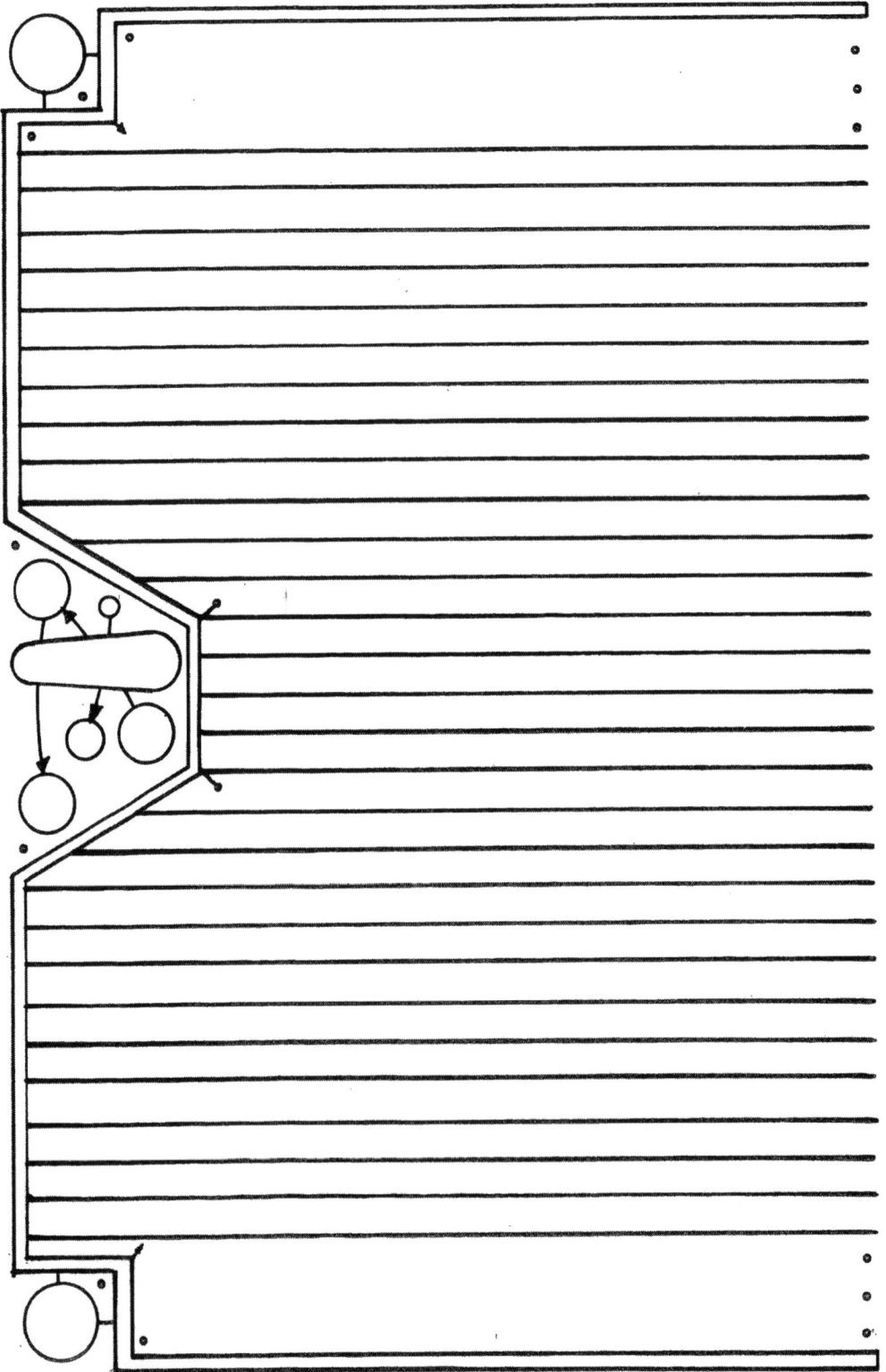

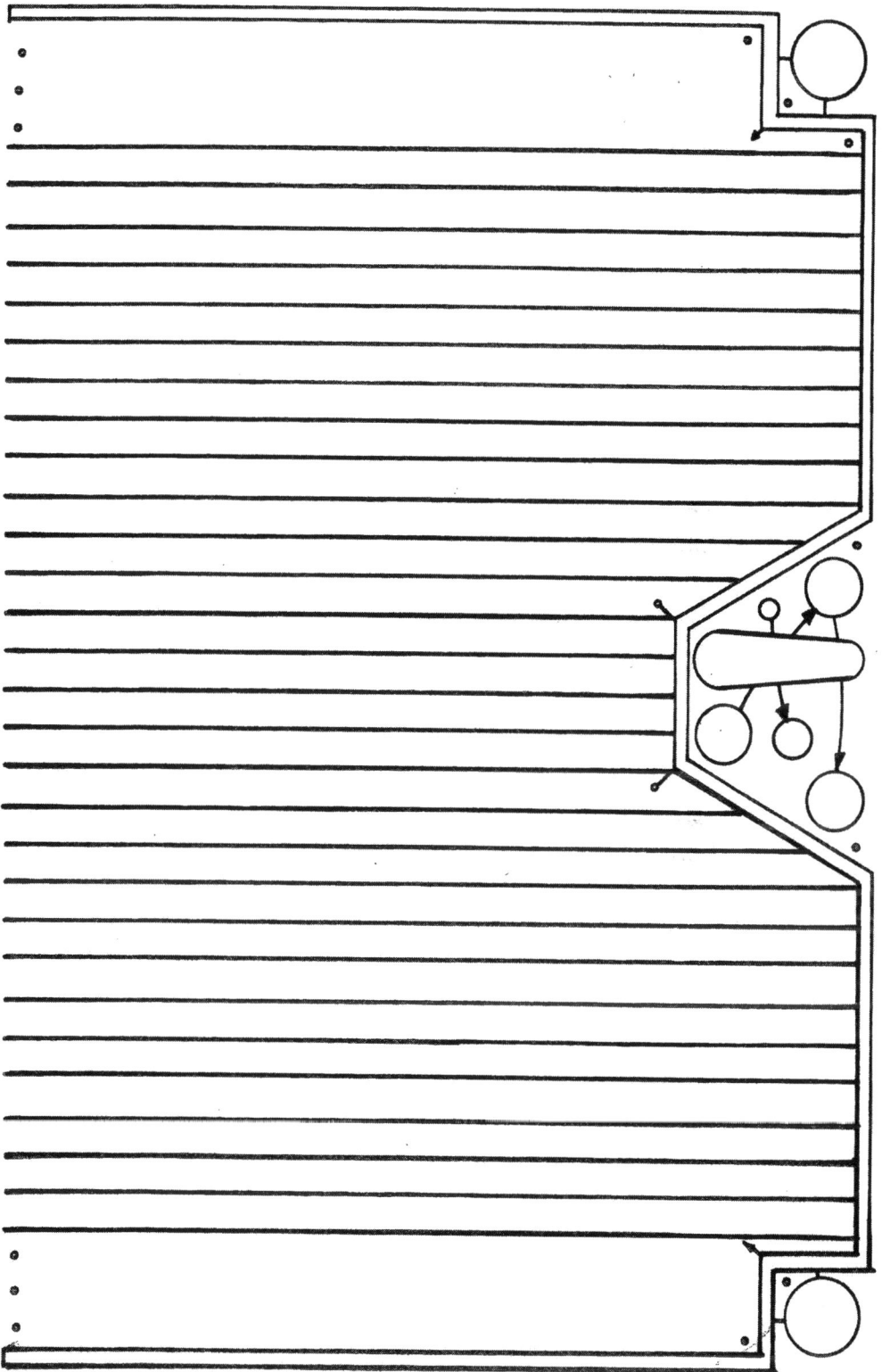

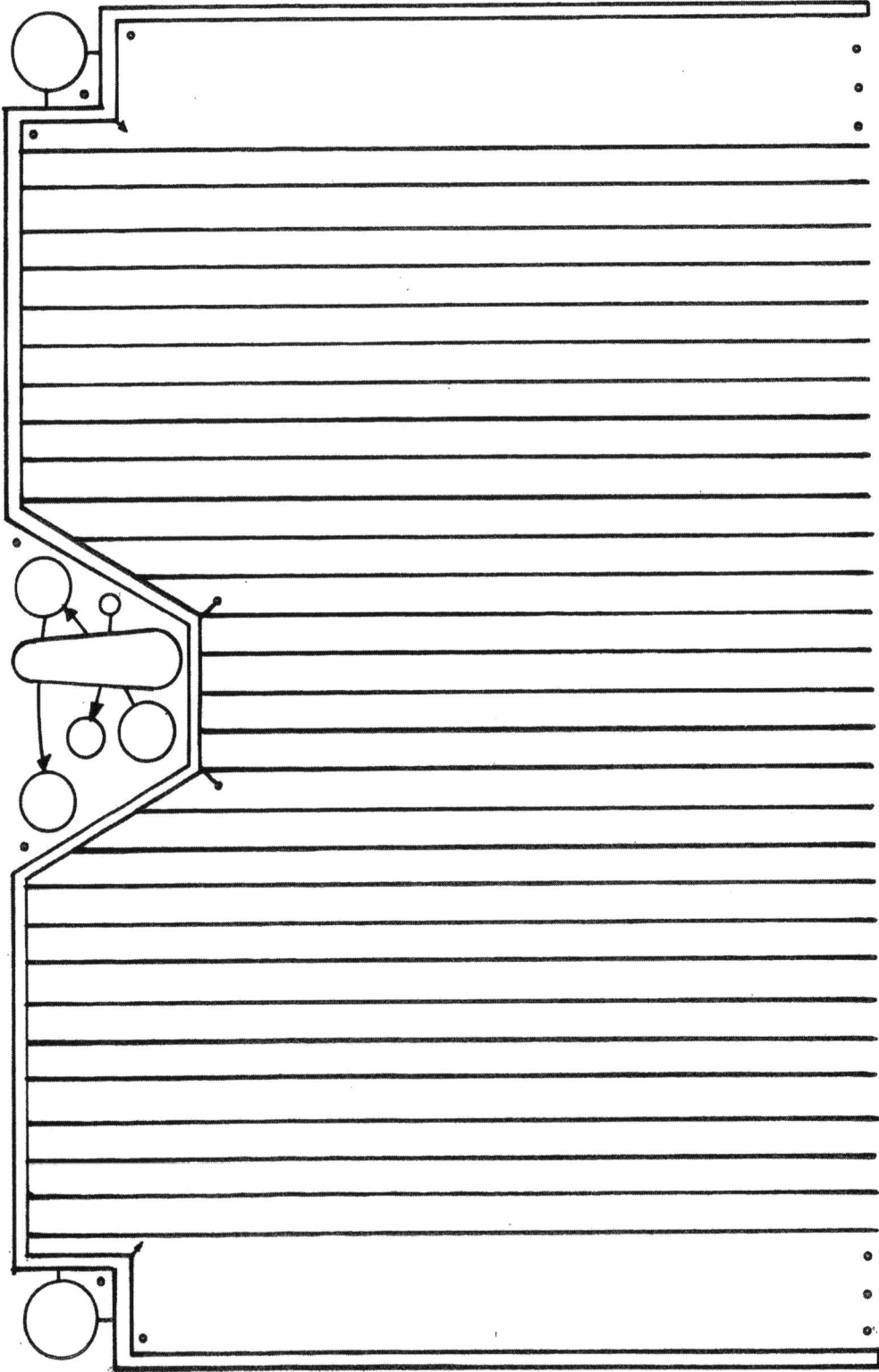

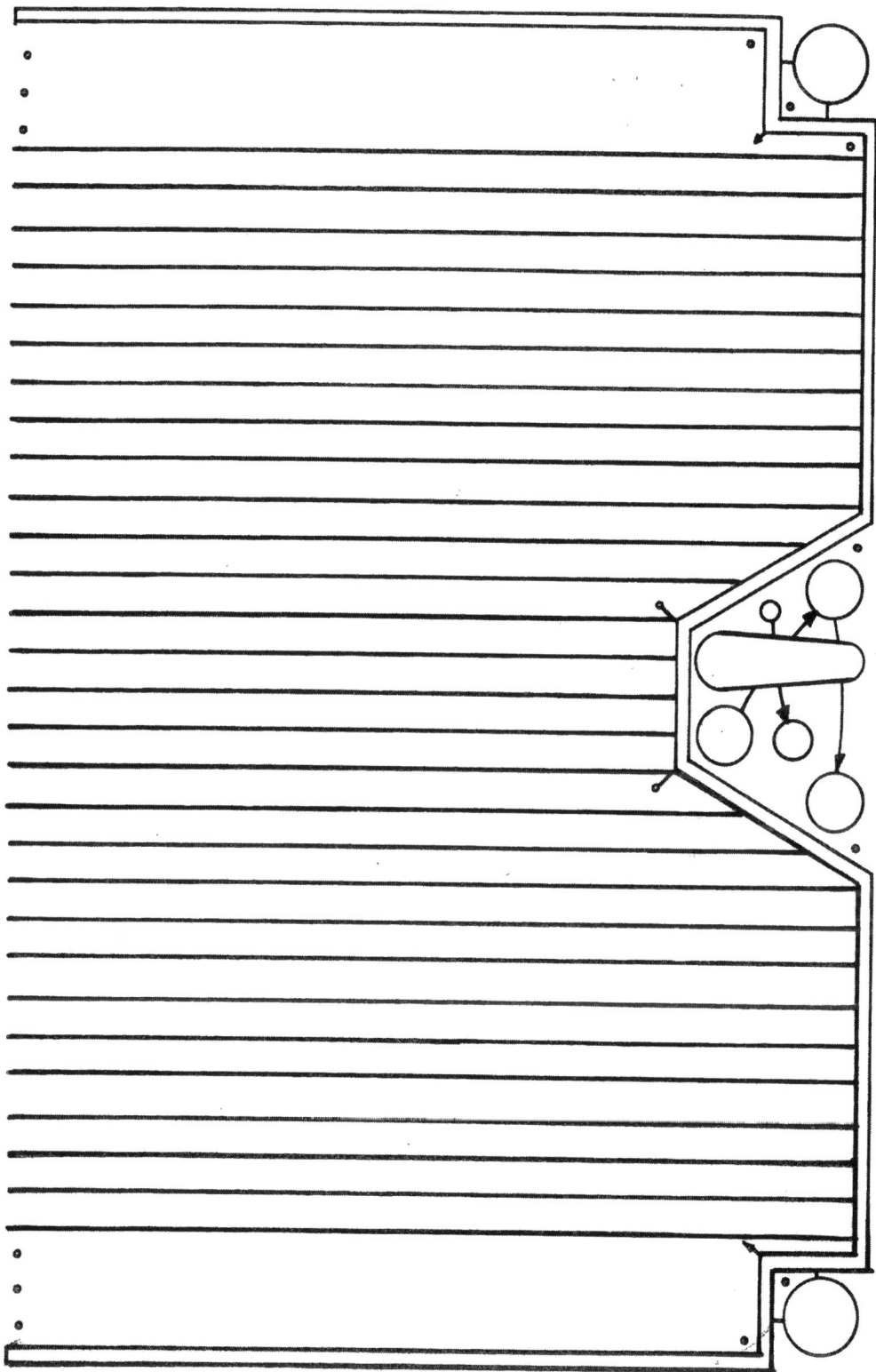

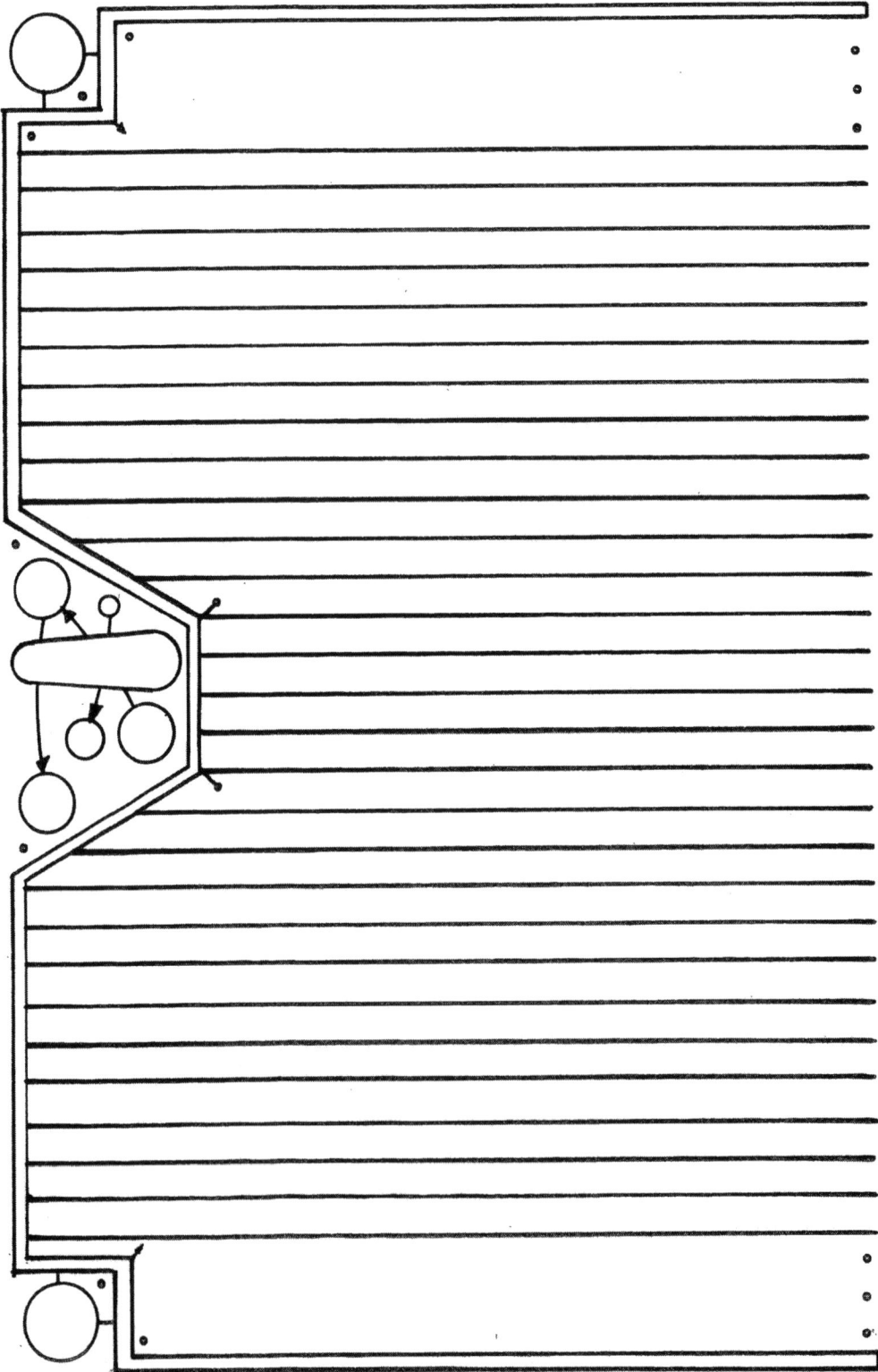

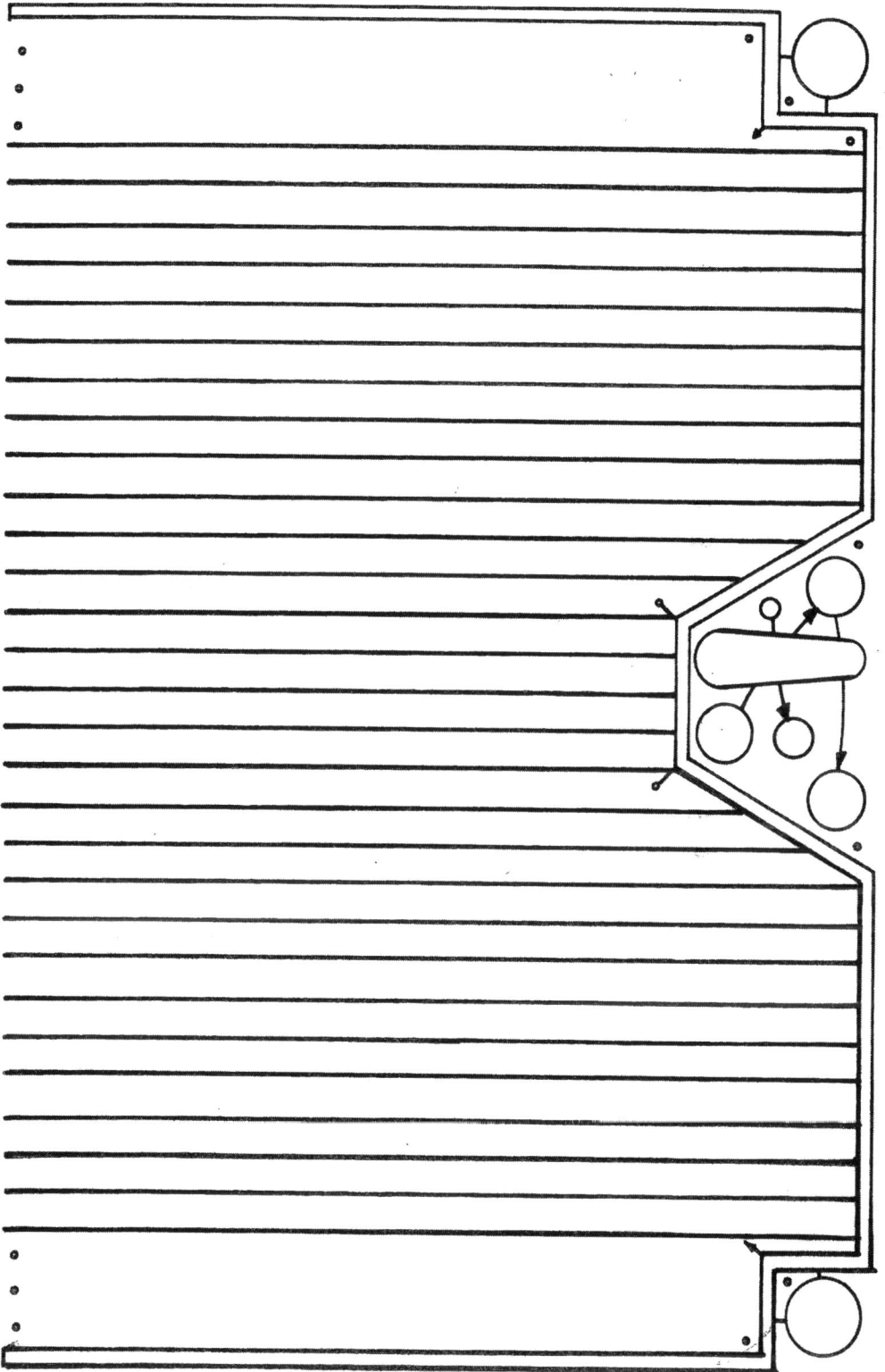

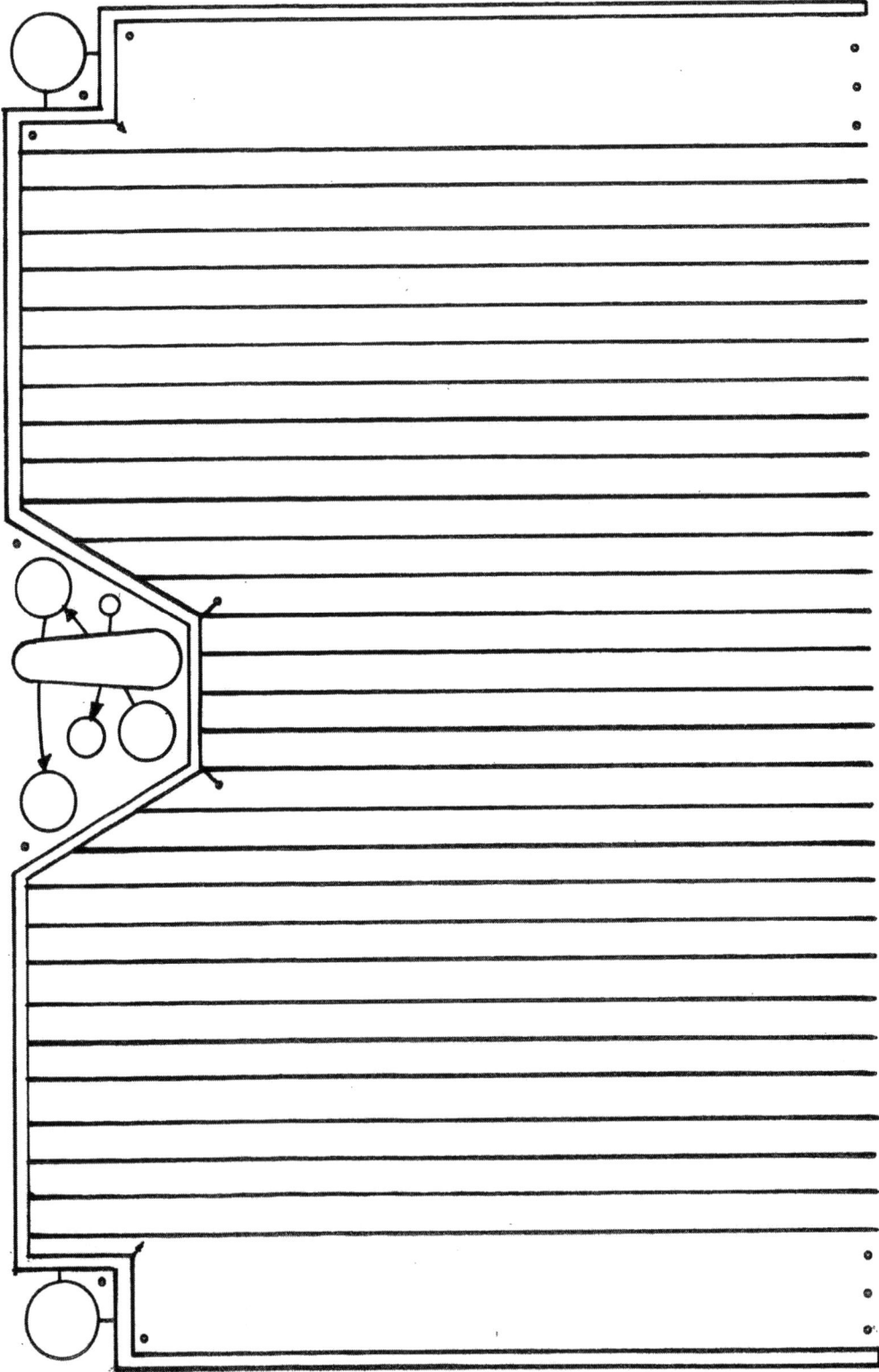

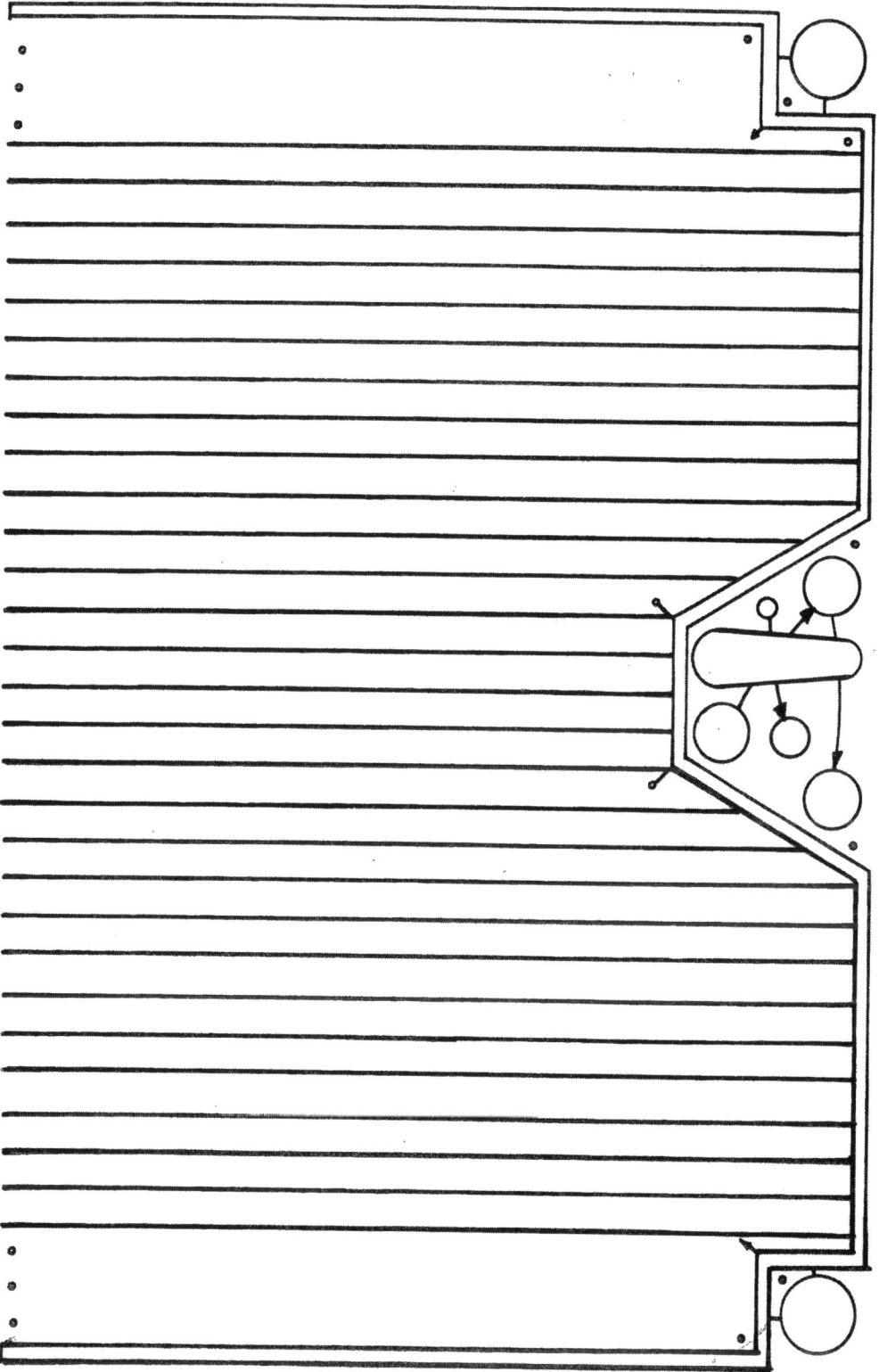

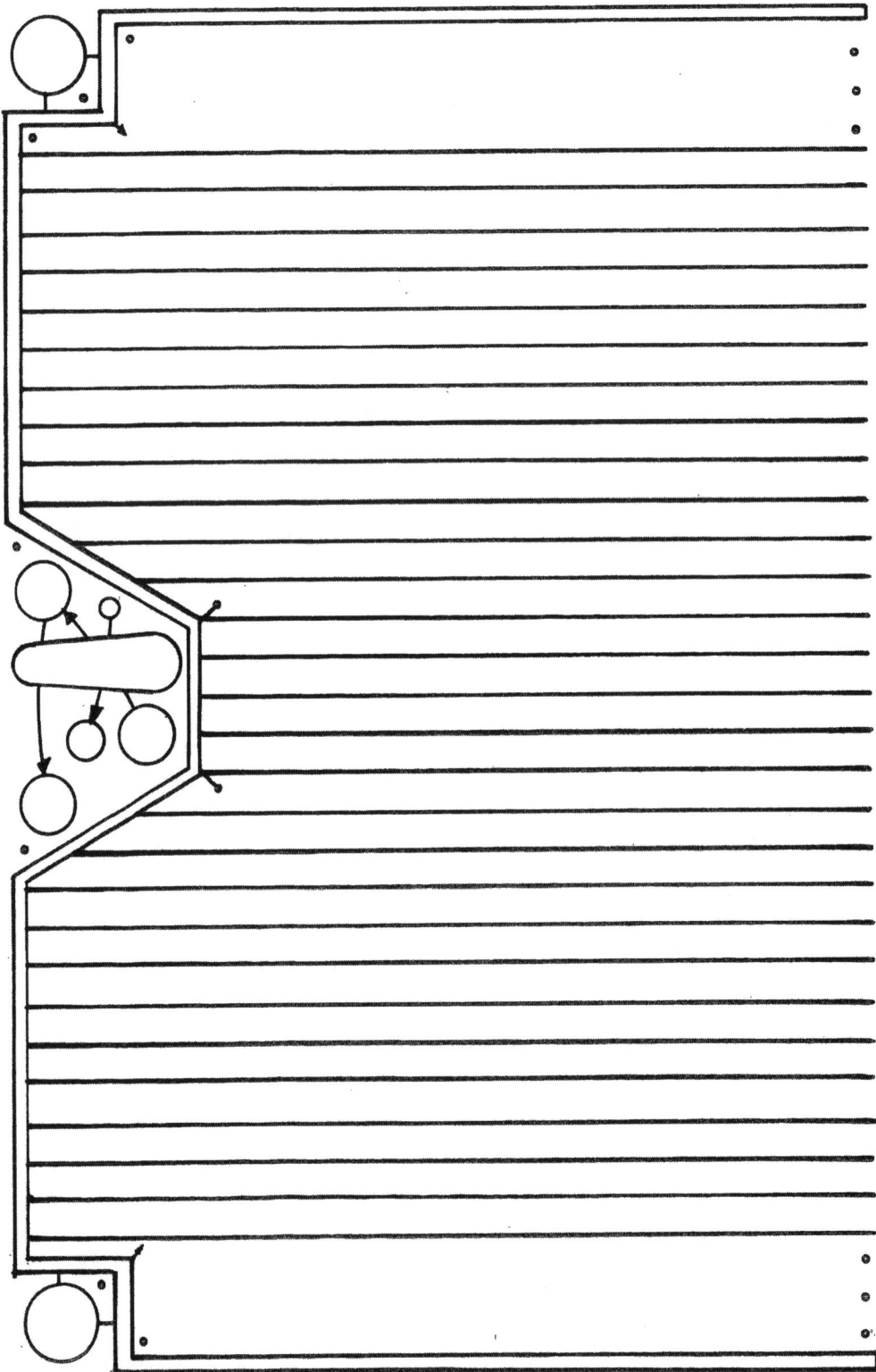

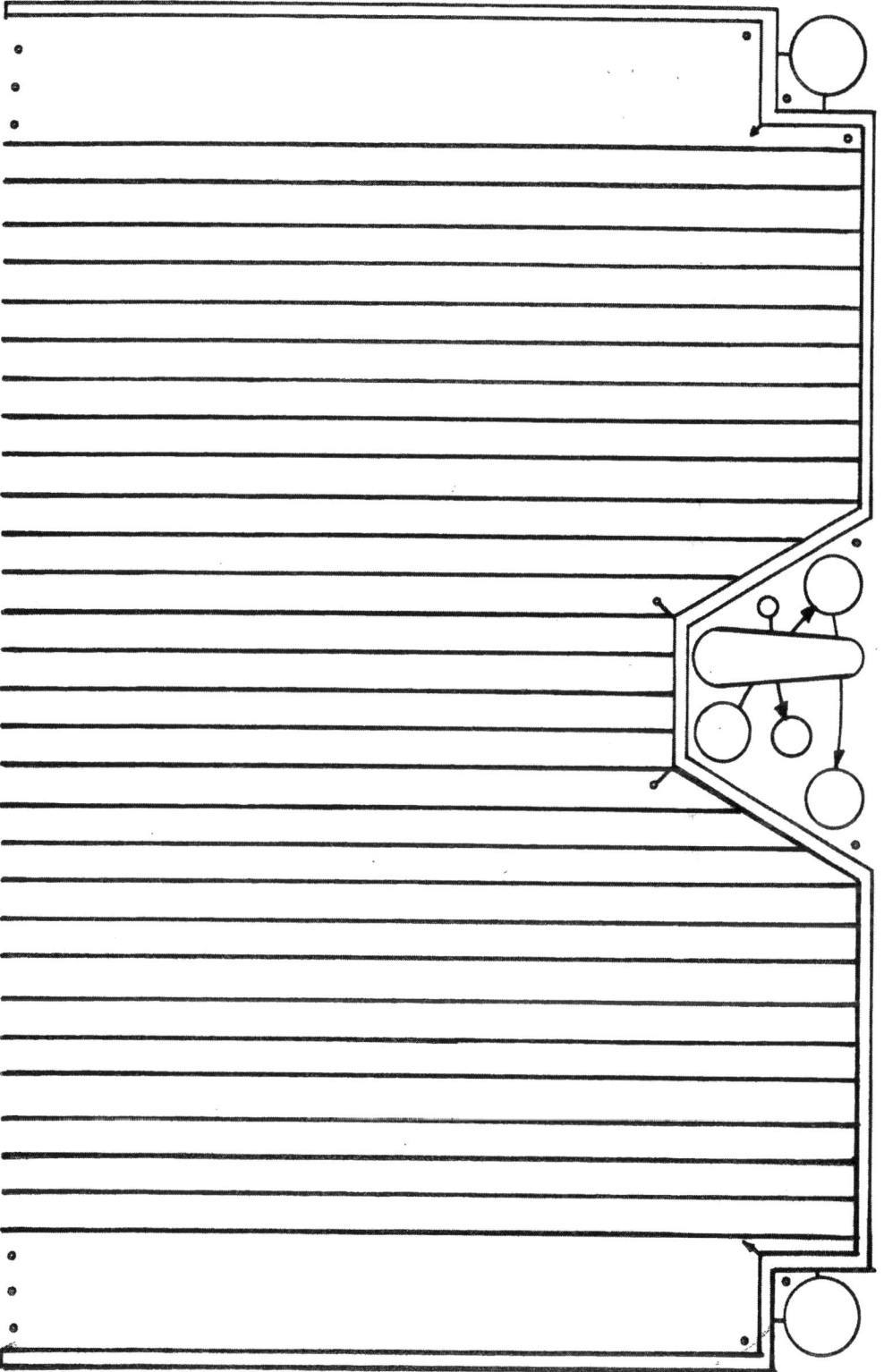

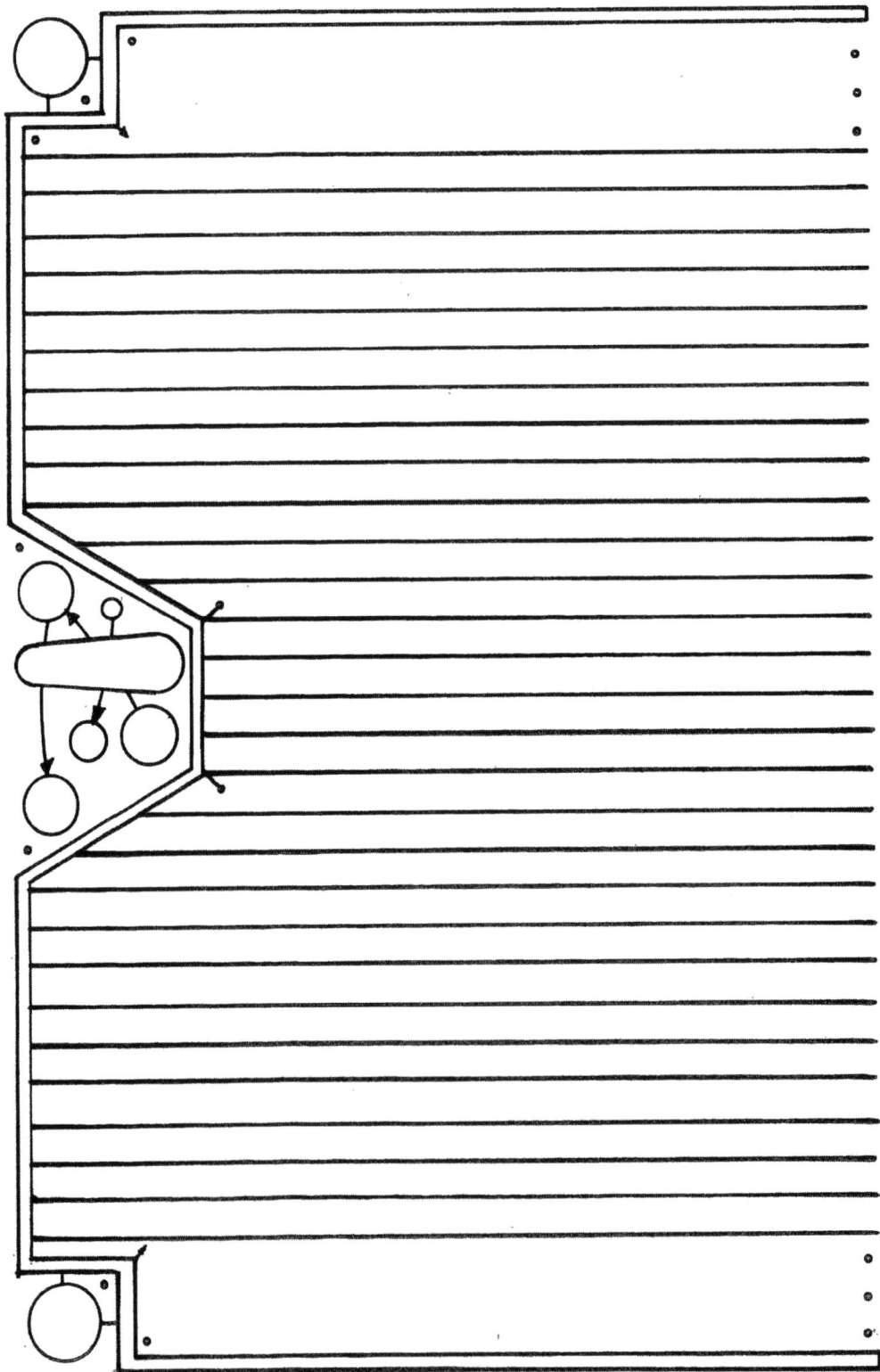

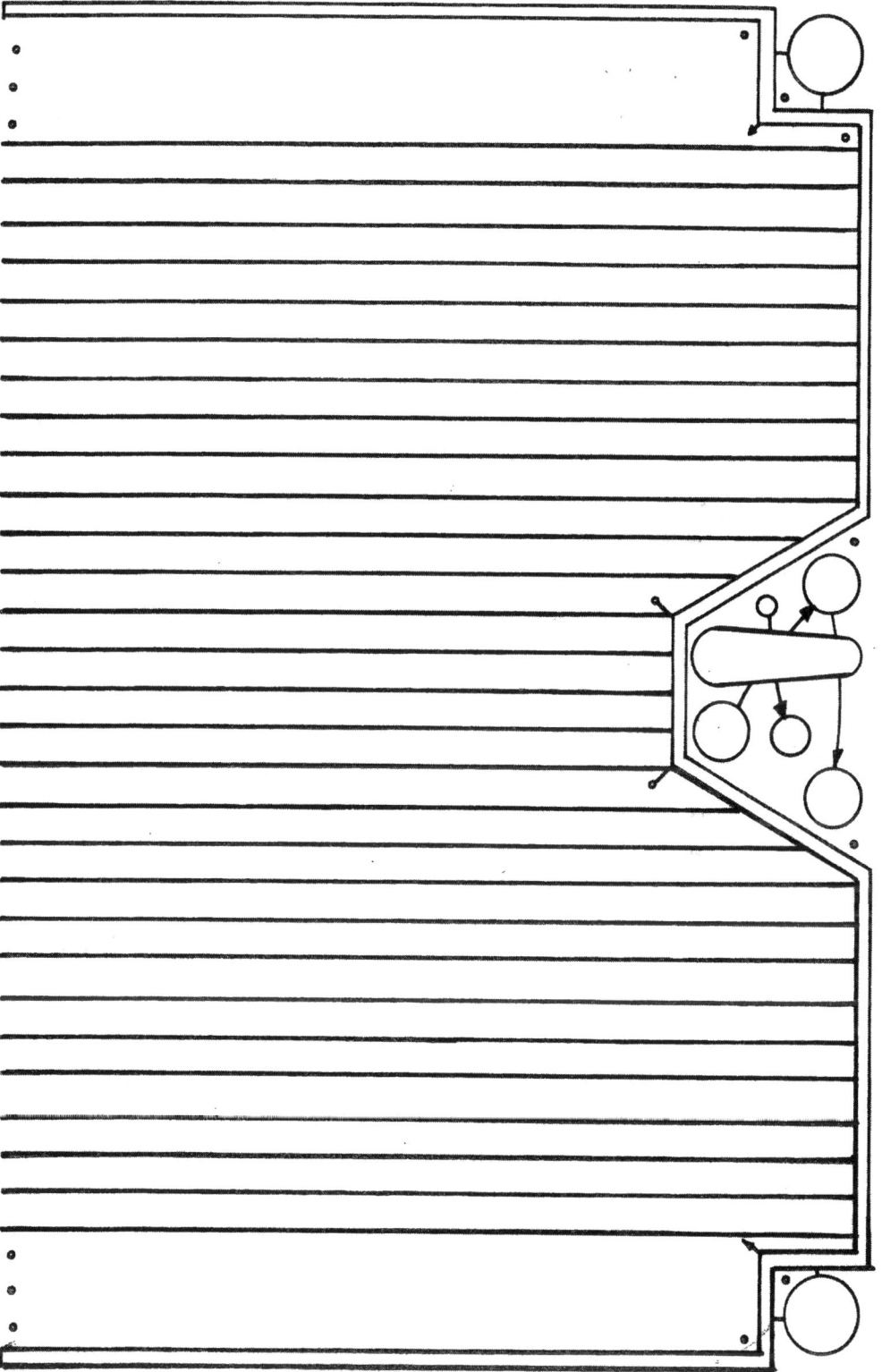

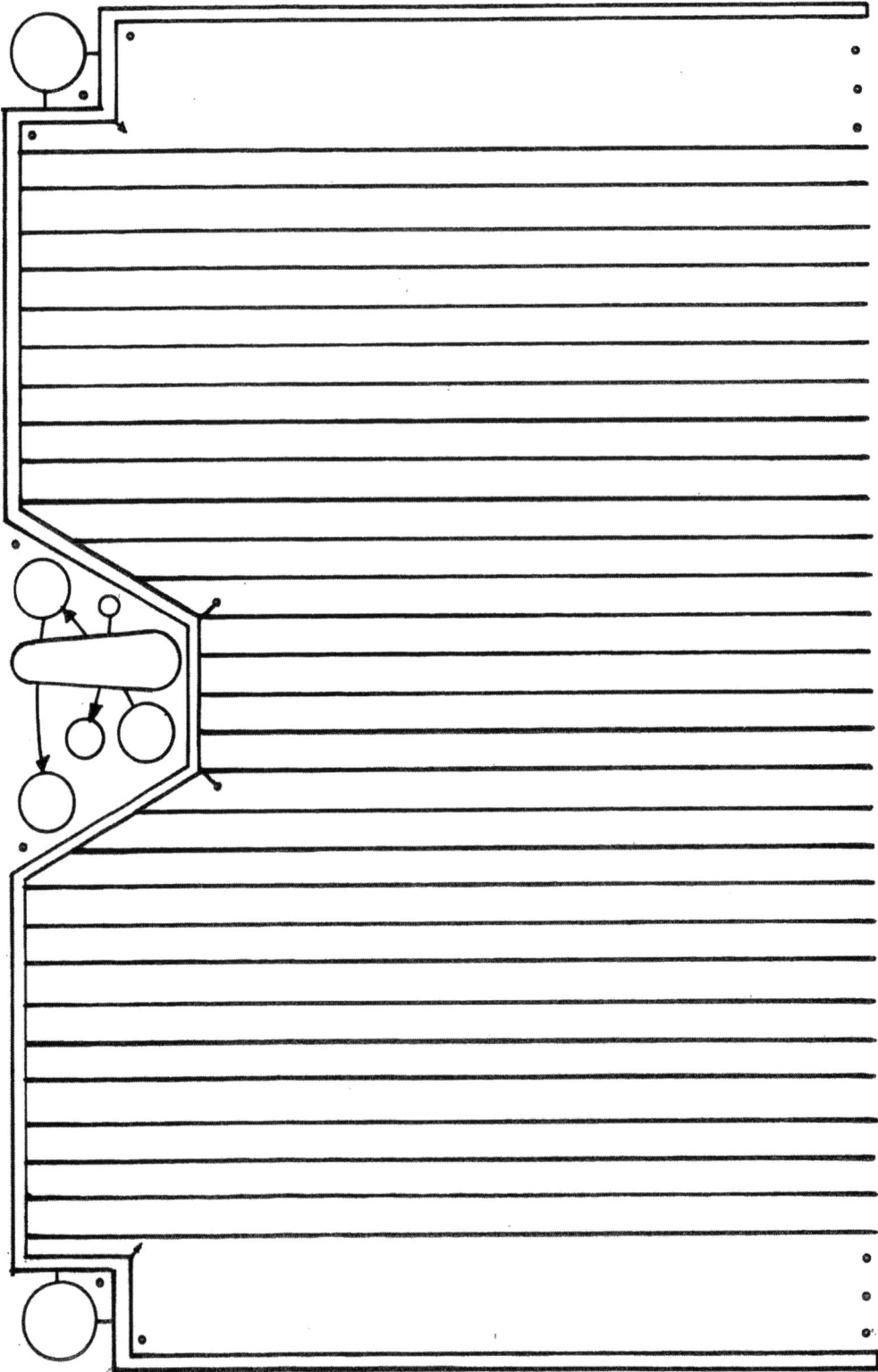

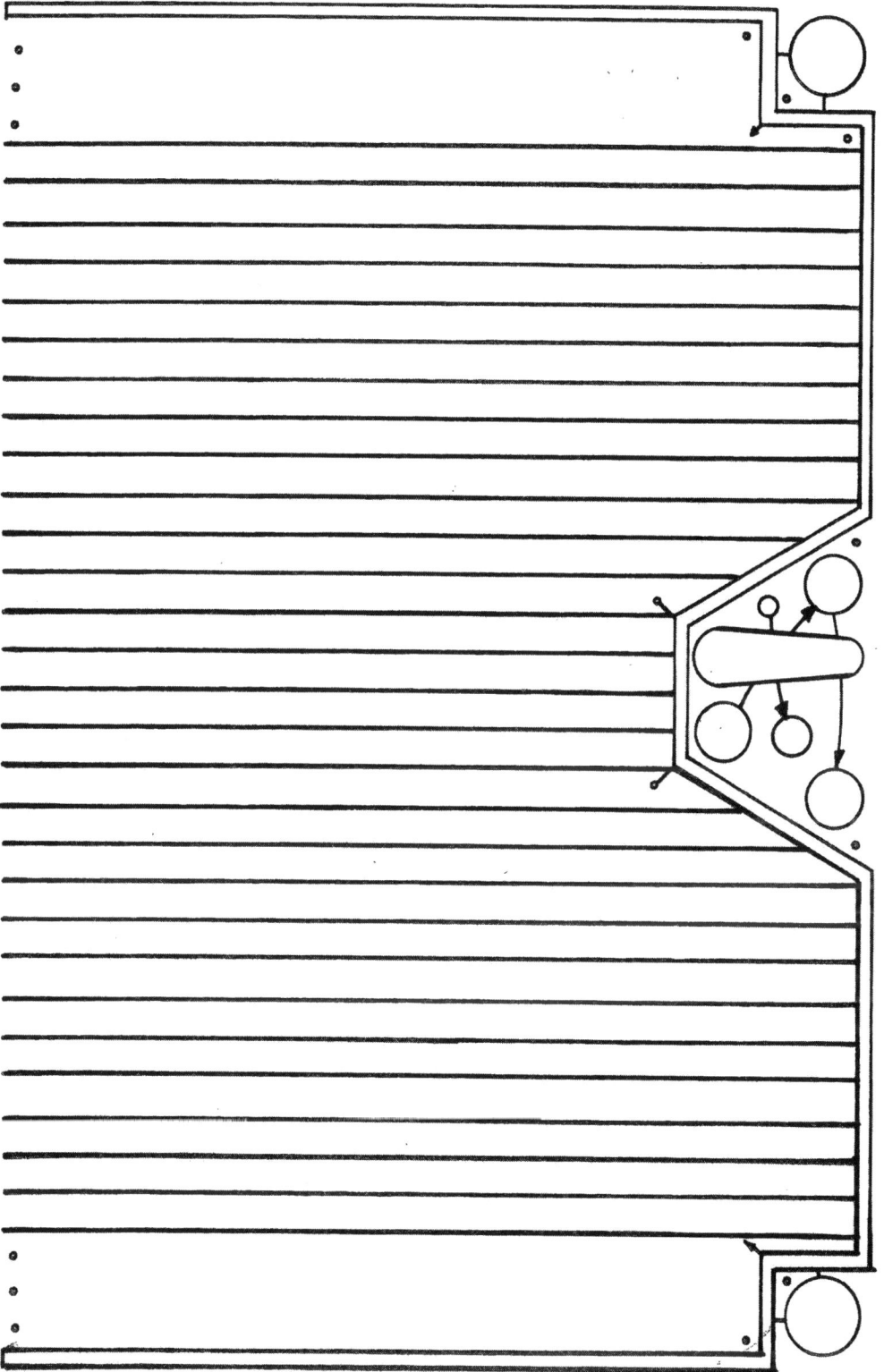

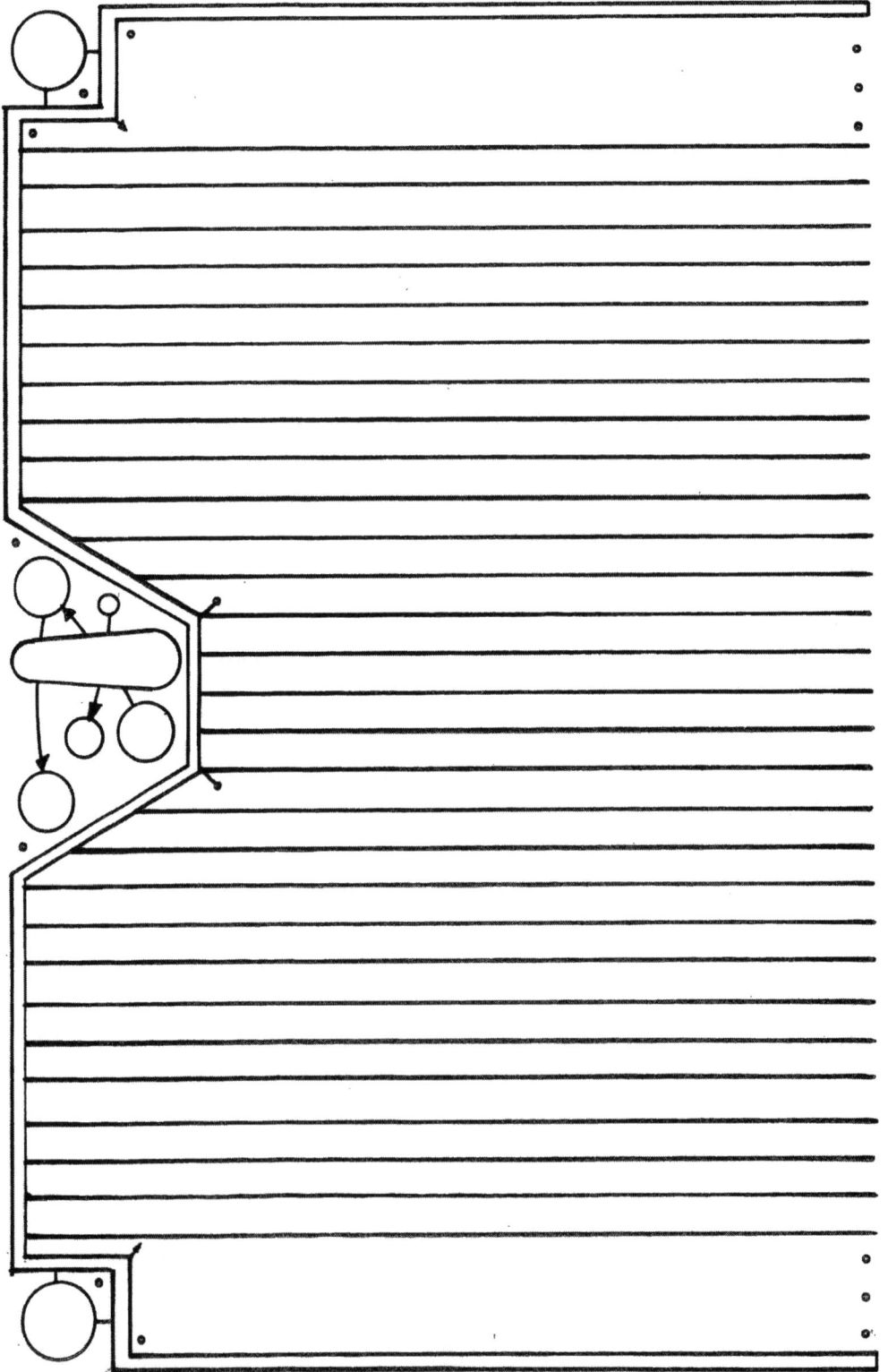

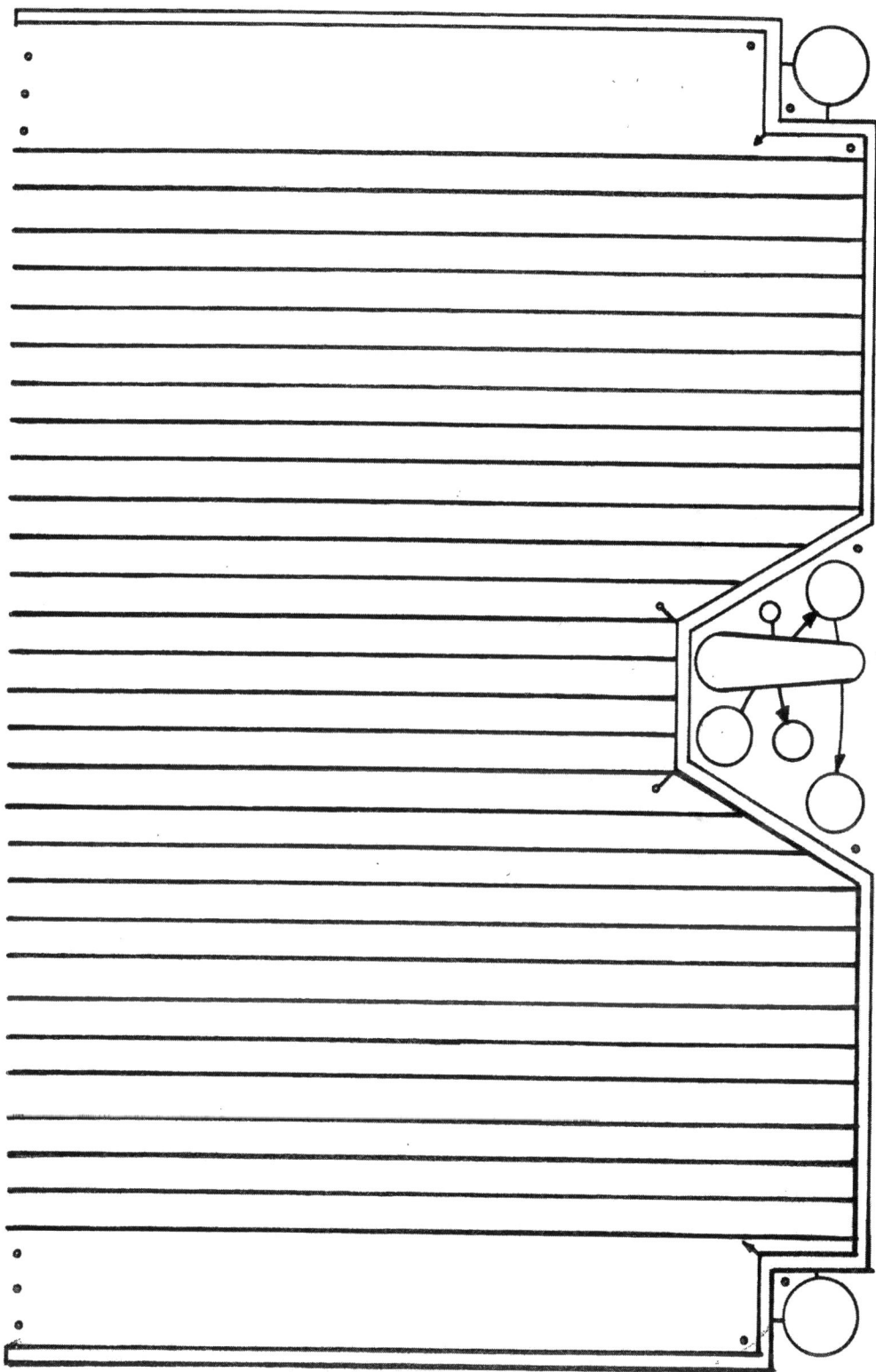

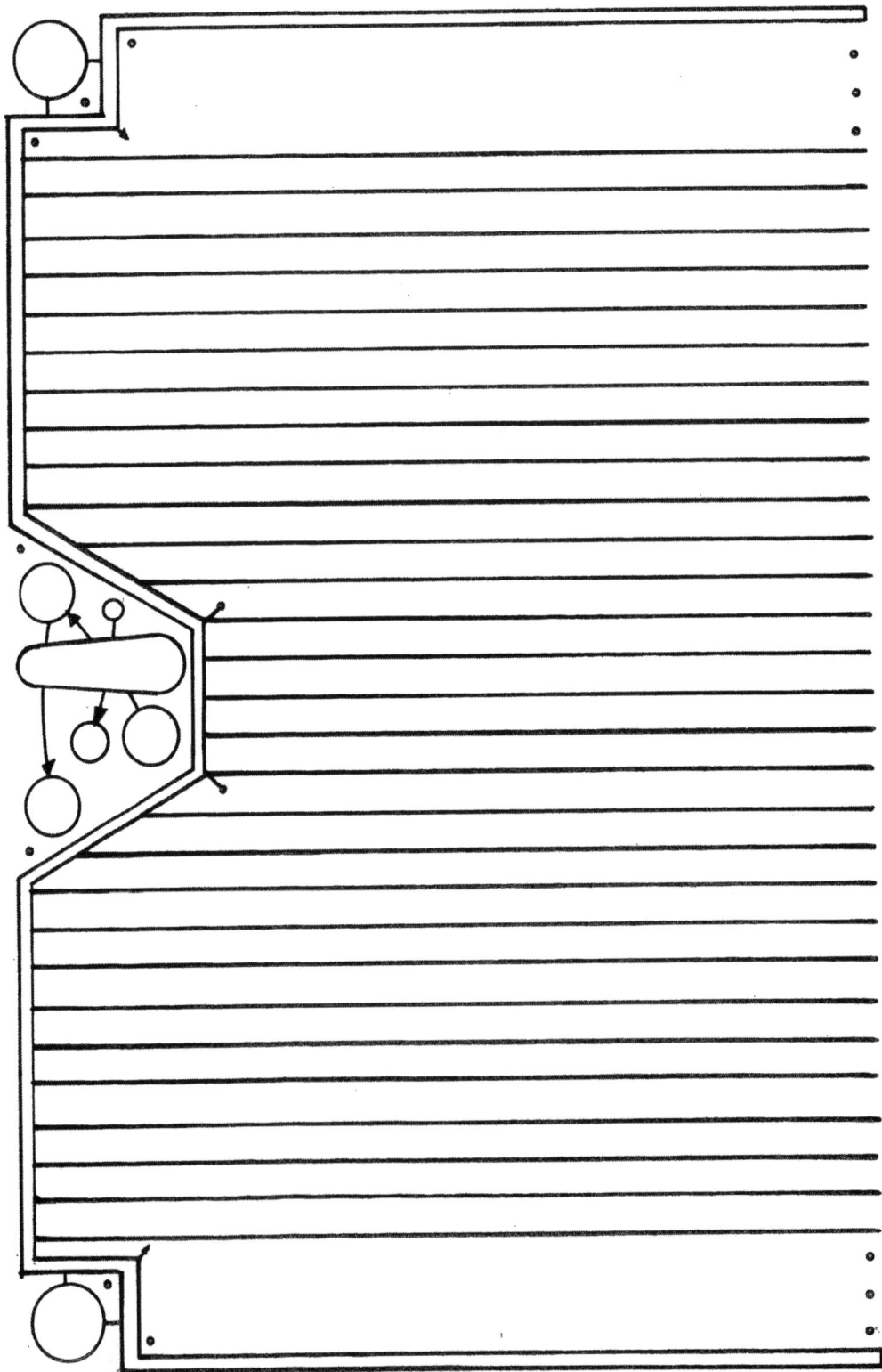

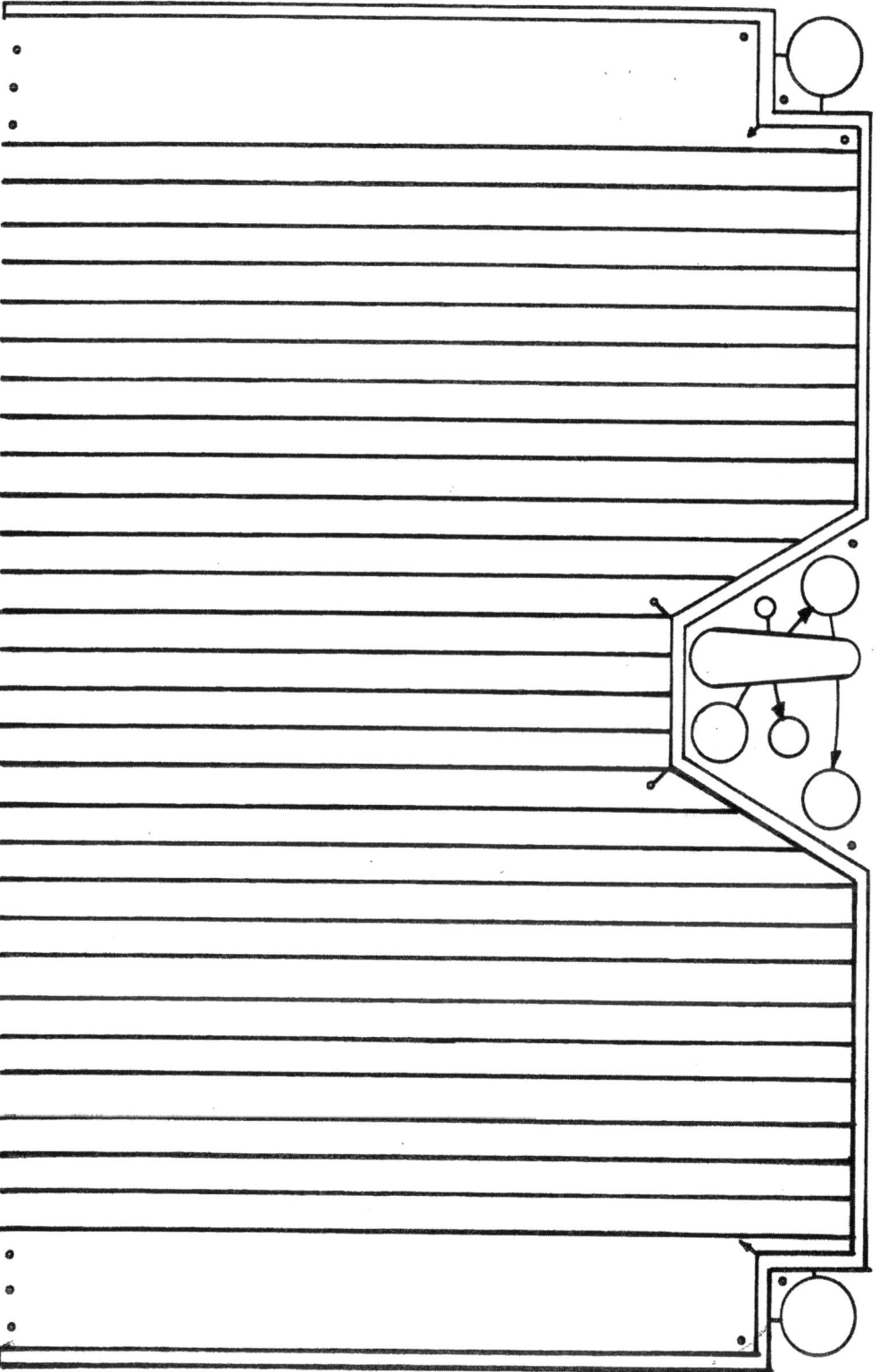

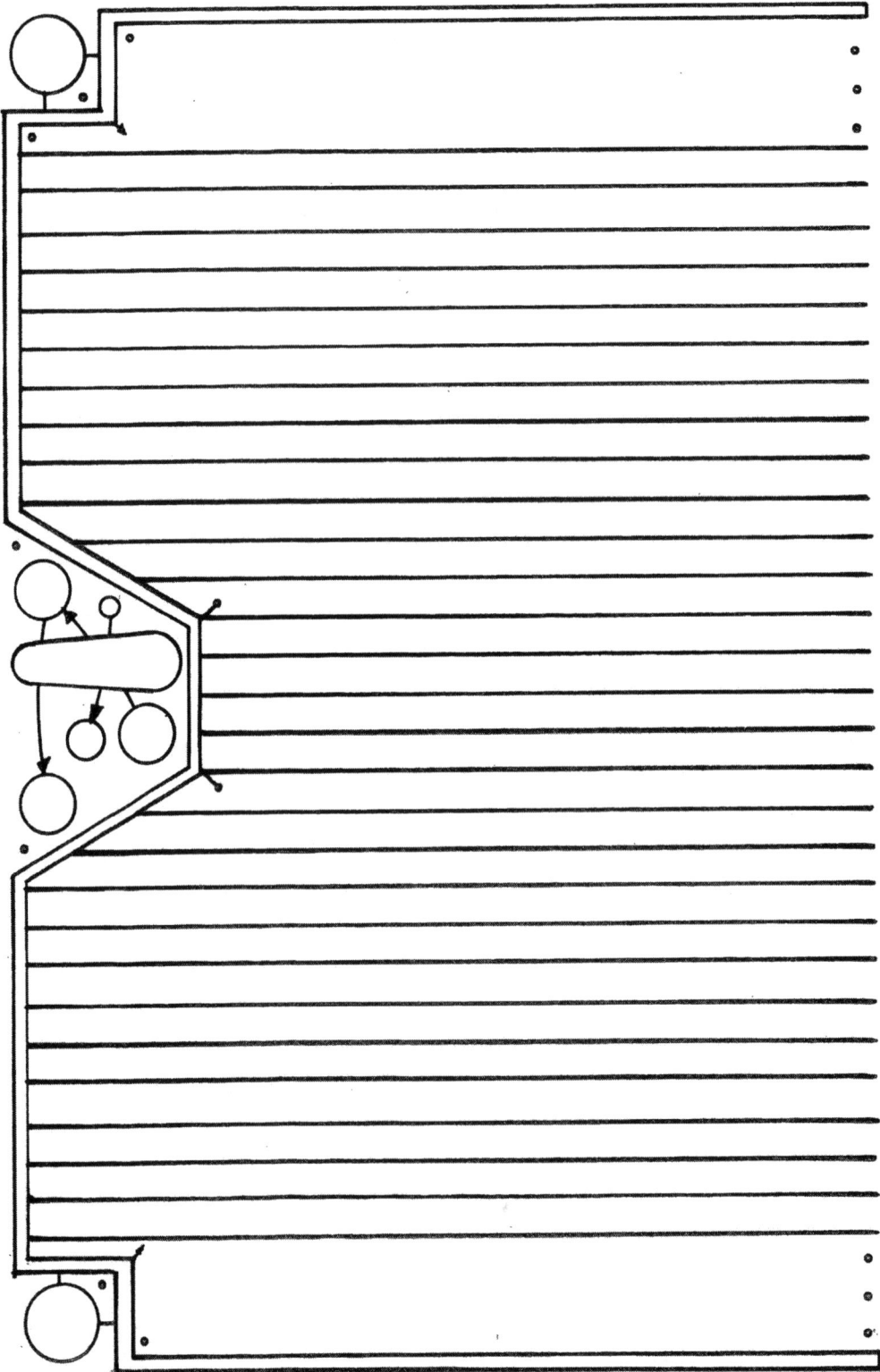

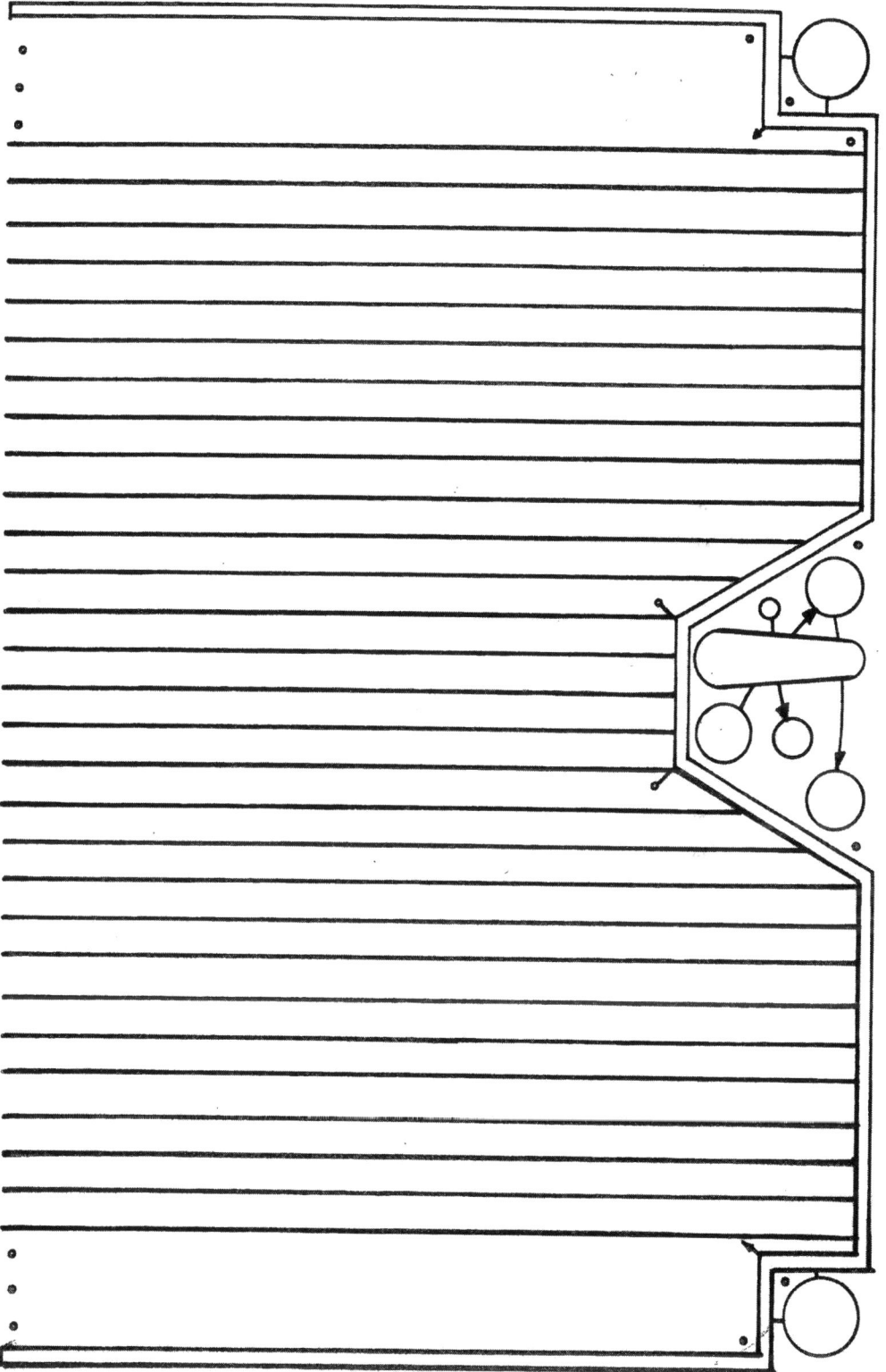

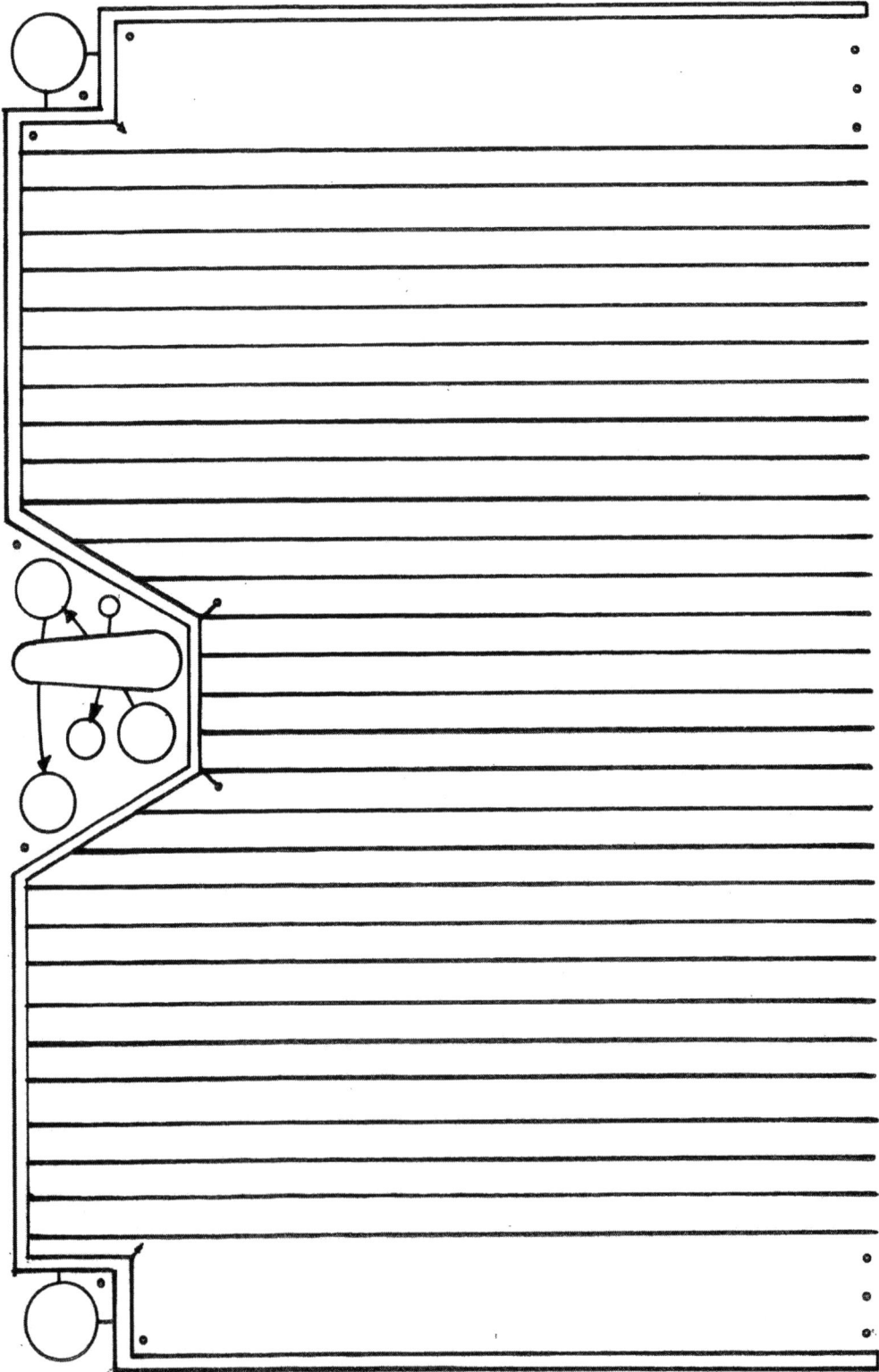

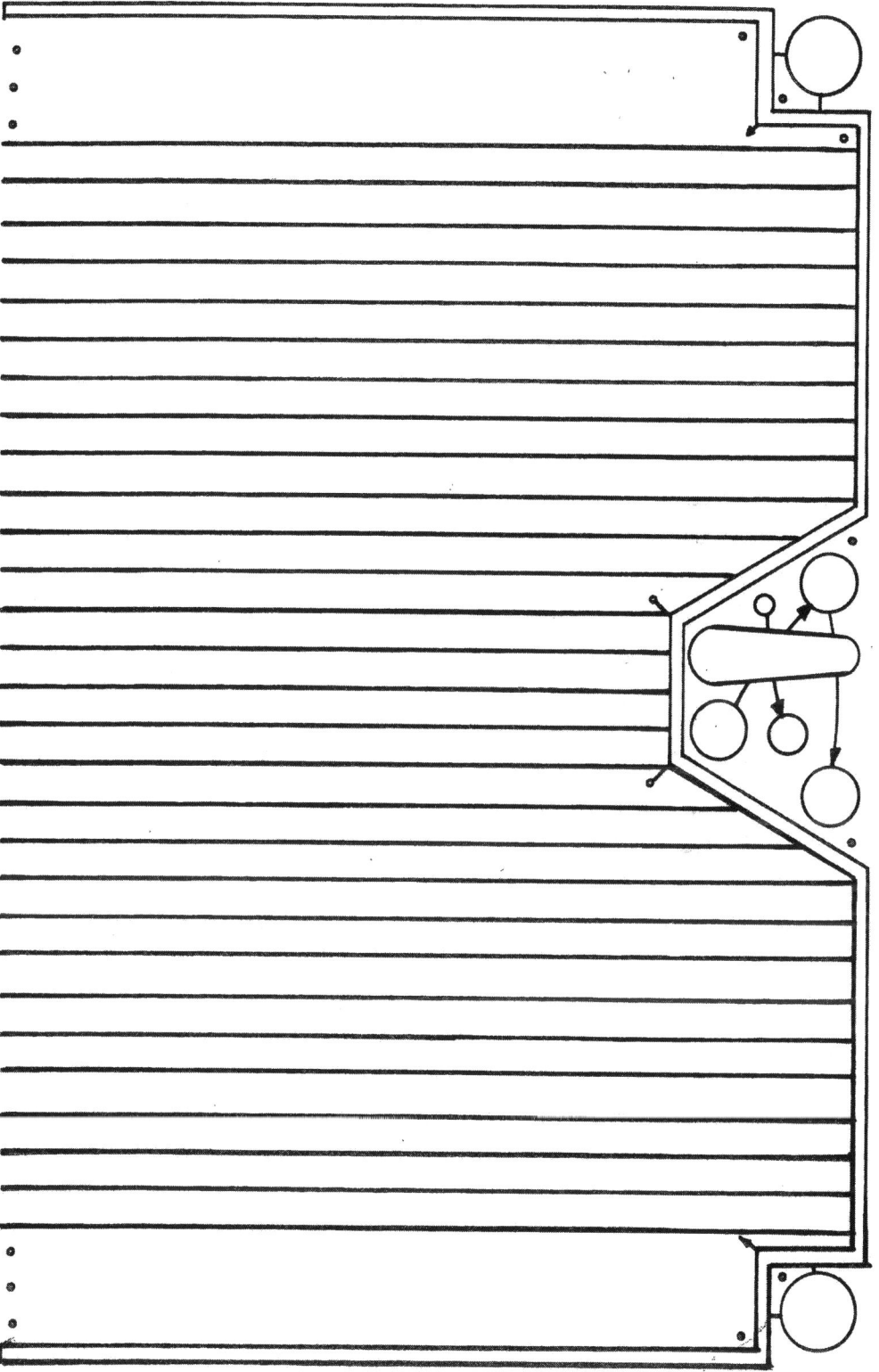

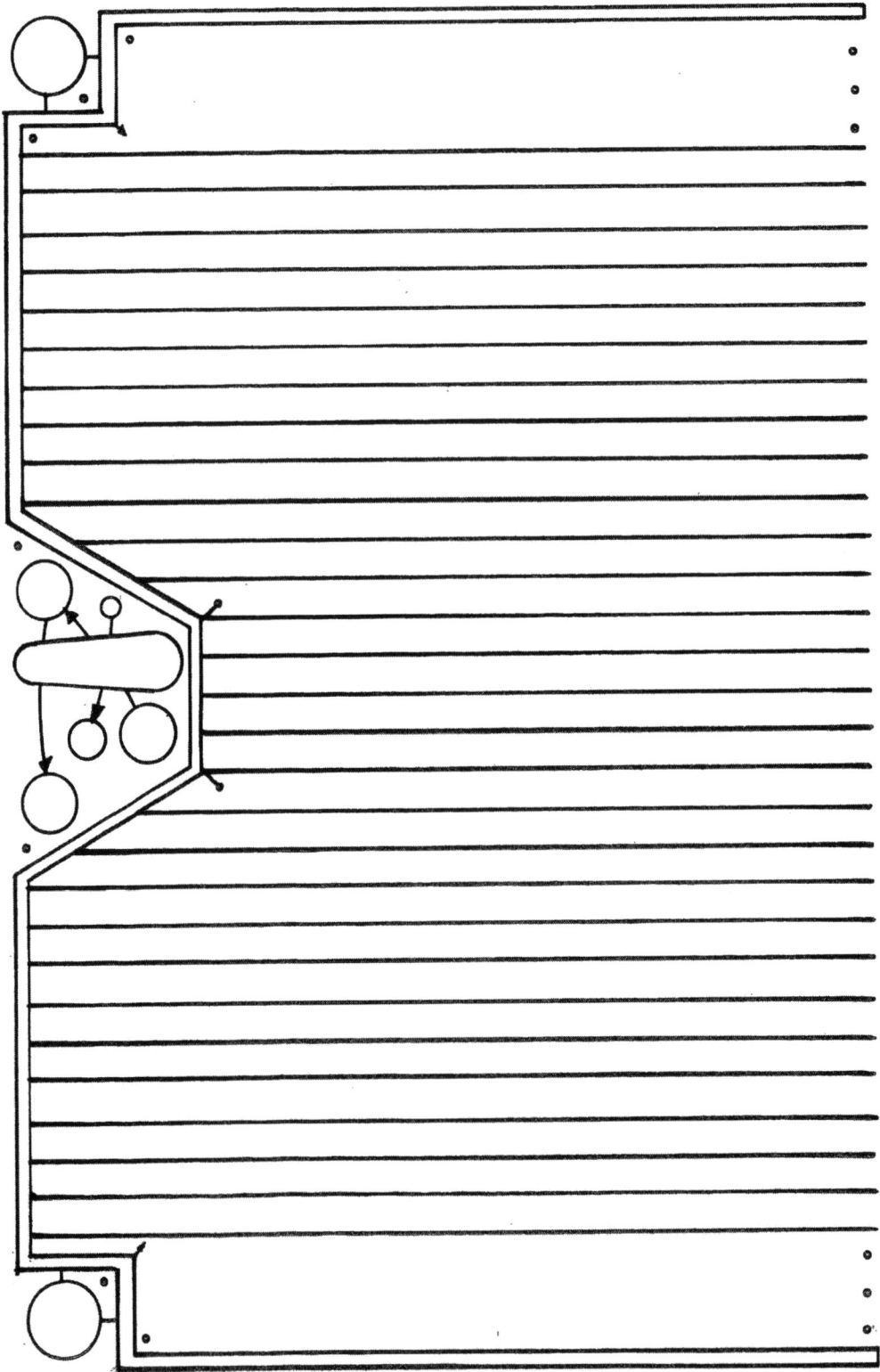

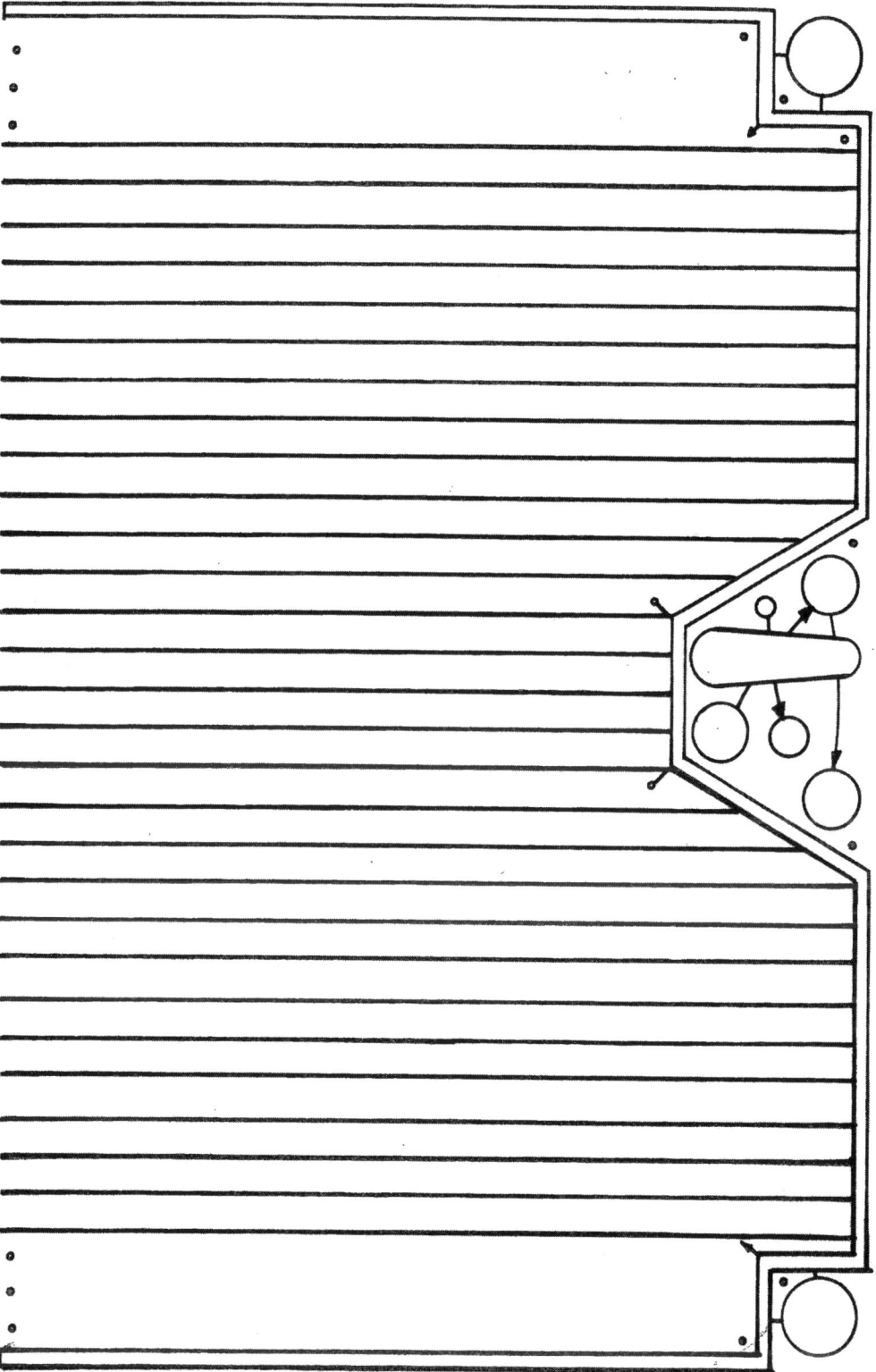

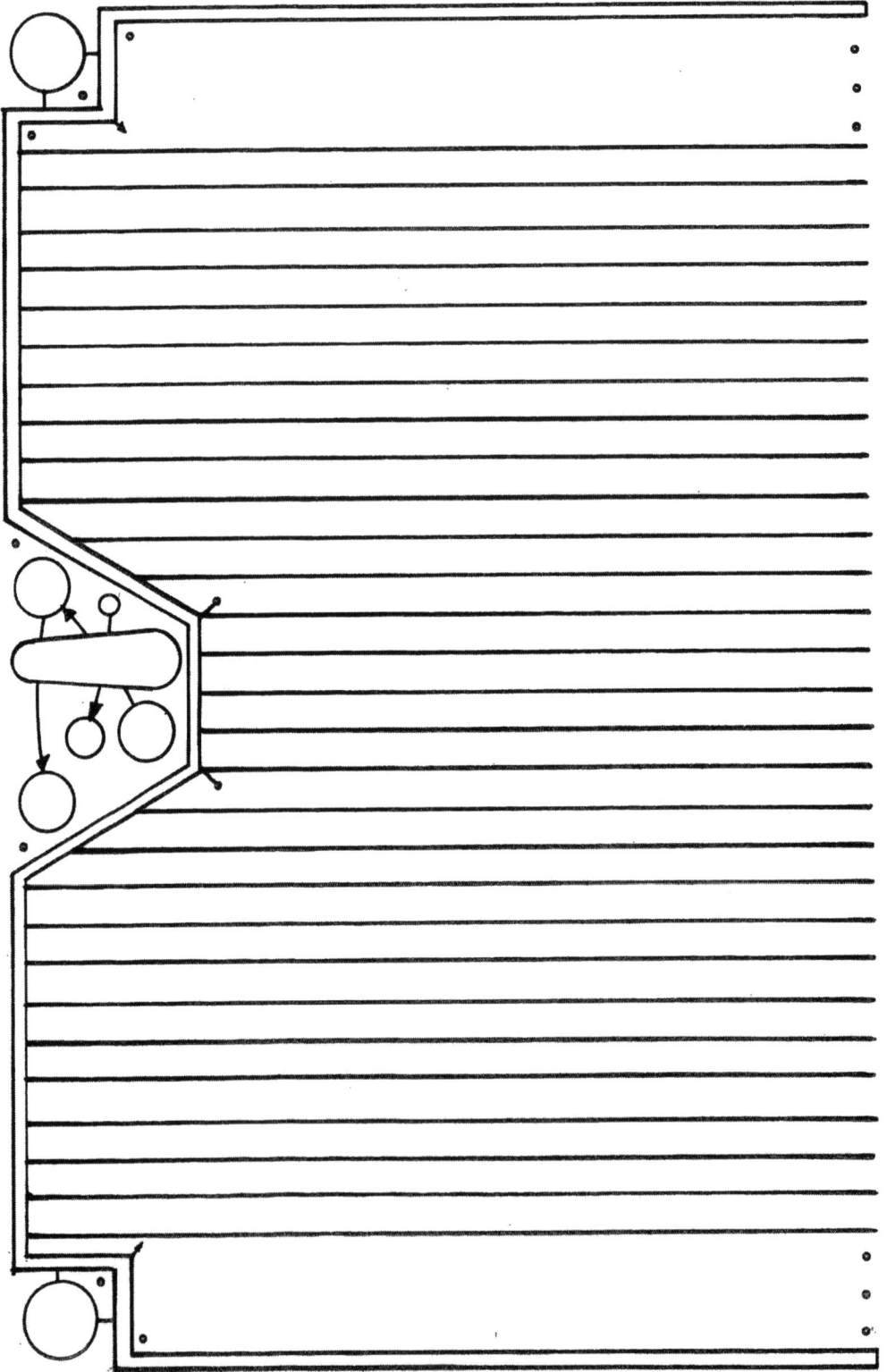

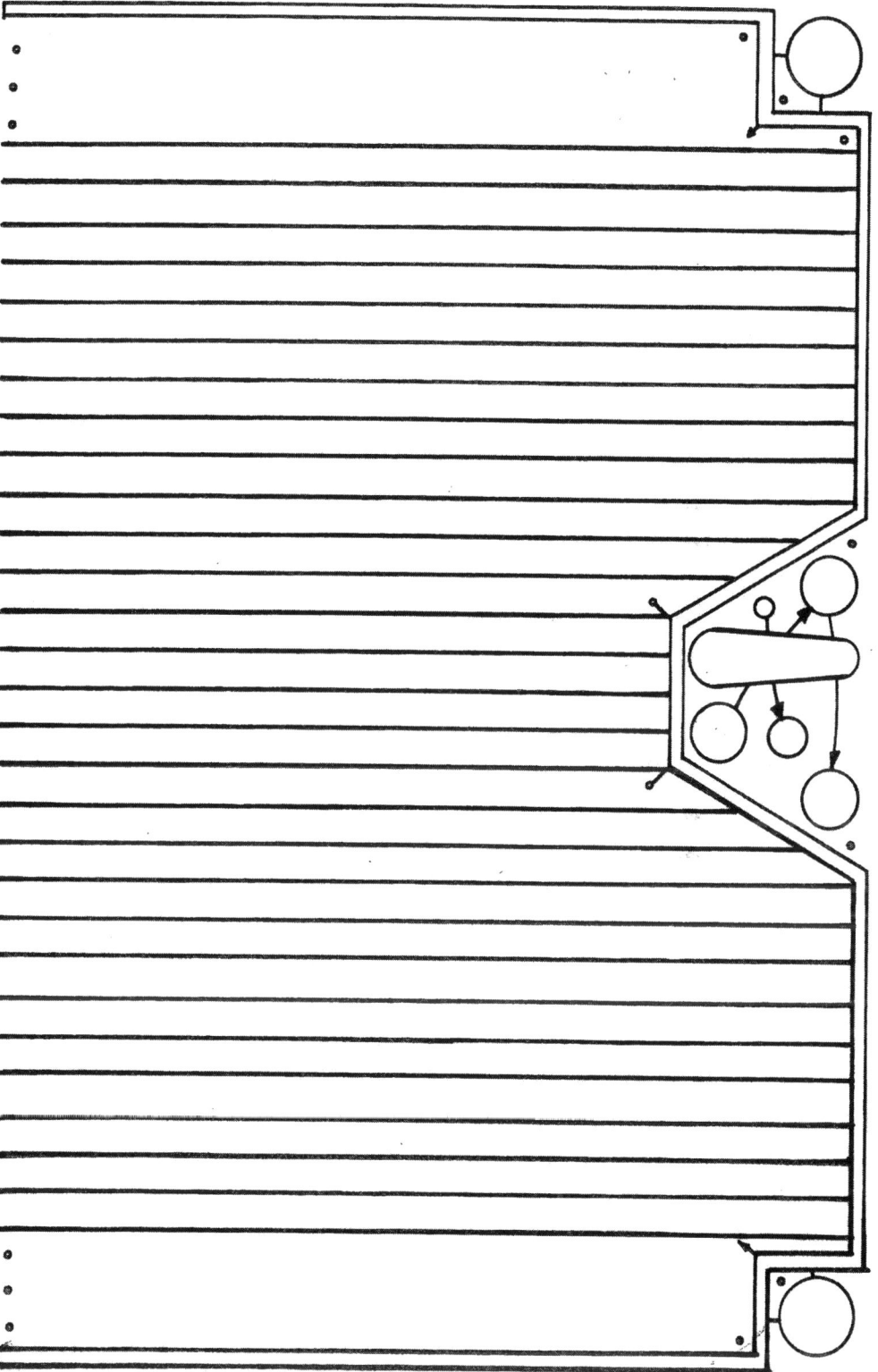

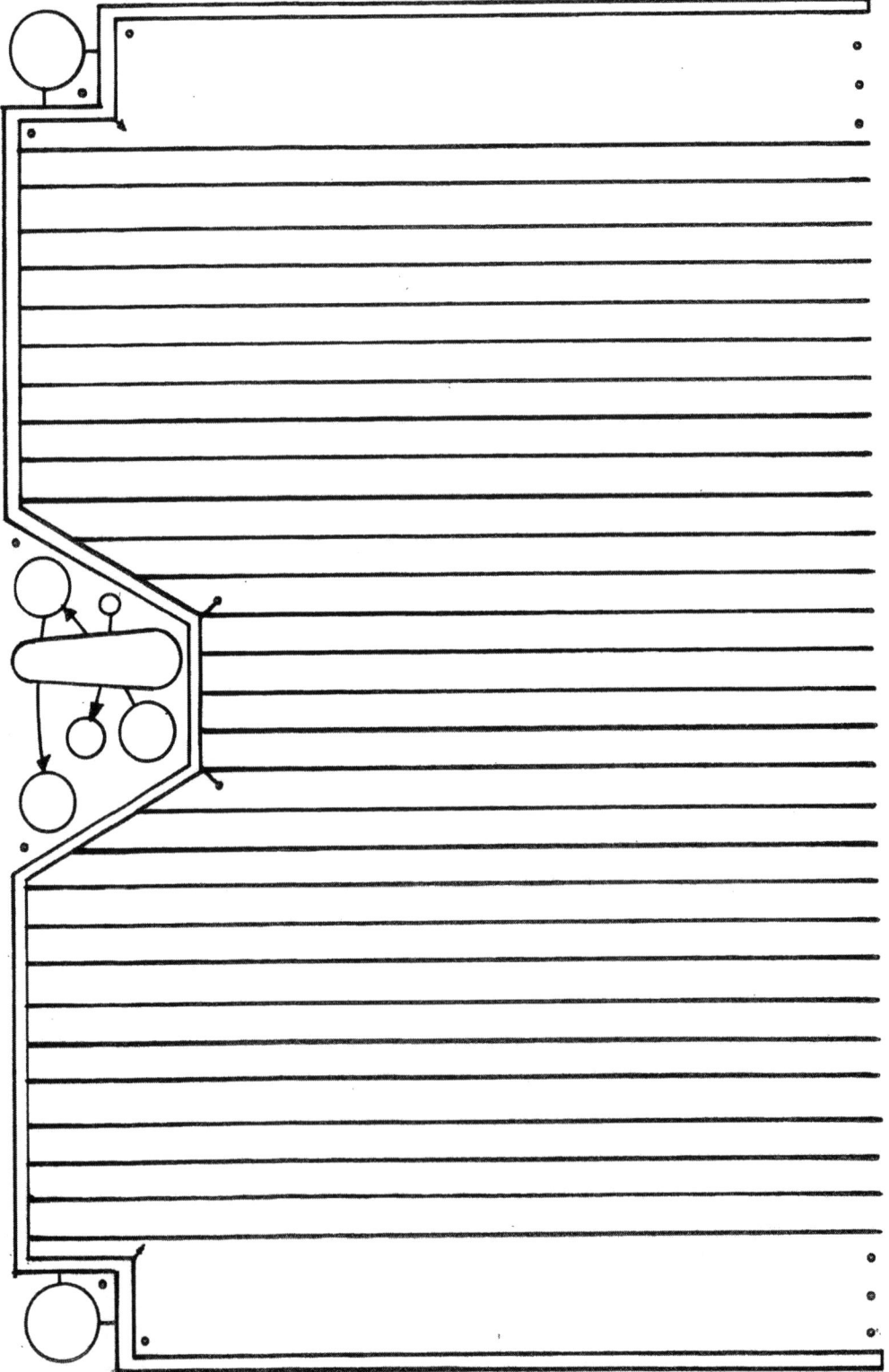

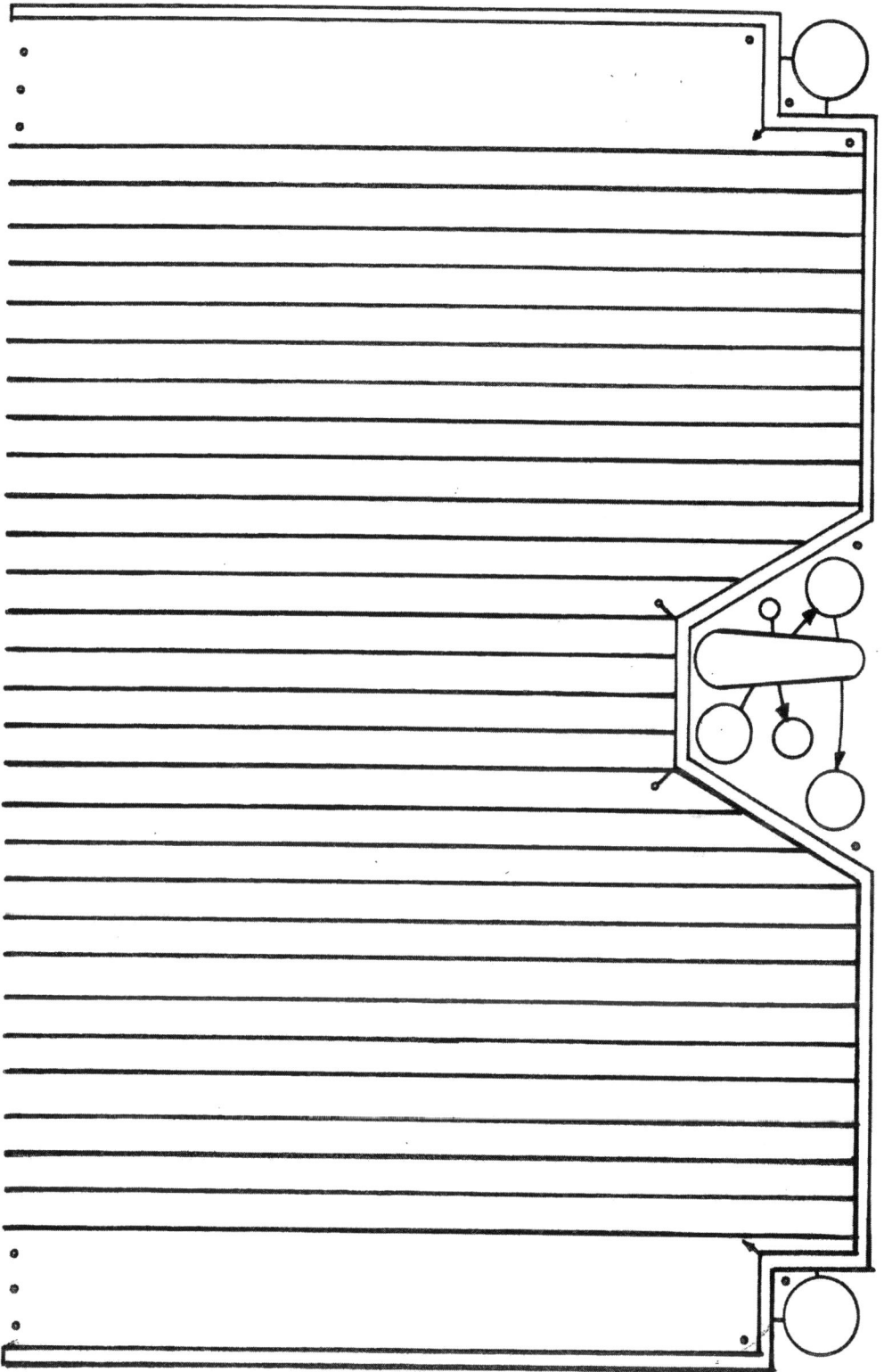

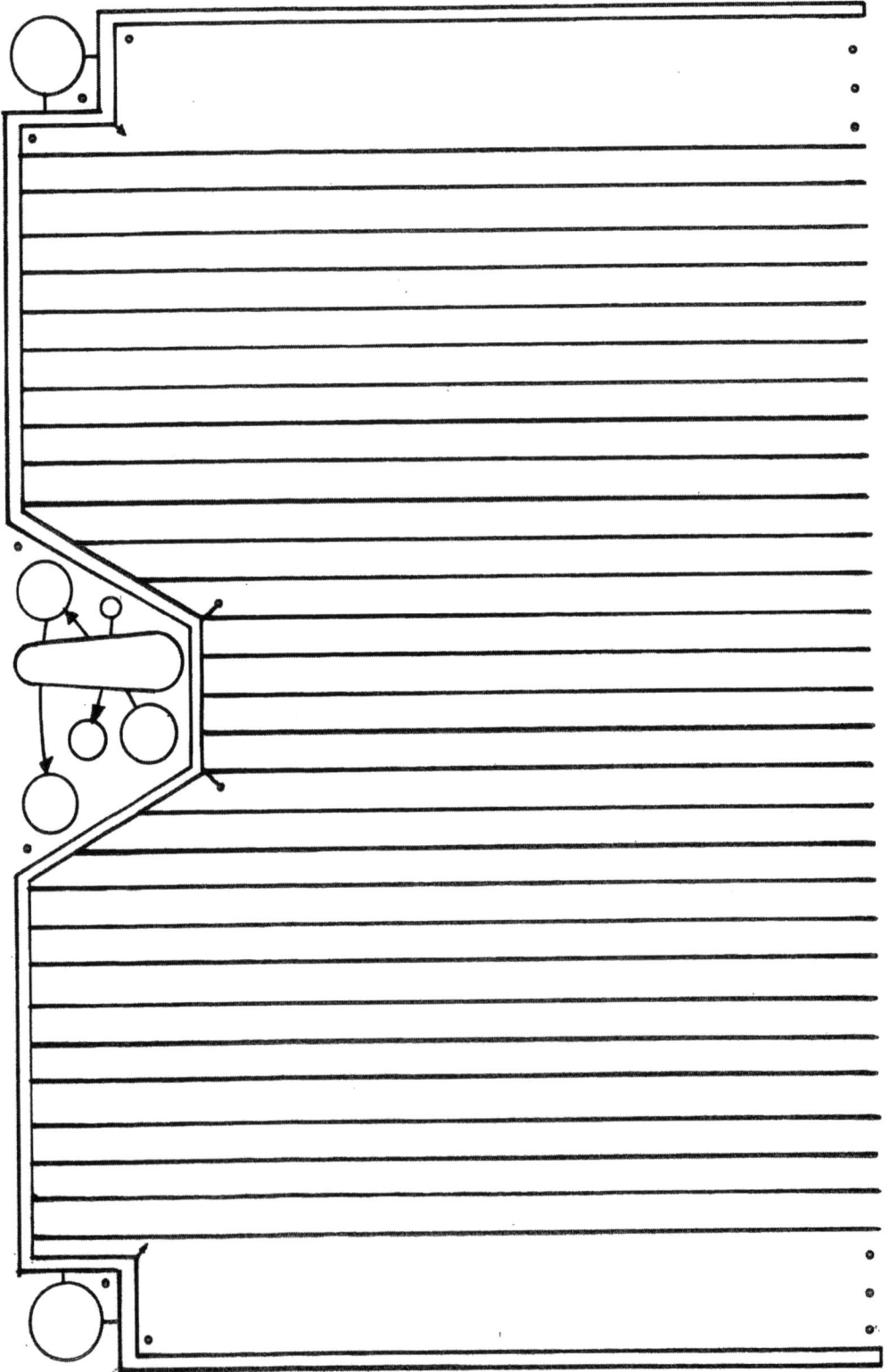

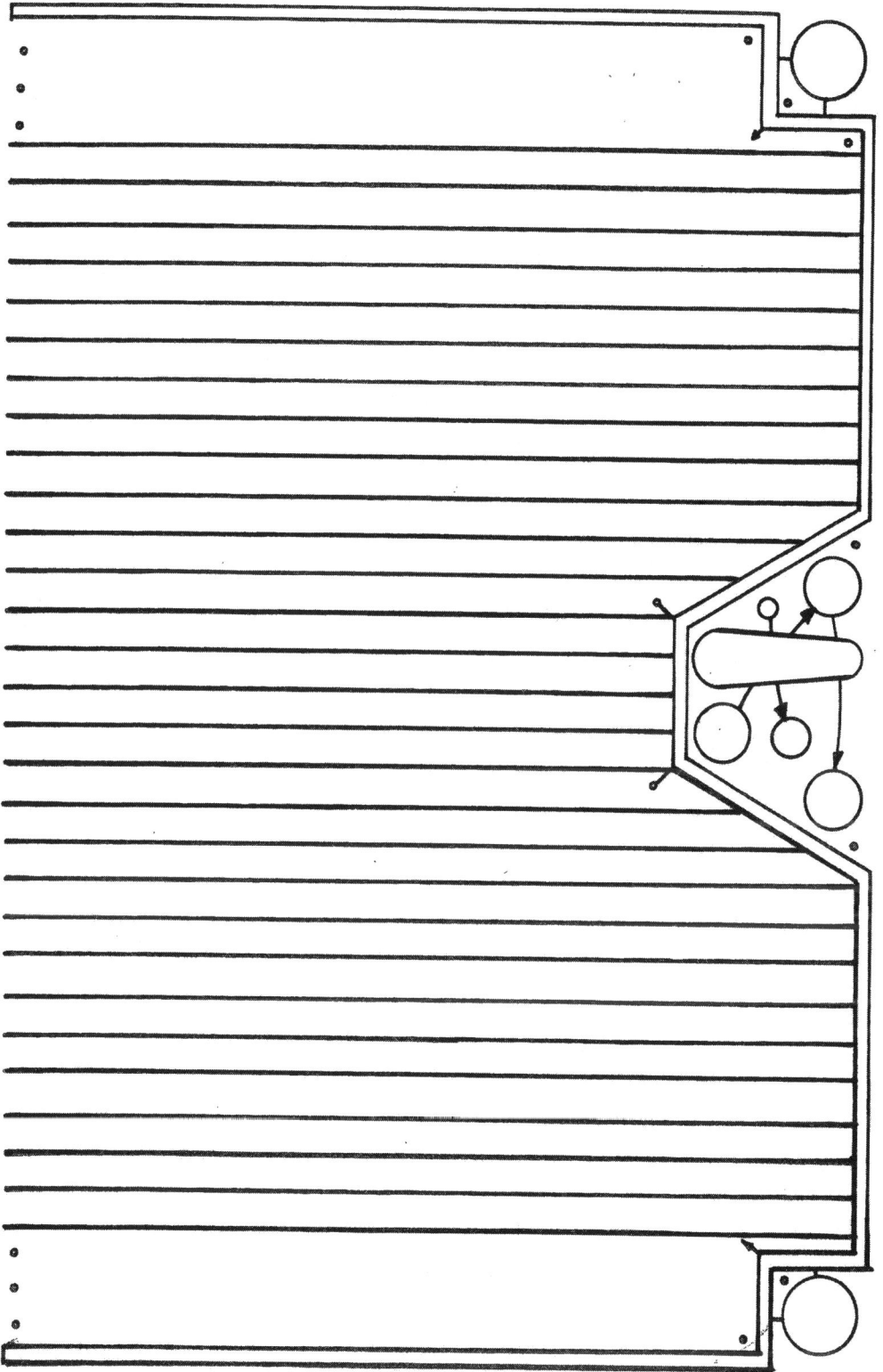

The Expansion series is all about Creation, Creativity, Imagination, Introspection, Growth, Authenticity, Expansion (of course) and the confidence to feel empowered in your greatest quality, YOU.

I.E.

INTROSPECTIVE EXPANSION

The idea behind Introspective Expansion is one's desire to write, journal, document, examine, creatively formulate and expand one's view of reality through consciously noting your observation of this wild ride along the journey. List keeping. Goal setting and smashing, etc. . .

Truly up to you on how you choose to express yourself. And you may as well do it in a dope book, deliberately created with gratitude and love that is fun and interesting to use, with a community centered heartbeat every step of the way.

So enjoy these sample pages of the full Introspective Expansion vol 02. Designed with your enjoyment of the experience in mind.

Expand your reality and discover the joy in the journey with the rest of the expansion series journals available now.

Go forth boldly and create deliberately.

INTROSPECTIVE EXPANSION
volume 02

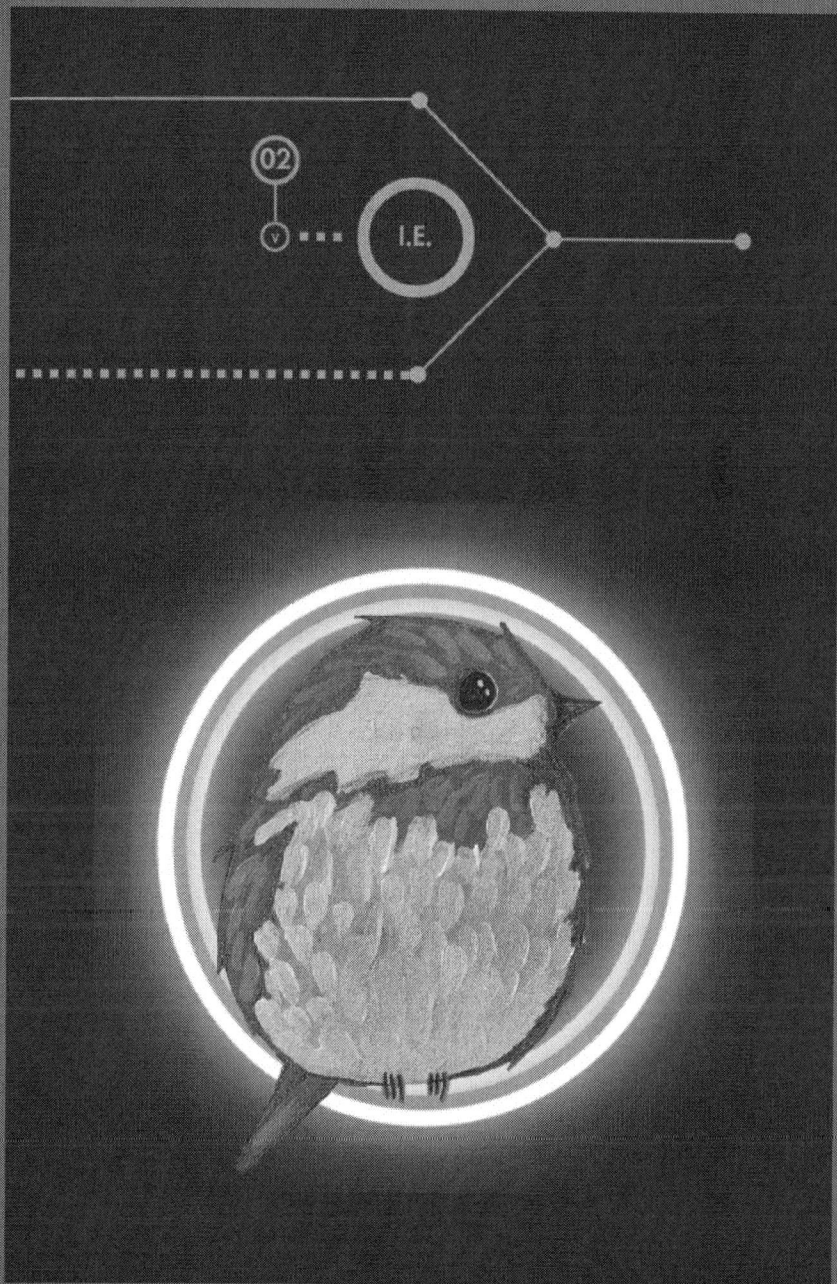

02

V • • • • I.E.

Cover art by Ashley Rose

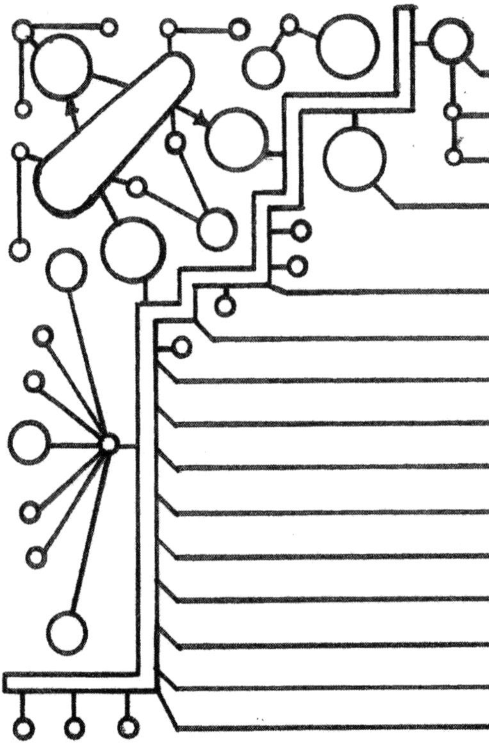

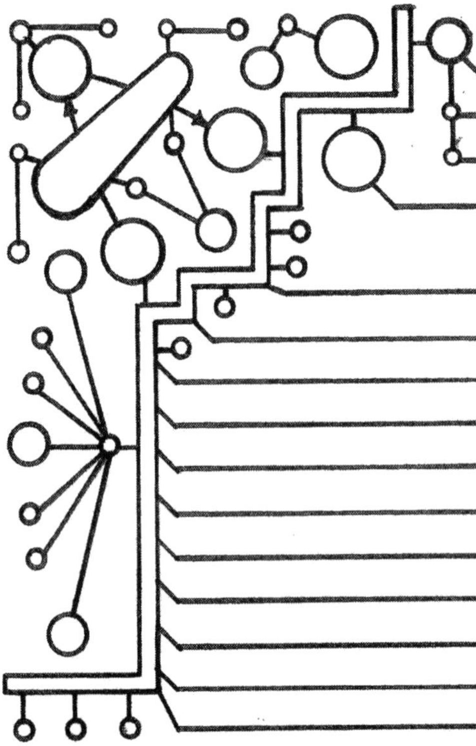

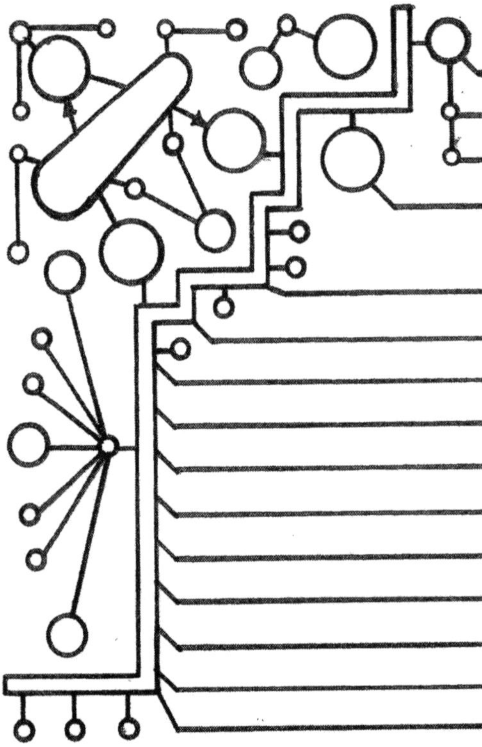

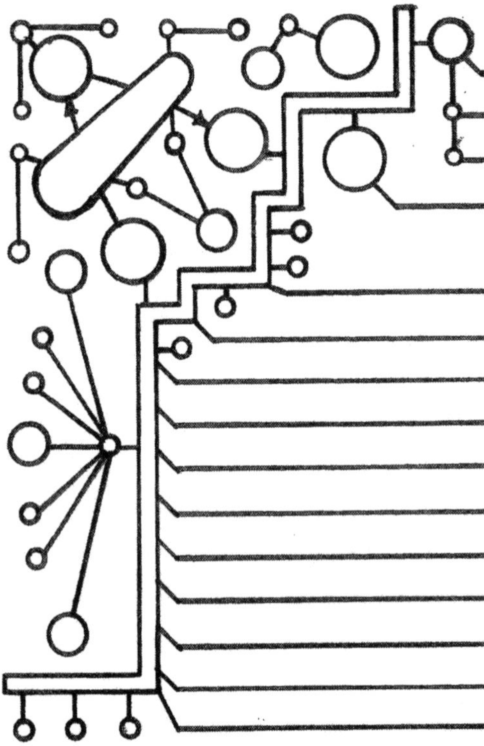

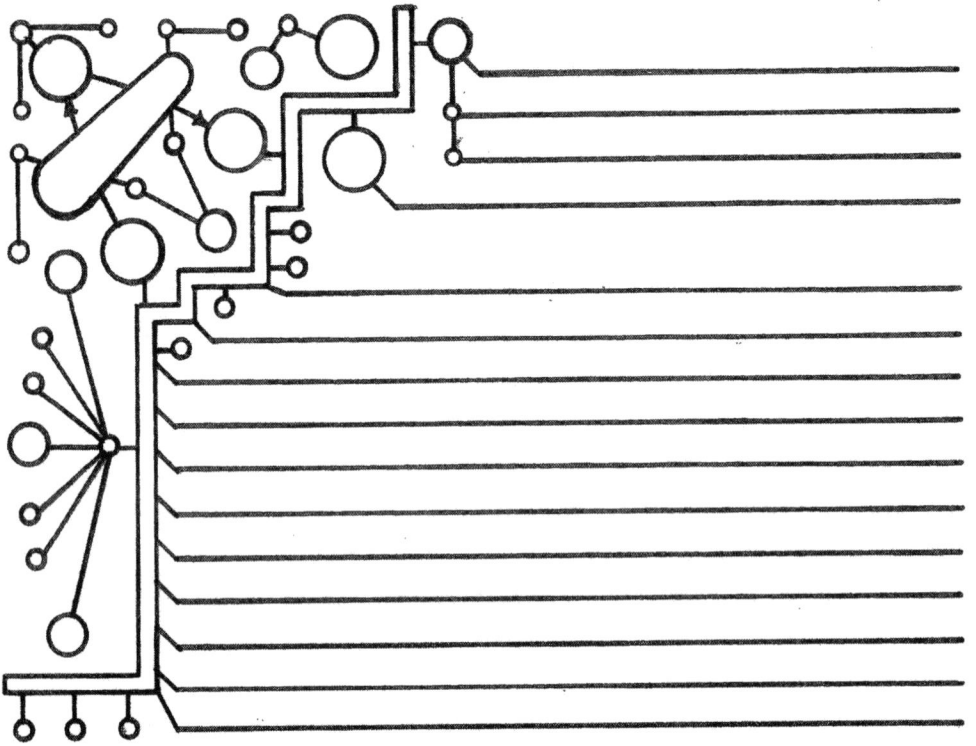

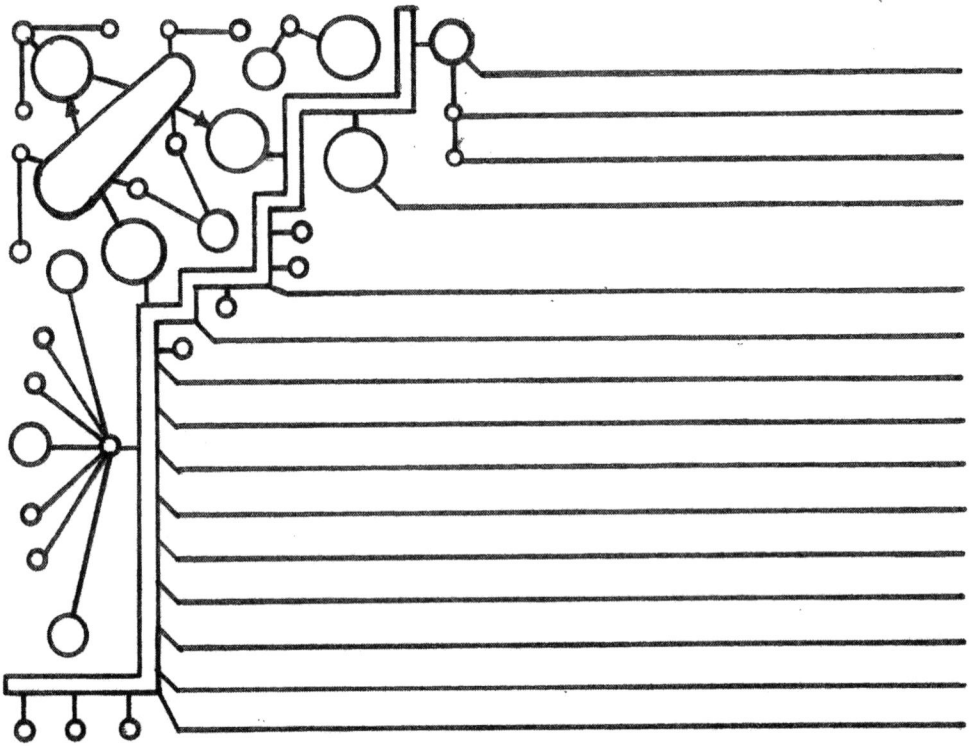

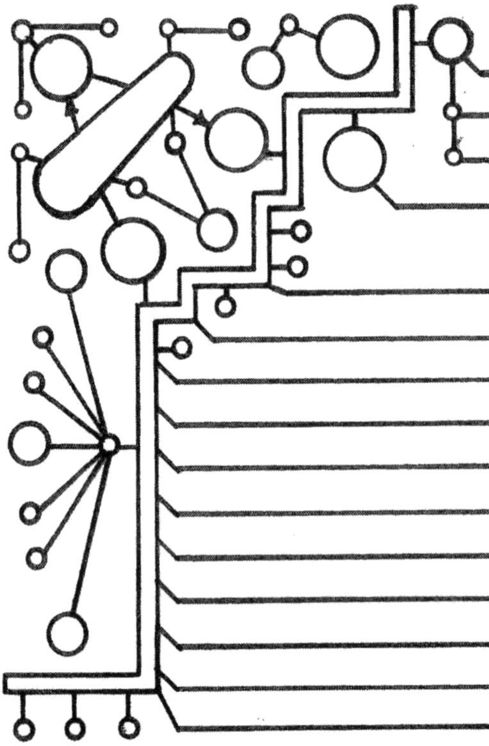

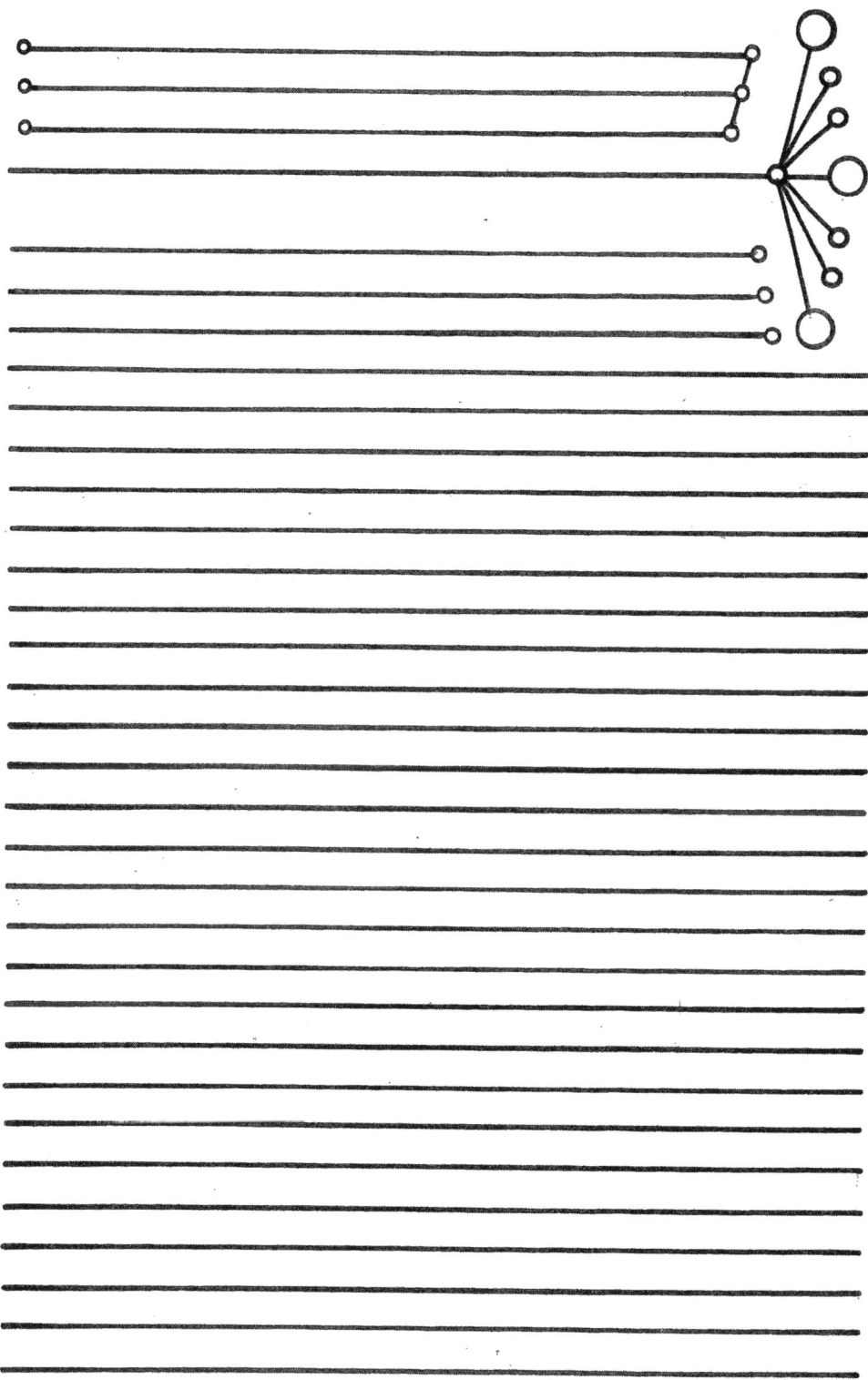

Thank you to all of the truly remarkable deliberate creators
who mindfully contributed their love, insight, perspectives
intention and positive energy to this expansive project.
This realm is far more enjoyable with you in it.

WITH GRATITUDE

THANKS
GOES TO YOU AS WELL,
FELLOW TRAVELER, FOR EXPANDING
YOUR REALITY INTO GREATER AND GRANDER
POSSIBILITIES OF EXPERIENCE.
WELL DONE.

INSPIRING COVER ART BY
| ASHLEY ROSE |
ashleyrosedesigns.net

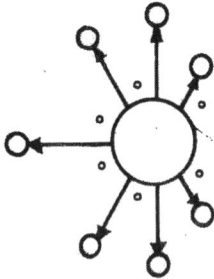

QUOTES, INSIGHTS AND ADDITIONAL
ENERGETIC ACCOMPANIMENT
CONTRIBUTED WITH LOVE BY. . .

RONALD KINSELLA \ thekinsellatwins.com
PHILP MANTLE \ flyingdiskpress.blogspot.com
LEWIS SNOOKES \ instagram.com/lewis.snookes
PAUL ASCOUGH \ facebook.com/paul.ascough.50
MARISA LOVE \ Instagram.com/the_ladybug_line
BEN TEJADA INGRAM \ instagram.com/anomalyhunterx
PHILIP KINSELLA \ thekinsellatwins.com
MARK GOBER / markgober.com
LESTER VELEZ / opusnetwork.org
DR DOUG MATZKE / deeprealitybook.com
DR IRENA SCOTT / facebook.com/irena.scott1
JIM PENNISTON / therendleshamforestincident.com
CHARLIE ROBINSON / theoctopusofglobalcontrol.com
MARK OLLY / facebook.com/markolly
MIKE RICKSECKER / mikericksecker.com
PRESTON DENNETT / prestondennett.weebly.com

Thank you as well to Cam Karri for his gift in the form of the words that look LIKE THIS
| CAM KARRI | cameron@masuyodigital.com

FEEL EMPOWERED TO REACH OUT AND SHOW THEM SOME LOVE.

Made in the USA
Monee, IL
09 November 2023